DOMIOAOIIIREY
DEPORTVGAL

Portugal

Edited by Alison Friesinger Hill
Directed and Designed by Hans Johannes Hoefer
Photography by Tony Aruzza

APA PUBLICATIONS

THE INSIGHT GUIDES SERIES RECEIVED SPECIAL AWARDS FOR EXCELLENCE FROM THE PACIFIC AREA TRAVEL ASSOCIATION.

PORTUGAL
First Edition

APA PUBLICATIONS

Publisher: Hans Johannes Hoefer
Managing Director: Julian Sale
General Manager: Henry Lee
Marketing Director: Aileen Lau
Editorial Director: Geoffrey Eu
Editorial Manager: Vivien Kim
Editorial Consultants: Brian Bell (Europe)
Heinz Vestner (German Editions)
Updating Coordinator: Hilary Cunningham (N. America)

Project Editors

Helen Abbott, Diana Ackland, Mohamed Amin, Ravindralal Anthonis, Roy Bailet, Louisa Cambell, Jon Carroll, Hilary Cunningham, John Eames, Janie Freeburg, Bikram Grewal, Virginia Hopkins, Samuel Israel, Jay Itzkowitz, Phil Jarrat, Tracy Johnson, Ben Kalb, Wilhelm Klein, Saul Lockhart, Sylvia Mayuga, Gordon McLauchlan, Kal Müller, Eric Oey, Daniel P. Reid, Kim Robinson, Ronn Ronck, Robert Seidenberg, Rolf Steinberg, Sriyani Tidball, Lisa Van Gruisen, Merin Wexler.

Contributing Writers

A.D. Aird, Ruth Armstrong, T. Terence Barrow, F. Lisa Beebe, Bruce Berger, Dor Bahadur Bista, Clinton V. Black, Star Black, Frena Bloomfield, John Borthwick, Roger Boschman, Tom Brosnahan, Jerry Carroll, Tom Chaffin, Nedra Chung, Tom Cole, Orman Day, Kunda Dixit, Richard Erdoes, Guillermo Gar-Oropeza, Ted Giannoulas, Barbara Gloudon, Harka Gurung, Sharifah Hamzah, Willard A. Hanna, Elizabeth Hawley, Sir Edmund Hillary, Tony Hillerman, Jerry Hopkins, Peter Hutton, Neil Jameson, Michael King, Michele Kort, Thomas Lucey, Leonard Lueras, Michael E. Macmillan, Derek Maitland, Buddy Mays, Craig McGregor, Reinhold Messner, Julie Michaels, M.R. Priya Rangsit, Al Read, Elizabeth V. Reyes, Victor Stafford Reid, Harry Rolnick, E.R. Sarachandra, Uli Schmetzer, Ilsa Sharp, Norman Sibley, Peter Spiro, Harold Stephens, Keith Stevens, Michael Stone, Desmond Tate, Colin Taylor, Deanna L. Thompson, Randy Udall, James Wade, Mallika Wanigasundara, William Warren, Cynthia Wee, Tony Wheeler, Linda White, H. Taft Wireback, Alfred A. Yuson, Paul Zach.

Contributing Photographers

Carole Allen, Ping Amranand, Tony Arruza, Marcello Bertinetti, Alberto Cassio, Pat Canova, Alain Compost, Ray Cranbourne, Alain Evrard, Ricardo Ferro, Lee Foster, Manfred Gottschalk, Werner Hahn, Dallas and John Heaton, Brent Hesselyn, Hans Hoefer, Luca Invernizzi, Ingo Jezierski, Wilhelm Klein, Dennis Lane, Max Lawrence, Lyle Lawson, Philip Little, Guy Marche, Antonio Martinelli, David Messent, Ben Nakayama, Vautier de Nanxe, Kal Müller, Günter Pfannmuller, Van Philips, Ronni Pinsler, Fitz Prenzel, G.P. Reichelt, Dan Rocovits, David Ryan, Frank Salmoiraghi, Thomas Schollhammer, Blair Seitz, David Stahl, Bill Wassman, Rendo Yap, Hisham Youssef.

While contributions to Insight Guides are very welcome, the publisher cannot assume responsibility for the care and return of unsolicited manuscripts or photographs. Return postage and/or a self-addressed envelope must accompany unsolicited material if it is to be returned. Please address all editorial contributions to Apa Photo Agency, P.O. Box 219, Orchard Point Post Office, Singapore 9123.

Distributors

Australia and New Zealand: Prentice Hall of Australia, 7 Grosvenor Place, Brookvale, NSW 2100, Australia. **Benelux:** Utigeverij Cambium, Naarderstraat 11, 1251 AW Laren, The Netherlands. **Brazil and Portugal:** Cedibra Editora Brasileira Ltda, Rua Leonidia, 2-Rio de Janeiro, Brazil. **Denmark:** Copenhagen Book Centre Aps, Roskildeveji 338, DK-2630 Tastrup, Denmark. **Germany:** RV Reise-und Verkehrsuerlag Gmbh, Neumarkter Strasse 18, 8000 Munchen 80, West Germany. **Hawaii:** Pacific Trade Group Inc., P.O. Box 1227, Kailua, Oahu, Hawaii 96734, U.S.A. **Hong Kong:** Far East Media Ltd., Vita Tower, 7th Floor, Block B, 29 Wong Chuk Hang Road, Hong Kong. **India and Nepal:** India Book Distributors, 107/108 Arcadia Building, 195 Narima Point, Bombay-400-021, India. **Indonesia:** Java Books, Box 55 J.K.C.P., Jakarta, Indonesia. **Israel:**
Steimatzky Ltd., P.O. Box 628, Tel Aviv 61006, Israel (Israel title only). **Italy:** Zanfi Editori SRL. Via Ganaceto 121, 41100 Modena, Italy. **Jamaica:** Novelty Trading Co., P.O. Box 80, 53 Hanover Street, Kingston, Jamaica. **Japan:** Charles E. Tuttle Co. Inc., 2-6 Suido 1-Chome, Bunkyo-ku, Tokyo 112, Japan. **Kenya:** Camerapix Publishers International Ltd., P.O. Box 45048, Nairobi, Kenya. **Korea:** Kyobo Book Centre Co., Ltd., P.O. Box Kwang Hwa Moon 1 658, Seoul, Korea. **Philippines:** National Book Store, 701 Rizal Avenue, Manila, Philippines. **Singapore:** MPH Distributors (S) Pte. Ltd., 601 Sims Drive #03-21 Pan-l Warehouse and Office Complex, S'pore 1438, Singapore. **Switzerland:** M.P.A. Agencies-Import SA, CH. du Croset 9, CH-1024, Ecublens, Switzerland. **Taiwan:** Caves Books Ltd., 103 Chungshan N. Road, Sec. 2, Taipei, Taiwan, Republic of China. **Thailand:** Far East Publications Ltd., 117/3 Soi Samahan, Sukhumvit 4 (South Nana), Bangkok, Thailand. **United Kingdom, Ireland and Europe (others):** Harrap Ltd., 19-23 Ludgate Hill, London EC4M 7PD, England, United Kingdom. **Mainland United States and Canada:** Graphic Arts Center Publishing, 3019 N.W. Yeon, P.O. Box 10306, Portland OR 97210, U.S.A. (The Pacific Northwest title only); Prentice Hall Press, Gulf & Western Building, One Gulf & Western Plaza, New York, NY 10023, U.S.A. (all other titles).

Chinese editions: Formosan Magazine Press Ltd., 6 Fl. No. 189, Yen Pin S. Road, Taipei, Taiwan, R.O.C. **French editions:** Editions Gallimard, 5 rue Sébastien-Bottin, F-75007 Paris, France. **German editions:** Nelles Verlag GmbH, Schleissheirner Str. 371b, 8000 Munich 45, West Germany **Italian editions:** Zanfi Editori SLR. Via Ganaceto 121 41100 Modena, Italy. **Portuguese editions:** Cedibra Editora Brasileira Ltda, Rua Leonidia, 2-Rio de Janeiro, Brazil.

Advertising and Special Sales Representatives

Advertising carried in Insight Guides gives readers direct access to quality merchandise and travel-related services. These advertisements are inserted in the Guide in Brief section of each book. Advertisers are requested to contact their nearest representatives, listed below.
Special sales, for promotion purposes within the international travel industry and for educational purposes, are also available. The advertising representatives listed here also handle special sales. Alternatively, interested parties can contact Apa Publications, P.O. Box 219, Orchard Point Post Office, Singapore 9123.

Australia and New Zealand: Harve and Gullifer Pty. Ltd. 1 Fawkner St. Kilda 3181, Australia. Tel: (3) 525 3422; Tlx: 523259; Fax: (89) 4312837.
Canada: The Pacific Rim Agency, 6900 Cote Saint Luc Road, Suite 303, Montreal, Quebec, Canada H4V 2Y9. Tel: (514) 9311299; Tlx: 0525134 MTL; Fax: (514) 8615571.
Hawaii: HawaiianLMedia Sales; 1750 Kalakaua Ave., Suite 3-243, Honolulu, Hawaii 96826, U.S.A. Tel: (808) 9464483.
Hong Kong: C Cheney & Associates, 17th Floor, D'Aguilar Place, 1-30 D'Aguilar Street, Central, Hong Kong. Tel: 5-213671; Tlx: 63079 CCAL HX.
India and Nepal, Pakistan and Bangladesh: Universal Media, CHA 2/718, 719 Kantipath, Lazimpat, Kathmandu-2, Nepal. Tel: 412911/414502; Tlx: 2229 KAJI NP ATTN MEDIA.
Indonesia: Media Investment Services, Setiabudi Bldg. 2, 4th Floor, Suite 407, Jl. Hr. Rasuna Said, Kuningan, Jakarta Selatan 12920, Indonesia. Tel: 5782723/5782752; Tlx: 62418 MEDIANETIA; Mata Graphic Design, Batujimbar, Sanur, Bali, Indonesia. Tel: (0361) 8073. (for Bali only)
Korea: Kaya Ad Inc., Rm. 402 Kunshin Annex B/D, 251-1 Dohwa Dong, Mapo-Ku, Seoul, Korea (121). Tel: (2) 7196906; Tlx: K 32144 KAYAAD; Fax: (2) 7199816.
Philippines: Torres Media Sales Inc., 21 Warbler St., Greenmeadows 1, Murphy, Quezon City, Metro Manila, Philippines. Tel: 722-02-43; Tlx: 23312 RHP PH.
Taiwan: Cheney Tan & Van Associates, 7th Floor, 10 Alley 4, Lane 545 Tun Hua South Road, Taipei, Taiwan. Tel: (2) 7002963; Tlx: 11491 FOROSAN; Fax: (2) 3821270.
Thailand: Cheney, Tan & Van Outrive, 17th Fl. Rajapark Bldg., 163 Asoke Rd., Bangkok 10110, Thailand. Tel: 2583244/2583259; Tlx: 20666 RAJAPAK TH.
Singapore and Malaysia: Cheney Tan Associates, 1 Goldhill Plaza, #02-01, Newton Rd., Singapore 1130, Singapore. Tel: 2549522; Tlx: RS 35983 CTAL.
Sri Lanka: Spectrum Lanka Advertising Ltd., 56 1/2 Ward Place, Colombo 7, Sr Lanka. Tel: 5984648/596227; Tlx: 21439 SPECTRM CE.
U.K., Ireland and Europe: Brian Taplin Associates, 32 Fishery Road, Boxmoor, Hemel Hempstead, Herts HP 1ND, U.K. Tel: (2)215635; Tlx: 825454 CHARMAN.

APA PHOTO AGENCY PTE. LTD.

The Apa Photo Agency is S.E. Asia's leading stock photo archive, representing the work of professional photographers from all over the world. More than 150,000 original color transparencies are available for advertising, editorial and educational uses. We are linked with Tony Stone Worldwide, one of Europe's leading stock agencies, and their associate offices around the world:
Singapore: Apa Photo Agency Pte. Ltd., P.O. Box 219, Orchard Point Post Office, Singapore 9123, Singapore. **London:** Tony Stone Worldwide, 28 Finchley Rd., St. John's Wood, London NW8 6ES, England. **North America &** **Canada:** Masterfile Inc., 415 Yonge St., Suite 200, Toronto M5B 2E7, Canada. **Paris:** Fotogram-Stone Agence Photographique, 45 rue de Richelieu, 75001 Paris, France. **Barcelona:** Fototec Torre Dels Pardais, 7 Barcelona 08026, Spain. **Johannesburg:** Color Library (Pty.) Ltd., P.O. Box 1659, Johannesburg, South Africa 2000. **Sydney:** The Photographic Library of Australia Pty. Ltd., 7 Ridge Street, North Sydney, New South Wales 2050, Australia. **Tokyo:** Orion Press, 55-1 Kanda Jimbocho, Chiyoda-ku, Tokyo 101, Japan.

B C D E F G

After returning to New York after her honeymoon in Portugal, **Alison Friesinger Hill** found that she had a new love other than her husband; she was overwhelmed with the warmth and beauty of this southern European country. She and her spouse, both writer/editors, collaborated on an article on Portugal for *McCall's* magazine, but Hill had much more to say on the subject.

Hoefer   *Friesinger Hill*   *Arruza*

Fortunately, APA Productions, headed by **Hans Hoefer**, was soon to give her the opportunity. APA Productions had begun the Insight Guide series in 1970 with its first title, *Insight Guide : Bali*. In 1984, it ventured into Europe, first with a grand tour, then country by country. And Portugal's turn had come. Associate publisher **Adam Liptak**, now an attorney, met with Hill in New York, and a contract was signed.

Hill has been writing and editing since receiving her degree in English Language and Literature from Harvard College. As a freelancer, she worked for many publications, including *The New York Times Book Review, American Health, New Woman,* and *Spy*. She and her husband have co-written a humor book called *Otherwise Engaged*. Hill was also the editor of *Insight Guide: Lisbon*. She has travelled in the United States, Switzerland, Greece, and Italy.

Hoefer already had in mind the photographer for the book: the man who had done such a beautiful job on *Insight Guide: Barbados*. **Tony Arruza**, based in West Palm Beach, Florida, already had thousands of photographs of Portugal in his collection—and was already in love with the country. He met with Hill in both New York and Lisbon, and he spent months and many long days capturing their mutual vision—dawns in tiny fishing villages, late nights in city nightclubs, perfect shots caught along highways and in the mountains. Arruza is particularly adept at that most elusive subject of photography: people. In the pages that follow, the reader can truly get to know the Portuguese, thanks to Arruza's skill.

The very first writer that Hill hired was, by no coincidence, another Hill—**Thomas Hill,** her husband. With his degree from Harvard in History and Literature, and his extensive writing experience, he was the perfect candidate to write Portugal's history. He also authored the article entitled "The Portuguese." In addition, he was recruited, both in an official capacity and in many unofficial instances, to assist his wife in endless editing, writing captions and whatever else came up.

For the section on Lisbon and its environs, and the section on the most important wine provinces, editor Hill found **Marvine Howe**. Howe spent her early years in China. Later, after graduating from Rutgers Journalism School, she covered the African independence movements as a stringer for *The New York Times*. In 1962, she discovered Portugal, and made Lisbon her base. Her many years there gave her both expertise and great fondness for the country. She writes about Portugal frequently for the *Times,* where she is now on the Metropolitan staff.

Sharon Behn, who contributed the article on the Algarve and also the feature on the *pousada* and manor-house system of inns, is another serious, well-travelled journalist. Born in Peru, she has lived in the U.S., England, Brazil, and of course, Portugal. Her travel history is endless, and she has written for publications which include *The Los Angeles Times* and Britain's *Independent*. She now freelances and is a stringer at the UPI wire service's Lisbon bureau.

The long article on the Alentejo was written by **Deborah Brammer,** a free-lance writer who lives in Lisbon. Although she did not venture out of her native England until she was 18 years old, she has had a case of the travel bug ever since. She and her Portuguese husband satisfy this between their longer holidays with domestic explorations to hidden corners of Portugal in their jeep.

Speaking of ramblers, few have covered as much ground in their wanderings than **Jeremy Boultbee** who wrote about Portugal's most remote sections, Trás-os-Montes and the Beiras. Boultbee, Canadian-born, lives in Sintra, Portugal, where he pursues careers as ceramicist, canoeist, and actor, as well as a writer. He formerly worked as a correspondent for Canada's *Maclean's* magazine.

Jenny Wittner wrote the sections on Coimbra and its surrounding areas, as well as compiling the very informative Travel Tips. As an undergraduate at Harvard College, she worked on the *Let's Go* travel series. She later moved to Coimbra and now lives in Lisbon, where she teaches English.

The feature on Portuguese art and architecture was lovingly written by **Ruth Rosengarten**, an artist herself who lives in Lisbon. Born in Israel, Rosengarten received her B.A. in Johannesburg and her M.A. in London, and has been teaching and practicing art since then. Though she was sure she would not fit in all there was to say, she managed to cover Portugal's dynamic, long artistic tradition admirably. She also offered editor Hill sound advice and support in Lisbon.

Peter Wise wrote "Trees of the Alentejo" and "Fishing Communities." Until 1974, he and his Portuguese wife were living in England, but after the Revolution they decided to return to her native country. Wise, who is also an expert on the complex subject of Portuguese politics, is currently a stringer for the AP wire service, and has written articles for *The Washington Post, The Boston Globe*, and many other publications.

To write about Portugal 's stunning wines, Hill recruited an experienced New York City sommelier. **Scott Carney,** of Gotham restaurant, already knew about Portuguese wines when he honeymooned there a number of years ago; he just wanted to see and taste for himself. It surpassed his high expectations, and since then Carney has kept up-to-date by constant reading—and sampling.

Jean Anderson probably has written more about Portugal's food than anyone in the U.S. Her new book, *The Food of Portugal*, is just one of

Hill

Howe

Anderson

Kim

Brammer   *Wise*

Simon   *Maschmeyer*

many cookbooks and magazine articles she has authored. The article she wrote for this guide is a lively introduction to the savoury eating found in Portugal.

The author of "Travelers to Portugal" is no stranger to Insight Guides. **Katherine Barrett Swett** edited *Insight Guide: Italy.* She also has contributed travel articles to several magazines. She is now working toward her Ph.D. at Columbia University in New York City. Tied down by her studies, her traveling has recently been of the literary sort, as she has explored the itineraries and impressions of other, earlier visitors to foreign lands.

The pseudonymous **Antonio dos Santos,** who contributed the article "Saints, Miracles and Shrines," is a Portuguese academic.

Among those who made contributions not in written words, Hill would like to thank **Antonio Madeira**, **Evelyn Heyward**, **Pam Brown**, and **Al de Sousa.**

Vivien Kim, APA's editorial manager in Singapore, struggled valiantly against tight deadlines and distance to supply the support and responsiveness that Hill needed. Kim's dedication and cool headedness has made *Insight Guide: Portugal* a success.

Editors **Audrey Simon** and **Gloria J. Maschmeyer** assisted Kim in all aspects of putting the final book together. Prior to joining APA,Simon was a free-lance writer for regional publications such as *Asian Business*, *South* and, *Asian Oil and Gas*. Writer and photographer Maschmeyer, an American currently living in Singapore, is widely published in the Asia Pacific region and a correspondent for a U.S. based travel magazine.

The editor would also like to thank production coordinator **Johnny Chng** and **Lim Peng Yam** who worked on all the maps in the book.

APA PUBLICATIONS

TABLE OF CONTENTS

OTHER INSIGHT GUIDES TITLES

COUNTRY/REGION

ASIA
Bali
Burma
Hong Kong
India
Indonesia
Korea
Malaysia
Nepal
Philippines
Rajasthan
Singapore
Sri Lanka
Taiwan
Thailand
Turkey

PACIFIC
Hawaii
New Zealand

NORTH AMERICA
Alaska
American Southwest
Northern California
Southern California
Florida
Mexico
New England
New York State
The Pacific Northwest
The Rockies
Texas

SOUTH AMERICA
Brazil
Argentina

CARIBBEAN
Bahamas
Barbados
Jamaica
Puerto Rico
Trinidad and Tobago

EUROPE
Channel Islands
France
Germany
Great Britain
Greece
Ireland
Italy
Portugal
Scotland
Spain

MIDDLE EAST
Egypt
Israel

AFRICA
Kenya

GRAND TOURS
Australia
California
Canada
Continental Europe
Crossing America
East Asia
South Asia

GREAT ADVENTURE
Indian Wildlife

CITYGUIDES
Bangkok
Berlin
Buenos Aires
Dublin
Istanbul
Lisbon
London
Paris
Rio de Janeiro
Rome
San Francisco
Venice
Vienna

PORTUGAL BECKONS

Portugal has always been the land on the edge, caught between traditional ways of living—fishing and farming—and the technology and integration that makes the world today so small. It is a cozy country, 34,332 square miles (88,944 square km) in total size and with a population of under 10 million. And it unquestionably has been blessed with some of the most beautiful landscapes in the world—endless beaches, like the Dona Ana near Lagos; craggy mountain ranges, including the Serra da Estrela with its top peak of 6,532 feet (1,991 meters); and the stark open plains of the southern central area, dotted with cork trees. All are crowned by stunning blue skies. It is a temperate country, both in weather and in mood; its people are gentle and warm, and generally an optimistic bunch.

The traveler is welcome in every corner of this marvelous land, from the *boites* in Lisbon, open for dancing until 4 a.m., to the most obscure village in Trás-os-Montes, with its simple ways of baking, spinning and farming. Sample whatever is to your taste—perhaps a little of it all.

This guide will start you off with a thorough lesson in Portugal's long and fascinating history, followed by a brief introduction to its people, insofar as it is possible to sum up any nation of individuals. Next, the Places section will take you on a tour of the entire country. The last section, features, will familiarize you with Portugal's foods and wines, with its wonderful *pousada* and manor house inns, and with its glorious art and architecture. Waste no more time here; read on to discover Portugal!

Preceding pages, the brilliant Serpa light; boat-watching at Cascais; the Alentejo plains; laundry day in Lisbon. Left, the god Bacchus in 17th-century *azulejos*

1147

1227

1762

1385

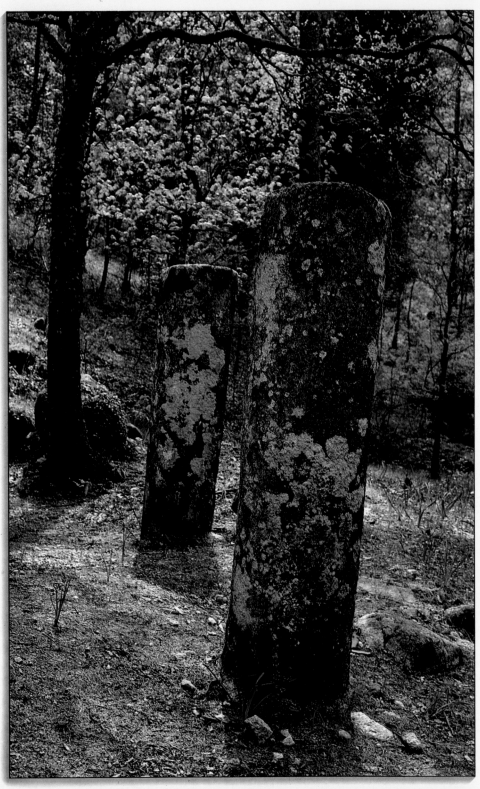

ANCIENT LUSITANIA

Portugal is something of an anomaly on the map of Western Europe. Not separated from neighboring Spain by any natural frontiers nor by a distinctive clime, the country's independence flaunts the dictates of geographical destiny. Each region of Portugal—the only exception being Lisbon's bay and its alluvial plains—corresponds closely to a region across the border. The northern Minho district is similar to Spanish Galicia; the southern Algarve and Alentejo districts to Andalusia and so on. The Tagus and Douro Rivers and the mountains of Beira Baixa extend into Spain. In fact, the natural division of the Iberian peninsula would divide not east from west, but north from south, the Atlantic culture and climate from the Mediterranean.

Yet Portugal exists, wholly an individual, politically and culturally. In fact, as its borders were established in the 13th century, it is one of the oldest nations in Europe. It has discovered and lost an empire, lost and regained its cherished autonomy and, in the last 25 years, stubbornly held and finally lost its last imperial colonies in Africa and the Indies.

A rich prehistoric culture has left its archaeological traces throughout Portugal. There is evidence of the earliest stages of human evolution and a large number of megalithic sites. The variety and quantity of these finds have led many scholars to a theory of maritime irradiation, supposing that cultural diffusion came primarily from overseas. Opponents of this notion point out that most of the megalithic sites are far from the coastline. They think the population grew via natural land routes of settlement which, not surprisingly, correspond to the paths invaders have taken throughout Portugal's history: across the Minho river from the north and over the Alentejo flatlands from the south.

In any case, by the second millennium B.C., the social organization was composed of scattered *castros*, garrisoned hilltop villages that suggest warfare between tribes. The people subsisted on goat-herding and primitive agriculture, and clad themselves in woolen cloaks. Some of their constructions are still standing, for example, at the Citânia de Briteiros near Guimarães. In the south, tribes came under the influence of ninth-century Phoenician and sixth-century Greek trade settlements. These early visitors made their presence felt throughout the south, both on the coast and in-

land, where metals were mined. Interestingly, it is only at this late point that there is evidence of a significant fishing economy among the indigenous people. Perhaps before then the rough-hewn and storm-beaten Atlantic coast was too intimidating for their small boats. During the 5th century B.C., the Carthaginians wrested control of the Iberian peninsula from these earlier traders, but lost it to the Roman Empire in the Second Punic War.

Wars of Conquests: The Romans called the peninsula **Hispania Ulterior**. Here, as elsewhere in the Empire, they combined their economic exploitation with cultural upheaval. They were not traders, after all, but conquerors, who quickly went to the business of founding cities, building roads, and reorganizing territories. They also implemented governmental and judicial systems. There was resistance among the inhabitants. The largest and most intransigent group were the Lusitani, who lived north of the Tagus, and after whom the area that is now Portugal was called Lusitania. Bitter guerrilla fighting was intermittent for two centuries. The most renowned rebel was a shepherd named Viriathus. He led uprisings until he was assassinated in 139 B.C. by three traiterous comrades who had been bribed by the Romans. It was during these wars of conquest that Roman troops are said to have refused to cross the Lima river, believing it to be the Lethe, the mythological river of forgetfulness. Their commander had to cross the river alone, then call each soldier by name to prove that the dip had not affected his memory.

Beginning in 60 B.C., Julius Caesar governed the province from the capital established at Olisipo (Lisbon). Cities were established and colonized at modern day Évora, Beja, Santarém, and elsewhere. Roads linked the north and south, aiding commerce and hastening the homogeneity of the area. Before the decline and fall, the Romans had infused the area with their language, legal systems, currency, agriculture, and eventually, with Christianity. The organization, of *latifundia* was particularly significant, it brought large-scale farming to the area for the first time, particularly in the south. The centers and routes the Romans chose have waxed and waned in importance, but today many are still geographic focal points. The most significant example, of course, is Lisbon.

With the conversion of the late Roman Emperors, the tenets and organizations of Christianity were spread throughout the fading empire. Bishoprics were established in a number of cities, notably Braga and Évora. As the church expanded it drew upon and later usurped the administrative power that had been developed by the Empire. Situated at the edge of Christian expansion, indeed, on the edge of the known world, pre-Portugal was susceptible to frontier rebellions against dogma. Heretical Christian doctrines held sway in Portugal during the 3rd and 4th centuries. In the early 5th century various groups of barbarians occupied the land. The Alani and Vandals each settled in for a short time, but by 419 the Suevi were in sole, if not steady possession of Galicia, and from there they conquered Lusitania and most of the Iberian Peninsula. The Suevi apparently assimilated easily with the existing Hispano-Roman population. But the tide turned on them in the form of the Visigoths. For the next 50 years, military conquest meant religious conversion. In 448, Rechiarius, king of a diminished

of Portugal was now a part of Moslem Spain, loosely organized underneath the Cordoba caliph. To them, this country was *Al-Gharb*, (the West), a term from which was derived the modern name of Algarve. The Moors soon ruled all of Portugal—Christianity was forced north of the Minho where it lay gathering strength for the *Reconquista*.

For centuries, the Moors ruled tolerantly, living in relative tranquility with Jews and Christians. They contributed new methods and crops to agriculture, including fruit orchards and rice fields. In 868, the first significant efforts to break from Spain began. A revolt was staged by a rich landowner nicknamed "The Galician," because he was a native of Spain whose family had converted to Islam. After three failed rebellions, he succeeded in founding a semi-independent state,

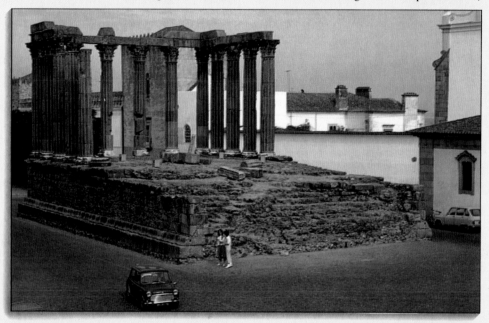

Suevi empire, converted to Catholicism, perhaps hoping to elicit aid from Rome in battling the Visigoths who were Christian but clung to the heretical Arianism. Rechiarius was killed in 457, but the Suevi kingdom survived, led by Masdra. In 465, Masdra's son Recchismundus converted to Arianism, probably to appease the Visigoths. By 550, the growing power of the Catholic Church led to a new round of conversions led by St. Martin of Dume, and apparently the Visigoths had finally had enough. The remnants of the Suevi were politically extinguished in 585.

Invaders from the South: Visigoth rule, an elective monarchy that soon bred internal dissension, was not seriously challenged until the Moors, who had arrived on the southern coast in 711, began their expansion northward. The south

in 885. His son took over after his death, but showed less fortitude, losing it all back to the caliph by 930.

Over the next decade, the overarching authority of the caliph decayed, and small kingdoms, *taifas*, took over. The decentralization naturally led to internal dissension, partly caused by the rise of a religious sect called Sufi. Sufism was a subversive and heretical brand of mysticism that grew popular in reaction to the formalism and rationalism of Islam. Its significance was two-fold: just as it allowed Christian forces to push the frontier lines downward from the north, it also allowed for radical Moslem military groups like the Almoravid and the Almohad to rise to power quickly.

The Almoravids, who had built an empire in

Africa, came north. After helping the Islamic rulers to force the Christians back, they decided to take over, to unify the *taifas* under them. By 1095 the Almoravids had succeeded, installing an austere military system and harsh government. As if that weren't enough, they were soon followed by the still more fanatical Almohads. The simmering Reconquista took on the aspect of a Holy War for both Christians and Moslems.

The stormy frontier in the center of Portugal that so threatened the Moslems had been gathering momentum for centuries. The first serious blows for a Christian return were struck in the mid-eigth century by marauders from Asturias-León (northern Spain). All of northern Portugal became a battleground. Slowly towns fell before the Christian armies. Oporto in 868, Coimbra in 878, and by 955, the king of León, Ordona III,

9th century, the area between the Lima and Douro Rivers was made into a separate territory named for its capital city, Portucale. The area was variously divided under the unstable feudal states. Stability came with a dynasty of *duces*, beginning with Gonçalo Mendes, so that the province was held by one family for a century beginning in 950. It was still under the supreme control of the Kingdom of León, but unlike León's other provinces, the power and autonomy of Portucale were on the rise.

Self-proclaimed Emperor: Fernando I of León was the great consolidating force of northern Spain during the 11th century. As part of his policy of centralizing authority, he tried to dismantle Portugal, dividing it into different provinces under separate governors. None of these efforts made a lasting difference. When

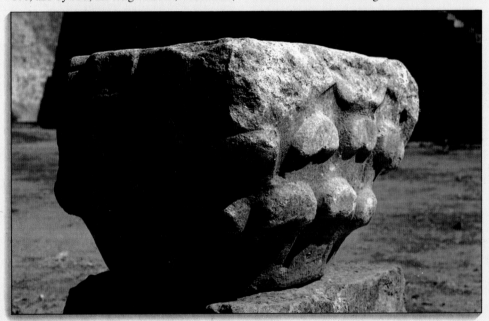

engineered a raid of Lisbon. Most of the victories below the Douro, however, amounted to nothing more than raids, as the territory was seldom held for more than a season or two.

Portugal's independence has been attributed to various causes, including the indigenous megalithic cultures whose borders were accepted by Rome and the resistance that the Suevi offered to the Visigoth hordes. However, it was during the Christian Reconquest of Iberia that Portugal first truly asserted its independent status and its leaders took on a sense of national destiny. Late in the

Left, the Roman temple in Évora, possibly dedicated to the goddess Diana, recently cordoned off to the public. Above, remnants of Visigothic pillar in Serpa

Fernando's successor Alfonso VI took upon himself the title of Emperor, it was over the kingdoms of León, Castile, Galicia and Portugal. "Emperor" was a bit of a stretch at this point, given the unstable ties of vassalage between the various players of the period, but it was an important claim because an emperor logically rules over kings. It was the lure of the title "king" that would inspire Afonso Henriques to battle, deal and connive for the autonomy of his particular *terra*, Portugal.

Afonso Henriques was the son of Henri of Burgundy and his wife Teresa. Henri was among a number of French knights who had arrived in the late 11th century to fight the infidels. They were mostly second and third sons, who, in the feudal system, were left with no real inheritance.

If they wanted land and riches, they usually had to travel abroad to win them. Henri's cousin Raymond, like Henri a fourth son, also came south. After proving his heroism in battle, Raymond married Alfonso VI's daughter Urraca, and was granted the territories of Galicia and Coimbra. With Henri's marriage to Teresa, who was Alfonso's favorite, though illegitimate daughter, he was given the territory of Portugal. With the death of Raymond and Alfonso VI, Urraca inherited that crown, but her second marriage, to another Alfonso, this one known as Alfonso I of Aragon, also set off a complex round of civil wars.

During this period, Henri made significant strides toward the autonomy of the state of Portugal. The most important of these was the support he offered to the archbishops of Braga in an

some of the nobility and her son. Continuing Henri's policies, Teresa schemed successfully to maintain Portugal's independence for awhile, but in 1127 she submitted to Alfonso VII's dominion after her army was defeated. It was in 1128 that the 18-year-old Afonso Henriques led his first rebellion, toppling his mother's rule at the battle of São Mamede, near their castle in Guimarães.

A King is Crowned: Over the next decade, Afonso Henriques vied with his cousin the emperor for ultimate control of Portugal. After a brilliant military conquest over the Moors in the Battle of Ourique, in 1139, he began to refer to himself as king. In 1143, the Treaty of Zamora was signed between them wherein Alfonso VII gave Afonso Henriques the title of King of Portugal in exchange for the usual feudal ties of mili-

ecclesiastical dispute with those of Toledo. Essentially, this rift was parallel to the growing political conflict. The Pope had granted the archbishop of Toledo dominion over all of the Christian Iberian Peninsula. The archbishop at Braga resisted the Roman decree, claiming a traditional right to autonomy, based on ancient ecclesiastical divisions. Henri's support served to solidify Braga's rights for practical purposes, and more importantly, served his own ends: to further solidify the political borders of Portugal.

In 1126 Urraca died and her son, Alfonso Raimundez, became the Emperor Alfonso VII. Henri had died and Teresa had retained Portugal as regent for her son, Afonso Henriques. Without wasting much time in mourning, she took a Galician count, Fernão Peres, as a lover, displeasing

tary aid and loyalty.

Though it was a victory, Afonso Henriques sought to fix the title more firmly by seeking recognition from Rome. Pope Lucius II refused, keeping to a policy of supporting Iberian union in order to better stem the tide of Islam. It was not until 1179 that Pope Alexander III, in exchange for a yearly tribute and various other privileges, finally granted recognition of the Portuguese kingdom to Afonso Henriques, who was by then nearly 70 years old.

By that late date, papal acceptance only served to formalize an entity that was not only well-established but growing. Afonso Henriques had enlisted the aid of crusaders and led the Reconquest over the Moors, adding his conquests to the emerging nation. Santarém and Lisbon were both taken in 1147; the first by surprise attack, the second in a siege that was supported by French, English, Flemish and German crusaders who were passing through Portugal on their way to the Holy Land. The inestimable assistance of these 164 ships of men was entirely fortuitous, and very nearly fell through when Afonso Henriques pronounced that he expected them to fight only for Christianity and not for earthly rewards. The English and Germans walked out; the king quickly rescinded, offering loot and land grants all around.

The Western Crusade: The bishop also added his aid here, providing theological assurance that these were the very same enemy that would be found in the Holy Land. However, this philosophical conundrum apparently plagued Afonso Henriques at times. His confessor questioned the

the Church that the "western crusade" was just as valuable as that to be found in Palestine. Another important development of the Reconquest was the founding of military-religious organizations like the Knights Templar and the Hospitalers. These groups were rewarded with land grants in exchange for chasing out the Moors. Both groups grew wealthy and powerful—uncomfortably so, for some later kings.

In 1170 Afonso Henriques fought his last battle, at Badajoz. The powerful Almohads had enlisted the aid of Fernando II of León, who felt that the Portuguese were recapturing not only the Moorish land, but land that was by right a part of León. The most renowned of Afonso Henriques' military cohorts was Geraldo Geraldes, a local adventurer who was dubbed *O Sem Pavor* (the Fearless) for his brilliant raids into Moslem terri-

diversion of troops from the Crusade, and legend has it that on the way to Santarém—with crusaders in tow—the King was besieged by guilt and anxiety because of the Moorish stronghold's reputation of impregnability. To soothe his torment, he vowed to St. Bernard that he would build the Abbey at Alcobaça in the Virgin's honor if the battle was successful. The battle was won: the Abbey still stands.

Convincing crusaders that one batch of infidel was as good as another was crucial to the Reconquista. Portuguese kings naturally argued with

tory. This national hero had taken a string of epic victories, but at Badajoz, the combination of Moorish and Leónese forces was too much for Geraldes and his king. The aging Afonso Henriques broke his leg in the midst of the battle and was captured. His release came only after he had surrendered the castles and the territories to both enemy parties. His retreat allowed the Moors to entrench along the battle zone. The founding king of Portugal's days of victory were over, with the final triumph of the Reconquista still a century away. Yet, with Afonso Henriques' monarchy a country was born, and whether this achievement

Left, two depictions of Afonso Henriques, first king of Portugal. Above, an 18th-century engraving of Afonso rallying his troops at the conquest of Lisbon in 1147

was truly an act of political will or simply a matter of historical confluence, the independence and individuality of the Portuguese nation was forever determined.

For a century after the death of Afonso Henriques in 1285, the first order of business was the slow riddance of the remaining, and still feisty, Moors. The *Reconquista*, now as good as sanctioned by the Church with various Papal bulls and indulgences as a "western crusade," was still very much underway.

The Knights Templar had arrived in Portugal with the crusaders stopping on their way to Palestine in 1128. They were soon followed by other military-religious orders: Hospitalers, Calatrava, and Santiago. These groups clung to the religious justification for their war-mongering and for their massive accumulation of land and loot. Still, the western crusade remained an awkward idea. Unlike Palestine, where the dividing line between Christians and infidels was clearly drawn, the south of Iberia had intermingled Moslem, Christian, and Jewish peoples in economic, cultural, and even political spheres. In 1197, papal indulgences were even promised in a war against Alfonso IX of Leon, a Christian, though at that time an ally of the Moslems. In truth, the *Reconquista* was, from the beginning, a matter of inheritance as much as religion. The Christians traced their ancestry, and their claims to the land, back to the age of Visigoth rule. They fought for the cities of man, not the City of God.

The frontier war proceeded steadily, if somewhat slowly. The first kings of the Burgundian line after Afonso Henriques continued to press the borders southward. Under Sancho II, the eastern Algarve and Alentejo were incorporated into the burgeoning nation. Under Afonso III, the western Algarve and Faro had fallen by 1249. The latter ruler also moved the capital south from Coimbra to Lisbon in 1256. These boundaries—essentially the ones that exist today—were officially and finally recognized by Castile in the Treaty of Alcañices in 1297. Thus, Portugal is one of the oldest countries in Europe.

Along with political settlement, the *Reconquista* brought Portugal fundamental social transformations. Having reclaimed the lands of the south, they now needed to recolonize and populate them. To do this, the Burgundian kings needed to balance their centralized, essentially military power with popular support. The need for popular and financial support forced kings to consult with *cortes*, local assemblies of nobles,

Left, Dom Dinis, whose reign saw the foundation of castles, forests, and the University of Lisbon, represented in a 17th-century screen made in China

clergy, and, somewhat later, mercantile classes. At the *cortes* of Leiria (1254), Afonso III conceded the right of municipal representation in questions of taxation and other economic issues. For the most part, the *cortes* were gathered whenever the king needed to raise money. João I would make particular political use of them. When later monarchs used trade and their own military orders to reap great and independent profits, the *cortes* fell into disuse.

Another result of the *Reconquista*, with the expansion of properties and the need for laborers who were willing to resettle, was an increase in social mobility among the lower classes. Distinctions fell away among the various levels of serfs as farm workers became a scarcer and so a more valuable commodity. Another, more general effect of the *Reconquista* was the beginning of amalgamation of the divergent cultures of north and south. The south was still marked by refinement and urbanity; it was a culture with a tradition of tolerance. In contrast, the northern culture had a rough arrogance, the attitude of invaders. They were, though they may have traced their lineages back to pre-Moslem Iberia, an emigrant nobility. Though the cultures of north and south would meld, differences remain even now.

The Church, naturally, rode the *Reconquista* to riches. The various orders were granted vast areas of land by the kings in return for their military aid. The church and clergy were also free of taxation, and were granted the right to collect their own "tenths" from the population. Their power was such that it soon threatened the monarchy. Afonso II was the first ruler of Portugal to defy the Church in attempting to curb their voracious acquisition of property. His efforts generally failed, as did those of his successor, Sancho II, who was finally excommunicated and dethroned in 1245 for his insistence on royal prerogatives.

It was the reign of Dinis, who was known as both the farmer king and the poet king, that truly cemented Portuguese independence, and at the core of independence, the power of the monarchy. It was his foresight and administrative genius that brought the nation into a new era. After briefly joining the nation of Aragon in war against Castile, Dinis ushered in a long period of peace and progress. Dinis encouraged learning and literature, establishing the first Portuguese university in 1288, first in Lisbon and later transferred to Coimbra. Portuguese, having distinguished itself from its Latin roots and from Castilian (which would become Spanish), established itself as the language of the troubadour culture, and the official language of law and state.

The troubadour culture—poetry and music spread by peripatetic minstrels—was greatly influential, more so than the official Church teachings of the University. Drawing upon the French tradition, and upon Moorish influences of, the Portuguese troubadours created a unique native literature. These song-poems of love and satire were often written by nobles, among them Dinis the "poet king", of course, and Sancho I as well. The singers were Moors, Jews, some lower nobles, and villeins, members of the free peasant class of the feudal hierarchy. Other forms of literary expression lagged far behind poetry. Neither history nor prose would offer any memorable achievements before the 15th century.

Dinis's rule also brought political progress. Landmark agreements were made to seal peace with Castile (the Treaty of Alcañices, 1297) and

finally began to shift the population center of the nation from north to south.

By now a monetary economy was well established, not only for international trade, but internally. Agricultural production was more and more geared toward markets, though self-sufficient farming did not disappear. Dinis encouraged the expansion of the economic system with fairs, large chartered trading centers that encouraged internal trade and thus allowed for greater specialization. Dinis was responsible for chartering 48 of these fairs, more than all the other Portuguese kings combined. The concentration of trade into fairs also, not coincidentally, allowed for a more systematic taxation.

The only section of the Portuguese economy to lag during this period was industrial production. In this case Dinis, and later kings, were counter-

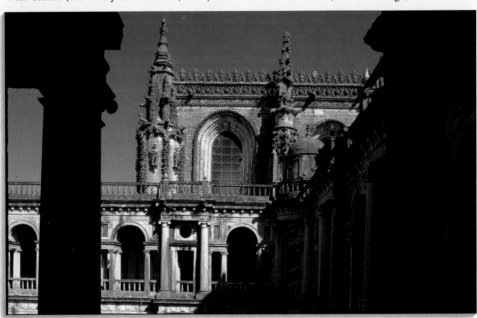

the clergy (the Concordat of 1289). The latter agreement was a major victory for royal jurisdiction in matters of property. During his reign, Dinis fortified the frontier by supporting and sometimes financing the construction of 50 castles. He organized the first national maritime organization, hiring skilled Genoese sailors for the task. In 1308 he signed the original pact of friendship with England that has been reconfirmed and expanded many times since. The "farmer king" also reformed the national agriculture, establishing forest plantations and other programs that soon allowed the export of grain, olive oil, wine and other foodstuffs. Portugal also profited from illicit trade with Islamic countries, acting as intermediary between them and the northern countries. These coastal developments

productive in their resistance to the idea of corporations. Craftsmen tended to work on their own, and thus confined themselves to local markets and limited quantities. There was a bit of goldsmithing, shipbuilding, and pottery done in commercial quantities, but for the most part craftsmen worked alone.

Perhaps the most significant of all of Dinis's accomplishments was his management of the disbanding of the Knights of Templar in 1312. The order was under fire throughout Europe; their demise was imminent. Dinis's triumph was to retain their great wealth within the country and to prevent the Church or any other order from taking over the material and land holdings for themselves. In 1317 he founded a new organization, the Order of Our Lord Jesus Christ. The Order

101 CASTLES

It is said that there are 101 castles in Portugal, most of which were built or rebuilt between the 12th and 14th centuries. King Dinis (1279-1325) began building or expanding more than 50 fortresses during his reign. His labors can be seen throughout Portugal, but the *Ribacoa*, a narrow strip of land along Portugal's eastern boundary, was where he concentrated his efforts. He strengthened the towns of Guarda, Penedo, Penamacor, Castelo Mendo, Pinhel and others, attempting to secure the area from the threat of Castile. He was rewarded: The Treaty of Alcanices, signed in 1297, gave Portugal the Ribacoa.

were on the sites of earlier forts: Morrish, Visiothic, Roman, or earlier. It is interesting to note developments in warfare that were reflected in physical features of Portugal's castles. Long verandas of wood, for example were in early days attached to the castles' walls. Later these were covered with animal hides so they could not be burned easily by flaming arrow, but were abandoned at the end of the 13th century. By then, the carved stone balconies, were used for the same purpose, with the added detail of the machicolation, which allowed defenders to repel attackers as they attempted to scale the castle wall. But the

Dinis provided the money for the castles, and even the exact measurements of the walls and towers. The castles of King Dinis were of a particularly fine construction, with decorations and designs not found on other buildings. Some of the towers were slender and elegant; many balconies elaborate, with detailed machicolations. Dinis often gave certain character or grandness to the structures, as in the 15 towers, he had built at Numao, or the delightful Torre do Galo, "Rooster Tower," at Freixo de Espada a Cinta, with its unusual and beautiful seven faces.

Many castles—built by Dinis and others—

Left, the Convent of Christ in Tomar, built by the Knights Templar and inherited by the Order of Christ. Above, the castle at Almourol.

most significant change came, with the advent of gunpowder and the artillery it brought. The heavy cannons required thicker walls to be built, sloped to resist the more powerful projectiles. Another reason for the thicker walls was so that the ramparts, running along the tops of the walls, could be wider. Earlier only men and their bows stood here, now the castles' heavy artillery was perched. Arrow slits, a common feature in castles, first became round to accommodate the new artillery, but were abandoned as impractical.

The sight of Portugal's charming castles will delight. Several of note are **Almeida**, east of Guarda; **Almourol**, perhaps the most romantic of all, set on its own small craggy island in the Tagus River and surrounded by myths; and, of course, **Guimaraes**, birthplace of Portugal's first king.

was granted all the former possessions of the Knights of Templar, but under royal, not papal control. It was as Grand Master of this Order of Christ that Prince Henry the Navigator would later have the resources to initiate and lead his renowned maritime trading and exploration.

Economic crises: Afonso IV succeeded Dinis. His administration was less sure, and hostilities with Castile waxed and waned. More significantly, his reign was burdened with the Black Plague. The first bout with the disease decimated the country, particularly the urban centers in 1348-9. Throughout the next century the pestilence would return again and again, causing both depopulation and despondency. Concurrently, various demographic and economic crises were beginning to undermine the nation. The attraction of the urban centers left the interior underpopu-

committed to maintaining total independence, and this, coupled with general social unrest, caused turbulence for Pedro I and his son Fernando, and finally brought down the House of Burgundy.

Betrothed to a Spanish princess, Pedro I instead fell madly in love with her alluring lady-in-waiting, Inês de Castro. It was not long before their dalliance became an open affair, much to the disgruntlement of his father, Afonso IV and powerful members of the court. Inês was no peasant though, in fact she was from a powerful Castilian family, and according to some, was manipulating Pedro for political ends.

Inês was banished in 1340, but upon the death of the princess Constanza in 1345, she returned to her lover. She lived in Coimbra with her children, secretly married to Pedro. The threat of a Castil-

lated. There was insufficient agricultural labor, leaving fields uncultivated and causing inflation in food prices. The kings tried to regulate the movements of the population to thwart migration to the cities, but their methods were ineffectual, based more on toothless coercion than on any persuasive economic motivation. The economic stagnation, whose dreary influence extended to literature, religion, and every element of daily life, would not truly end until the beginnings of the maritime empire.

Politics of this period, despite the independence of Portugal so well established under Dinis, were motivated largely by fear of Castilian domination. In fact, continual intermarriage between the two royal families did keep the possibility of unification open. But the Portuguese were

ian heir was intolerable to Afonso, who finally sanctioned her brutal assassination in 1355.

After being rebuffed in a brief civil war, Pedro, later known as "the Cruel" for his half-mad administration of justice and government, waited patiently for his revenge. He assumed the throne upon his father's death in 1357 and quickly tracked down his lover's assassins. They were brought before the king, who ordered their hearts torn out. In 1361, more than five years after her burial, Pedro ordered Inês to be exhumed, dressed in royal robes and crown, and placed next to him on the throne. Each member of the court was then forced to pay homage by kissing the dead queen's decomposed hand.

Aside from its immediate political consequences, this gruesome tale also later proved to be inspirational for historical dramas, romantic chronicles and poems. Adapted by writers such as Camões (in *Os Lusiadas*) and Antonio Ferreira (in *Castro*), the legend became a central legend for the Portuguese literary imagination. Today, the tombs of Inês de Castro and Pedro I, both in intricately detailed Gothic style, can be seen in the Santa Maria Monastery in Alcobaça.

Despite the instability of the monarch himself, the reign of Pedro I was marked by peaceful coexistence with Castile. Social and political growth was seen as the country recovered from the convulsions of the plague. However, the growing power of the nobles, the clergy and the emergent bourgeoisie, all represented in the cortes, would break loose in active social discontent during the reign of his son and successor, Fernando I.

Fernando tried to unite Portugal and Castile under his rule, engaging the country in a series of unpopular and unsuccessful wars with its neighbor. Even more disastrously, the wars provided a way for France and England to join the turmoil, using the Iberian peninsula as a theater of the Hundred Years' War. In 1373, Enrique II of Castile attacked Lisbon, burning and pillaging the city and forcing Fernando to pledge his alliance. To add to the confusion, the "Great Schism" divided the Catholic Church under opposing popes beginning in 1378, and Fernando alternated his loyalties frequently. The wars had ravaged the whole country, leaving the populace both tired of war and angry at the nobility they blamed for causing it.

Fernando had further alienated his subjects with his unpopular marriage to Leonor Teles, who was perceived to represent the landed gentry. Riots broke out at the marriage and again in 1383 when Fernando died, leaving his widow (with her lover, the Galician count, João Fernandez Andeiro) to rule as Queen-Mother.

Andeiro was assassinated within weeks by João, the illegitimate son of Pedro I and the Master of Avis, one of the national military-religious orders. In the ensuing civil war for the throne, Leonor had the support of most of the nobles and clergy, while João relied upon the support of the middle class. He depended upon the deepening resentment the people now felt toward Castile— Leonor had fled to Juan I of Castile after Andeiro's death—and rode this growing wave to victory. The final military conflict was the Battle of Aljubarrota, a decisive victory for João's troops, despite being outnumbered—thanks in large part to the contribution of a squadron of English archers.

Left, Dom Pedro I waits the Day of Judgement in his tomb at Santa Maria Monastery in Alcobaça. Above, the portal to the unfinished chapels at Batalha

A number of stories and legends surround this battle. The "Holy Constable" Nuno Álvares Pereira was captain of João's small squadron. As he valiantly led his charges in the battle, Nuno was agonizingly thirsty, with no water to be had anywhere on the plain. He swore that no traveler would ever go thirsty here again, and since 1385 a small pitcher of water has been daily placed in a niche of the Aljubarrota chapel of São Jorge. João, too, made a vow. Seeing that his army was vastly outnumbered he felt that victory would require a miracle, he swore to build a great church in the Virgin Mary's honor if his cause won the day. As the Castilian army turned tail and fled, João hurled his lance into the air to choose the place for the construction that would be the great Monastery of Batalha. If the story is true, João had a real good arm, because the battlefield is

some 10 miles from the Monastery.

The rule of João I, founder of the House of Avis, represented a new political beginning. The disputes with Castile continued, but they were winding down. The unsteady Anglo-Portuguese alliance was cemented by the Treaty of Windsor in 1386, a document which has been called to account as recently as World War II, when Britain invoked it to gain fueling way stations for airplanes and seacraft in the Azores.

João I brought stability, but the change of order could not be mistaken for a social revolution. New political representation was established by the mercantile class, but in time it was clear that only the names had changed among the landed aristocracy who still held real power. The new dynasty was much like the old.

EMPIRE BUILDING

João I ruled from 1385 to 1433, fending off the demands of a resurgent nobility by installing his sons Duarte, Pedro, Henry, Fernão, and João in powerful positions as the leaders of military-religious orders. Henry the Navigator, for example, was made Master of the Order of Christ. It was under João I that Portugal first began to look across the seas for solutions to their internal economic and political problems. Trade and exploration would serve both to occupy the nobility and to boost commerce. João's successor, King Duarte, initially continued with overseas expansion, but drew back after a disastrous failed attack on Tangiers. In 1438, Duarte died, setting off a brief civil war to determine who would be regent to his young son Afonso V. Pedro, relying on the support of the bourgeoisie and lower classes, defeated Queen Leonor (yes, another scheming Leonor, this one Duarte's widow) and her noble backers, for a time seemed to have effected a political turn of sorts. When Afonso V came of age, however, he gave his allegiance to the parties that had opposed Pedro. In one last futile attempt, Pedro fought the King at Alfarrobeira, in 1449, and Pedro and most of his followers were killed.

Two of Afonso's uncles were particularly trusted advisors, and stand as symbols of the ideals Afonso held throughout his reign: Henry the Navigator, leader of conquest, and Fernão, the Duke of Bragança and leader of the newly strengthened nobility. Each was granted a large share of independent power. For himself, King Afonso held the honor of his position, remaining above the fray of administration. He did not rule ineptly, but he was a chivalric soul, a debonair leader in an era where politics had been sullied and complicated by the growing power of mercantilists and low nobility. He concerned himself largely with martial glory, which he found crusading in North Africa. In 1471 he took Tangiers. Another of his accomplishment was the minting of the first *cruzado*, the gold coin that became a symbol of the wealth flowing in from the voyages. Unlike many coinages of the era, the *cruzado* was a remarkably stable currency, becoming a form of propaganda for Portuguese domination of world markets.

In 1475, there was civil discord in Castile because of a dispute for the crown. Afonso decided to marry Juana, one of the claimants, and

thus unite Portugal and Castile under his monarchy. He invaded in support of her claims, occupied León, but failed to hold his ground. He tried to enlist the aid of King Louis XI of France in support of his claims to the Castilian throne, traveling to France to make a personal plea. He arrived in the midst of Louis XI's tumultuous rivalry with the Duke of Burgundy and proved to be a hapless diplomat, quickly alienating both sides. Frustrated, he abdicated his throne to go on a pilgrimage to the Holy Land, but even this quixotic voyage was thwarted. Louis prevented the Portuguese monarch from embarking, virtu-

ally arresting him, and the despondent Afonso was deported to his homeland. His son, the future João II, stepped down from the throne, letting Afonso resume his nominal position, though thenceforth the rule was shared.

Under these kings, the overseas expansion began in earnest. It began, but no one prepared or knew how to prepare for the empire that was to come. It is important to remember that the discoveries were never systematic: they were sporadic, unplanned and limited. The little policy that existed was a strange mix of crusading ideals, romantic curiosity, and profit motive. Charting the world was always a secondary matter. It was less important, for example, than the search for the odd figure known as Prester John.

A mythical priest and king, Prester John was

Left, detail of a Japanese screen (ca. 1593) commemorating the arrival of Portuguese traders. Above, a statue of the Infante D. Henrique in Lagos.

supposed to have been the leader of a vast and powerful Christian empire located somewhere in the African interior. His legend was elaborated with tales of a kingdom that was an earthly paradise peopled with a bizarre menagerie of chimeras and mythical characters. Strange as it seems, this tale had an enormous influence on early exploration of Africa. In fact in 1455, after the Portuguese had established their dominance all along the northern coast, a Papal bull granted them the sole right to discovery and conquest of all of Africa except those parts ruled by Prester John. It was only later, by the early 16th century that Portugal's explorers began to realize that spice and gold were more accessible goals, and the voyages in and around Ethiopia were replaced with more profitable itineraries.

Another goal of seafarers was the still-popular

to be a debilitating obsession, diverting attention from surer if less spectacular sources of profit. These lesser goals were nevertheless an impetus for exploration from the start. Fishing ships had circled further and further out in search of richer waters. Moroccan grain, sugar, dyestuffs, and slaves were all found in Africa. These were eventually joined by the spices and rare woods of India and the Orient.

Preliminary to any exploration, of course, the technical aspects of navigation had to be discovered and mastered. Shipbuilding in Portugal took lessons from the Moslems and Italians, refining and strengthening their central-ruddered ships. They soon developed the wide-hulled *caravela* that was ideal for long-voyages with cargo. Key inventions like the compass and portulan chart (a kind of atlas) had vastly improved sailors' ability

slaughter of the infidel. Attacking Moslems wherever they could be found gave the voyages all the benefits of a crusade: the effort was legitimized, and the church lent its financial resources, to some extent, along with spiritual support, in the form of indulgences and martyrdoms. The sanctions of Rome, like the Bull of 1455, would become an important factor when maritime competition intensified.

Economic and social needs undoubtedly lay at the base of the voyages, but it is difficult to precisely unravel these motivations. Certainly there was a shortage of gold all over Europe. Without it, coinage was severely debased and the growth of commerce was retarded. Gold from Africa, America, and India eventually did find its way into the coffers of Lisbon, but it also proved

to plot and keep a course. Map-making was advancing, although some discoveries were jealously guarded. It is speculated that the Portuguese knew about Brazil some time before Cabral blew off course and officially noticed it in 1500.

Henry the Navigator is often credited with leading the discoveries, masterminding them while surrounded by expert astronomers and shipbuilders at his school of navigation in Sagres. The truth is more humble. His financial sponsorships and enthusiasm made him a definite influence, but discovering the world was beyond the scope of any one man.

With many hands at the tillers, the enterprise was not well-coordinated. Of course, no one knew exactly where they were headed in the first place. The main goal was to press the crusade forward and eventually to reconquer Jerusalem. Obviously, they had other goals as well. Maps were accurate enough to suggest that getting to Jerusalem via Brazil was definitely the scenic route. So Portugal took the world as it came, never quite planning what to do with it all.

Prince Henry's main goal was actually the taming of the North African coast, which meant the banishment of the Moors. He never traveled further than Morocco himself, although some of his brothers did. Records show that he devoted most of his time to squeezing profits out of his various tithes, monopolies and privilege revenues. Apparently, the income generated by the Order of Christ was a pinch; his household spendings and military expeditions to Africa consumed every cent he obtained. Only later in life, with increasing reports of wondrous and far-off places

benefit of their homeland.

Of course, popular history also makes some dubious claims for Portugal's heroes, for example, that they were the first to discover America. Afonso Sanches, blown off course on a trip to the East Indies, is said to have landed on an uncharted western coast, and on his return, shared the log of his misadventure with a certain Genoese navigator named Columbus.

Perhaps the first indisputable hero of the discoveries was Gil Eanes. Madeira and the Azores, along with the north of Africa, had been charted. The islands had begun to be colonized. The fabulous tales of the edge of the world and the various horrors of the south seas were soon connected with the stormy promontory of Cape Bojador, on the west coast of Africa. It became the boundary. Finally, in 1434, Gil Eanes, a pilot commissioned

to inspire him, did Henry give the discoveries his full attention. When he did, it was with the possibilities of early profit firmly in mind.

Epic heroes: It is easy to see why popular history might accord undue credit to an individual like Henry. The Age of Discovery was a time for heroes and adventurers, and also a time for the rebirth of knightly ideals. Fearless mariners sailed off into the unknown realms of sea monsters and cannibals. Their voyages were imbued with noble intentions: for the greater glory of the Church, in the service of knowledge, and for the

Left, the four winds blow hard and steady for the Portuguese Discoverers in this unusual 1519 map. Above, Cabral happens upon Brazil.

by Henry the Navigator, broke the barrier. He found more coast and safe water behind. He returned to Portugal triumphant, bringing wild roses plucked from the land beyond as proof, dubitable as it may have been, of his accomplishment. The next year he led voyages further down Africa's coast, and the way was open for the many who followed. They searched primarily for the legendary *Rio do Ouro* (River of Gold). Some of that precious ore was found, and the trips soon became profitable.

In 1482, Portuguese ships explored the mouth of the Congo River. In 1487, Bartolomeu Dias rounded the Cape of Good Hope. In 1494, Papal intervention in the growing competition between Spain and Portugal resulted in the famous Treaty of Tordesillas, which divided the newly discovered, as well as the still unknown lands between the two countries. This treaty granted Portugal the lands east of a line of demarcation 370 miles (592 km) west of the Azores. This put Brazil within Portugal's sphere. In 1497-99, Vasco da Gama sailed to Calicut in India and back, immediately throwing Portugal into competition with Moslem and Venetian spice traders. In 1500, Cabral officially discovered Brazil. In 1519-22, Ferdinand Magellan, a Portuguese in the service of Spain, led the first voyage to circumnavigate the globe, though he died before the journey was completed.

The expeditions opened the seaways, but there were battles to be fought to establish trading posts in the Indies. Arabs, protecting their own trade interests, fought the Portuguese wherever they could. The Portuguese, of course, were still intent

on eradicating such infidels from the face of the earth. So although Portugal had no intentions of land conquest, by simply striving to establish and maintain a monopoly of the high seas, they were constantly at war.

Succession of conquests: The great leader of these campaigns was Governor-General Afonso de Albuquerque, a brilliant strategist and, in essence, the founding father of the empire in Asia. His victories allowed garrisoned ports and fortresses to be built in key locations. Goa, in India, conquered in 1510, became the center for all operations. Malacca fell in 1511 and served as the East Indies hub, while Ormuz came under Portuguese control in 1515, proving the ideal seat from which to dominate the Persian Gulf. Later, in 1557, Macão was established on a kind of perma-

nent lease with China, extending Portugal's reach to the Far East.

Albuquerque administered these new holdings with a basic policy of colonization rather than exploitation. All the major cities, Goa in particular, were converted by architecture and government into European towns. Interracial marriages were encouraged and Catholic missions established.

The growth of Goa was extraordinary. By 1540 there were 10,000 European-descended households and the town was the seat of a bishopric. However, these few altered cities and the battles of the Indies were in marked contrast to the general policy of peaceful coexistence that Portugal used wherever it could. In Africa, Brazil, and the various islands and archipelagos, they tried to set up trade stations without interfering with local customs or politics.

It is, however, the exceptions that proved the most interesting: in the Congo, for example, where a number of missions were sent. The people of the kingdom there were quite taken with their European visitors, though they could provide little of interest to the tranders. The Portuguese had begun by overestimating the political and cultural sophistication of these people, and once the Congolese were exposed to certain Western practices, they embraced them. They took to Christianity, if their own version of it, and imitated the manners and fashions of the Portuguese. Their first Christian monarch dropped the unwieldy *"Nzinga a Nkuwu"* and renamed himself João I. His son took the name Afonso, and from that point into the 17th century the land was ruled by a succession of native Henriques, Pedros, and Franciscos.

The Congo, though it did provide both ivory and slaves, was not of central economic importance. The Portuguese *caravelas* were too busy reaping bounty elsewhere to pay much attention to cultural matters: spices were carried from the Indies, gold was found in the Sudan and other parts of Africa, sugar and wine was brought from Madeira, sugar and dyestuffs came from Brazil.

The wealth reaped overseas made for a stable economy, but it did not make Portugal rich. Individuals and the monarchy—taking its royal fifth of all trade revenues—became rich, but even they eventually found it difficult to hold or build their fortunes. Neither the relatively sudden rise, nor the long fall of the Portuguese trade empire is easy to encapsulate. There are many points of debate. Still, certain influences may be safely outlined.

At its beginning, the "empire" demanded little

Above, Vasco da Gama stands tall in Sines, the town where he was born. Right, Afonso de Albuquerque in a portrait (ca. 1509) by an unknown artist.

O COVERNADOR AFFONÇO E ALBOQVERQVE SVÇEDEO NA INDIA
A DOM FRANCISCO D ALME＿＿＿IDA EM NOVEMBRO DE
509 TOMOV DIAS VEZES ＿＿＿A CIDADE DE GOA FAS DE MALA
E TE ORVZ E FEZ A FORTALEZ＿＿＿A E CALECVT E FOI A PERÇIA E AO
ESTRETO DE ORMVZ E＿＿＿MAR ROXO

33

from its diminutive fatherland. Like other small trading centers in Italy and like the later Dutch empire, organization and central authority were more important than mere size. Furthermore, the early expeditions required little manpower. It was only later, when they found themselves trying to enforce their worldwide trade monopoly, that Portugal's small population began to tell. It has been suggested that a crucial deficiency was Portugal's lack of a middle class—quashed by royal and noble dominance of commerce—a group that might have provided qualified and educated planners, pilots and administrators.

In explaining the empire's failure, some have pointed to widespread corruption or to the foreign control of profits garnered from Portuguese expeditions. How great an effect they had is arguable. Certainly the religious efforts that went hand in

hand with Portuguese voyages did not make the wheels of commerce spin any more freely. Whether fighting Moslems with whom they had once peacefully coexisted, or trying to force Christianity down the throats of local populations, the Portuguese lost time and focus from the business of business. Whatever the causes, it is clear that the potential benefits of the burgeoning overseas trade were not being reaped by Portugal. Deflation in Europe stifled trade. Domestic agricultural production, hampered by a lack of manpower, lagged, occasionally causing serious shortages of meat and grain. Even the Crown was in debt, as the cost of the trading empire was, surprisingly, more than its revenues.

It was, of course, many years before these flaws and inabilities truly sank the empire. Trade

continued for several centuries, although it steadily deteriorated. Portugal eventually turned away from the Indies and poured their efforts to maintaining Brazil.

Before the slide began, the lively age of empire did bring sufficient peace and prosperity for Portugal to fortify truly great eras of artistic and humanist achievement. João II had taken over from the flighty Afonso V in 1481. Revitalizing the throne, he managed to take up where Henry the Navigator, who died in 1460, had left off. João turned away from the nobility, minimizing their rights and calling upon the *cortes* for support. A conspiracy soon gathered against the king, but he learned of the central traitors soon enough to strike back. In 1484, the Duke of Bragança was briefly tried and beheaded. When other members of the nobility fled the country for their lives, their titles and holdings reverted to the crown. The Duke of Viseu unwisely mounted a second plot, and was stabbed by the king himself. Another group fled the country, and João II was in the catbird's seat.

The prestige and authority that these fierce, Machiavellian tactics had given to the monarchy would stand undiminished for centuries. However, João's successor, Manuel I had to steer a course between the ferocity of his predecessor and the idealistic nobility of Afonso V. This was accomplished with diplomatic and farsighted administration. The estates of the noble families were largely restored, though this did not restore their political power. Judicial and tax reforms worked to bring authority to government on both the national and local levels. The postal system was instituted. Public services like hospitals were centralized. And essentially, Manuel lifted the power of the monarchy above both the nobles and the *cortes* , launching the first era of enlightened absolutism.

Importance of education: Manuel also fostered contacts with the Renaissance humanism then spreading throughout Europe. There were many trade, religious and cultural contacts with Italy, in particular, and young Portuguese men began to seek educations abroad, at the universities in France or Spain. In fact, Manuel actually tried to buy Paris's renowned Saint Barbara College. Though he failed, it became a center for Portuguese students. By 1487 a printing press had been established in Lisbon. Portugal entered the 16th century with a rush of new cultural currents.

New colleges and educational reforms at home were fundamental elements of the next century's progress. Teaching methods were modernized and curriculum expanded. There was more opportunity for specialization and dialectic. The students were drawn from a larger pool, now including aristocrats and wealthy bourgeois in addition to the young members from the religious orders.

CAMÕES

Luís de Camões did not live to reap the celebrity of his poetry. He began and ended life poor, though he did find romance and adventure in between.

After attending the University at Coimbra, the young poet's prospects were good. However, many twists of fate lay ahead. An affair with one of the Queen's ladies-in-waiting caused his banishment to North Africa, where he lost an eye in military service. Returning to Lisbon, Camões was involved in a skirmish that wounded a magistrate. He ended up in prison and then was banished again, in 1553, this time to Goa in India. It was 1570 before he returned to Lisbon. Having written poetry and plays for many years with some success, he published *Os Lusíadas* in 1572. The poem's worth was recognized immediately, and as a reward Camões received a small royal pension. His final illness, however, was spent in a public hospital. When he died, in 1580, he was buried in a common grave.

The title *Os Lusíadas* means the sons of Lusus, the mythical founder of Portugal: poetically, then, it means "the Portuguese." Echoing classical models, the poem chronicled the voyages of Vasco da Gama, before a panorama of strangely mixed Christian and pagan images.

Os Lusíadas has been hailed throughout Europe (Lope de Vega and Montesquieu were early admirers) sometimes to the detriment of Portugal's other literature, Portugal's one masterpiece. Under Salazar, *Os Lusíadas* became an icon of Portuguese nationalism. Speeches and propaganda were peppered with quotes drawn from the great book, providing a mythos for imperialism, without reflection upon the differences between the 16th and 20th centuries.

The 18th-century verse translation by W. J. Mickle, quoted below, though tinged with the lyrical romanticism of that era, captures the proud spirit of the poem from the opening lines:

Arms and the heroes, who from Lisbon's shore,
Thro' seas where sail was never spread before,
Beyond where Ceylon lifts her spicy breast,
And waves her woods above the watery waste,
With prowess more than human forc'd their way
To the fair kingdoms of the rising day.

In the second canto the treacherous Moslems—"faithless race"—*prepare to attack:*
On shore the truthless monarch arms his bands,

And for the flee's approach impatient stand:
That soon as anchor'd in the port they rode
Brave Gama's decks might reek with Lusian blood:
Thus weening to revenge Mozambique's fate,
And give full surfeit to the Moorish hate...

In the world of the discoverers, the enemy forces take their strength from the netherworld:
As when the whirlwinds, sudden bursting, bear
Th' autumnal leaves high floating through the air;
So rose the legions of th' infernal state,
Dark Fraud, base Art, fierce Rage, and burning

Hate:
Wing'd by the Furies to the Indian strand
They bend; the Demon leads the dreadful band,
And in the bosoms of the raging Moors
All their collected living strength he pours.

At Vasco da Gama's request, the chronicler aboard the ship retells Portugal's history, and, in this section, recounts the "glad assistance" brought by the crusaders who helped take Lisbon from the Moors.

Their vows were holy, and the cause the same,
To blot from Europe's shores the Moorish name.
In Sancho's cause the gallant navy joins,
And royal Sylves to their force resigns.
Thus sent by heaven a foreign naval band
Gave Lisboa's ramparts to the Sire's command.

Left, the library at the University of Coimbra, decorated with baroque gilt and chinoiserie japanning. Above, a bust of Camões that once graced a ship's bow.

The purposes and potential of these changes was not without its crises. The University of Lisbon had a cultural and political influence that was threatening to the crown. It was difficult to impinge upon their traditional autonomy, but Manuel, as part of his general process of centralization, tried to force change through economic and legal pressure.

Finding great resistance, he turned to the idea of founding a new University elsewhere, without success. João III continued these efforts and finally more or less quashed the University, shifting it to Coimbra, and sapping its political strength in the process. Later in the 16th century this conflict culminated in João III's giving control of national education to the Jesuits. It was a victory for the monarchy. There would be no university in Lisbon again until 1911.

Nonetheless, the century inspired a broad-ranging intellectual vigor, a fitting counterpart to the great voyages of discovery. Some of the works produced were directly attributable to the expeditions. Travel books, of both scientific and cultural themes, were a rich vein of literature. Tomé Pires wrote *Suma Oriental* (1550), which described his voyages in the East. Many of these wandering writers were Jesuit missionaries, whose concerns with converting the natives led them to make careful sociological and ethnological observations. The most renowned traveler, the Marco Polo of Portugal, was Fernão Mendes Pinto, whose *Peregrinaçam* (Pilgramage) brought imagination and lively style to the form. Among the historians of this period, who adopted modern concern for accuracy and some

measure of objectivity, were Fernão Lopes, who wrote a history of João I's reign, and João de Barros, who chronicled the conquests in Asia.

The courtly verses typical of King Dinis's reign were still very popular, but the strong influence of the Italian Renaissance broadened the themes of poetry. Out of the troubadour tradition, but going far beyond it, was Gil Vicente, the founder of the Portuguese theater, who wrote scores of satirical and comic one-act plays. Vicente began life as a goldsmith, and in *Farsa dos Almocreves* he writes himself into a farce about an impoverished nobleman who can never pay his entourage or creditors. When the goldsmith asks, eloquently, for long overdue payment, the nobleman procrastinates:

"How most cunningly inlaid
And enamelled is each word!
I rejoice not to have paid
For the sake of having heard
Phrases with such skill arrayed."
(A.F.G. Bell translation)

In the second half of the 16th century, a new group of writers emerged, including António Ferreira, Diogo Bernardes, and, the most renowned of all, Luís de Camões. *Os Lusiadas* Camões's masterpiece, is an epic national poem celebrating the discoveries that was first published in 1572. It is rightfully renowned as a classic of world literature. (See box story.)

However, these great writers aside, Portugal's main contributions to the intellectual ferment of the Renaissance were in science, particularly (and naturally) in navigation, astronomy, math, and geography. Their contribution was not the mere accumulation of facts from foreign places. New methods amounted to a kind of skepticism, a science based on experience rather than recorded facts. Having disproved a dozen theories of the shape, limits, and contours of the earth, the Portuguese felt free to question the other dogmas of antiquity.

Yet even as new writers and new sciences were coming to the fore, a Counter-Reformation (though there had been no real Reformation, the Portuguese Catholics having an essential antipathy to the simplifying and icon-destroying Germanic philosophies) was casting a pall of religious conformism over learning and creativity. In addition, the political threat to Portuguese autonomy—the future union with Spain was already an undercurrent—hung over all these achievements. In fact, Camões, Vicente and many of the others actually wrote as much as half their works in Castilian, the rest in their native Portuguese.

Portuguese Inquisition: João III ruled from 1521-1557. He continued Manuel's expansion of the trade empire and royal authority. Perhaps his most significant act was the establishment of the Inquisition in Portugal. The Inquisition was intended to be a tool of the monarchy, and for a time it was. Eventually, however, it took on a direction and authority of its own. The Papacy knew that there was no real need for the Inquisition, no menaces to the unity of faith in Portugal, so it was resisted for many years. João III used every diplomatic intrigue at his disposal and finally won approval for a greatly limited version of the Inquisition in 1536. In 1547 those restrictions were lifted.

With this turn of events the rule of João III turned, too—away from the humanist influences of Europe and toward religious fanaticism. The bureaucracy of the Inquisition expanded quickly, its main target being the converted Jews known as New Christians. The victimized group was persecuted as much for their role as middle-class mercantilists as for religious deviation. The power of the Inquisition grew quickly, with the

The ascension of King Sebastião in 1568 only exacerbated these excesses. His regency, from 1557-1568, was a period of stability, though marked by signs of trouble to come. The Inquisition grew in power. The *Casa da India*, the national trade corporation, went bankrupt in 1560. Then the 14-year-old Sebastião took the throne. An unstable and idealistic king, with a dangerous streak of chivalry like Afonso V, he took upon himself the crusade against the Moors of North Africa. A lack of funds prevented him from undertaking the task for many years. In the meantime he surrounded himself with cohorts no older and no more sensible than himself, dismissing the warnings of older, more prudent statesmen. Finally sensing that the time was right, he spent every *cruzado* he could raise on mercenaries and outfitting his troops. He set sail for Mo-

inquisitor-generals taking orders only from Rome. The inquisitor-generals also carried the right of excommunication, and utilizing the public and spectacular *autos-da-fé*, soon had an influence far beyond their legal authority. The influence of the Inquisition, with its rigid orthodoxy, vengeful judiciary, and general intolerance, was equally deadening to both culture and commerce. Many of the bourgeois leaders of trade were targets. Later, the Inquisition would virtually govern Portugal, usurping the authority of the monarchy during the union with Spain.

Left, detail from a portrait of João III by Christovão Lopes. Above, an engraving of the *auto-de-fé* processional; a festive affair for everyone, or almost everyone.

rocco in 1578. Sebastião was no better a military leader than administrator, madly dismissing stratagem and planning as cowardice. He refused, for example, to consider the possibility of retreat—and therefore had no plan for it. Outnumbered and outmaneuvered at the Battle of Alcacer-Quiber, his army of 18,000 men was destroyed. Some 8,000, including Sebastião and most of Portugal's young nobility, were slaughtered. Only 100 or so escaped death or capture. With this debilitating disaster, the way was open for Spain to step in. From 1578-1580, Cardinal Henrique was king, occupied primarily with raising the ruinous ransoms for the captured soldiers of Alcacer-Quiber. In 1580, Philip II of Spain invaded and within a year was installed as Philip I of Portugal.

THE CONQUERORS ARE CONQUERED

Throughout their rule over Portugal, the Spanish Habsburg kings faced many challenges to their authority. Not the least of their problems was that King Sebastião kept rising from the grave. After the massacre at Alcacer-Quiber, a devastating blow to national pride, there arose a popular belief that their lost king would rise again to restore all that was lost. Consequently, a number of false Sebastiãos tried to reclaim the throne. Though they satisfied the wild hopes of the lower classes, none of these rabble-mongers made a significant play for the crown.

At the root of both the accomplishment and the

continuation of the Iberian Union was the support provided by merchants and traders. The Dutch and other countries were strongly challenging Portuguese shipping, slicing into vital profits. It was supposed by the bourgeoisie that by combining Spanish and Portuguese interests, the maritime empire could be reclaimed; or at least what was left could be better protected. The "alliance" with Spain would also open up inland trade. At any rate, there were few options: Portugal's treasury was empty.

Politically, the union was accomplished by Philip II of Spain. After Alcacer-Quiber, a number of candidates aspired to take the Portuguese throne. Philip II, though his genealogical claim to the throne was more tenuous than his competitors', was a far more viable ruler than any of them.

He was the grandson of Manuel I, which proved adequate, given his political wiles and power. The majority of the populace was opposed to the Spanish king, but the relatively impoverished nobles, clergy, and upper bourgeoisie saw that Philip could provide fiscal and military stability. Ironically, the most powerful group to resist the union were the *Spanish* ruling classes, who saw the danger of untrammeled Portuguese trading within their traditional markets.

Part of Philip's appeal was that he promised to maintain Portugal's autonomy in many specific ways: no Spanish representation in Portuguese legislative and judicial bodies; no change in official language; the overseas empire would still be ruled by Portugal; no grants of Portuguese assets to non-Portuguese; and so forth. In fact, Philip would more or less fulfill these promises. On this platform, after chasing out a small army who supported the claims of António, Manuel's son, Philip took up residence in Lisbon. In 1581 he summoned the *cortes* to declare him king with the title Philip I.

After the years of mismanaged government, the efficient bureaucracy of the union provided relief for Portugal's uneasy finances. However, with the succession of Philip II (III of Spain), the Spanish began to press their powers too far. Lacking Philip I's diplomatic savvy, they bungled relations between the two countries, and tried to correct their mistakes through force. Resistance grew. Philip III managed to succeed to the throne in 1619, but the union continued to erode. Spain was weakened by its involvement in the Thirty Years' War with France. Portuguese troops were forced into battle and taxes were pressed upwards.

The 60 years of union with Spain did nothing to protect Portugal's empire. The Dutch and the English usurped one after another of their former strongholds. Naturally, Portugal tended to blame the Spanish administration for these defeats, rather than reacting constructively. Between 1620 and 1640, Ormuz, Baia, São Jorge da Mina and many more trade centers fell. In 1630 the Dutch established themselves in Brazil; in 1638 they took Ceylon. There were still ports and territories controlled by the Portuguese traders, but the "monopoly of the seas" was a dream quickly fading from memory. What's more, to a country once intent upon ridding the earth of the last vestige of the infidels, it was particularly devastating to surrender their missions to the Dutch, purveyors of the heretical Protestantism.

For the Portuguese, each of the three Philips who reigned over them was worse than the last.

The Spanish domination became less respectful and more grating on the populace. Philip II did not even deign to visit the country for years after his coronation. Philip III systematically breached all the guarantees put in place by his grandfather. The incipient revolution was aided by insurgents and secret diplomatic agents sent by the French, who were still embroiled with Spain in the Thirty Years' War.

The Bragança regime: On December 1, 1640, a coup in Lisbon capped the growing revolutionary fervor. The palace was attacked and the reigning Spanish governor, the Duchess of Mantua, was deposed and arrested while her strongman, Miguel de Vasconcelos, was fatally defenestrated. The Duke of Bragança, though he had been reluctant to lead the revolt, was declared king within a few days as João IV. So was ushered in Portugal's final royal period, as the House of Bragança would hold power until the 20th century and the First Republic.

Most of João IV's 16-year reign was occupied in hapless efforts to form diplomatic ties in Europe. France, England, Holland, and the Pope all refused to confirm Portuguese independence. Only Spain's preoccupation with other battles, some heroicPortuguese military stands along the frontier, and a well-organized national administration managed to hold their restored independence. One of João's most important long-term achievements, though he was at least partly forced into it, was turning emphasis away from trade with the Indies and toward Brazil.

On his ascension to the throne in 1656, Afonso VI was still a minor, though his youth was the least of his problems. Later, married off to a French princess, he behaved like a roustabout, associated with base criminal elements and, worst of all, proved to be impotent, a fact elicited from the scandalous public inquiry that was necessary to annul his marriage. Both his wife and his throne were eventually usurped by his brother, who ruled as Pedro II.

Until then, Queen-mother Luisa acted as Afonso's regent, and political control resided for the most part in the nobles who had been established in João IV's administration. War with Spain waxed and waned from 1640 until 1655. It was 1668 before the Spanish officially recognized Portugal's independence. During this period diplomatic efforts continued in the hopes of making vital alliances. In 1654 a treaty of friendship and cooperation was signed with England, a useful link, but also the first step down a primrose path that guaranteed Portugal's economic subservience to Britain for centuries to come. In 1661 a

treaty was also signed with Holland, and the alliance with England was sealed by the marriage of Princess Catarina to Charles II. Included in her dowry gifts to England were Tangier and Bombay. These moves sparked a new round of battles with Spain, but the two sides were quickly exhausted, both economically and politically. In 1665 a decisive Portuguese victory at Montes Claros ended the fighting.

Pedro II became prince-regent to his brother in 1668, was officially crowned king in 1683 and ruled until 1706. His long reign, though stable, was deeply marked by an unrelenting economic depression. The primary cause of this long decline was the dissipation of maritime commerce. The spice trade was almost entirely taken from out of their hands, while sugar and slaves went through periods of both competition and crisis

when Portugal could ill afford such instability. On the mainland, olive trees and grape vineyards offered good profits, but they were largely controlled by British interests, and they took up land that would have been better devoted to grain production. Grain shortages were common throughout the era.

Economists of that age who analyzed world trade patterns and studied the new doctrines of mercantilism dictated industry as Portugal's future. Two of Pedro's finance ministers, the Count of Ericeira and the Marquês of Fronteira helped plan numerous factories. Glass, textile, iron, tiles and pottery industries were all supported by the state in an effort to balance national trade deficits.

The mercantilist approach made some headway, but what finally dispelled the economic

Left, one of the movers and shakers of the Restoration, Antão de Almada. Above, Pedro II, a more potent leader than his brother Afonso VI

gloom was neither industrialization nor reorganization of any sort, but the discovery of gold in Brazil. With a constant stream pouring in, Portugal could once again rely on the exports of wine, olive oil and sugar. The infant industries sputtered and halted. The Count of Ericeira committed suicide, while Fronteira renounced his previous economic philosophy. Eventually, when Brazil began to hold onto its own mineral wealth, the various manufacturers started again, but it was only under Pombal, after mid-century, that they prospered.

Before the gold strikes of 1693-95, Brazil had been considered a second-rate colony. Portugal had hoped, given Spain's strikes in Peru and Mexico, that its piece of South American would yield the precious ore, but effort after effort came up empty. Despite these disappointments, when

Portugal had to retract the bounds of its empire, it wisely chose to defend Brazil and let the Asian trade go to the free market.

Even before gold, Brazil offered a number of valuable commodities: sugar, brazilwood, cotton, tobacco, and some spices and dyestuffs as well. The husbandry of cattle started slowly, but by the end of the 17th century, was providing lucrative exports of meat and leather.

The Jesuit missionaries were extremely influential in Brazil, as both explorers and settlers. Among other things they held the brazilwood monopoly for over two decades (1625-49). More importantly, they were successful in winning over the native populace to Christianity, and in large part, preventing their enslavement. The abundant colonial economy naturally had much

need for native labor, and the Jesuits were pressured to step aside, though they had the clear support of Rome in the form of a Papal bull (1639) that threatened excommunication for the trading of natives. Oddly enough, the Jesuit's humanitarianism did not extend to the African slaves, who were imported in great numbers to work the expanding sugar plantations.

In 1706, João V succeeded Pedro II, and began to spend the Brazilian gold with a vengeance. Taking his cue from other monarchs, particularly the French court of Louis XIV, he quickly earned the moniker "the Magnanimous." Palaces, churches and monasteries were erected, and support was granted to the arts and to education. Along with this extravagance came a moral profligacy. Convents around Lisbon were converted from religious houses into aristocratic brothels, while the inhabitants were still nuns, more or less. Among the royal constructions were palaces to house João's numerous bastard sons, born of various nuns. The instability of the monarch's life was in more or less inverse proportion to the economic and political stability of Portugal.

When João died in 1750 his son José succeeded him, but proved to be more interested in opera, a recent Italian import, than in matters of state. The full power of the crown was entrusted to a diplomat and member of the lower aristocracy, Sebastião José de Carvalho e Melo, who eventually earned the title by which he is better known, Marquês de Pombal.

Enlightened absolutism, as typified by the ministry of Pombal, represented both a beginning and an end. The enlightment ideal of rationalism meant a leap toward modernity, while the concomitant republican ideal of social equality meant that royal absolutism was on its last legs. Pombal's insistence on exercising royal prerogative sounded a death knell for the political power of nobles and clergy alike, and, quite unintentionally, allowed the bourgeoisie to take over administrative and economic control. His was an oppressive, dictatorial rule, though he was careful never to claim any personal power. The crown, which embodied all law, was omnipotent; he was merely its officer

The great earthquake: In 1755, on All Saints' Day—just as Mass was beginning—Lisbon was destroyed by a massive earthquake. Estimates vary, but at least 5,000 people were killed in the initial impact, many while attending morning services. Many more died of secondary and aftereffects. Fallen church candles quickly ignited the wreckage around them. Survivors rushed from

Above, urban renewal in one fell swoop as Lisbon topples in the earthquake of 1755. Right, a 19th-century political cartoon satirizing Napoleon's deviltry

41

the blaze toward the safety of the Tagus, only to be met by a massive tidal wave. In the weeks afterwards infected wounds, epidemics and famine also took their toll. The final count may have been as high as 40,000.

The Jesuits tried to fix the blame for this divine retribution upon Pombal's wayward and "athiestic" policies. (He had angered them by his hard line policies in Brazil, curbing their control over their native protégés.) He weathered both their criticism and their plot to assassinate him. The Jesuits' power throughout Europe was dissolving, and in 1759 they were officially disbanded and exiled from Portugal.

The catastrophe that shook the country's faith allowed Pombal's policies of secularization and rational government to take firm hold. He took absolute control, declaring "close the ports, bury

was first used, derisively as well, the word *estrangeirados* means "imitators of foreigners". It referred to Portuguese expatriates as well as those who had returned. Both groups were influential, particularly in defining a cultural identity for Portugal that was distinct from Spain. They undertook a conscious cultural split from Spanish influences, turning toward Europe and America. One *estrangeirado*, Correia da Serra, a diplomat and man of letters, became Portugal's first envoy to the United States, where Thomas Jefferson would later offer him the presidency of the University of Virginia.

As Pombal's sponsor-king José neared the end of his reign, the Marquês plotted to force the crown-princess Maria to renounce her rights so that her son José, a disciple of Pombal, could continue the policy of despotism. The efforts

the dead, feed the living," and setting the city to the task. José granted his minister emergency powers (which were not rescinded for some 20 years) and Pombal used them to rebuild Lisbon according to an eminently neoclassical plan, both neatly geometric and functionally sound. University reforms weakened religious elements. The social and legal distinction between old and "new Christians" (Jews) was abolished. Pombal's economic reforms helped Portugal remained stable when Brazilian gold production waned around 1760. And he managed to rebuild Lisbon without depleting the state treasury.

Pombal was one of the *estrangeirados*, a group of Portuguese who were educated in Europe, and looked toward Europe when planning their country's future course. Literally, and when it

failed and Maria, a pious, but somewhat imbalanced woman with no sympathy for Pombal's oppressive rule ascended in 1777. She immediately tried the former minister of various crimes against the state and found him guilty, confining him to his estate rather than prison, out of deference to his age. Though she revived religious elements of a government and culture that had been increasingly secular, she allowed most of Pombal's very necessary economic and administrative reforms to stay in place. Her reign was conservative in tenor, allowing the governmental underpinnings established by Pombal to provide steady, if slow, economic progress.

Both Maria's political and personal health were badly shaken by news of the French Revolution in 1789. In 179 1ong after her behavior had become an embarassment, she was declared insane. Her son João, an awkward and nervous man, took over the crown as regent, officially becoming king after Maria died in 1816 (his older brother José, had died in 1788).

The Portuguese monarchy and nobility feared that the French Revolution, and to a lesser extent, that of America, might be contagious. They were particularly wary about the possibility of democratic insurgency in Brazil. Though gold exports from that country were on the decline, they were quickly being supplanted by beef, cotton and tobacco. In 1793, Portugal sent troops to fight revolutionary France, further aligning itself with England and against French-controlled Spain. In 1801, Spain invaded in the War of the Oranges. Portugal ceded various political concessions, and forever lost the town of Olivença.

In July 1808, Britain came galloping to the rescue under the leadership of the master military tactician, Sir Arthur Wellesley, who was later dubbed the Duke of Wellington. The Peninsular War, sometimes called the War of National Liberation, lasted two years, expelling the French, but devastating the country. There were three waves of attacks set back by Portuguese victories at Roliça, Vimeiro, Buçaco, and the lines at Torres Vedras. The wars left the country in rocky shape. Portugal's capital was now located across the ocean in Rio de Janeiro and the nation's general weakness fostered Brazil's claims for autonomy. In 1815 Brazil was declared a kingdom on equal footing with Portugal.

The French (and English) had sacked many national treasures in Portugal, stealing paintings, sculptures, jewelry, books—all of which were

In 1807, Napoleon delivered an ultimatum to Portugal, a bad tiding to receive at a time when the Little Corporal was considered invincible. It was demanded that Portugal declare war on Britain, and, specifically, that it close its ports to British shipping. But Portugal could not possibly turn on its long-term allies. Napoleon was defied. While the royal family scooted off to Brazil for safety, the French General Junot marched into Lisbon. Initially, the Portuguese government offered no resistance.

Left, while Carlotta Joaquina led the debaucheries at Queluz, above, the citizens rallied in the streets, for the Liberal Revolution of 1820

especially lamentable losses for such a small country. The regency in Lisbon showed no intelligence in their rule, governing with uncoordinated despotism, ignoring the burgeoning democratic groundswell. The monarchy's blindness to contemporary political ideas fostered the revolution that would break in 1820.

The British military occupation, under the leadership of Marshal William Beresford, though necessary and sometimes appreciated, had further undermined Portuguese self-determination. British control, particularly in the economic realm had been growing throughout the 18th century. The Treaty of Methuen (1703) had established their dominance of the wine industry and generally served to stifle industrialization in Portugal. Various treaties continued this relationship, and in 1810, Portugal was forced to cede to Britain the right to trade directly with Brazil, eliminating its role as middleman, which had been an economic mainstay. Portugal was taking on all aspects of a British protectorate with Marshal Beresford wielding dictatorial control.

The roots of the liberal revolution of 1820 lay in the French influences, picked up by various military and secret societies, especially a Masonic lodge called Sinédrio. One of the primary events that coalesced the movement involved a plot by one of these clandestine groups against the British rule. A dozen conspirators were accused of plotting to assassinate Marshal Beresford in 1817. All of them, including the alleged leader, Lieutenant-General Gomes Freire de Andrade, were summarily tried and executed. This brutal reprisal heated Portuguese resentment and fos-

document was ahead of its time, with broad guarantees of individual liberties and no special perogatives for nobles or clergy. It lasted only two years, but did succeed in finally legally banning the Inquisition, which, though very nearly defunct, had lingered on and on.

Greedy for power: Portugal's profoundly conservative streak made the revolution not a time of competition among rival factions, but a simple split between republicans and absolutists. New charters and new efforts to restore full-bodied monarchy kept the country unsettled throughout the first half of the 19th century. In 1824, for example, João VI resisted a conspiracy of royalist extremists led by his own wife Carlotta and his son Miguel.

João's queen was the notorious Spanish princess Carlotta Joaquina, who had made herself an

tered support for the Liberal movement. The tyranny of the regime could no longer be denied, and it was becoming equally apparent that only violent means could force a change.

In 1820, the Spanish Liberal movement had won control of their government providing further inspiration, as well as political support for Portuguese Liberal forces. The moment arrived for Portugal when Beresford left the country to go to Brazil on a diplomatic mission to discuss the growing problem. His absence was the spark, and the Portuguese military revolved. The uprising began in Oporto, and eventually forced João VI to return from Brazil where he had been trying to ignore the turmoil at home. By the time he arrived, the new constitutional ideology was firmly in place. A constitution was adopted in 1822. The

epitome of the "old regime." She tried her best to make a Versailles of her palace at Queluz, surrounding herself with absolutists and engaging in outrageous royal decadence, begetting numerous children by various lovers from among her entourage. Her flamboyant leadership of the absolutist cause made her popular among a substantial following. However, the failure of her conspiracy to dethrone her husband in favor of her son, after which Miguel was banished to Brazil, marked the end of her influence.

The politics of the next 50 years were endlessly

Above, King Carlos and Prince Filipe, now honored in death, were reviled and assassinated by revolutionaries in 1910

complex, and this served to distract national attention and energies, which only further burdened Portugal's economic deceleration. In 1826 João VI died, leaving Pedro, his eldest son, who was still in Brazil, as heir to the throne. After failing to unite the two kingdoms through political maneuvers, he chose to stay in Brazil, abdicating the Portuguese throne to his seven-year-old daughter, who became Maria II. Pedro's plan was that the girl would marry her uncle, the exiled Miguel, who would rule as her regent under a moderate constitution.

Miguel had other ideas. Upon his return he abolished the constitution and invoked a counter-revolutionary *cortes* to name him king. There was considerable popular support for these moves, but still enough sympathy for constitutional ideas that Pedro could return and eventually defeat his brother in what were known as the Miguelist Wars. Pedro had abdicated his Brazilian empire so that he could defend his appointment of Maria II. Though this "War of Two Brothers" did little to resolve the deep conflict between absolutist and republican ideologies in Portugal, in fact it marked the last time that absolutism was ever in official power. Constitutional monarchy—though practically absolutist at times—would hold sway until 1910.

Pedro died in 1834 and his daughter, now 15, finally took the throne as Maria II. She reigned until 1853, during which time the first political parties developed. The liberals, victorious over absolutism, divided into conservatives and progressives. The *Septembrists*, given their name for their revolutionary victory in September of 1836, came into power first. They initially restored the constitution of 1822, but then adopted a more moderate constitution. They were opposed by *Chartists* who took their stand, and name, from the conservative charter of 1826.

In 1839, as the Septembrists were suffering from internal dissension, the Chartists came to the fore. Supported by the Queen, they were led by Costa Cabral and took power in 1839. Costa Cabral's government was authoritarian, and, though it provided stability, became more and more corrupt and autocratic. In 1846 the popular uprising known as the revolution of Maria da Fonte demanded his downfall. Maria II tried to replace him with the equally conservative Duke of Saldanha, a grandson of Pombal, and the country stood at the edge of civil war. English and Spanish intervention prevented mass violence, but resulted in Costa Cabral being returned to power. In 1851, without a war, Costa Cabral was ousted for good and Saldanha took his place.

The early period of Saldanha's rule was a period of transformation out of which came the political divisions that would exist throughout the century. Saldanha introduced a compromise to the constitutional debate that allowed his new party, *Regeneraçao*, to encompass both the old Chartists and the moderate progressives. The amendments to the constitution allowed for direct elections and an expanded electorate. Those who were still more radical, a small group at first, would become known as the *Históricos* and then *Progressistas*.

In 1853 Maria II died in childbirth. Her husband, the German Duke Ferdinand of Saxe-Coburg-Gotha, ruled as the regent until their son Pedro V, came of age in 1855. Pedro, a young but wise ruler, died in 1861 and was succeeded by his brother, Luís I. Constitutional monarchs tend to be judged best by those who stayed farthest from politics, and the change from the meddling Maria to the literary Luís was a clear victory for the republican government. Among his other accomplishments, King Luís translated Shakespeare into Portuguese.

The reign of Luís lasted until 1889 and was a period of relative peace. Conservatives and liberals alternated in controlling the legislature. Portugal's external affairs were more or less dictated by England, their protector under the Congress of Vienna's partitioning of smaller countries under major powers. Portugal was, however, tenacious in holding onto many of its colonial claims and territories in Africa. The high expense of maintaining those colonies was a burden to the rickety national economy, but it would stand them in good stead when the holdings finally did pay off during the 20th century. In the meantime, Portugal's finances were a muddle. The havoc wrought by the peninsular and Miguelite wars, on top of the loss of Brazil, was insurmountable. In 1889, Carlos I became king, setting African expansion as his primary goal, but his efforts were unsuccessful. In 1892, Portugal declared bankruptcy.

Carlos, still dreaming of restoring the empire, could do little to defuse the growing anti-monarchical sentiment. Socialism and trade unionism were growing influences. The legislative *cortes* had degenerated into a powerless assembly full of obstructive and self-promoting debate. Corruption and inefficiency were rampant.

In 1906, struggling to maintain some form of control, Carlos appointed João Franco as Prime Minister, endowing him with dictatorial powers. He quickly dissolved the useless legislature. In 1908 unknown parties, either members of a republican secret society or isolated anti-monarchical fanatics, assassinated Carlos as well as his son Luís Filipe, heir to the throne. In the assault upon the royal carriage, Manuel, the king's second son, was wounded but survived. In the next two years Manuel II tried to save the monarchy, offering various concessions, but the assassination had served to fortify the republican movement. The long-decrepit House of Bragança finally tumbled into dust.

REVOLUTION AND EVOLUTION

The paths of Portuguese cultural development in the 19th century followed many of the same byways as the country's politics. The influence of the rest of Europe was both heavily felt and intermittently resisted. The slow turning from conservative romanticism to modern rationalism that seems so natural in retrospect was experienced as a series of shocks.

Arts and literature were greatly influenced by politics, even during the romantic period. The energies of both liberal and conservative intellectuals were turned outward; they were forever in the process of "rebuilding" their nation. Thus, the best Portuguese prose was in essay form, the best poetry and drama was in satire, and historical writing flourished. Among the celebrated literati of the era were Alexandre Herculano, who wrote both historical fiction and a monumental history of Portugal, and Almeida Garrett, who was best known for his drama, but also was a writer of political, legal, and critical essays.

The conflicts of the 19th century were encapsulated in the "Coimbra question." Two groups of university scholars stood divided. The older group, led by the blind poet Castilho, advocated the virtues of the status quo, while the "generation of 1870," as they became known, called for revision of both intellectual and spiritual values. They were rationalist, anticlerical, and antimonarchist. In their writing could be heard the first strains of emerging socialist thought. Their daring critiques, however, were suppressed by the government in 1871.

But the rising tide of republicanism could not be stymied forever. As the century drew to a close, the democratic ideal was combined with a nationalistic utopian vision, a shift that was hoped would raise Portugal to its long-lost glory. The national anthem that was adopted in 1910 echoed the theme of resurgence: "*Oh sea heroes, oh noble people...raise again the splendor of Portugal...may Europe claim to all the world that Portugal is not dead!*"

The assassination of Carlos sealed victory for Republicanism; but it took time for the various parties and coalitions to sort themselves into a workable government—practically speaking, they never did. Between 1910 and 1926 there were 45 different governments, with most of the changes being brought about by military intervention rather than parliamentary procedure. The

The First Republic is proclaimed in 1910 and Joaquim Teófilo Fernandes Braga forms an anti-clerical government

SALAZAR

António Oliveira worked as an overseer for absentee landlords around the small village of Santa Comba, halfway between Viseu and Coimbra. He was known for his austerity, strong faith and stringent supervision and was known as *O Manholas*—"The Crafty One." His first son, António de Oliveira Salazar, (born in 1889) took the conservative values of his father far beyond the small rural world that formed them: indeed, finally making the whole nation of Portugal into his image of what it should be.

Salazar, as a professor of economics at Coimbra, was an active polemicist for the right, expressing some pride in that mark of cultural purity. In the same way, Portugal steered through international affairs with neutrality wherever possible. His own conservative values of piety, economy, and fatalism were also imposed on his country, even where it meant that the technological and cultural advances of the 20th century passed by. He lived quietly, taking modest vacations by the shore or visiting farms around the countryside. He remained unmarried, though he had a close but apparently celibate relationship with his lifelong housekeeper, Dona Maria de Jesus Caetano, who raised his two adopted daughters.

pressing his political faith in the slogan "Nothing against the nation, all for the nation." Nonetheless, for years he resisted various invitations to political positions until 1928, when General Carmona, as Prime Minister, offered Salazar the role of Finance Minister with absolute power over national finance. In 1932, having founded the National Union party, Salazar became Prime Minister. Though there were periods of serious opposition, and various plots on the dictator's life, his pervasive influence on Portugal would not truly lift until the April revolution of 1974, six years after his retirement and four years after his death.

Salazar's character is best read in the character that he imposed upon the nation. An introvert, he seldom traveled out of Portugal, perhaps tak-

On September 6, 1968, at the seaside in Estoril, Salazar's deck chair collapsed. The Prime Minister hit his head, developing a stroke that left him an invalid. With little turmoil, Marcelo Caetano, a former loyal of the regime turned critic, was made Prime Minister.

For the duration of Salazar's life, less than two years, he lived with few visitors and little attention. Strangely, those close to him chose not to tell him the truth about his position and the succession of Caetano. Sparing him the harsh reality, they fabricated a Portugal still led by Salazar. When Dona Maria tried to convince him to retire during those final years, he refused and, in a last pathetic boast that displayed the egomania which had grown over the years, he said that he had no choice, for there was no one else.

early leadership pressed their radical antichurch and social reforms too hard, causing a reaction that revived the influence of the Catholic church. Labor movements sprang up with the best intentions, but often paralyzed industry. First and foremost, the republicans were unable to deliver promised financial reforms and stability, both through their own ineptitude and, later, because of the international depression of 1920s. It was their economic failure that most significantly eroded their popular support.

Afonso Costa rose to leadership of the Republican factions, but the hard stance of anticlericalism caused too much ill feeling to allow stability. The political structure was intransigent, so military coups became standard. General Pimenta de Castro grabbed control briefly, but democratic forces deposed him. Sidónio Pais formed a dicta-

until 1951, but it was not his leadership but that of his most influential appointee that made that stability possible. In 1928, Carmona named António de Oliveira Salazar to the post of Finance Minister, with wide-ranging powers. Salazar had made his first political impact as the youthful leader of the Centro Acàdemico de Democracia Crista (Academic Center for Christian Democracy) a Catholic intellectual group that opposed the anticlerical and individualistic philosophy of the Republic. An economics professor, Salazar stayed out of the fray until his time was ripe. He resisted accepting any political position until he could be assured of what quickly amounted to complete control. By 1932, Salazar was made Prime Minister, a position he would retain until 1968.

Salazar's regime: Miraculously, Salazar imme-

torial government in 1917, but was assassinated in 1918.

Portugal, initially neutral, joined the Allies under Britain's influence in 1916, but World War I meant little to them except further financial upheaval. In 1926, the democratic government was overthrown by military forces and the constitution was suspended. Leadership passed through various hands and finally to General Oscar Carmona. He would remain as President

Left, Salazar delivers a public address. Above, shrine of Fátima, which gave the New State a foreign policy and encouraged domestic obedience.

diately straightened out the country's disastrous financial morass, mostly through an austerity that reflected his personal ideals. Having done what no leader had been able to do for a century, Salazar used his political capital to form what amounted to a dictatorship, taking Mussolini's Italy and Primo de Rivera's Spain as his models in the call for national order and discipline.

The "New State," as it was called, was a fascist regime, though nominally a corporative economic system under a republican government. The National Union was the only political party. It was authoritarian, pro-Catholic, and imperialist. A state police organization, the PIDE, were notorious and vigilant watchdogs against subversion. Censorship, rigid and effective, settled like a thick fog over all literature, journalism and art.

Nothing negative or critical could find its way into print. An example of the absurd extremity of the New State's repression was when a censor in Mozambique replaced the word "muddy" with "blue" in the sentence "...*the South African fleet had arrived in the muddy waters of the bay on a courtesy visit to Lourenço Marquês.*" The formerly lively national journalism withered away. And in blatant doublespeak, the government often referred to itself as a dictatorship without a dictator.

There was some resistance. In reaction to the powerful militaristic control of the country, there were numerous attempted coups and an underground Communist party that grew in power, leading the clandestine opposition. However, Salazar's leadership was never strongly challenged. Still essentially rural, relatively backward, and mostly conservative, Portugal accepted Salazar's fascism as a kind of defensive posture to the worldwide technological explosion of the 20th century. His conservative and at times reactionary attitudes toward industrialization, agricultural reform, education and religion kept Portugal out of the traumatic turbulence of the age. His attitude that Portugal was a naturally poor country—good for living but not for producing anything—was widely held. Catholic cults, like that of Our Lady of Fátima, were encouraged and turned into propaganda for the regime. Salazar also drew upon the romanticized history of the Portuguese exploration and trade, inculcating a generation of schoolchildren to the self-aggrandizing idea of Portugal's manifest destiny as an "empire." They turned inward, though still holding their colonies where possible, and tried to ignore the changing face of world politics. It was a comforting if finally debilitating attitude. Portugal, after all, would eventually have to catch up.

Putting self-preservation ahead of ideology, Salazar pretended to adhere to the League of Nations' nonintervention policy during the Spanish Civil War, because he could not afford international censure, but actually sent a great legion of soldiers—as many as 20,000—to aid Franco's Nationalist forces. The effort was well-conceived. Franco's victory served to validate the authority of Salazar's own regime.

The minor flourishing of culture of the republican era, when democratic ideals had encouraged efforts at mass education, a proliferation of journalism, and a few writers of modern fiction and poetry, was slowed by political upheavals, and effectively quelled with the advent of the New State. The greatest writer of the period, the poet Fernando Pessoa, was not "discovered" until after World War II, when most of his works were first published, posthumously. Few others transcended the romantic nationalism of the era, as formidable barriers to the larger currents of European culture were created. In any case, the censor-

ship of the New State slowed original thinking to a trickle, and most of that was devoted to political subversion. Of course, this was nothing new to a country that had been dominated by the Inquisition for so many years. In the whole 500-year history of Portuguese publishing, only 80 years have been free of oppressive censorship of one kind or another.

During World War II, the New State again sensibly concentrated on self-preservation. Though Salazar admired Hitler, Portugal's traditional political and economic ties with Britain demanded at least neutrality. However, Portugal did supply the Axis with much needed wolfram (the ingredient necessary to alloy tungsten steel) almost until the end of the war. On the other hand, the Allies were granted strategic bases in the Azores. In fact, the war's main effect—though it was not widely advertised—was to replenish Portugal's coffers as they did business with both sides. The defeat of the fascists did serve as a signal to Salazar, a warning to mute his totalitarianism, but he was by now firmly entrenched. The changes over the next decade served primarily to protect the dictatorship still further from democratic insurgency.

In the 1950s, opposition to the New State solidified into two blocs. The one, legal, took advantage of the relaxed censorship in the month preceding elections (the state's way of giving the impression of free elections) to run independent candidates. The other, furtive, organized various protest actions and engaged in what propaganda they could. These means kept resistance vital, forcing Salazar's hand. Their actions required new rounds of repression, deceit, and constitutional changes that eroded both Salazar's authority and popularity.

In 1958, General Humberto Delgado, a disenchanted member of the regime, ran for President, announcing among other things that he would use the constitutional power of that position to dismiss Prime Minister Salazar. Despite the mass demonstrations in his support, and his apparently successful campaign, the "official count" elected instead Admiral Américo Thomás, a Salazar loyal. Afterwards, further constitutional decrees were enacted to prevent the repetition of such an election, making the presidential election not by popular vote, but by an electoral college of the National Assembly, which was Salazar-controlled. Delgado was assassinated in 1965, while attempting to cross the Spanish border into Portugal, a murder generally attributed to PIDE operatives.

Portugal's entry into the United Nations had been prevented by the Soviet bloc and by oppo-

Right, the headline of April 25, 1974: Military strike—The Armed Forces Movement Takes Action at Dawn.

ANO VII ... Nº ... — 1974 — QUINTA-FEIRA, 25 DE ABRIL — PREÇO 2$50

A CAPITAL

EDIÇÃO ÀS 12 HORAS

Director: HENRIQUE MARTINS DE CARVALHO
Subdirector: JOSÉ JÚLIO GONÇALVES

PROPRIEDADE, S.G.C. • SOCIEDADE GRÁFICA DE «A CAPITAL» • R. JOAQUIM ANTÓNIO DE AGUIAR, 66 • LISBOA-1 • TELEFS. 688125/6/7 • END. TELEG. ACAPITAL • TELEX 12306

GOLPE MILITAR

"MOVIMENTO DAS FORÇAS ARMADAS" DESENCADEIA ACÇÃO DE MADRUGADA

(PÁGINA 2)

nents of Salazar imperial colonialism until 1955. Membership was finally granted not because of any real change, but by a successful diplomatic effort to whitewash his colonial despotism. Salazar would not actually alter his policies because despite the increasingly higher cost of maintaining military rule in the colonies, they were very profitable for the homeland. Subsistence crops were increasingly neglected in favor of crops like cotton, to feed the mills of Portugal while the native Africans went hungry. The policy of *assimilado*—claiming that the national goal was to assimilate the local culture into Western, Portuguese culture—allowed Portugal to exploit these "citizens" as virtually free labor. Despite international pressure, and increasing agitation within the colonies, the regime—steeped in the ancient idea of the glorious empire—fiercely resisted any incursions on its colonial outposts, to extreme and sometimes ridiculous lengths. For example, in 1961, the territory of São João de Ajudá consisted of a decrepit fortress and the governor's estate, a tiny enclave surrounded by the country of Dahomey. That year Dahomey had become independent from France, and had delivered an ultimatum to Lisbon to return Ajudá. Waiting until the last possible minute to surrender this tiny sliver of territory, the Portuguese governor spitefully burned down the buildings before departing.

Of course, Salazar's imperial intransigence had far more serious consequences elsewhere. An explosion of African nationalism was set off by a violent 1961 Angolan native uprising that had been brutally crushed by the Portuguese military and civilian reaction. Throughout the 1960s, the government was more and more economically and militarily involved in maintaining the colonies, which actually had been renamed "provinces" in a 1951 decree that semantically underscored the insistence on a permanent Portuguese settlement. Meanwhile, the stagnation of Portugal's home economy grew more oppressive. Hydroelectric power projects were successful, but industry and agriculture grew more and more backward compared with international standards. Emigration, mostly in search of employment, began to take a serious toll on the country's demographic resources.

Many young men were conscripted, and popular support for the wars in Africa waned quickly. Angola continued to be an economic boon, but the other colonies were a drain. Salazar, in response, trusted fewer and fewer members of the regime, taking on more direct responsibilities for continuing the wars. He also relaxed his former policy of fiscal austerity, and increasingly relied on foreign credit to finance the overseas operations.

Acting Prime Minister: In 1968, a deck chair collapsed under the 79-year-old Salazar. He suf-

fered an incapacitating stroke, and the long awaited succession had arrived. Because Salazar had made no provision for a successor—unwilling to face his own mortality—major upheavals were expected. But the transition to "acting" (while Salazar lived his final years in seclusion) Prime Minister Marcelo Caetano was relatively smooth.

Caetano, once a protégé of Salazar, had resigned seven years earlier over conflicts with his superior. Now called upon to resolve the national crisis, he saw the need for balanced change and stability. But he was not bold enough. Though many of the gravest injustices of the old regime were righted, other changes were superficial, and the colonial issue was not confronted. When his early efforts at liberalization failed to appease opposition unrest, Caetano returned to the oppressive hostility of the former regime.

Discontentment among all ranks of the military over the continual and ineffective wars in the colonies led to the formation of the Armed Forces Movement (MFA) in 1973. In 1974, General António de Spínola published *Portugal and the Future*, a stinging and comprehensive critique of the current state of affairs that recommended a military takeover to save the country. The book's messages had been heard before, but never from so high up the power structure. Though many factors had built toward the revolution, this famous publication lit the fuse. Caetano himself felt its importance, saying later that he began reading it in the late evening and "*did not stop until the last page, which I read in the small hours of the morning. And when I closed the book I understood that the military coup, which I could sense had been coming, was now inevitable.*" Like many revolutions, however, this one was as much a collapse of the old as it was a triumph of the new.

Two months later, on April 25, 1974, after a few premature uprisings, a nearly bloodless coup began in Lisbon. It was led in part by Spínola and fellow General Costa Gomes, and by all the "angry young captains" who commanded the 27 rebel units that seized key points throughout the city. One of the signals that was used to coordinate the coup's launch was the playing of a song on the radio. The song, "Grandola, Vila Morena," which was about a town where the people governed themselves, became an unofficial anthem of the movement. Caetano and other ranking government officials took refuge in the barracks of the National Republican Guard, a building that was once a convent. The formal surrender came after a young officer threatened to crash a tank through the gates. The rebel takeover was quickly accepted throughout the country. The revolution took the red carnation, then in season, as its symbol, and sparked nationwide celebration, including joyous mass demonstrations on the first of May.

The initial government was a National Salvation Board of military men, designed to give way to a constituent assembly as soon as it was practical. A provisional government was soon in place, and negotiations with African liberation movements went ahead. The government was divided over the new overseas policies, and an odd *coup* within the *coup* developed, with Spínola attempting to wrest control from his opponents. It was unsuccessful and liberal forces continued to divest colonies. Guinea-Bissau, Mozambique, the Cape Verde Islands, São Tomé and finally Angola were granted independence. One of the disastrous results of this sudden change was a mass immigration of Portuguese nationals back to their homeland. As many as 500,000 people flowed into Lisbon and other urban centers.

In 1976, with the economy in dire straits, a Pintassilgo. At the end of 1979, a coalition of the right took power.

In 1982 the long-awaited revision of the constitution finally arrived. The Democratic alliance and the far right were determined to quickly rid that document of its Marxist taint. They were partially successful after a period of nationwide demonstrations, strikes, and resignations. The Council of the Revolution, a powerful overseeing branch of the former arrangement was eliminated, but the hope for a classless society remained a signal goal, mentioned in Articles 1 and 2 of the document.

In the past few years, the country has witnessed a general conservative shift, away from socialism and toward capitalism. Though veteran socialist leader Mário Soares was elected President in 1986 (the first civilian to hold the post in over 60

socialist-influenced constitution was adopted, and Mário Soares, leader of the Socialist party, was appointed Prime Minister. The next decade brought little stabilization. The Socialists fell in 1977, then rose again as part of a coalition government with the Social Democratic Central Party. But it fell again the next year, replaced by a government of technocrats that lasted just 17 days. Small, powerful groups were ranged throughout the political gamut, keeping the government in turmoil. Among the various short-lived governments was an interim period led by the first woman Prime Minister, Maria de Lurdes

Above, Prime Minister Mário Soares signs and makes official the long-awaited entry of Portugal into the EEC in 1986.

years), the more capitalistic Social Democrats made Cavaco Silva prime minister in 1987

The political flux will never be completely over, but at least the variations are more contained. This relative stability, has allowed Portugal to emerge from its long financial doldrums. In 1986, it joined the European Economic Community (EEC). Among Silva's most successful programs has been the reprivatization of many companies and industries that had been nationalized under Communist pressure after the Revolution. These poorly managed national resources are regaining vitality as private enterprises. For a change, the Portuguese are looking within for economic viability—expanding industry, agriculture, education—putting their glorious but obsolete history of adventuring and colonizing behind them.

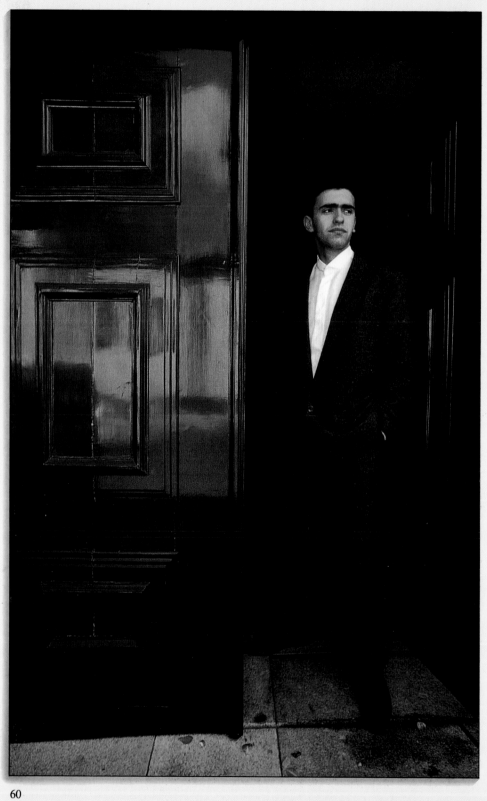

THE PORTUGUESE

Defining a national character is never simple, and Portugal presents no exception. Travelogues tend to portray the Portuguese as easy-going, smiling, patient, good-natured, but imbued with an inner *saudade*, a feeling variously defined as a nostalgia or melancholy. Certainly the Portuguese are perfectly suited to dealing with touring foreigners, whether the visitors are in search of sunny beaches, medieval architecture, or folklore. The native forbearance allows for cross-cultural missteps and halting phrase-book Portuguese. For the visitor, the only character flaw is the innate reluctance to consider time. Shopkeepers, gas station attendants, or postal clerks, no one is in a hurry, or even close.

The Portuguese have also faced more serious criticism. Writing in the 30s, the great modern poet Fernando Pessoa criticized their "provincialism", meaning their naively uncritical appreciation of all things "modern" and "civilized": big cities, new fashions, etc. Dr. Salazar, whose 50 years of oppressive rule still effect Portugal's character today, once commented bluntly, and unfairly, "The Portuguese are not a very intelligent people."

From childhood: Paul Descamps, a Frenchman writing earlier this century, isolated permissive childrearing as a key to understanding the national character. Though this may seem a specious argument, its conclusions make sense. Portugal is a matriarchal society and having been spoiled by mother, the Portuguese learn to operate by cajolery rather than diligence, to favor patience over perseverance. Raised permissively, they grow up without great self-discipline, with only the vaguest sense of time constraints, and generally with a streak of independence and an unsinkable self-esteem.

Generalities are great liars, however. It is, after all, 10 million individuals that make up this great country that is both ancient—the oldest national boundaries in Europe—and newborn—after the Carnation Revolution of 1974. And there may even be a prompt shopkeeper or two.

In the bucolic backways of Trás-os-Montes and the Beiras, it is possible to feel that one has stepped back in time. Indeed, ways of life from Europe's past are alive throughout Portugal. There are windmills on grassy knolls, cobbled roads from Roman times, and horse-drawn

farmer's carts—some with handmade wooden wheels—that look extremely picturesque when piled high with the grape harvest.

The people in rural areas generally distrust Lisbon and all that it stands for: political turmoil, taxes, police functions, bureaucratic regulation, centralized education, etc. They would rather keep their distance. Able to sustain themselves, if sometimes meagerly, by their harvests, they have no patience for worrying about the EEC, inflation, or trade deficits. They are self-reliant.

This is not to say that national pride is any less vigorous here. It seems that even the smallest

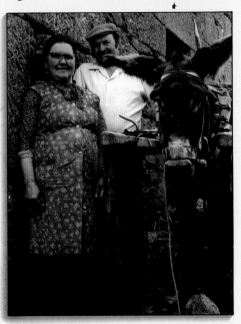

town will boast its own museum, scenic church, or historical monument, and the residents are anxious that you visit and appreciate them.

In both city and country, there are ingrained social classes, but there is also a broad sense of equality. Every man expects to be treated with dignity. Manners tend to be elaborate, especially in forms of address. "Your excellency" is a common tag. Handshakes are exchanged at every chance, in addition to a parting wave on turning out of sight.

The fairer sex: Women, on the other hand, are on a separate footing. Feminist ideas are only beginning to be heard. A ground-breaking feminist collection of poems letters and stories, *New Portuguese Letters* was written and attacked in 1972. Now there is more freedom of ideas, but a

Preceding pages, a Portuguese-French immigrant in the Upper Minho; Maria Lusa, Bruno, Marco, Eva and friend in Grandola; a lone traveler in Monsaraz. Left, a Braga resident. Above, a couple in Aldeia Solveira.

long way to go before attitudes change.

Throughout Portugal the general attitude—which English and Americans might consider cynical—is that there is no objective basis for laws or government. The assumption is that leaders and legislators are most dedicated to furthering their own interest. Anyway, history and current events dictate against forming strong attachments to current leaders—there have been 16 governments in the past 13 years. Change is all that can be depended upon. All this instability keeps politics lively and fills the daily papers.

Beneath the ever-shifting face of contemporary politics are the proud contours that are Portugal's history. Os *Lusiads* is hailed as the seminal Portuguese work not only for its beauty and literary influence, but for its paeans to the Discoveries and to national pride. In fact, this

agriculture, with 35 percent in industry. Naturally, many are employed at the ports all along the coast, especially Oporto and Lisbon, and fishing remains a strong vocation, as it has been for centuries (see page 191). The major agricultural products are olives, potatoes, and wine grapes among others. Trees provide numerous cork products, resins, and lumber (see page 164).

Portugal is still Europe's poorest country. The gross national product per capita in 1984 was US$1,970. That of Spain, hardly a rich country, was $4,440. However, the economic statistic that is more likely to be cited is growth rate, which is one of Europe's fastest. The natural optimism of the Portuguese is, for now, well founded.

Family ties: Home and family life is much more stable cultural framework than politics or economics. Kinship, in fact, can be a powerful

Portuguese identity—as explorers, colonizers, a world power—lent itself to dangerous illusions during Salazar's regime. The tendency to look overseas for answers to internal woes and weaknesses is only now being overcome as Portugal turns inward to develop.

Industries: The control of many industries was usurped by the state in 1974, and though the trend over the last few years has been toward reprivatization, many remain state-owned. Unemployment, rampant in the 1970s, is still high, particularly among young people seeking first jobs. Long-term emigration in search of steady work causes strange demographics; almost as in wartime, young and old are left behind as workers part from their families and send home wages. As of 1985, 31 percent of the workforce was in

influence in finding employment and aligning the many splintered political parties. The extended family is a common living situation, as grandparents help care for the children, and young adults—without any other housing option—often live at home until they are married.

Portugal is predominantly a Roman Catholic country (see page 68), with only a few Protestant communities, and a few Jews and Muslims, too. One interesting sub-group of the Catholics is the *Marranos*, the hereditary Jews who converted during the 16th-and 17th-century prosecutions, and who retain some Jewish rituals and practices in combination with their nominal Catholicism.

Television is a state monopoly called RTP (*Radiotelevisão Portuguesa*) offering two channels. However, within the past year there has been legislative activity towards allowing private broadcasting. The country owns 1.5 million TV sets (15 sets per 100 people; the US figure is 63 per 100.) The country counts a total of 31 daily newspapers and 379 movie theaters among its other distractions. Smoking is supposed to be on the decline, but it is still very evident and always accepted. Crime rates are relatively low and the prison population is a scant 6,000 or so. Capital punishment has been abolished.

Drive, baby, drive: The Portuguese may be easygoing by nature, but behind the wheel of a Mercedes, a BMW, or even a Morris Mini the locals are possessed by an irresistible urgency to get around that grape truck. Whether on winding mountain roads or the Lisbon-Oporto highway, the Portuguese drive with the bravado of immortals. Unfortunately, they are quite human and in

Pre-school is an option for three-to-six-year-olds, while basic mandatory education is six years during the ages six to 14. In the age group six to 12 enrollment is 97 percent. Secondary education is not compulsory. Numerous universities and polytechnical colleges offer higher education.

Illiteracy has been the scourge of progressive reformers, but recently the efforts of public education have made some headway. Over the last decade adult illiteracy has declined from 29 percent to just over 20 percent.

No portrait of the Portuguese would be complete without taking note of the differences between the South (Lisbon and below) and the North. First of all, the racial cast of the people is slightly different. In the North the basic Iberian strain—dark, thick-set—has been leavened with Celtic blood, while in the South, Jewish, Moorish

fact have the dismal distinction of one of the highest accident rates in Europe.

Military service is compulsory, for either 12-15 months in the army or 18-20 months in the navy or air force. The armed forces total 68,252. Though soldiers in uniform are certainly a common sight throughout Portugal, the defense budget is relatively small: 86 million e*scudos* in 1985, compared with 115 million spent on national health the same year.

Education has been thoroughly modernized.

Far left, a carrier in Caria. Left, time out for the latest gossip. Above, graduation day at the University of Coimbra. Following page, the Portuguese Cup Final packs the stadium

and African ancestors are evident.

The North is generally more conservative, both politically and culturally. It is the bastion of Portuguese Catholicism. The south has a tradition of liberalism and adaptation.

The two temperaments—the warm Mediterranean and cool Atlantic—wash over each other across Portugal. The people are as varied as the land that drinks at the banks of the Tagus and Douro rivers: bursting with verdure in Sintra, rippling with stark beauty in the Alentejo, and thundering up into the craggy Serra da Estrela. There is a folk saying that "Coimbra sings, Braga prays, Lisbon parades, and Oporto works." Nothing is that simple, but it is true that traveling here unveils not only a beautiful landscape but a beautiful panorama of character and humanity.

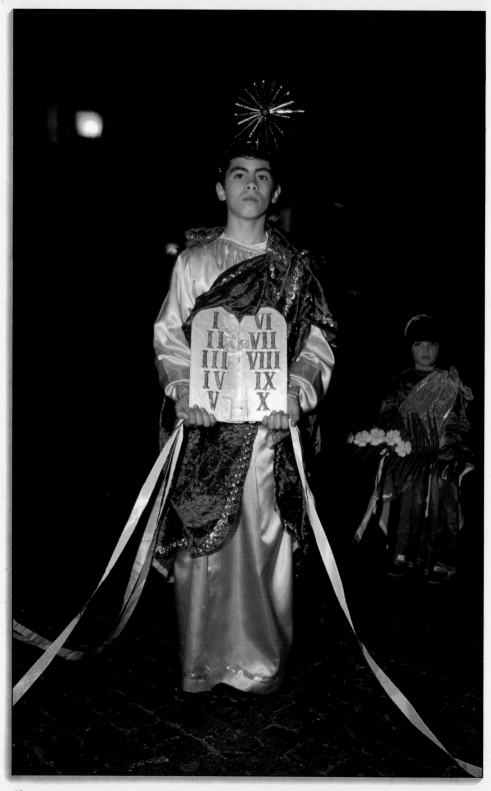

Saints, Miracles And Shrines

In the first decade of the 6th century, a young monk named Martin arrived in Braga. This former Roman capital was now the political and religious stronghold of the Suevi, the barbarian tribe that had adopted Arianism, a heretic form of Christianity. Martin, inspired at the shrine of St. Martin at Tours, was determined to convert these rulers to Catholicism.

Martin's parents came from Panonia (modern day Hungary), the original home of the Suevi, so he was well suited for this particular mission. And he succeeded. Martin founded an abbey at Dume, became a bishop, and, in 559, converted the Suevi king Theodomirus.

Martin found a further challenge, however, among the general population of the area. Although practicing Catholics since their conversion under the Roman Empire, the masses had incorporated many local beliefs and customs into their religion. To Martin, this amalgam was unacceptable, and in a written sermon entitled *De Correctione Rusticorum* (On the Correction of Peasants), he called for the cessation of the use of charms, auguries and divination, of the invocation of the Devil, of the cults of the dead, fountains and stars.

In this St. Martin of Dume did not succeed, nor have 14 centuries of similarly inclined zealots and reformers. All these elements are present to this day as an obstinate strain within the orthodox Catholic traditions in many areas of the country. The north, in general, is the most devout section of Portugal—over 40 percent of adults attend Sunday Mass as opposed to about ten percent in the south.

Naturally, there is still much wrestling over these issues between the church hierarchy and the practicing parishes—recently the bishops banned Padre Miguel, a priest from an isolated northern mountain parish who was supposed to have healing powers. Yet, though frowned upon by the orthodox Church, this spontaneous, independent Catholicism should not be seen as a form of pagan superstition or magic; rather, it is evidence of a vigorous religious tradition.

What are some of these still-current beliefs? When a newborn child proves healthy, it is said that it was conceived when the moon was waxing. The states of the moon are believed to be very influential in the way all vegetables, animals and humans grow. Similarly, certain fountains are reputed to have particular healing powers. And under many of these, beautiful Enchanted Mooresses are said to be hiding, watching over great treasures.

A variety of beliefs function to reassure people during the most frightening moments of the human life cycle. For instance, many practices have evolved that are meant to protect children as they gestate in their mothers' wombs, or just after they are born. Thus, a newborn should not be taken out of the house during certain hours, to protect it against the "evil air"; and its father's

trousers should be placed over the cot to frighten away witches; and the mother should not eat while breastfeeding, as the child may grow up to be greedy.

Midnight Baptism: One of the more dramatic folk practices is the Midnight Baptism. This happens when a pregnant woman is prone to miscarriages or when her previous child was stillborn. The "baptism" takes place at midnight in the middle of a bridge that divides two municipalities—a powerful place that is neither one place nor another, at the moment that is neither one day nor the next. Certain bridges, such as the Ponte da Barca in Minho, are famous for this and still secretly sought by hopeful parents. When all is ready, the father and a friend, armed with sticks, stand guard at the ends of the bridge. They are

Preceding page, the Fátima devout in a candlelit procession. **Left**, solemnity at Good Friday in Braga, while **above**, St. Anthony's festival rollicks in Lisbon warding off cats and dogs—which may be witches or the Devil in disguise. The first person who passes after the church bells strike midnight must perform this rite. He (or less frequently, considering the late hour, she) pours river water over the expectant mother's belly and baptizes the child "in the name of the Father, the Son and the Holy Ghost…" but the final "Amen" must not be uttered. The child must wait to be born to be properly and completely baptized by the priest in church. Thus, the healing powers of baptism are extended to cover this dangerous period.

The church is the central meeting place of the whole parish, as most gather there on Sundays. At Easter, the cross that represents the resurrection of Christ is taken out of the church to visit successively all the households of the parish. The cross is kissed as it enters each house in the company

they have the power to hear or see a procession of the ghosts of those parishioners who have recently died. This procession is seen leaving the cemetery, with a coffin in its center. When it returns, the ghost of the parishioner who will be the next to die will be in the coffin. Thus these seers predict how many people are going to die soon—but they cannot reveal their names if they themselves want to remain alive.

The use of religion to establish a communal identity is most clearly shown by the celebration for the local patron saint. An organizing committee busies itself all year collecting money, planning decorations, arranging events. Whether it is a rural parish, a small village, or a middle-sized town, the importance of these celebrations is immense. They represent and solidify local pride. The *festa* is a joyful occasion heralded by fire-

of the priest and sacristan. This process may take days. When the cross returns to the church, it is a symbol of the new life shared by all in the community.

Similarly, on All Saints' Day and All Souls' Day (1st and 2nd of November), the celebrations at the parish cemetery are attended by all. Lamps are lit, tombs are cleaned and decorated with flowers. Friends and neighbors visit tombs. The whole parish celebrates this strongly felt sense of continuation with the past, praying together for "their" dead.

Perhaps the strongest evidence that the feeling of community extends beyond this life is the common belief in the "procession of the dead." This belief is found in the whole northwest section of the Iberian Peninsula. Certain people claim that

crackers—a familiar noise to those traveling the northern countryside in summer, when most of these occur—and by music blaring from loudspeakers placed on the church tower. The pivotal event is the procession after the Mass, when the image of the patron saint, along with other images, is carried with great pomp in a brightly decorated stand in a roughly circular, traditional path.

After that the lay celebrations begin. These usually involve a great deal of dancing to traditional brass bands, folk-dance groups, and nowadays, rock bands. Much wine is consumed and the occasion is indispensable for young people, who use these opportunities as social mixers. It is this section of the celebration that the priests have always opposed. For the people, however, the two aspects are deeply connected and cannot be disassociated. There is no sense of disrespect for the sacred part of the celebrations, simply that religion is fully integrated into their lives.

Popular attitudes to saints differ from Church doctrine not so much in content as in emphasis. The people place great importance on material benefits and personal, reciprocal relationships with saints. They pray to specific saints for specific problems—St. Lawrence for toothache, St. Bráz for sore throat, St. Christopher for traveling, Our Lady of the Conception for infertility, the Holy Family for family problems, and so on. Also, people will have unique devotions for particular saints that they have developed over time. If the believer's prayer has been answered, this proves that the particular image addressed is a singularly sacred one, a favored line of commu-

saint something in return. A wax heart might be given for a successful engagement or a wax pig if the pig has fully recovered. If the promise is not fulfilled, the saint may well aveng himself.

If one visits churches in northern Portugal, these kinds of offerings are often seen hanging on the walls of the sacristies alongside other gifts such as bride's dresses, photographs, written testimonies or women's braids. Shrines of great fame such as Bom Jesus and Sameiro, near Braga, or the Senhor de Matosinhos, near Oporto, have large displays of votive offerings. In Fátima (perhaps the most important shrine in the country), wax gifts accumulate so quickly that special furnaces have been installed to burn them.

Wax gifts are not the only kind of offering. Jewelry, money, flowers, and objects associated with the disease in question (crutches, glasses,

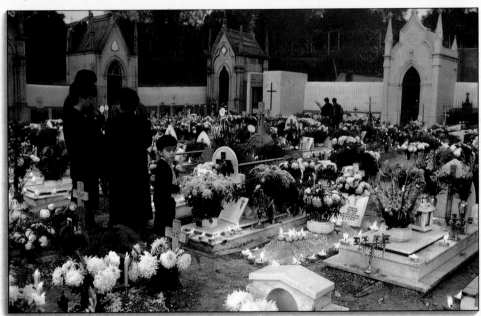

nication. In this way shrines develop, whether personal, family, or even national, with images famous for their miraculous powers.

The notion of the miracle in popular religion is also more loosely interpreted than in the Church. Essentially, a miracle is considered to have taken place every time a specific prayer is positively answered. The believer must then "pay" the saint whatever he or she had promised.

Wax Offerings: When a prayer to St. Anthony involves a loved one or a pig to recover from a bout of ill health, a promise is made to give the

wheelchairs, etc.) are also used. There is also another kind of gift: a personal sacrifice. Recently, the Church has been strongly critical of this, but until the late 1960s, it was strongly encouraged. If one visits the shrine of São Bento da Porta Aberta (St. Benedict of the Open Door), in the beautiful mountain landscape of Gerês near the dam of Caniçada on the 13th of August, one will find men and women laboriously circumambulating the church on their knees. There is a path especially laid out in cement for this, to avoid even more painful natural surfaces.

This scene is even more striking as these people are surrounded by others celebrating the day with song, dance, eating and drinking. It must be remembered that those on their knees are celebrating, too—because the saint answered their

Left, the much-kissed crucifix makes another stop on its Easter Sunday rounds. Above, cemetery candle-burning on All Saints' Day.

prayers. As São Bento da Porta Aberta often is called upon in cases of fatal disease, these people may have a great deal for which to be grateful.

Another shrine associated with such practices is Fátima, near the town of Leiria, in the center of Portugal. It deserves special mention, as it is one of the largest shrines in Western Europe. On May 13th, 1917, the Virgin is supposed to have appeared to three children on top of a tree (one of the children is, incidentally, still alive, an incarcerated Carmelite nun). This event is said to have been repeated on the 14th of each month until October of the same year, and each time, the Virgin spoke in a vague and allegorial way about peace in the world. Fátima soon became a rallying point for the revival of Catholicism in the 1930s and 1940s. Today, from May to October the roads around Leiria are lined with pilgrims,

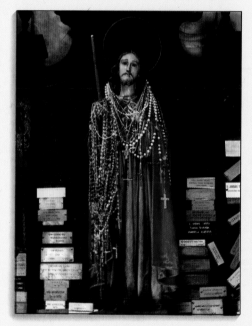

many of whom have come on foot from great distances to "pay" the Virgin for her favors.

Another kind of "payment" to the saints has all but disappeared now due to strong Church opposition. In the parish of Senhora da Aparecida in Lousada, for example, before the main procession leaves the church, another procession takes place. This is the procession in which 20 or so open coffins are carried—containing live people, their faces covered with white handkerchiefs. Some coffins are dark brown and lined in white satin; some are tiny white coffins for children. Those who ride in the coffins are offering a false burial to the saint who saved them from having to participate in a real one. The occasion, therefore, is a joyful one. There are plenty of light-hearted comments, and the participants mingle

with the others afterward, drinking and dancing for the rest of the day.

The cult of the dead, another morbid religious tradition, and one of the targets of St. Martin of Dume during the 6th century, remains the object of popular fascination in the 20th. Occasionally, a body is buried but does not undergo the normal process of decay. Such people often are considered by the Northerners to be saints. There are a number of such grim shrines where the corpses are exposed. The Church nearly always opposes these cults at first, but eventually tolerates them as they grow in popularity—three such are the *Infanta Santa* in Arouca, the *São Torcato* near Guimarães, or the *Santinha de Arcozelo* near Oporto. Even in an unlikely spot like the small urban cemetery of the elegant neighborhood of Foz in Oporto, a shrine of one of these "saints" can be found.

Along rural roads one will frequently find pretty little shrines. These contain an image of Christ or the Virgin or a saint. At the bottom, little molded flames surround barely dressed figures who represent the souls of sinners suspended in Purgatory. These shrines are there to protect travelers.

Portuguese history is full of examples of the continuing conflict between the spontaneous and all-embracing religiousity of the less educated class and the more restrictive attitudes of the theologically learned. The tense embrace between these two traditions is an essential facet of the national character, and both the naive and the orthodox elements have often had a direct influence on politics. From the early days of the "Western Crusade" to the Knights Templar and their ilk to the dark days of the Inquisition, religion has vied with national authorities. Imperialism, like the early exploration, was seen as a form of religious crusade—each victory along the way was considered a miracle performed by the saints. Most extraordinarily of all, Salazar's regime presented its policy of neutrality during World War II as based on the reported sooth-sayings of the Virgin at Fátima.

Finally, it is important to realize that while Portugal is very much a Roman Catholic nation, there has always been opposition to the orthodox hegemony, from both within and without the Church, from both naive and sophisticated sources. These have ranged from the passive and popular forms that St. Martin campaigned against (and which still have their adherents) to the more active and intellectual rebellion of the victim's of the Inquisition and the anti-clerical forces of the 1910 and 1974 revolutions.

Above, the plaques are gifts from grateful supplicants. Right, a floral offering to the Virgin in Lamego's Cathedral

CENTRO SOCIAL JOÃO PA O I
(2ª FA.)

APROVEITAMENTO DESTA CASA PARA

"For me Lisbon was a very agreeable surprise," Evelyn Waugh wrote in his travel book *A Bachelor Abroad*. "There is no European capital of antiquity about which one hears so little." Without realizing it, Waugh was echoing the impressions of others before him, among them Dorothy Quillinan, daughter of the poet Wordsworth. In 1845, she had written, "There is, I believe, no country in Europe that is less thoroughly familiar to me."

The visitor to Portugal has always believed himself to be a discoverer of the one exotic land left in well-visited, well-described Europe. These revelations, however, have accumulated over the centuries; so frequently in fact that Portugal has developed from these preceptions a literary persona to complement—and occasionally contradict—her historical and geographical images. That is, a country that the rest of the world is just about to discover. And is it true? Is Portugal about to be discovered by the world? Yes, and it probably always will be.

Crusaders: Those ancient Greek and Roman sailors who made it to fair Lusitania left few written records of their impressions or opinions, noting only their belief that the sun off the Atlantic coast hissed when it set. In the centuries before Christ, the Greek historian Polybius remarked upon the fat tuna off the coast of Lusitania, and the geographer Strabo reported that the Cabo de São Vicente, the westernmost point of continental Europe, was shaped like a ship. Both these men were unknowing oracles of Portugal 's future maritime greatness. The 4th-century poet Avienus left us *Ora Maritime*, iambic verses in Latin about his sea journey along the Atlantic and Mediterranean coasts of Iberia. This poetic sea log would inspire the intrepid Englishwoman Rose Macaulay more than 1,500 years later to retrace part of his route in *Fabled Shore*, her book about Spain and Portugal.

The earliest full-scale account of travel to Portugal dates from the Crusades, reputedly jotted down by a British priest named Osbern. Before this bard ever set eyes upon Portugal, he had to make the crossing from Britain to the Iberian peninsula, a trip that was legendarily unpleasant. Frequently, on their way to the Holy Land, Crusaders would stop at Santiago, in western Spain, to visit the shrine of St. James of Campostella. The discomforting effect of the voyage on the constitutions of the pious through what Byron

would later called "Biscay's sleepless bay," is depicted graphically by one unnamed medieval poet:

> *Men may leve all gamys,*
> *That saylen to seynt Jamys!...*
> *Thys mene whyle the pylgryms ly,*
> *And have theyr bowlys fast theym by,*
> *And cry aftyr hote maluesy,*
> *"Thow helpe for to restore."*

After the physically and spiritually restorative visit to the sacred bones of St. James, the pilgrims would continue south, eventually entering the Mediterranean through the strait of Gibraltar.

In 1147 a band of Crusaders—English, German and Flemish—broke their Atlantic journey in Oporto (they were shipwrecked, in fact) and were then persuaded by the new king of Portugal, Afonso Henriques, to join him on a sidetrip to seize Lisbon from the Moors. The chronicler Osbern sang the beauties of Lisbon first seen by the Britons—from the sea, of course. Her fertile countryside, lush with figs and vines, epitomized the seductive pleasures of the south. The 17-week siege led to victory for the Christians. A number of English settled along the Tagus: the first Bishop of Lisbon, Gilbert of Hastings, was an Englishman. This was neither the first nor the last of such stopovers for the Crusaders, but it was the most celebrated. It even became the subject of a poem written by the 18th-century-translator of Camões, William Mickle:

> *The hills and lawns to English valor given*
> *What time the Arab Moors from Spain were driven,*
> *Before the banners of the cross subdued,*
> *When Lisboa's towers were bathed in Moorish blood*
> *By Gloster's Lance—Romantic days that yield*
> *Of gallant deeds a wide luxuriant field*
> *Dear to the Muse that loves the fairy plains*
> *Where ancient honor wild and ardent reigns.*

The Portuguese themselves had less happy memories of the Crusaders from the north, whom they generally considered a loud drunken lot, given more to piracy than to piety. But the British, with their superior size and martial skills, would long feel a condescending pride in their Portuguese achievement, expecting gratitude and not a little obsequiousness from their allies to the south.

If the British Crusaders were given bad marks for their plundering and their fondness for the local wine, the Portuguese could not be praised for their later persecution of British "heretics." From its establishment in 1536 to its final dismantling under Pombal in the 18th century, the Inqui-

Left, early tour group, like these Crusaders, did not have the luxury of buses and occasionally kicked up a fuss about accommodations

sition got its unpleasant hands on a number of Englishmen. One of the first of these was the 16th-century Scottish humanist George Buchanan, who went to Portugal in 1547 to join the colony of educated men at the recently established University of Coimbra. The death of his protector, André de Gouveia, left Buchanan vulnerable to the attacks of his enemies. He was then made to suffer many months in a squalid prison, ignorant of both his accusers and his crimes. He was brought before the inquisitors and interrogated numerous times. His crimes, he finally discovered, were writing impious verses against Franciscans, eating flesh during Lent, and being critical of the monks. After a year and a half he was sentenced. In his autobiography (written in the third person) he sounds surprisingly forbearing about the whole affair: "They enclosed him

several months in a monastery, so that he could be taught by the monks, men indeed neither inhumane nor evil, but completely ignorant of religion."

Buchanan fared better at the hands of the Inquisition than others who were unwilling to deny their religion to escape the horrors of the torture chamber. The Roman Catholic church was not, after all, Buchanan's sworn enemy, as it would be for later visitors from Great Britain. While the Enlightenment, with its principles of reason and tolerance, lit up England, the fires of the *auto da fé* still raged in Portugal. In 1770, John Marchant compiled an anthology of monstrous experiences of the Inquisition in Spain and Portugal called *The Bloody Tribunal*, or *An Antidote Against Popery*. In it he states the rationalist view of the Inquisi-

tion: "Conviction can only be wrought by reason and argument; a convert by necessity is no better than a hypocrite."

Marchant includes the horrifying account of Mr. John Coustos, a British entrepreneur. Coustos came to Lisbon in 1743 to get a passage to Brazil, where he wanted to trade diamonds. His fierce loyalties to Protestantism and free-masonry inspired the wrath of the inquisitors. Coustos wrote:

"I considered that, being a Protestant, I should inevitably feel, in its utmost rigor, all that rage and barbarous zeal could infuse in the breast of monks; who cruelly gloried in committing to the flames great numbers of ill-fated victims, whose only crime was their differing from them in religious opinions; or rather who were obnoxious to those tygers, merely because they thought worthily of human nature."

Coustos, willing to die in the claws of these "tygers" rather than renounce his religion, managed to survive being tortured nine times.

For the most part Portugal was not a popular stopping place of the Grand Tourists of the 18th century. The modest list of ladies and gentlemen who published accounts of their travels in Portugal cannot compare with the massive catalog of writers offering narratives about France or Italy. Henry Fielding, who might have left a worthy literary tribute to the Portuguese, instead bequeathed only his grave to Lisbon. The novelist, who went to Portugal in 1754 in hopes that the mild climate would help his dropsy, survived only two months. His lengthy *Journal of a Voyage to Lisbon* is devoted to the journey itself and offers no impressions of the country, except to say that Lisbon was "the nastiest city in the world." Not very charitable, but then, he was dying. Nevertheless, his grave in the English Cemetery in Lisbon has been a pilgrimage spot for generation of travelers. The 19th-century missionary George Borrow wrote in his idiosyncratic and brilliant travel book *The Bible in Spain* that the cemetery was "Pere-le-chaise (the famous burying place of Paris) in miniature." He added that travelers, "if they be of England…may well be excused if they kiss the cold tomb, as I did, of the author of *Amelia*."

Beckford—The Grandest Tourist: Without a doubt, the most flamboyant of 18th-century visitors to Portugal was William Beckford, who set up sumptuous housekeeping in Ramalhoa near Sintra in 1787. He inspired Byron's Childe Harold, whose first stop on his pilgrimage to Portugal was to wander through Sintra conjuring Beckford's ghost and meditating on the brevity of life and pleasure:

"There thou too, Vathek! England's wealthiest son

Once formed thy Paradise, as not aware
When wanton Wealth her mightiest deeds had

done,

*Meek Peace voluptuous lures was ever wont to
shun.*

*Here didst thou dwell, here schemes of pleas-
ure plan*

*Beneath yon mountain's ever beauteous brow:
But now, as if a thing unblest by man,
Thy fairy dwelling is as lone as thou!*

Beckford first visited Iberia in 1787 shortly
after the publication of his Gothic novel *Vathek*.
The unorthodox Englishman, who had left England in the wake of a scandal over a homosexual
affair, caught the fancy of the extremely pious
Marquis of Marialva, who was convinced
Beckford would convert to Catholicism.
Beckford, meanwhile, as we learn from his diary,
was desperate not for the salvation of his soul but
for an introduction to the court of Queen Maria.
England's ambassador Walpole had refused to
perform this service for his disgraced country-
man. The Marquis guaranteed an introduction if
Beckford would become Catholic and abandon
England. Beckford had no such intention and he
left, petulant, without being presented to Queen
Maria. By the time he was finally presented at
court in 1795, Maria had long been insane.
Beckford's *Sketches of Spain and Portugal,
Recollections of An Excursion to the Monasteries
of Alcobaça and Batalha*, and his diary give an
idiosyncratic, slightly bitchy, aesthetically sensitive view of Portuguese art, music, nature and
society. Beckford's Portugal is a land of the
senses—he describes the haunting, erotic song
called the *modinha* and the luxuriant beauty of the
vegetation. (English plants he imported to his
quinta in Ramalhoa grew strangely large and
luxuriant in the southern clime.) Beckford's diaries and travel journals provided a brilliant, if
haphazard guide to aspects of the art and climate
of Portugal.

Byron: Beckford offers a pleasant alternative
to the vitriolic portrait of Portugal left by the 19th
century's greatest promoter of travel outside of
Thomas Cook: George Gordon, Lord Byron. The
poet left two accounts of Portugal, neither favor-
able: one in his letters home during his visit there
in 1809, the other in Childe Harold's pilgrimage,
Canto I. His hatred for the Portuguese has mysti-
fied and disturbed scholars and admirers of Portugal since it first appeared in print in 1812. There
is no record of an encounter during his brief stay
there that would have led to such dislike. Some of
Byron's criticisms reveal a typical Anglo-Saxon
ambivalence toward the South. Robert Southey, a
romantic and the future English Poet Laureate,
visiting Portugal 25 years earlier, had also been

torn between his disapproval of the filth of Lisbon, the discomfort of the country inns, and the
corruption and superstition of the priests; and his
delight in the sensual orange groves, long lazy
days and lush, fertile fields. William Mickle, an
unqualified admirer of Portugal's "genial clime"
contrasted the "gloomy mists" of England to the
"sun-basked scenes…where orange bowers in-
vite." This view of Portugal differs little from
reflections on other southern lands—Italy or
Spain or the south of France. But while elsewhere
Byron admires the southern spirit, his image of
Lisbon is of a false and faithless harlot of a town,
a southern siren who glitters beautifully from the
water but who reveals, on closer contact, only
filth and treachery:

*"But whoso entereth within this town,
That, sheening far, celestial seems to be,*

*Disconsolate will wander up and down,
Mid many things unsightly to strange ee;
For hut and palace show like filthily…
Poor paltry slaves! yet born 'midst noblest
scenes—"*

Byron's summary of Portugal is that it is a fair
land that has been peopled by beasts. The most
likely explanation for his anger is that the Portuguese felt resentful rather than grateful towards
the British for their help in expelling the French
invader, "Gaul's locust host," from their country
during Napoleon's Iberian campaign. Compli-
cating emotions further, Byron probably, many
of his countrymen, felt shame that at the
Congress of Cintra (Sintra), Arthur Wellesley
(later the Duke of Wellington) allowed the defeated French to evacuate with their loot, many of

**Left, George Buchanan looking a little tense, as
well he should. Above, Henry Fielding, author of
Tom Jones and despiser of Lisbon**

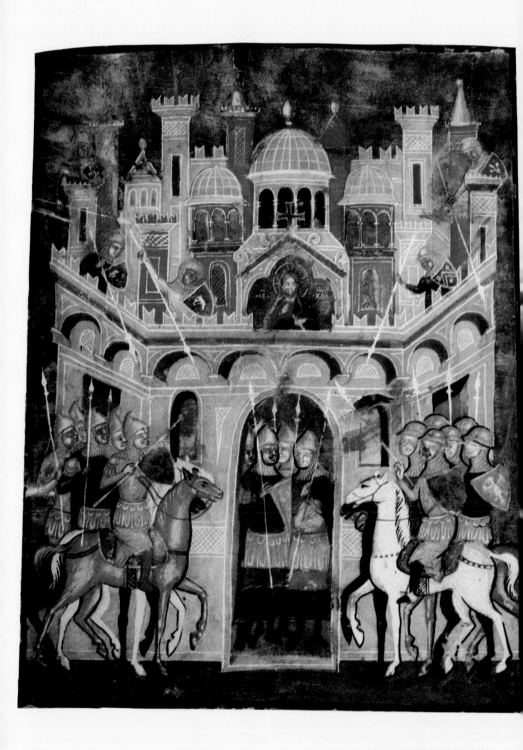

Portugal's treasures.

That the Portuguese felt resentment rather than gratitude toward their northern liberators is testified to by another Englishman, George Borrow. Traveling in 1835 he was miffed by the ingratitude of the Portuguese. Borrow, an eccentric itinerant minister, once left New Testaments and tracts next to the smouldering charcoal and broken liquor bottles of a bandit campsite in the wild back country of Portugal. His impatience with Portuguese hostility to the English is similar to the way many Americans felt after World War II about French criticism of the United States: "I could not command myself when I heard my own glorious land traduced in this unmerited manner. By whom? A Portuguese! A native of a country which has been twice liberated from horrid and detestable thraldom by the hands of Englishmen." He complains that the English "who have never been at war with Portugal, who have fought for its independence on land and sea, and always with success, who have forced themselves by a treaty of commerce to drink its coarse and filthy wines…are the most unpopular people who visit Portugal." But, unlike Byron, the pious if irascible Borrow attributed this not the Portuguese nature but to "corrupt and unregenerate man."

Borrow is a wonderfully comic traveler, especially in his belief that after just two weeks he could speak fluent Portuguese. His advice to novices speaking a foreign language is the sort of wrong-headed lesson that tourists of all times can never seem to forget. He advises, "Those who wish to make themselves understood by a foreigner in his own language should speak with much noise and vociferation, opening their mouths wide." Borrow's account of Portugal, less famous than the nasty stanzas from Byron, is a most original and evocative description. Borrow is a great reporter of human eccentricity and his account is extremely entertaining. He is also quite enthusiastic about the beauties of Portugal, comparing them favorably to other more visited countries. Lisbon, he claims, "is quite as much deserving the attention of the artist as even Rome itself." Sintra, praised lavishly even by the disagreeable Byron, is "a mingled scene of fairy beauty, artificial elegance, savage grandeur, domes, turrets, enormous trees, flowers, and waterfalls, such as is met with nowhere else under the sun." It is truly, Borrow writes, "Portuguese Paradise."

Byron's attacks on Portugal led predictably to a positive reaction. In 1845 Dorothy Quillinan, William Wordsworth's daughter, set out to contradict "Childe Harold's rash and unlordly sneer." Her *Journal of a Residence in Portugal*, she had hoped, would "assist in removing prejudices which make Portugal an avoided land." Unfortunately her call was not heeded by many, and with the exception of the Danish Hans Christian Anderson's *A Visit to Portugal 1866*, which was never very popular in his time, none of the great 19th-century travel writers put down their thoughts about Portugal.

Mrs. Quillinan was hoping to inspire Americans to visit as well, but the closest any 19th-century American writers came was when Mark Twain visited the Azores Islands. Read today, *The Innocents Abroad* displays Twain's deep streak of jingoism and blustery intolerance. Every land he visited crumbled when compared to the United States. He also tends to look at the natives as if they were the foreigners. He comments upon the backwardness of the Portuguese islanders: "Oxen tread the wheat from the ear, after the fashion prevalent in the time of Methusalah." He continues with the real horror: "It is in communities like this that Jesuit humbuggery flourishes." The phony relics irk him. To Twain, backwardness is neither quaint nor romantic, but ignorant and un-American.

For 20th-century travelers, disenchanted with the progress which Twain htouted with such vehemence, Portugal has provided an escape from modernity. Close to a hundred years after Twain visited the Azores, the Irish writer Leonard Wibberly would also comment on the backwardness of the Portuguese agricultural methods, in his charming and funny account of a year in Portugal, *No Garlic in the Soup*. He found much wisdom in sticking to the old ways. For the 20th-century visitor, Portugal satisfies a nostalgia for the past. It is, after all, the last country in Western Europe to engage in full-scale modernization and industrialization. Wibberly devotes an entire chapter to "The Language of Oxen" in which he describes the mysterious way the farmers talk to their oxen when they're plowing the fields: "Here was one of the most ancient agricultural cries in the world . . . .It was a cry which Vasco da Gama, should he return to Portugal, would recognize immediately." The plow, he also notes, resembles those used by the Saxons in the dark ages. Wibberly cannot resist asking the farmer why he doesn't use a metal plow. His answer: "There must be work for the oxen to do."

What may seem charming and quaint to the traveler is often the source of hardship and poverty to the native. Portugal is fast modernizing. The traveler will have to look a little harder for the land where Moorish minarets inspired the blood lust of the Crusaders or where William Mickle wandered through orange groves that stretched to the horizon, or where Beckford "trifled away the whole morning, surrounded by fidalgos in flowered bee-gowns and musicians in violet-colored accoutrements. . ."

Left, invasion by the Crusaders

PORTUGAL

50 km

N

Orense
VIGO
Valença do Minho
Minho Valley
Caminha
Lindoso
UPPER CÁVADO VALLEY
MINHO
Paradela Dam
Bragança
Lima
Ponte de Lima
PENEDA GERÊS
Viana do Castelo
Cávado
Chaves
Barcelos
Bom Jesus
TRÁS-OS-MONTES
Braga
Tâmega
Mirandela
Miranda do Douro
Póvoa de Varzim
Guimarães
Romeu
Dam
Vila do Conde
Amarante
Vila Real
Picote Dam
Azurara
DOURO
Serra do Marão
Sabor
Leça do Balio
Mateus
DOURO
PORTO
Paço de Sousa
Vila Nova de Fozcoa
Moncorvo
Lamego
Freixo de Espada à Cinta
DOURO VALLEY
Penedono
Barca de Alva
Vila da Feira
S. João de Tarouca
Sernancelhe
Figueira de Castelo Rodrigo
Arouca
BEIRA ALTO
Torreira
Aguiar da Beira
Trancoso
RIA DE AVEIRO
Pinhel
Aveiro
Caramulo
Viseu
Mondego
Ilhavo
Manguald
Guarda
Buçaco Forest
Varziela
Manteigas
Belmonte
Cantanhede
Oliveira do Hospital
Sabugal
ATLANTIC OCEAN
Montemor-o-Velho
COIMBRA
SERRA DA ESTRELA
Figueira da Foz
BEIRA LITORAL
Conimbriga
Serra da Lousã
Zêzere
Monsanto
Pombal
Cabril Dam
BEIRA BAIXA
Figueiró dos Vinhos
Leiria
Fátima
Castelo Branco
Batalha
Ourém
TAGUS
Nazaré
ESTREMADURA
Cruz da Légua
Tomar
Alcobaça
RIBATEJO
Castelo do Bode Dam
Berlenga Island
Peniche
Caldas da Rainha
Abrantes
Castelo de Vide
Óbidos
Almourol
Marvão
Alpiarça
Santarém
Portalegre
Serra de São Mamede
Alter do Chão
Ericeira
Mafra
Avis
Sintra
Vila Franca de Xira
ALENTEJO
Colares
Queluz
Estremoz
Elvas
Badajoz
LISBON
Arraiolos
Vila Viçosa
Cascais
Estoril
Montijo
Evoramonte
Palmela
Montemor-o-Novo
Évora
Sesimbra
SETÚBAL
Alcácer do Sal
Monsaraz
Viana do Alentejo
Sado
Grândola
GUADIANA
Miróbriga
Santiago do Cacém
Ferreira do Alentejo
Moura
Sines
Beja
Vila Nova de Milfontes
Mira
Odemira
Mértola
Alcoutim
Cachopa
SEVILLA
ALGARVE
Castro Marim
Cabo de S. Vicente
Portimão
Tavira
Lagos
Albufeira
Praia da Rocha
Vila Real de Santo António
Sagres
Faro
Olhão

PLACES

There's no *wrong* way to explore Portugal—except to make too many plans in advance. A car is the handiest means because, although the trains are good and the buses adequate, they won't allow you the freedom to go just over the next hill…and the next, and the next. Portugal is wonderfully seductive, and if you give in to her, you'll never regret it.

There are surprisingly few roads in Portugal—a typical full-size road map shows virtually every tiny lane. In the mountains of the center and north, the roads are sometimes poorly maintained, and of course filled with curves as they wind up and down—another reason to take your time when traveling Portugal.

Lisbon (pg 95) and its environs are most certainly the best starting point for the traveler. Even just a few days there will give a good feel for this old European capital. From there, if the weather is fine, you may want to simply head south, a few hours on the very good highway, to the glorious beaches of the **Algarve** (pg 131), long an attraction for international beachlovers, and not far from some great golf courses as well. After relaxing here for a few days, you might begin meandering back up through the Portuguese countryside. Begin by exploring the expanse of the **Alentejo** (pg 147), spectacular plains with the charming ancient town of **Évora** in its midst.

Cutting back toward the Atlantic, still heading north, you can visit the old university town of **Coimbra** (pg 173) and some of the surrounding sights. You might also look in on some of the traditional fishing communities along the coast here. To the north is the Douro River and the **wine districts** (pg 200) of Douro and Minho. Here, world-famous port, the delightful *vinhos verdes* (pg 211), and other wines are produced—and shipped to the city of **Oporto** (pg 211) at the mouth of the Douro.

The far interior north of Portugal is called **Trás-os-Montes** (pg 221), a primitive, remote area that is hauntingly beautiful. And below Trás-os-Montes, still somewhat in the mountains, is the **Beira Alta**; below that, the plains of the Alentejo have crept up into the province of **Beira Baixa** (both, pg 235).

Now your tour is done. Are you lost? Don't worry, you've nearly come full circle. Lisbon is just a few hours to the west, and a little to the south.

Preceding pages, a traffic jam in the streets of Carvicais; the calvary parades in Belém on April 25th; the *cavaleiro* expertly plants the *farpa* mid-gallop

LISBON

Parque de Eduardo VII

R. do Arco do Carvalhão

Auto-   Estrada   Av. Eng. D. Pacheco   Av. Joaquim   A. d. Aguiar   Praça do Marques de Pombal

Castilho

Ave

Rua   das   Amoreiras

Rua Silva Carvalho

Rua de S. Filipe Nery

Rua Rodrigo de

Rua Braamcamp

Rua Castilho

Avenida

Hercu

250 m

Campp   de   Ourique

R. da Anunciação

Borges

Ferr.

Rua   Carvalho

Silva

Rua do Cabo

Rua   do   Sol   ao   Rato

Carvalho

de

Largo do Rato

Rua de São Bento

R A T O

Alexandre

Rua   Fonseca

Rua Castilho

Rua   do   Salitre

Rua   Saraiva

† †
† †

Carvalho

Av. Pedro Alvares Cabral

Rua de São Bernardo

Rua da Escola

Faculdade de Ciências

Politecnica

Jardim Botânico

Rua   de   S.

Jardim da Estrêla

R. da Imprensa Nacional

Rua de S. Marçal

Praça do Príncipe Real

R. Conce

R.D. Pe

Rua da Rosa

Av. do Infante Santo

Rua da Estrêla

Basilica da Estrêla

Caláda

Rua   de   S.

Rua Bela Vista

da

Século

R.d.S. Ciro

Aires

Rua Borges Carneiro

Parliament

Estrêla

Rua   de   São   Bento

B A I R R O A L T O

do

R. de S. Domingos   a Lapa

Buenos

Rua   da   Lapa

Rua   das   Pracas

Santa Catarina

Calçada   do   Combro

Rua da Rosa

Calhariz

Rua   Garcia   da   Horta

Carlosl

Calçada Marquês de Abrantes

R. da Boavista

IIIII IIII

IIII

Largo de Santos

Avenida   Vinte   e   Quatro   de   Julho

Avenida   Dom

Rua   Dom   Luis I

Market

R. das Janelas Verdes

Museu Nacional de Arte Antiga

Av.   Vinte   e   Quatro   de   julho

Cais do Sodré Station

Cais do Sooré

Doca Alcântara

← Tagus

Rue de Loulé
Rue Gomes
Dona
de
Joaq. Bonifacio
Rue José Estéfão
Rua de Arrolos
Rua
Almirante
Marquês da Silva
R. Cesário Verde
Rocadeção

Luciano
Cordeiro
Rue Gomes Freire
Execlito
Rua
R. da Escola
Largo de Santa Bárbara
Rua dos Anjos
Reis
Palmira
Avenida Zaire
Rua
Cam. do Forno do Tejolo
Rua da Penha de França
General

Rua do Passadiço
Luciano
Cordeiro
Freire
Gomes
Paço da Rainha
Almirante
Rua
Baptista
Rua a. Vidal
Rua H. Salgado
Avenida

Rua da Fé
San José
Largo do Mitelo
R. Renato
Avenida
Rua Maria da Fonte
R. Damasceno Monteiro
Rua da Graça
Rua dos Sapadores

Rua de S. Lázaro
Rua da Palma
Rua do Benformoso
R. das Olarias
R.S. de Monte
Rua Senhora da Glória
R. Leite de Vasconcelos

Praça dos Restauradores
Teatro Nacional
Praça Dom Pedro IV (Rossio)
Praça da Figueira
R. d Cavaleiros
Calç. de Santo André
Largo da Graça
N. S. da Graça
R. da Veronica

Convento do Carmo
Elevador
Rua
Rua
Rua
BAIXA
IIII Castelo
Rua da Costa do Castelo
Castelo de São Jorge
São Vicente de Fora
Santa Engrácia
Santa Apolónia Station

rett
do
Garrett
Teatro São Carlos
Rua de Ouro
Augusta
Prata
R. de S Mamede
da
Nicolau
R. das Escolas Gerais
Museum of Decorative Arts
ALFAMA
Rua dos
Military Museum
Remédios

Town Hall
Madalena
Cathedral (Sé Patriarcal)
Praça do Comércio
(Terreiro do Paço)
Rua da Alfândega
João Evangelista
Rua

Tagus

LIS

LISBON

Lisbon, once the center of the world's last great colonial empire, nostalgically holds to the past as it tries to come to terms with Portugal's role as a new member of the European Economic Community (EEC).

A sense of history and tradition permeates downtown Lisbon, giving it a leisurely, old-world quality. The Portuguese still make pilgrimages to the monuments of Vasco da Gama and Prince Henry the Navigator. They still gather in the evenings in small wineshops in the Alfama quarter to sing of lost glories and lost loves. They browse for poetry in the dusty bookstores of Bairro Alto and pause for flowers and coffee on Rossio Square. They buy fresh fish at the Ribeira Market from *varinhas* imperiously wearing their wares like crowns. They bask in the shade of tropical gardens, stroll along the palm-lined mosaic sidewalks of Avenida da Liberdade and while away the time dreaming by the great olive-green Tagus River.

The Portuguese seem to have more time than most people to relax. Meals are a serious affair, and *siestas* are observed whenever possible. Shops tend to open at 9 a.m., take a long lunch break, and close at 6 p.m. Dining hours are reasonably early around 7:30 p.m. or 8 p.m., unlike the excesses of their Spanish neighbors. Weekends are sacred, perhaps a legacy of the British allies. The shops that do open Saturday generally close at 1 p.m. The only sure places to shop evenings and weekends are the shopping malls.

Lisboetans retain a certain formality that has long since disappeared from other European capitals. In business relations and even between friends and relatives, there is still much use of the third person. Titles of respect, such as *Senhor Doutor* or *Senhor Engenheiro, Excelentissimo Senhor* and *Vosa Excellencia* are used widely.

Appearances are very important. There's a popular expression, *"para Ingles ver,"* which loosely translated means "putting up a good front for the foreigners."

Contemporary heroes still tour the world, not as seafarers but as soccer players, cyclists and runners. The Portuguese characteristics of persistence and agility, which served the ancient explorers well, have made their descendants winners in modern international competitions.

Lisbon has felt the winds of change.

Many dilapidated palaces and mansions have been tastefully renovated and turned into elegant restaurants and bars, fashionable boutiques, art galleries and discotheques. Crumbling houses in the old quarters are beginning to be restored. In outlying neighborhoods, there are new hotels, a controversial shopping mall, office complex and a handsome modern museum. Beyond that is the inevitable monotony of satellite dormitories.

The first view of Portugal's capital should come from the great suspension bridge on the Tagus, one and-a-half miles long and clearly inspired by San Francisco's Golden Gate. It was originally called the Salazar Bridge after the late dictator António de Oliveira Salazar, under whose auspices it was completed in 1966. It has been rebaptized the **25th of April Bridge**, in honor of the bloodless 1974 revolution which restored democracy in all of Portugal.

Lisbon possess few architectural wonders, yet is a pleasing city to tour. The ensemble of buildings, with their faded elegance and harmonious arrangement on the hills and valleys along the northern shore of the Tagus, make it one of the loveliest capitals in the world. Located a few miles from the Atlantic Ocean, Lisbon is really a Mediterranean city: pastel and white buildings, orange tiled roofs, luminous sea and sky, mild winters and hot summers. But from time to time, the Atlantic prevails, bringing a dark opaque mist, chill rains and threatening waves.

With a population of about two million, Greater Lisbon has absorbed many Portuguese from rural areas, and many refugees from Portugal's former colonies, the last of which, with the exception of Macau and East Timor, gained independence in 1975 as a result of the Revolution. The influx of overseas Portuguese, Portuguese-Africans and Portuguese-Asians has made Lisbon a cosmopolitan and dynamic city.

History: According to Portuguese tradition, it was Ulysses who founded the city and gave it its original name, Olisipo. The Phoenicians, who occupied the area around 1200 B.C., are said to have called it Alis Ubbo, or "delightful shore." The Romans established the Lusitanian province by the end of the 1st century B.C. and named the site **Felicitas Julia**. Remains of their rule are seen in the **Castelo de São Jorge**, the castle that still overlooks the city, but the ramparts are essentially Visigoth, dating from the 5th century A.D.

The city became increasingly important under Moorish rule, from the 8th to the 12th centuries, when it was called **Al-Ushbuna**. The period of the Moslem-Christian wars of the 12th and 13th centuries was a time of great building. This is evident in many residential palaces.

It was only after 1255, when Afonso III drove the Moors out of the southernmost region of Portugal, that Lisbon became capital of the kingdom. Under the long reign of King Dinis (1279-1325), urban life flourished. But the Black Death, which is thought to have invaded Lisbon from the sea in 1348, decimated the capital.

In the 15th century, Lisbon became an important trading center and seat of a vast empire, rivaling Italy's Genoa and Venice. In 1497 Vasco da Gama opened the sea route to India, and Portuguese navigators began to establish trading posts around the world. By 1499, King Manuel I assumed the new title "Lord of the conquest, navigation and commerce of Ethiopia, Arabia, Persia and India."

Lisbon's golden age was the 16th century. She sent out countless ships to the colonies and many, although certainly not all, returned—ladened with riches to glorify the Portuguese court.

Although Portugal's fortunes declined with the costly colonial expansion, royal feuds and 60 years of Spanish rule, Lisbon's glory continued, reaching a new apogee from King João V's reign (1706-1750) through the first half of the 18th century, thanks to the gold and diamonds from the wealthy colony of Brazil.

Then came the terrible earthquake of 1755, followed by devastating fires. The total catastrophe took as many as 30,000 lives and left most of Lisbon in ruins. Voltaire's *Candide* bears witness to the devastation: *"The sea rises boiling in the port and shatters the vessels that are at anchor. Whirlwinds of flame and ashes cover the streets and public squares, the houses crumble, the roofs are tumbled down upon the foundations and the foundations disintegrate."* Lisboetans would not be happy with Candide's companion's consoling response: *"All this is for the very best. For if there is a volcano in Lisbon, it could not be anywhere else."*

An Enlightenment minister, the Marquês de Pombal, entirely rebuilt downtown Lisbon into, more or less, the form visitors see today: an imposing, cleanly designed 18th-century city. The grid design of the downtown quarter makes it easy to negotiate.

City center: Lisbon is a walking city of pleasant esplanades with kiosks, cafes,

Praça do Comércio seen from the southeast

benches and belvederes. The black-and-white limestone mosaic sidewalks are decorative, if treacherous for high heels.

For handling the hills, there are plenty of reasonably priced, black-and- green taxis—except when it rains. A support network exists of bright yellow *eléctricos* or street cars, buses (some double-decker) and a modest subway.

The heart of the city is a vast square directly on the Tagus River called **Praça do Comércio**. This gracious space has been compared to Venice's Piazza di San Marco, but, unhappily, now is used as a parking lot. On the south, marble stairs lead down to a broad section of the river known as the *Mar de Palha* or Sea of Straw. Along the other three sides of the square are stately rose-colored 18th-century government buildings. Occasionally, English-speaking visitors refer to Praça do Comércio as "Black Horse Square" because of the large equestrian statue (now green because of its patina) in its center. The figure astride the horse is King José, the ruler at the time of the 1755 earthquake.

It was on the northwest corner of this square, opposite the main Post Office, that King Carlos and his oldest son and heir, Luís Felipe, were assassinated in 1908, leading to the abolishment of the monarchy two years later.

Praça do Comércio is also the center of Lisbon's port, a 15-mile (24-km) stretch of docks and warehouses. From a landing on the square, red ferryboats briskly ply back and forth. All kinds of sailing vessels are seen going up and down the river: long flat river barges loaded with coal or steel, container ships, the world's great cruise liners, as well as NATO gunships.

Unfortunately for the capital, there are no great promenades along the quay, no attractive riverside restaurants or cafes. It is clearly a working port. But from April to late October, there are daily afternoon boat excursions. These provide wonderful views of the city and the busy river life. Arrangements may be made at the main hotels or at the pier, on the southeast corner of Praça do Comércio.

Northwest of this square lies the **Praça do Municipio**, where the imposing 19th-century **City Hall** stands. In the center is a fine 18th-century pillory, which used to be symbol of authority. Atop the spiral is the Manueline sphere, a symbol from King Manuel I's reign seen frequently in Portuguese architecture (and on the country's flag). The banded globe recalls Portugal's

Moon rising over Castelo São Jorge.

conquests around the world.

A little further west, the **Cais do Sodré railroad station** is the starting point for the electric riverside train that goes to Estoril and other resorts. Here, too, is the **Ribeira**, the dock where fishing boats come in with their catch.

Across the road, the **Mercado de 24 Julho**, with its cathedral-like dome, has an overwhelming, lush display of fresh fish, fruits and vegetables. Lunch in the market's restaurant is a delightful experience, with tasty local swordfish, fresh grilled sardines or steamed bass, depending on the season and the catch.

Returning to Praça do Comércio, one goes through the triumphal arch on the north side of the square. This leads to **Rua Augusta**, which, like a number of side streets, has been closed to traffic and turned over to cafes, street vendors and shoppers.

This area is called the **Baixa,** or lower town, and forms part of Pombal's well-planned grid of streets. Pombaline architecture is relatively simple and graceful; the handsome color-washed buildings have carved corners and broad stone-framed windows. Now mainly an area of banks, offices and shops, the Baixa used to be divided into crafts. **Rua d'Ouro** and **Rua da Prata**, the streets of gold and silver respectively, still exist, and still claim quite a few jewelry shops, but they are now joined by a variety of other stores, including an inexplicable proliferation of shoe shops. On the eastern side of the Baixa, **Rua dos Fanqueiros**, which means "street of haberdashers," is now a street of textiles, yard goods and inexpensive clothing.

The Baixa leads into a square that everybody calls Rossio but is formally named the **Praça de Dom Pedro IV**. Once bullfights and executions were held in the Rossio; today it's a peaceful scene where old men feed pigeons, flower sellers preside over an elaborate display of seasonal blooms, and people of all ages congregate at the sidewalk cafes. The two fountains in the center were brought from Paris in 1890.

At the north end of the Rossio, the **National Theater of Dona Maria II**, built in the middle of the 19th century and restored in 1964, is a handsome rose building with arched windows and classic columns. The company generally gives quality performances of Portuguese and foreign plays in Portuguese. Standing to the west of the National Theater is a wonderful mock-rococo structure, the **Rossio railway station**. Trains leave from here for Sintra and

Roses, carnations, daisies and more for sale in the Rossio.

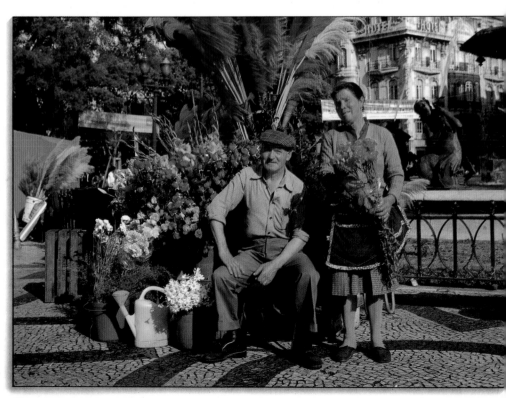

Rossio is linked to another square called **Praça dos Restauradores**, with an obelisk in its center honoring the leaders of the 1640 movement against Spanish domination. Under the square there's a convenient underground parking lot.

On the eastern side of the Restauradores square is the post office. The street running behind this large pale pink building is **Rua das Portas de Santo Antão**, where shoeshine men practice their art with a flourish while their clients sit splendidly on throne-like chairs. This is an area of popular, cheap chicken-on-the-spit restaurants and some expensive seafood places.

Back across Restauradores, the Ministry of Tourism is located in the lovely rose-colored **Palácio Foz**. An office on the ground floor is open to visitors daily with maps, brochures and counsel.

To the north lies Lisbon's Champs Elysées, the **Avenida da Liberdade**, a broad boulevard lined with palm trees, pools and benches. This splendid thoroughfare was laid out in 1879. It terminates at the **Praça de Marquês de Pombal**, with a tall statue of the man who built new Lisbon.

About halfway up the avenue on the left, a secluded square called **Parque Mayer** has

several pleasant, very Portuguese restaurants not aimed at tourists. Here, too, are several popular theaters that specialize in Portuguese musical comedy: known as *revista*, it is really a kind of political burlesque show with girlies, songs, comics and sharp satirical comments on current events, all unfortunately, only in Portuguese. During the dictatorship and press censorship, the *revista* was the only place where the regime was openly criticized.

The eastern hills: The best way to approach Alfama, the oldest quarter of Lisbon, is to take a taxi to its highest point, the **Castelo de São Jorge** and then wend one's way down on foot. On close view, the Moorish castle and medieval ramparts have been perhaps too perfectly restored; but it is a pleasant site, with a shady cobblestone terrace and peacocks and other colorful birds walking about. The view of Lisbon, the bay and the surrounding countryside is spectacular. Within the ramparts lies a small village with a shady square and a church.

Descending a little, one reaches the **Largo das Portas do Sol**, with another terrace providing a splendid vista over Alfama's orange-tiled rooftops, maze of television antennae and the river.

In a lovely 17th-century palace on the

The Marquês de Pombal surveys the Avenida da Liberdade

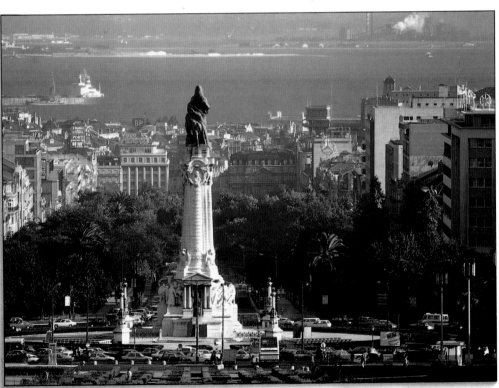

Largo is the **Espirito Santo Foundation** and **Museum of Decorative Arts**. Philanthropist and banker, Ricardo Espirito Santo established the foundation in 1953 to preserve the skills of Portugal's master craftsmen. Each Wednesday the workshops are open to the public, and visitors may see artisans working in leather, ceramics, wood, iron, bookbinding, carpet restoration and other crafts. The small church of **Santa Luzia** has some interesting old tiles, including a large panel outside depicting Martim Moniz, a soldier, helping to take Lisbon from the Moors. The *miradouro*, or lookout, is especially charming, with benches and trellised flowers. Portuguese often come here to meet friends or read.

Continuing downwards, the **Rua do Limoeiro** leads past the palace prisons of **Aljube** and **Limoeiro**, where many of Salazar's political opponents sojourned. They are now for common criminals. One should stop at the **Sé** or Cathedral, with its handsome Romanesque doorway, two square towers and rose window. The cloisters date back to the 13th century. They contain a variety of remnants, including some particularly interesting column fragments. The Sé was badly damaged by earthquakes in the 14th century and has been largely restored.

There are two other churches on the way down: **Santo António da Sé**, built in 1812 on the birthplace of Lisbon's unofficial patron saint, St. Anthony of Padua; and the **Church of Madalena**, built in 1783, with a fine Manueline doorway.

Another way to visit Alfama is to begin at the bottom, starting from the main square near the Tagus, **Largo do Chafariz de Dentro**. There's no particular way to go, just up: along the narrow winding alleys and stairs, past peeling facades and lines of well-scrubbed laundry, pausing in the shady cobblestone squares. **Rua de São Pedro** is a quintessential Alfama street, and it can lead one to the **Beco do Mexias**, a tiny alley with an inner court where women come to do their washing.

This aimless journey through Alfama can be a rewarding experience anytime for someone with a camera. But in summer, particularly June, every night seems to be a festival in Alfama. The street and squares are decorated with colored lights and streamers, and the air sparkles with fireworks. It seems that the whole city converges on Alfama to eat grilled sardines and sausages, drink wine and declaim poetry just for fun. The most important festival is

A much-needed shoeshine after a rough day on the cobbled walks

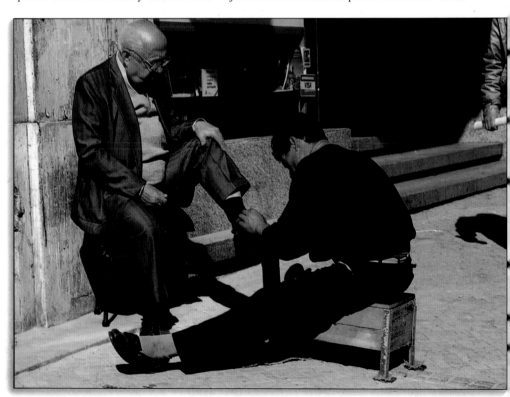

the nights of St. Anthony, June 12-13. Neighborhood groups parade down Avenida da Liberdade with colorful costumes and floats and end up singing and dancing in the squares of Alfama.

To the North of Alfama rises a hill called **Graça**, well worth the taxi ride up. The *miradouro* gives yet another magnificent view of the city. The Baroque church **Nossa Senora da Graça** has very fine tiles.

There are three other remarkable churches on the eastern heights, outside of what was, in the Middle Ages, the town walls of Lisbon. The churches are visible from the Alfama lookouts, but it is wise to take a taxi—the labyrinth of the ancient streets can tangle one's sense of direction. The 16th-century church of **São Vincente de Fora**, whose huge dome was restored after the 1755 earthquake, now serves as the Pantheon of the royal house of Bragança. Most of the members of Portugal's last royal family are buried there, including Dom Manuel II, who found exile in England in 1910 when the Portuguese monarchy was overthrown. King Carol of Rumania, who spent his last years in exile in Portugal, is also temporarily buried here, as is his morganatic wife, Madame Lupescu.

The National Pantheon is located in **Santa Engrácia**, nearby, and contains representative tombs of national heroes: Prince Henry the Navigator, Afonso de Albuquerque, Nuño Álvares Pereira, and Pedro Álvares Cabral, among others. The church was begun in the 16th century. According to popular legend, a merchant was wrongly accused of stealing the host from Santa Engrácia and put to death around 1630. It was said that he cast a spell whereby the construction of the church would never be completed. Whether due to a spell or not, the structure remained unfinished. Thus the Portuguese expression: *"obras de Santa Engrácia,"* meaning a task never done.

Salazar, however, took up the challenge and had the church restored in 1966. Some people wish he had not bothered, as it is not considered as one of Lisbon's loveliest monuments.

On the outskirts of town beyond the **Santa Apolónia railroad station**, the old monastery of **Madre de Deus** has been converted into the **Museu dos Azulejos**, the Tile Museum. Founded in 1509 by Queen Leonor, the monastery now boasts one of the best collections of Portuguese tiles of the 16th to 18th centuries. Among the most outstanding tile scenes are a panorama of Lisbon from 1730 and the life of St. Anthony, about 1780. The church, connected to the museum, is decorated with rich gilded woodwork, huge panels of fine paintings, and, of course, tiles.

The western hills: The quickest way to get to **Bairro Alto**, or the high neighborhood, from the city center, is by using the **Santa Justa Lift**. This mini-Eiffel Tower on Rua Santa Justa, just off Rua d'Ouro, was built by the noted French engineer. For a small fee, one can ride to the top of the hill to the ruins of the 14th-century **Carmo Monastery**. The roof and other sections of this building were destroyed by the 1755 earthquake; what remains provides a dramatic setting for summertime concerts. The monastery serves as an archaeological museum as well, with marble bas reliefs, tombs from the 13th century and prehistoric pottery.

Then there's the slow approach, strolling up the **Chiado**, Lisbon's most fashionable shopping area. From Rossio, one takes **Rua do Carmo**, recently turned into a pedestrian mall, which leads into **Rua Garrett**. Here are the best boutiques, shoe shops, silver and porcelain shops and bookstores. Here too is the **Brasileira**, a venerated institution, the favorite cafe of Lisbon's artists and politicians.

On the south side of the Chiado is another great view of the city, the river and São Jorge, from the **Largo da Biblioteca Nacional**.

Nearby, the opulent **Teatro São Carlos**, built in 1792 and inspired by La Scala of Milan, has a rich season of international and Portuguese opera, ballet and concerts. Around the corner, the less ornate municipal theater of **São Luiz** also presents good concerts and the National Ballet Company.

At the top of the **Rua do Alecrim** is a small square with a romantic statue of Portugal's cosmopolitan 19th-century novelist Eça de Queirós embracing his scarcely clad muse.

Rua Garrett leads into the **Largo de Chiado**, with two churches of interest: 17th-century **Nossa Senhora de Loreto**, with some nice marble and wood sculptures, and **Nossa Senhora de Encarnação**, rebuilt in the 18th century with a lovely painted ceiling and an entire wall of blue tiles.

Adjoining the Chiado is the large **Praça de Camões** with shady elms and a monument to the great epic poet Luís de Camões, who died in obscure poverty in Lisbon in 1580. John Dos Passos compares Camões' monumental poem, *Os Lusíadas*, which glorifies the Discoveries, to the *Odyssey*: "An epic of the sea, full of the smell of pitch and creaking timbers and the spray screaming off the caps of the ocean waves ."

Nearby is another 16th-century church, **São Roque**. The facade, however, was largely destroyed in 1755 and has been restored without great ability. The interior is notable for its fine tiles, painted wood ceilings and beautiful marbles. One of its side chapels is the fabulous **Chapel of St. John the Baptist**, with columns made of lapis lazuli. Adjacent to this is the **Museum Of Sacred Art** with a very small collection of fine 17th- and 18th-century silver, paintings and embroidered altar pieces.

Moving up **Rua São Pedro de Alcântara**, noted mainly for its antique shops, one arrives at another shady terrace with an admirable view of the city and the São Jorge castle crowning the opposite hill. Just across the street is the **Port Wine Institute** located in an 18th-century palace. Its cozy bar offers an unbelievable selection of port wines.

Here on the left is Bairro Alto proper, a picturesque maze of cobblestone alleys and old tenements. This quarter was built on solid rock and generally withstood the great earthquake. Some of the buildings have peeling facades or worn blue tiles but are

Mass at the São Roque

decorated with fine wrought-iron balconies, flowerpots and birdcages.

In the old days, Bairro Alto was known for its good *fado* houses. There are basically two kinds of *fado* : the tragic epic song born in the former African colonies of hardship, full of *saudade* or bittersweet nostalgia; and the joyous *fado corrida* , sung usually after bullfights.

Fado is still a rite and visitors should obey the rules requiring dim lights and absolute silence during the performance. Most Portuguese go to *fado* houses after dinner (the food in *fado* houses is generally not outstanding), drink wine and lose themselves in nostalgic reflections for the rest of the evening. Today, many of the *fado* houses have become blatantly commercial, offering foreign guests songs like "*The Yellow Rose of Texas*."

Some mansions in the Bairro Alto have been restored and turned into fashionable restaurants, discotheques and art galleries. Avant-garde Portuguese art can be seen and purchased—for a price, of course—in two recently converted elegant galleries, **Os Cómicos** and **Emi-Valentim Carvalho**. Another fine gallery is located in **São Mamede**, on **Rua da Escola Politécnica**.

The Portuguese are excellent gardeners so naturally Lisbon is laced with parks and gardens and other green spaces. Perhaps the finest of them all is the **Jardim Botánico**, one of the richest botanical gardens in Europe. Created in 1873, just off the Rua da Escola Politécnica, the garden has a magnificent wall of 100-year-old palm trees, banana trees, bamboo and water lilies and many exotic tropical plants.

Northwest of Bairro Alto is another hill with the charming **Estrêla Gardens** and splendid 18th-century **Basilica of Estrêla** with its great dome and pink, yellow and blue marble interior. Here can be found the remarkable room-sized crib carved by Machado de Castro. This neighborhood is a kind of Anglo-Saxon oasis. Close by is the British hospital, the little English **Church of St. George**, and the adjacent English cemetery where Henry Fielding, the author of *Tom Jones* is buried. Descending the hill on **Rua São Domingos á Lapa**, and turning to the right, one finds the **American Ambassador's Residence**, splendid old-rose palace and garden with a marvelous view of the river. Further down the hill is another rose palace housing the **British Embassy** and just beyond, the **British Ambassador's Residence** in a 17th-century convent.

Left, wedding music at São Roque. Right, the Estrêla Basilica

There are a number of ways to get to the **Palácio de São Bento**, where the national assembly is located. One may take the **Calçada Do Estrêla** downhill, or climb the **Avenida Dom Carlos I**, which begins on the riverfront road just west of the central market. Although special permission must be obtained to enter São Bento, visitors should take a look at it simply because so much of modern Portuguese history took place here. Originally built as a monastery, the palace was transformed into the parliament at the end of the 19th century. It was renovated in 1935 and decorated with rich sculptures and paintings.

This was the universe of former dictator António de Oliveira Salazar. He lived and worked in a small house behind the palace, hidden by a high wall. It was here in 1975 that Portugal's new leaders drafted their revolutionary constitution, which has since been amended. At São Bento political parties from the extreme left to the far right have painstakingly fashioned a dynamic European democracy.

Going back to the river road and continuing westward, one reaches the **National Museum of Ancient Art**, commonly called *Janelas Verdes* or the Green Windows. The museum is located in a fine 17th-century palace with a tasteful modern extension. On display are many fine pieces of 16th-century porcelain brought back by Portuguese sailors from India, Japan and Macão. Upstairs is the masterpiece attributed to the 15th-century Portuguese painter Nuno Gonçalves, a polyptych depicting St. Vincent, Lisbon's patron saint, and a select group of admirers including a figure presumed to be Prince Henry the Navigator, who wears a large black hat.

There are also fine wood and terra cotta figures by the great 18th-century sculptor, Machado de Castro. Foreign works include Pierro Della Francesca's *St. Augustine*, Hans Memling's *Virgin And Child*, Raphael's *St. Eusebius* , Bosch's dizzying *The Temptation of St. Anthony* and Durer's *St. Jerome*.

Leaving the museum one can move a short distance westward, and climb the Avenida do Infante Santo. There, on the left is a pre-earthquake royal palace, called the **Palácio das Necessidades**, originally a monastery. This fine building in Lisbon's ubiquitous rose-colored stone has a magnificent view and lovely gardens. It is now the Portuguese Ministry of Foreign Affairs. Although not open to the public it can be seen from the front courtyard.

Two views of Eduardo VII park

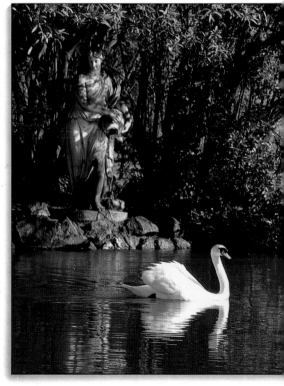

The northern hills: New Lisbon rises on the hills to the north of the city like a many-tiered fan. The Praça de Marquês de Pombal can be used as a point of reference for various tours.

Directly north of this circle rises the **Parque de Eduardo VII**, commemorating a visit by the British king to Lisbon in 1902. At the top of this grassy sloping lawn with box hedges in geometrical design is one of the finest views directly down to the city and the harbor. On the northwestern corner of the park lies the **Estufa Fria**, or Cold Greenhouse, a kind of tropical jungle, protected by bamboo slats and a joy to stroll in.

Overlooking the park on the west are residential apartments and several of the city's best hotels. Across the park stands the large **Pavilhão dos Esportes** with its elaborate yellow- and-blue tile scenes, where sports events, concerts and political rallies are held.

Driving in a northwesterly direction from the Marquês de Pombal Circle on Rua Joaquim António de Aguiar, (the road will run into the main highway towards Sintra.) One suddenly comes upon a group of startling pink- and-blue towers called **Amoreiras**. The vast complex of hotels, offices, apartments and shopping center looks like some futuristic fairyland. Architect Tomás Taveira's other shocking canary, black or multicolored edifices are increasingly disrupting the rows of drab conformist structures that characterize much of Lisbon's modern architecture.

On the hill at the northern end of Eduardo VII park stand the picturesque old penitentiary and the sleek new court building. Beyond lies the neighborhood of **Benfica**, known mainly for its stadium and as the home of Portugal's favorite soccer team. Even if one isn't a soccer enthusiast, it's worth trying to get into the **Benfica Luz stadium**, to see the fighting spirit of the fans when Benfica plays a foreign team, particularly the English or Spanish.

Here, too, is found the **Jardim Zoológico** which is not an ordinary zoo but rather a garden with animals. Founded in 1905 in the **Quinta das Laranjeiras**, the zoo is known for its magnificent rosebeds and flowers from around the world.

One area recently developed is the **Praça de Espanha**, slightly to the northeast of Pombal and the park. Here is the splendid new **American Embassy** in a renovated old palace.

Nearby is a conventionally handsome modern complex, the **Calouste Gulben-**

The futuristic Amoreiras shopping and office complex

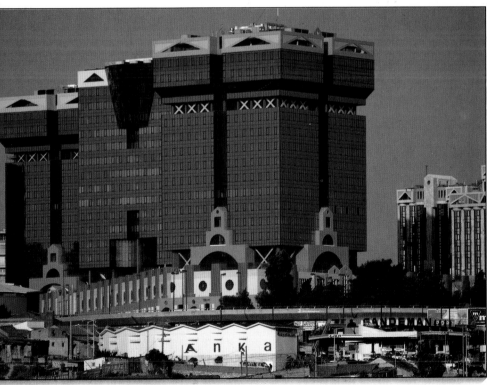

kian Foundation and Museum and the **Center of Modern Art**. Gulbenkian, an Armenian oil magnate from Turkey who personally owned five percent of Iraq Petroleum Company, spent the last 13 years of his life in Lisbon. He died in 1955. Besides supporting artists around the world, the Gulbenkian Foundation sponsors a comprehensive year-round program of lectures, ballet and concerts at its headquarters in Lisbon.

The Gulbenkian Museum contains what is said to be one of the richest formerly private collections in the world. Outstanding is the section of Middle Eastern and Islamic Art, which includes an alabaster bowl from Egypt's Old Kingdom (about 2,700 B.C.) and an Assyrian bas-relief representing the *Genius of Spring* in alabaster dating back to the 9th century B.C. There are Syrian mosque lamps and glass items from the 14th century, and many richly illuminated Armenian manuscripts from the 12th - 14th centuries.

The Greco-Roman section includes an outstanding collection of Greek gold and silver coins from the 6th century B.C. to the 1st century A.D. Among the Oriental pieces are fine Chinese porcelains of the 17th century, jades of the 18th century and Japa-nese prints and lacquers of the 18th and 19th centuries.

In the European collection, there are paintings by masters such as Carpaccio, Van Dyck, Ruysdael, Colbert, Rubens and Rembrandt. There are splendid 16th-century Italian tapestries and furniture by the finest French *ébénistes* of the 18th century. Also, there's an unusual display of the flamboyant jewelry and glass by the dean of Art Nouveau, René Lalique.

A well-tended park with ponds, paths with modern sculpture and an outdoor auditorium connect the Gulbenkian Museum with the newly built **Center of Modern Art**. Here are the works of many of Portugal's finest contemporary artists. There are several paintings by Maria Helena Vieira da Silva, who made her reputation in Paris. But other talented artists deserve to be better known abroad as well, such as the powerful first generation of modernists—José de Almada Negreiros, Eduardo Viana and Jorge Barradas—and the talented painters that followed, including Julio Pomar, Maria Ines Menez, Julion Rezend. There is Carlos Botelho who prints the soul of Lisbon; and sculptor João Cutileiro, creator of the slender frolicking women with big breasts and bushy hair that are increasingly

Lisbon's bullfights are in the Campo Pequeno

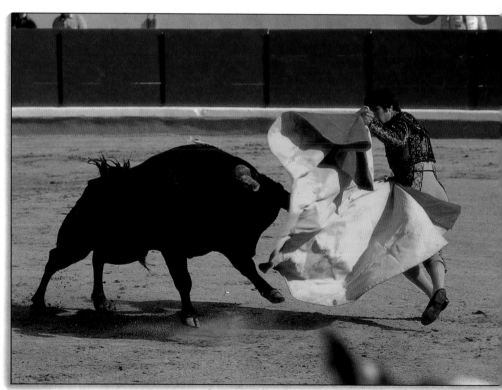

visible in the city's parks and gardens.

The easiest way to get to northeastern Lisbon and the "new avenues" is by taking Avenida Fontes Pereira de Melo again, from Pombal circle. On the left, the tall yellow tile Sheraton Hotel looks like the office building that it was originally meant to be.

Across the way, the large modern convention hall called **Picoas**, with a cafeteria, bookstore and bank, also has exhibition facilities.

Along Avenida da República, one cannot miss the large red bull ring, called **Campo Pequeno**, built in 1892. More sensitive visitors may enjoy Portuguese bullfights, called *touradas*, because unlike the Spanish, the Portuguese don't kill their bulls—at least not in public.

Across the street, the **Feira Popular** is essentially an amusement park, but it's a good place to get snails in butter and grilled sardines when they are in season (from June to October).

The avenue runs through **Campo Grande**, a shady promenade with a small lake. On the left stands **Cidade Universitária**, a group of pleasant if not spectacular modern buildings. The university campus is generally quiet and orderly these days although there was a time, just after the 1974 revolution, when the students to a large degree took the law into their own hands.

Attached to the campus is the **Biblioteca Nacional**. The National Library was founded in 1796, but moved to this huge new building in 1969. Its collection are extensive; visitors can get glimpses by viewing the two small exhibitions that change monthly.

At the end of Campo Grande, one may turn right to the airport, or visit two museums. In an 18th-century palace, the **Museu da Cidade**, or Municipal Museum, has an interesting collection of archaeological pieces and old engravings relating to Lisbon's past. About a mile down the road to Lumiar, the **Museu do Trajo**, or Costume Museum, located in an old manor with delightful gardens, is said to have one of the best collections of Portuguese costumes.

Belém: In a green, spacious zone by the river, on the western side of Lisbon, a number of monumental buildings stand as a reminder of Portugal's maritime and colonial past. This area is called **Belém**, which translated means Bethlehem in Portuguese. The name reflects the involvement of the Portuguese rulers and the religious orders with the crusades.

Without doubt, Lisbon's most glorious monument is the **Monastery of Jerónimos**, built in memory of Vasco da Gama and his successful journey to India in 1499. King Manuel personally laid the cornerstone of the Hieronymite monastery in 1502 at Belém, on the site of a chapel founded by Prince Henry the Navigator. It was here in the cloisters of Jerónimos that the ceremony was held on January 1, 1986, that marked Portugal's entry into the European Economic Community.

This vast limestone building is a masterpiece of Manueline or Portuguese baroque architecture with its opulent decoration. Notable are: the two tiered cloisters completed in 1517, the southern door, with multiple carved statues and the Templar cross, and two windows with carved rope, anchors and other seafaring symbols. The grand interior has six great octagonal stone columns with ornate decoration which have withstood time and the earthquake of 1755. Also of special interest are the finely chiseled modern altars, brilliant stained glass windows, and monumental carved tombs. Here are the tombs of two national heroes, Vasco da Gama and Camões. Today the church is a favorite place for weddings and is open to all.

Some critics complain that Jerónimos has been too thoroughly cleaned because its golden patina is gone. Critics also lament the recent construction of a wing in rather poor Manueline imitation, obscuring a fine door. Built on the western side of the church in the latter part of the 19th century, this wing houses the **National Museum of Archaeology and Ethnology** with an interesting collection of folk art, dating to the Stone and Bronze Ages. On the other end of this wing, the **Museu da Marinha**, the Navy Museum, tells the story of Portugal's seafaring discoveries with paintings, models, sculpture and maps from the empire that stretched from China to Brazil.

Across the park and to the west on the river stands the **Torre de Belém**, on the site from where Vasco da Gama and other navigators set forth on their explorations. This exquisite little 16th-century fortress is another fine example of the unique Manueline style with its richly carved niches, towers and shields bearing the Templar cross.

Back a short way towards city center stands the modern **Monument to the Discoveries**, built in 1960 to honor Prince Henry the Navigator. It is a stylized caravel with figures representing the Portuguese who took part in the great adventure, standing on the prow, looking out to sea.

Across the way rises the ornate rose-colored **Palácio de Belém**, which once served as a royal retreat and is now the Presidential palace. Decorated with lavish Oriental and European furnishings, this palace is where the President of the Republic has his offices and gives official receptions. The palace and gardens, with an interesting blend of ancient and modern sculpture, are open to the public periodically.

Adjacent to Belém Palace in what was once the royal riding-school is the **National Coach Museum**, housing one of the finest collections of its kind in Europe. The museum contains a 16th-century coach that once belonged to King Philip II of Spain and a number of well preserved gilt carriages of the 17th and 18th centuries, royal litters and sedan chairs and an ecclesiastical throne.

Behind the palace is the wonderful but rather neglected **Colonial Garden**, with all kinds of exotic plants and shady walks.

On the eastern side of Belém Palace, up the Calçada da Ajuda hill is the immense **Palácio da Ajuda**, built after the earthquake as a royal palace but never completed. The palace is sometimes used for concerts, and some of the rooms with lovely unusual ceilings, fine tapestries and lavish furnishings are open to the public.

Left, south portal of Jerónimos Monastery; right, the now-serene Torre de Belém

CASCAIS AND ESTORIL

It is officially known as the Costa do Sol, but the locals simply call it the *Marginal*. It is a wonderful 18-mile drive along the northern bank of the Tagus River to the Atlantic.

A delightful way to make the trip is by the electric train that leaves from Lisbon's Cais do Sodré station and wends its way along the coast as far as Cascais. It's about a half-hour ride, with stops. Particularly in the spring the bank along the train track is filled with colorful wildflowers. A leisurely yellow tramway also runs from the **Praça do Comércio** as far out as the resort of Cruz Quebrada.

And there's the inland *autostrada* or superhighway, almost as lovely. It starts at Marquês de Pombal Circle, runs past the Amoreiras shopping complex, through the valley of Alcântara, parallel to the grandiose **Aqueduto das Águas Livres**. The 11-mile aqueduct was built in the 18th century as the main source of water for the capital, and it still supplies water for public parks and fountains. The highway goes through one of

Salazar's finest legacies, the park of **Monsanto**, a vast area of eucalyptus trees and umbrella pines, pleasant winding roads and belvederes with magnificent views over Lisbon and the river. Beyond the park, the highway continues through gentle hilly countryside as far as Caxias, where it turns south to join the Marginal.

The river road starts out at the Praça do Comércio as the Avenida de 24 de Julho, changes its name to the Avenida da India and becomes the Marginal at the 25th of April Bridge.

As the road passes by the working quarter of **Alcântara**, some dramatic political art is visible. These murals are mostly the work of the Portuguese Communist Party and Marxist-Leninist groups, usually calling for peace and the ouster of whatever government happens to be in power. In the early days of Portugal's 1974 Revolution, there was more of this kind of political graffiti all over town. Some of Portugal's NATO allies and many tourists were quite alarmed at how aggressive the wall slogans appeared. But now the country has taken a more conservative line; many of the angry epithets have been cleaned up and what remains worries only visitors.

Further on, there is the **International**

Preceding pages, scenes from Cabo Espichel. Below, the beach at Estoril

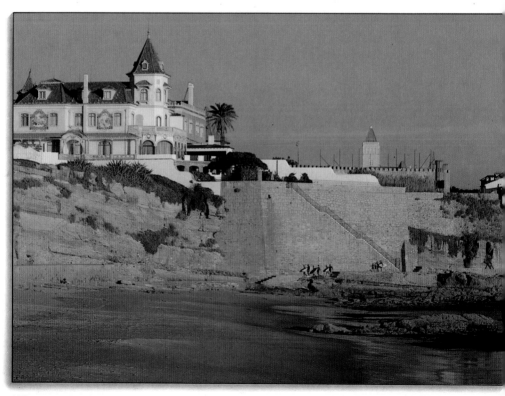

Fair Building, which frequently presents trade fairs and exhibitions. Then comes Belém with its historical monuments and parks.

Just beyond lies the elegant hillside neighborhood of **Restelo**, where many embassies and diplomatic residences are located. **Algés** is the first town outside the city limits, and it is here that taxi drivers turn off their meters and start counting the fare by kilometers.

A string of picturesque riverside towns follow. **Dáfundo** has several fine old mansions standing in sad contrast alongside dilapidated rent-controlled housing. It also boasts the **Vasco da Gama Aquarium**, with its fascinating world of sea turtles, eels, barnacles and all kinds of fish. **Cruz Quebrada** is the site of a lovely stone-seated stadium built for international soccer matches. **Caxias** is known for its flowering villas, 18th-century gazebos and an infamous hillside prison-fort. **Oeiras** has a fine 18th-century baroque **church**, lovely park, modern apartment blocks and an austere 16th-century fort. Just beyond lies the 17th-century fortress of **São Julião da Barra**, marking the point where the Tagus River meets the Atlantic. **Carcavelos** has several moderate hotels and a broad sandy beach.

Finally, **Estoril** is the first point of what has often been called the Golden Triangle and includes Cascais and Sintra. A flowering, palm-lined, pastel resort, Estoril first gained fame at the turn of the century for its therapeutic spring waters. During World War II, Estoril became known as hunting grounds for international spies. Later, this corner of the Atlantic, with its mild weather, gentle people and gracious lifestyle, became home-away-from-home for European royalty and other refugees fleeing the political upheavals after World War II. Among the Triangle's illustrious residents were former King Simeon of Bulgaria, former King Umberto of Italy, and Antenor Patiño of Bolivia. Others, like the Count of Paris, kept summer homes in the area.

With the changing times and passing royalty, local aristocrats are beginning to sell or rent their villas. More and more Portuguese, and foreign business and professional people come to the Triangle either to live, retire or keep summer homes. Estoril has now become a cosmopolitan playground with its celebrated casino, first-rate hotels, restaurants and international tennis and golf tournaments.

The **Casino** is a low white modern building with immaculately kept gardens. A passport or identity card is necessary to enter the casino as the minimum age limit is 18. There is everything in the way of games from slot-machines to blackjack, roulette and baccarat. Some people go to the Casino to see the show, usually a colorful international extravaganza. There is also an elegant dining room, an art gallery, a cinema and a bar.

Estoril has an active night life, with a variety of nightclubs, discotheques and very English bars. There are also several rather good *fado* houses in the area.

The **Estoril Music Festival** takes place from mid-July to mid-August. Concerts and recitals are held in the **Estoril Cathedral** and the **Cascais Citadel**, and also in the Jerónimos cloisters at Belém and the Lisbon Cathedral.

In recent times, the **Handicrafts Fair** has become a major production, lasting throughout the months of July and August. Located near the railroad station, the fair features arts, crafts, food, wine and folk music from all over the country. But a word of warning: Korean objects are showing up and are sometimes taken for local craft.

At this writing, the famed **Estoril Beach** and in fact all the beaches along the Costa do Sol are badly polluted, and crowded in summertime. Foreigners tend to swim in hotel pools on the coast and the Portuguese who can, go elsewhere: to **Guincho** nearby on the Atlantic; further north to **Praia Grande**; or to **Caparica** on the peninsula south of Lisbon. There's an ambitious program in the works to clean up all the beaches along the coast, but it will take a long time.

There is a lot to do in the way of sports in the Triangle. The **Estoril Golf Club**'s course, on the outskirts of town, is one of the loveliest in Europe. It was laid out by McKenzie Ross on a hillside dotted with pine and eucalyptus groves. The smaller **Estoril-Sol Golf Course** is located in a pine wood at **Linhó** near Sintra. Overlooking the Atlantic coast just beyond Cascais is the **Marinha Golf Club**, with swimming pools, tennis and riding facilities and a course designed by Robert Trent Jones. The **Estoril Autodromio** or automobile race track, located inland on the road to Sintra, draws large crowds for the Grand Prix Formula One races. It is also the site for the start and finish of the annual international Port Wine Rally.

Cascais has its own bull ring—the largest one in the country—but not many fights are scheduled. The main problem is that it is very windy: according to the locals, it would have made a better place for a windmill.

There's horseback riding at the **Escola da Equitação de Birre**, on the road to Sintra and at the **Hippodromio da Quinta da Marinha**, inland from the Guincho Beach. The Marinha Club also has mini-cruises of Cascais Bay. The **Cascais Naval Club** has facilities for water skiing, wind-surfing and sailing, and holds the Star Class Sailing World Championship.

Although it was once a royal resort, Cascais doesn't have the glitter of Estoril. In 1870, King Luís I established his summer residence in the 17th-century **Citadel** on the Bay of Cascais. Before that, it was known only as a fishing port. The locals claim that a fisherman from Cascais, Afonso Sanches, actually discovered America in 1482, and Christopher Columbus merely repeated the trip 10 years later and got all the glory. In 1580, the Duke of Alba attacked the village as part of Spain's claim to Portugal. And in 1589, the English arrived here as retaliation for the Spanish Armada's 1588 foray. But for the most part, Cascais has been as quiet as it is today, with the two principal attractions of the fishing village being the comings and goings of the colorful fishing boats in the bay and the noisy nightly **auction** at the central fish market.

There are several lovely old churches and chapels in Cascais, including the 17th-century **Church of the Assumption** with its plain facade, lovely tiles and marble nave. It houses several paintings by Josefa de Óbidos. On the pedestrian mall, attractive shops and boutiques offer elegant fashions, jewelry and authentic fishermen's sweaters. A weekly market displays nice handicrafts as well as fresh fruits and vegetables.

A lovely hotel in the region is the **Albatroz**, built for the royal family in the 19th century. On the outskirts of town in an exotic garden, lies the **Castro Guimarães Museum** with a nice display of 17th-century Portuguese silver, tiles and furniture, and good 19th-century paintings.

Beyond Cascais lies the wooded rocky Atlantic coast. Lisboners flock here on weekends for the popular seafood restaurants, particularly at **Boca do Inferno**, where they can sit and watch the waves pound the rocky inlet and fish for their own lobsters. Some hardy people swim at the broad clean beach of Guincho, where the waves can be wild and the undertow fierce. Others come to shop in this unlikely spot where vendors often appear to sell colorful woven rugs, sheepskin carpets and craftwork. And some people simply like to take the long road to Sintra, through the pines and along the bleak rocky coast.

Right, windsurfing at Praia do Guincho

SINTRA

With its lush forests and gentle surrounding plain, Sintra has long been a favorite summer resort for Portuguese and foreign aristocrats and vacationers. People delight in the area because of its sheer natural beauty, in spite of man playing a few of his tasteless tricks.

Lord Byron, who could find little good to say about the Portuguese, was enamored with Sintra and likened it to "Elysium's gates." In *Childe Harold*, he wrote: "Lo! Cintra's glorious Eden intervenes in variegated maze of mount and glen."

Byron, Southey, Beckford and others who have written eloquently of the charms of Sintra would probably be horrified by some recent signs of "development." The most conspicuous mistake is the Tivoli Hotel, a huge graceless block, incongruously placed beside the imposing National Palace. The romantics would be dismayed by the recent growth of small, new, rainbow-colored houses below Sintra where there used to be large estates or wooded countryside.

Some 20 miles (32 km) to the northwest of Lisbon, Sintra is another world with its own special climate and almost bucolic way of life. The most practical way to go is by train from Rossio. If one drives, rush hour traffic should be avoided if at all possible. It seems that most of the inhabitants of Sintra commute to Lisbon on weekdays and vice-versa weekends. The road to Sintra from Lisbon starts at the Pombal Circle and is well marked. Avenida Duarte Pacheco runs into the *autostrada* or super highway that leads out of town, past the Aqueduto das Águas Livres, up the hill through Monsanto Park, turning right to join the highway to Sintra.

A slight detour to visit **Queluz** is well worthwhile. The town has become a rather drab Lisbon dormitory. The **Palace**, however, is a marvelous rose-colored edifice with a monumental facade. It was first built as a simple manor for King Pedro in the mid-17th century and enlarged when the court moved there. Most of the palace is Baroque, but the courtyard and formal gardens were modeled after Versailles.

The palace is used as a government guesthouse for special visitors, such as Queen Elizabeth II and former President Dwight D. Eisenhower. In summer, concerts are sometimes held in the **Music Room**. At other times, the public may visit the lavishly decorated **Throne Room** with its fine painted wood ceiling, the **Hall of Mirrors**, **Ambassador's Room**, and others. The great kitchen, with its stone chimney and copperware, has been turned into a luxury restaurant called Cozinha Velha.

Back on the main road, one continues along rolling hills, past modest white-washed villages and rich *quintas*, or manors, to arrive at the **Serra de Sintra**. At the base of the mountain lies the village of **São Pedro de Sintra**, where on the second and fourth Sunday of each month, a wonderful country fair takes place. On display are all kinds of crafts from primitive wood carvings and ceramics to fine antique furniture, as well as the latest plastic utensils and polyester tablecloths. São Pedro is also known for its popular *tavernas* , with spicy sausages, hearty codfish and heady wines.

The road climbs slightly and curves around the mountain to reach the center of town. Here is the office of Turismo with permanent exhibition halls and a number of silver and craft shops. Also nearby, the **Estalagem dos Cavaleiros**, formerly called the Hotel Lawrence, where Lord Byron stayed in 1809. Despite official pressures, the owner, as of this writing, has still not been persuaded to open the building to the public.

Two 12th-century churches in town, **Santa Maria** and **São Martinho**, have both been much altered over time. There is also a **Municipal Museum**, which offers a pleasant way of getting acquainted with Sintra's history.

The centerpiece of Sintra is the former royal palace, now called the **Palácio Nacional**, parts of which date back to the 14th century. Broad stairs lead up to the stately building with Gothic arches, Moorish windows and two extraordinary chimney cones. Of special interest on the guided tour of the palace are: the **Sala dos Brasões**, with its remarkable ceiling panels painted in 1515, which show the coat-of arms of 72 Portuguese noble families. (Note that actually only 71 exist; that of the Távoras was removed after the conspiracy against King José in 1758); the **Sala dos Arabes**, with marble fountain and 15th-century Moorish tiles; the **Sala dos Cisnes**, an enormous reception hall with swans painted on the paneled ceiling; the **Sala das Pegas**, whose ceiling is covered with magpies brandishing banners reading *"Por Bem."* It is said that when Queen Philippa caught King João I courting a lady-in-waiting, he claimed it

Preceding page, the eccentric Pena Palace. Below, Queluz, Portugal's Versailles

was an innocent kiss. "*Por Bem*," he said, which loosely translated means: "All for the good."

Sintra's other palace-museum, the **Castelo da Pena**, dominates the town from the top of the mountain and is best visited by taxi or horse-and-carriage. The road winds up steep rocky slopes through thick woods to the castle, built on the site of a 16th-century monastery. For many visitors, Pena is better viewed from afar, where it gives the impression of some medieval stronghold. Close at hand, the castle is an architectural monstrosity, a potpourri of various styles and influences. Arabic minarets, Gothic towers, Renaissance cupolas, Manueline windows. It was commissioned by Prince Ferdinand of Saxe-Coburg-Gotha, husband of Queen Maria II, and built by German architect Baron von Eschwege around 1840. At the entrance of the castle, a tunnel leads to the ruins of the original monastery. The old chapel walls are decorated with fine 17th-century tiles and there is a splendid altar of alabaster and black marble by 16th-century French sculptor Nicolas Chanterene. But the best thing about the castle is the view. Below lies **Pena Park**, with lakes and black swans, tangled forest and tile fountains. When Richard Strauss visited the park, he supposedly said: "*I know Italy, Sicily, Greece, Egypt, but I have never seen anything equal to Pena.*"

Across the way, another mountain-top castle, the **Castelo dos Mouros**, is now only ruins of a Moorish fortress, dating to perhaps the 11th century. The fortifications visible along the mountain ridge were restored in the middle of the 19th century. To the southwest rises the highest peak called **Cruz Alta**, 540 meters (1,772 feet) high and marked by a lovely stone cross.

The mountainside is a luxuriant mass of vegetation—subtropical plants, boulders covered with moss, giant ferns, walnut, chestnut and pine trees, and rhododendron bushes.

One of the strangest sights on the mountain is the **Convento dos Capuchos**, a 16th-century monastery built entirely out of rocks and cork. Some say the monks lined their cells with cork to obtain absolute silence—but there is little noise in the forest other than bird sounds. More likely, the cork helped the monks bear the long and humid winters.

On the outskirts of town stands the **Palácio de Seteais**, which means "The palace of the seven sighs" clearly a reference to the great beauty of the surroundings. Built

he Throne
oom at
ueluz

by a Dutch diamond merchant in the 18th century, Seteais is remembered as the site where Generals Junot and Dalrymphe signed the Convention of Sintra in 1809, after the defeat of Napoleon's forces by British and Portuguese forces. The palace was restored and turned into a luxury hotel and restaurant in 1955 and should be seen, if only for tea or a drink. The parlors are decorated with crystal chandeliers, wall-hangings, murals and antique furnishings. From the gardens, with sculpted hedges and lemon trees, one has a magnificent view of the countryside. At the *quinta* of *Penha Verde*, not far from here, João de Castro planted the first orange trees in Portugal after retiring as viceroy of India in 1542.

Nearby is the **Quinta da Monserrate**, a strange Moorish-type villa built in the 19th century by Sir Francis Cook. The property is now owned by the State but poorly maintained. The villa is closed but the exotic garden and greenhouse are worth seeing. The wild jungle includes trees and plants from all over the world: palm trees, bamboo, cedars, magnolia trees, cork-oaks, pines and giant ferns.

Once part of the Monserrate gardens, the **Quinta de São Thiago** is a 16th-century manor owned by a retired Englishman and his Spanish wife. It has a lovely chapel, majestic kitchen, cell-like bedrooms, garden and pool. Like other gentry, the Braddells found taxes and utilities prohibitive and, in 1979, opened the *quinta* to paying guests.

The main cultural event of the area is the annual **Festival of Sintra**, generally running three weeks in July. First class recitals, concerts and ballet are presented in the National Palace, Queluz Palace and some of the great *quintas* of the region. And all summer long, there is a "Sound and Light" program presented on weekend evenings at the National Palace.

For a delightful excursion, the **Colares** Road leads through vineyards, white-washed hamlets and stone walls to the sea. Enroute, it is possible to visit the **Adega Regional**, a traditional winery. Colares grapes grow in sandy soil with humid maritime climate. The wines are dark ruby and very smooth.

Cabo da Roca is a wild desolate cape, known as the westernmost point of continental Europe. Visitors receive a certificate for their trouble. Camões described it as the place *"where the land ends and the sea commences."* Heading north, there are several beaches frequented mainly by Portu-

Left, the conical chimneys of the Royal Palace. Right, the Seteais.

120

guese: broad, sandy **Praia Grande** and **Praia das Maçãs**. The fishing village of **Azenhas do Mar** has natural rocky swimming pools.

Another excursion goes to **Mafra**, the immense palace-convent which is almost as large as Spain's Escorial. One follows the road for **Ericeira**, a beach resort and fishing village, and then drives inland for six miles.

Mafra rises just like some dark mirage across the plain from the modest low-lying houses that make up the village of the same name.

Originally a Capuchin monastery stood on the site. João V erected the new collection of buildings, on quite a different scale, in fulfillment of a vow he made in hopes of having an heir. Work began on the palace in 1717 and ended 18 years later. Estimates of the total of the project vary, but it is said that more than 50,000 workers and 1,000 oxen were employed. Planned to house 13 friars, the final result could easily fit 280—and many novices as well.

Mafra's construction drew so many artists from so many countries that João decided to found the School of Mafra, utilizing these talented artisans as masters to local apprentices. The most famous teacher was probably Joaquim Machado de Castro.

The Limestone facade is massive, 220 meters long. From its center is the **church**, with two tall towers and an Italianate portico. The interior of the church is decorated with the finest Portuguese marbles of different colors. The 14 large statues of saints, located in the vestibule, are carved from Carrara marble—they were made by Italian sculptors. The church contains a generous supply of organs—six.

Part of the monastery is off-limits, being used by the military, but many sections can be visited. The most impressive room is the **library**, full of Baroque magnificence and light. Among its 35,000 volumes are first editions of *Os Lusíadas* by Camões and the earliest edition of Homer in Greek.

Other areas open to the public include the **hospital**, with original decorations and fittings, the **pharmacy**, the **audience room**, painted with a *tromp l'oeil*, and the oval **chapterhouse**. There are three cloisters. The north tower can be climbed, and the two **towers** together contain more than 100 bells, some of which were cast in Belgium.

The town of Mafra is also the site of the church of **Santo André**, which contains the tomb of Diago de Sousa. Pedro Hispano was priest here before he was elected Poe John XXI in 1276.

he library t Mafra

SETÚBAL AND THE ARRÁBIDA PENINSULA

Lisboetans call it *Outra Banda*, the other shore, meaning the southern bank of the Tagus River, long neglected because of the sheer inconvenience of getting there. This all changed after 1966 with the completion of what was then Europe's longest suspension bridge, the 25th of April Bridge. The region, known as the **Arrábida Peninsula**, has developed rapidly, and not always wisely.

Directly across the river is the unassuming ferryboat port of **Cacilhas**. Its main charm is a string of riverfront fish restaurants with a great view of Lisbon. About five km west of the bridge is **Trafaria**, the whole town, since rebuilt, that was burned to the ground on the harsh orders of Pombal in 1777, official punishment for resisting press gangs. Most visitors tend to drive through the neighboring industrial town of **Almada**, except those who want to examine the **Christ the King** monument close at hand. Christ seems dwarfed by his pedestal—irreverent Portuguese say some priest must have dipped into the till before the statue

was completed. Visitors may go up to the top of the pedestal by elevator and stairs for a magnificent view of Lisbon. Almada also contains the monastery of **São Paulo**, founded in 1568.

Most people avoid the Outra Banda dormitory district by taking the superhighway leading directly from the bridge. After a few miles, a turnoff leads to **Costa da Caparica**, a series of broad Atlantic beaches with moderately priced hotels and restaurants. This popular resort is cleaner than the Costa do Sol, and the currents are safer than those of the Atlantic north of the Tagus.

Continuing south on the highway, one passes new factories where there used to be only fields, pine forests and vineyards. The road marked **Palmela** leads to a small town with a great **medieval castle**. This has been restored and converted into a luxury *pousada*, with a lounge in the cloisters, elegant dining room in the old refectory, and antique furnishings. The attached **church** is a beautiful, simple Romanesque structure. The walls are covered with 16th- and 18th-century tiles. The church contains the tomb of Jorge de Lencastre (1431-1550) natural son of João II.

Built by the Moors, the castle was reconstructed in 1147 as a monastery and the seat

The Igreja de Jesús

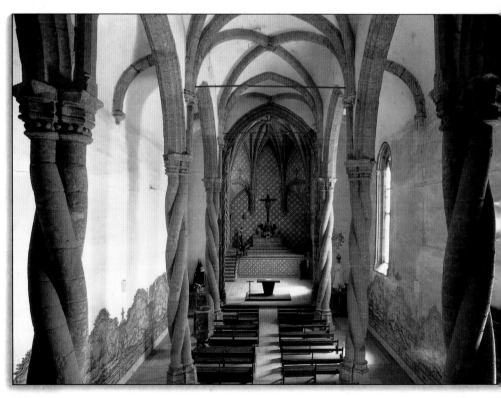

of the Knights of the Order of Saint James. In 1484, the bishop of Évora, Garcia de Meneses, was imprisoned in the dungeon here for his role in conspiring against the king, João II. He died a few days later, probably of poison. Palmela castle was badly damaged by the 1755 earthquake, but the monks rebuilt and remained until the abolition of religious orders in 1834. It is said that much of the town of Palmela was built from pieces of the old castle. At the foot of the castle stands the church of **São Pedro**; its interior is lined with tiles showing the life of the saint.

Just outside of **Setúbal** rises another great castle-turned-pousada, **São Filipe**, with a magnificent view of the **Sado River** estuary. Philip II of Spain ordered the construction of the strategic castle in 1590 to keep a watch over the area—Portugal was under Spanish rule at the time. Starting in 1766, the fortress-castle was used as a prison until its conversion into a pousada in 1965. The castle's **chapel** is decorated with tiles that recount the life of Saint Philip (not Philip of Spain), signed by the master painter Policarpo de Oliveira Bernardes and dated 1736.

According to local legend, Setúbal was founded by Tubal, the son of Cain. It is said that Phoenicians and Greeks, finding the climate and soil of Arrábida similar to their Mediterranean homelands, brought their grapes and started vineyards. Setúbal is known to have been an important fishing port since Roman times.

Today Setúbal is an industrial town, a center of ship-building, fish-canning, and the production of fertilizers, cement, salt and moscatel wine. Nevertheless, there are a number of interesting sights in town and in the region. Setúbal's pride is the **Church of Jesus**, a spectacular monument dating back to 1491. The church was designed by Diogo Boytac, known as the founding master of the Manueline style of architecture. It is considered one of his finest works. The narrow building has a high arched ceiling supported by six great stone pillars that look like coils of rope; its apse is etched with stone and lined with tiles. Arrábida marble was used, and the pebbled, multi-colored stone gives the whole a distinct appearance. There are also lovely tile panels along the walls. The **cloister** has been turned into a museum with an exhibition of rare 16th-century Portuguese and Flemish primitives, numismatics, jewelry and archaeological discoveries from the region.

Nearby is the **Praça do Bocage**, with palm trees and a statue honoring one of the town's illustrious sons, 18th-century sonneteer, Manuel Barbasa du Bocage. Off the square stands the church of **São Julião** with a handsome Manueline doorway built in 1513. The inside walls are decorated with 18th-century tiles showing the life of the saint and popular fishing scenes. Also of interest is the **Ethnographical Museum**, with models depicting the city's main industries: fishing, farming and textiles. The church of **Santa Maria de Graça**, at the east end of town has 17th-century paintings.

One of the great scenes is **Setúbal Harbor**, particularly in the morning with the arrival of brightly painted trawlers loaded with fish. Then there's the continual show of fishermen mending nets and working on their boats. Best of all is the lively fish auction.

Setúbal is the main point of departure for the peninsula of **Troia**. From Setúbal's dock, ferryboats make the 20-minute crossing frequently in season; there is also a hovercraft service. Troia, a long narrow spit jutting out into the Sado estuary, is said to be the site of the Roman town of **Cetóbriga**, buried by a tidal wave in the 5th century. Substantial ruins have been found but little has been excavated besides a temple and tombs. Underwater, one may see the walls of Roman houses. On the northern end of the peninsula, there is a rather unattractive modern beach resort with large apartment blocks, hotels and villas. The **Troia Golf Club** has an 18-hole course designed by Robert Trent Jones. On the southern end of the peninsula, however, there are still miles of pine forest and fine empty beaches and dunes.

Many Portuguese and foreigners regret that the Portuguese authorities did not see fit to protect this City of the Dead in its natural state, as the Greeks have done with Delos.

At the mouth of the Sado, about three miles (five km) southwest of Setúbal, is the **Torre do Outão**, originally a Roman temple to Neptune, which offers a great view. Another delightful excursion from Setúbal goes along the ridge of the **Serra da Arrábida** which rises to 2,000 feet (606 meters). As one leaves the city, the only sight that mars the natural beauty of the coast is the cement factory, usually spitting out black smoke. From the belvederes, there are majestic views of the mountain slopes. A cluster of whitewashed hermitages and chapels, built around 1542, lie almost lost in the dense mass of greenery, oaks and pines, ferns and wildflowers. Far below, ochre cliffs drop into the turquoise sea.

A road descends to **Portinho da**

Arrábida, a popular bathing beach with transparent waters, white sand and the splendid **Grotto of Santa Margarida**. Hans Christian Andersen, who visited the region in 1834, marveled in his diaries at this cave with its imposing stalactites. Scuba diving is popular here.

But it was Robert Southey, a young traveler who was very difficult to please, who consecrated Arrábida for English readers, calling it "a glorious spot." In his letters, he recounts going swimming at the base of the mountain and writes: "I have no idea of sublimity exceeding it."

Regaining the ridge, one continues along the skyline drive, which is reminiscent of the Amalfi coast. The next turnoff leads to **Sesimbra**, a lovely fishing village and resort with several notable sights. The castle above the village, although known as Moorish, has been entirely rebuilt since that time. Afonso Henriques captured it in 1165, but the Moors utterly razed the structure in 1191, following a scorched earth policy. King Dinis almost certainly helped with the rebuilding, and King João IV again added and repaired in the 17th century. Inside the walls are ruins of a Romanesque church, Santa Maria, and the old town hall. King João IV also ordered the fort of São Teodo-

sio built, to protect the port from pirates.

In town is the Misericórdia, constructed in the 15th century, with a painting attributed to Gregório Lopes. The 16th-century parish church contains a noteworthy 18th-century gilded wood alterpiece.

But the most fascinating sight is the port with its fishermen, always busy either going out to sea, coming back, or selling their catch. There are several simple bistros near the port where one may eat fresh fish—swordfish is the local specialty—and enjoy the show.

Going westward about seven miles (11 km), the road ends at **Cabo Espichel**. This promontory with the shrine of **Nossa Senhora do Cabo** used to be an important pilgrimage site, as shown by the long rows of dilapidated pilgrims' quarters on either side of the church. There is still a fishermen's festival here each October. On the edge of the high cliff is the small fisherman's **Chapel of Senhor de Bomfim**, in a rather desolate state but with a breathtaking view of the Atlantic coast.

The road back to Lisbon goes through **Vila Nogueira de Azeitão**, sometimes simply called Azeitão, which means large olive tree. In the center of this charming village is the stately **Távora Palace**, where

The endless beach at Troia Peninsula

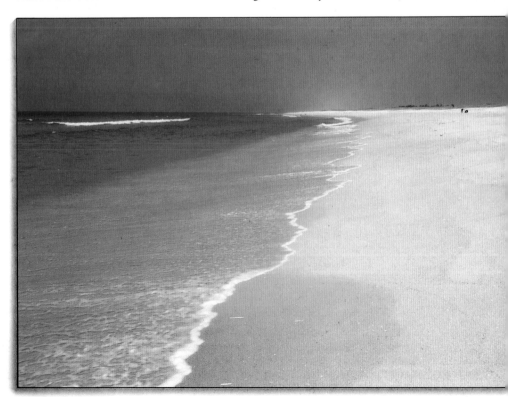

the Duke of Aveiro and his friends are said to have plotted to overthrow King José. The Duke, and his friends, were burned at the stake for their troubles, in Belém in 1759. Townspeople plan to restore the palace and turn it into a museum. Lovely Baroque fountains border the town's main street. The **Church of São Lourenco** has been restored and boasts of beautiful 18th-century altars, paintings and tile panels.

The **Azeitão fair**, held in the central square on the first Sunday of the month, became so popular that it caused havoc and had to be moved to the outskirts of town. Less picturesque now, it is still a major attraction with stands offering everything from shoes and pottery to furniture. There is also a large section devoted to livestock and poultry.

In the village, stands the original **José Maria da Fonseca winery**, founded in 1834. The old family residence, which now houses a small museum, stands nearby. The winery still produces one of Portugal's best red table wines, the soft rich Periquita, as well as Setúbal's popular moscatel wines. Moscatel is a sweet aperitif wine, topaz in color with 18 to 20 percent alcohol.

Da Fonseca also coproduces **Lancers**, one of Portugal's best known table wines, in new modern installations on the outskirts of town. Visitors are welcome to tour the factory and see its assembly-line production.

Not far from town stands one of the oldest inhabited manors in the country, the **Quinta da Bacalhoa**, built in 1480. It had fallen into ruins and was saved by an American woman from Connecticut, Mrs. Herbert Scoville, who bought it in 1936 and restored it scrupulously. The gardens, which are open to the public, are admirable with their clipped boxwood in geometric design, orange and lemon groves, and pavilion with beautiful tile panels. One of these scenes, showing Susanna and the Elders is dated 1565, and said to be the earliest known dated panel in Portugal.

Another attractive manor, the **Quinta das Torres**, stands just outside the neighboring village of **Vila Fresca de Azeitão.** This 16th-century *quinta*, decorated with tile panels and set in a romantic garden, has been converted into a cozy inn and restaurant and is an ideal spot for tea.

In the village, there is yet another charming church, **São Simão**, with more ancient tile walls and polychrome panels.

The easiest route back to Lisbon is to take the old national highway, N10, which runs into the superhighway.

Cabo Espichel sweeps into the Atlantic

ALGARVE

Separated from the rest of Portugal by smooth rolling hills, the Algarve, a southernmost province, seduced the ancient Phoenicians with its abundance of sardines and tuna, which they salt-cured for export almost 3,000 years ago. Four centuries later, around 600 B.C., the Carthaginians and Celts arrived, which in turn attracted the Romans.

The Romans adopted the Phoenician practice of curing and exporting fish—the precursor to Portugal's large tinned sardine industry. They built roads, bridges, and spas, such as that in Milreu. They also enjoyed the springs of Monchique.

But the Algarve really blossomed under Moorish rule, which began in the early 8th century. Its name comes from the Moorish **Al-Gharb** meaning "The West".

The Moorish period was one of vivacious culture and great strides forward in science. Moorish poets sang of the beauty of Silves, while the more practical settlers introduced orange crops, and perfected the technique of extracting olive oil, still very much an important Portuguese product. The blossoming almond trees in February remains one of the most beautiful sights to behold in the Algarve thanks to the passion a Moorish king once held for a northern princess.

Legend has it that the princess, pining for the snows of her homeland, slowly began to waste away. Distraught, the king ordered thousands of almond trees to be planted across the region, then one February morning carried her to the window where she saw swirling white "snow flakes" carpeting the ground—the white almond blossoms. She quickly recuperated, and the two as you might guessed, lived happily ever after.

King Afonso Henriques led the Portuguese conquest of the Algarve in the 12th century, and later his son Sancho I was to lead the siege against Silves and its estimated population of 20,000 people with the help of the Crusaders. It took 49 days before the Moors of Silves surrendered. In 1192 they reconquered the city and remained there for another 47 years. It was Sancho II who, supported by military religious orders headed by Paio Peres Correia, finally crushed the Moors. The last major city to fall was Faro in January 1249.

But the Arabic influence is visible even today: town names, words beginning with the "al" prefix, and Tunisian blue is still used in trimming the whitewashed homes, terraces atop houses used for the drying of fruit, and the white-domed buildings still popular in many towns. The Algarvian sweets made of figs, almonds, eggs and sugar called *Morgados* or *Dom Rodrigos* are yet another reminder of the area's ancient heritage.

For centuries almond, fig, olive and carob trees represented a major part of the Algarve's agriculture, as they are suited to the dry inland areas. Recently, citrus fruit has taken on greater importance, changing the region's typical agricultural cycles.

Thanks to the area's different climates—coastal, inland and mountain—the Algarve also produces pears, apples, quince, loquats, damask plums, pomegranates, tomatos, melons, strawberries, watermelon, peas, lima beans and green beans.

The export of wine from the Algarve—began during the Muslim occupation and reached its peak in the 14th and 15th centuries. Lagos, Portimao, Lagoa and Tavira are the primary wine centers. The Lagos *Algar Seco* is a very dry aperitif wine, served chilled. The region's dry and sweet *Moscatel* wines are both aged in oak barrels for at least seven years and have an alcohol gradient of 18 to 19 percent. The dry wine should be served chilled as an aperitif, while the sweet is essentially served as a dessert wine.

Afonso III is a very dry wine from Lagos, served chilled, while the *Cruz de Portugal* is a sweet red wine, normally aged eight to 10 years, that should be served at room temperature with desserts. From Tavira comes the sweet, dark and fruity *Licoroso de Tavira* which should be served at room temperature in a port glass.

Medronho is a clear brandy-type of drink made out of wild strawberry of the same name and is famous throughout the Algarve. It has an alcohol gradient similar to the kick of a mule, and is available everywhere, but especially in the roadside *tascas*, or bars, where it is served in small Port glasses. The best Medronho is homemade. In the tiny village of Cachopo lost in the inland eastern part of the Algarve, a tiny pixie-like old widow soberly dressed in the obligatory black will be quite happy to usher you into the back of her house (if you can find her) and tip herself almost upside down into her huge medronho barrels to fill your empty bottles with her own special make. Another favorite in the Algarve is *Brandymel*, a type of honey-brandy

Typical handicrafts are fading fast, but you can still find soft yellow *esparto* or matgrass baskets, hats, mats and hampers and so on in Loulé. This is traditionally made by women who pick and dry the *esparto* in May, then shred it into thin strips which are soaked before worked.

Lovely *esparto* rugs are also made in Albufeira, Monchique and Vila Real de Santo Antonio. Cane basketry is almost exclusively made by men and is most popular in Alcoutim, Castro Marim, Odeleite, São Brás and Aljezur. These stiff baskets are used to carry eggs, or are sometimes transformed into fish traps.

Lagor, Loulé, Tavira and Martinlongo are reknowned for pottery, including the two-handled big-bellied water pitchers that resemble Roman amphoras, as well as various bowls, plates and tiles, and the famous white lace-like chimney tops that embellish the Algarve's skyline. Dark wrought-iron railings are the work of ironsmiths from Silves, Portimao, Loule and Tavira, while the art of beaten copper, similar to that of Northern Africa, is most seen in Lagos and Loulé. An excellent example of this is the *cataplana*—grandmother of the modern pressure cooker.

The copper *cataplana* is a wok-like cooking dish with a hinged lid which has become a symbol of the Algarve. Originally used by hunters, it is now used to make a series of seafood dishes like *Ameijoas na Cataplana*: a delicious dish of fresh steamed clams mixed with chopped onion, pork, parsley, green peppers and oil. One warning: Pollution has increased drastically in the past few years due to the tourist boom, and this with the heat has affected clams and mussels, so only eat them in reputable restaurants in the summer, and never eat one that has not opened.

Other handicrafts include woodwork, such as the wooden spoons of Aljezue, or the colorfully painted mule-drawn wagons. Beautiful hand-made bobbin-lace is on sale in Olhão, Fuzeta, Castro Marim and Azinhal. Wool-weaving is more typical in the mountainous regions, and some flax-weaving is still practiced in Monchique. Driving south of Monchique you can also see stoneworkers hand-cutting blue and white stone squares used to make the striking mosaic-like pavements seen around Portugal.

There are various ways of getting to the Algarve. The most direct is to fly to the Faro International Airport, a half-hour hop from Lisbon. Faro is the Algarve's capital, thought to have been founded by the Phoe-

nicians, then used by Greeks and Romans as a trading post before it became a flourishing Moorish town. It was largely demolished by the violent 1755 earthquakes, and its architecture reveals a hodge-podge of styles and eras.

Faro: The city surrounds an attractive yacht basin. Off to one side is the beautiful Renaissance **Arco da Vila** archway that leads to the old part of town and the Renaissance-Baroque **cathedral**. The second chapel in this cathedral has a lovely panelled depiction of the Biblical flight to Egypt in Dutch tiles. Another 15th century chapel, dedicated to Our Lady of Conceiçao, also has a lovely collection of 17th century tiles. The red Chinoserie organ in the main part of the church dates from the 15th century.

A most bizarre and macabre sight can be found in the **Carmelite Church**. Within this 18th century structure is the **Chapel of Bones**, built entirely out of skeletons and lined with grinning skulls, said to have been created out of a nearby over-crowded cemetery.

The museum in the former **Clarissas Convent** has a good selection of Roman artifacts from Faro and the ancient Roman site of Milreu to the north. The **Ethnographic Musem** in the Praça Alexandre Herculano is also interesting, with detailed replicas of a typical Algarvian home as well as handicrafts from all over the province. The **Nautical Museum** in the Port Authority building is worth a quick visit for the history of Algarve fishing, complete with models of ancient fishing boats.

The rest of town is divided into different quarters with one quieter 18th century section and other scattered historical features, but overall Faro has lost some of its old-fashion charm in growing into a bustling resort town. However, a number of lovely villages are within driving distance from here.

Estói, for example, is a tiny place where archaeologists have found artifacts dating from Paleolithic times down to the Bronze and Copper Ages. Not far are the remains of the Roman settlement of **Milreu**. There is usually a guide to show you around the ruins of baths believed to have belonged to an important Roman noble. Some of the original mosaics depicting leaping blue dolphins and fish are still visible, and the walls of an old Roman temple, presumably built to honor the god or goddess of the baths, still stand.

North of Estói is **São Brás de Alportel**, founded by the Moors, and topped by a large hill that has a great view of the lower

Algarve. Some eight miles (13 km) west is **Loulé**, a charming white washed town whose old quarter, the *almedina* (like the *medinas* or *casbahs* of north Africa) is a maze-like array of streets full of shops selling regional handicrafts. The old **parish church** here was built by King Dinis (1279-1325). Worth a visit is the *Mae Soverana* or **Sovereign Mother shrine** built in the early 16th century—today overshadowed by a modern dome-shaped cathedral—whose interior is covered in 17th century tiles and frescoes.

North again and off the beaten track is the **Serra do Caldeirão**. This range of hills, reaching 1,800 feet (545 meters), has been left largely untouched by the tourist explosion; areas of it are still home to some not very friendly wild boars. Walks through these mountains can be wonderfully peaceful after the summer bustle of the coastal resorts, and it is a great place for picnics under the cork trees, holm oaks and pink and white blossoming oleanders. Sheep, goats, and their shepherds are the only inhabitants of this area. The plain white houses with their small windows and simple tiled roofs reveal the hardworking and gentle character of the shepherds.

Another route into the Algarve is to drive from Lisbon, through the Alentejo. The main road passes through the lovely mountain village of **São Marcos da Serra**. There is a terrific roadside restaurant here—ignore the rough edges on the outside and go inside where they serve fresh fish, chicken and meat grilled on a wood fire.

The road then leads to **São Bartolomeu de Messines**, whose small 15th century red sandstone **church** is filled with 17th century tiles. Drive on then to the coastal resort town of **Albufeira**. Once a small fishing village favored by the Romans and Moors, Albufeira today is a populous tourist spot with an active nightlife, hundreds of bars crushed next to each other blasting rock music, plenty of restaurants ranging from La Pizza to more typical regional fare, and late-night discos.

The old part of town is still very attractive, as are the rock-protected beaches where the fishermen keep their boats, gaily painted with large eyes (to ward off evil), as well as stars and animals. There is a bustling seafood market near the fishermen's beach and a fruit, meat and vegetable market in the main town square held daily except Mondays.

The distance between towns east or west of Albufeira is negligible, the roads being

Mixing business and pleasure on the beach of Albufeira

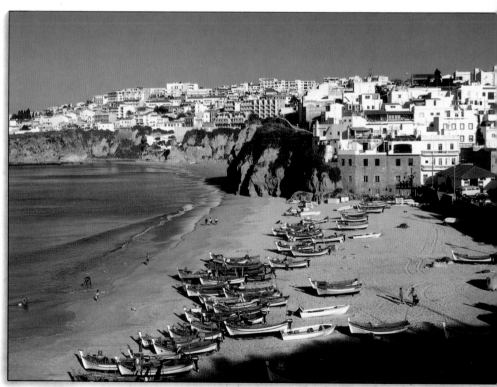

boring but easy to drive; and the relentless tourist industry has built so much in between that it is hard to tell when you have left one town and entered another. Unfortunately, much of this area has been ruined with massive billboard advertising and bad urban planning.

However, veering off to the shore you can still find some uncrowded beaches. One good alternative is to hire a boat (and a fisherman) for the day, fill the boat up with food and drink, and go exploring the coast for the deserted beaches and grottoes that dot this rocky coastline that can only be reached by sea.

Most of the well-known golf courses lie east of Albufeira, such as Quinta do **Lago**, a 27-hole course, **Vale do Lobo**, and **Vilamoura**, which was originally designed by Frank Pennink and is part of a 4,000 acre (1,600 hectares) tourist development. Penina, designed by three-time British Open champion Henry Cotton, is west of Albufeira, closer to Portimão. More than 120,000 golfers visit Algarve's six courses every year.

Northeast of Albufeira is Alte, a naturally elegant village lying at the foot of woolly hills huddled around its parish church. The church of **Nossa Senhora da Assunção** dates from the 16th century and has magnificent 18th-century tile panels. Within, the tiles in the **Our Lady of Lurdes Chapel**, considered the best in the Algarve, are of 16th century Sevillian origin. Alte is perhaps one of the most typical villages of the province with its delicate laced white chimneys, simple white houses and timeless serenity.

A nearby brook (to which people come from miles around to gather water) has transformed the area into an oasis amid the region's sometimes scrubby landscape. It's a lush garden of oleanders, fig and loquat trees and rose bushes. The blue- and-white tile panels around the **Fonte da Bicas** or fountain, contain poems by Candido Guerreiro. This area is perfect for long walks or picnics, or a donkey ride up the Pena hill where you can visit the **Moors' Cave** (*Buraco dos Mouros*). Further up the mountain is **Rocha dos Soidos**, a cave filled with intricate stalactite and stalagmite formations.

Northwest of Albufeira is **Silves**, the oldest town in the Algarve, settled in the 4th century B.C. Although the city was important in Roman times, it reached its greatest splendor under the Moors, who made it the capital of the Algarve. You can drive to Silves, or sail up the Arade River from Portimão—the same route used by the crusaders centuries ago—stopping on the way to see the **Ibne Ammar** and **Algar** caves, or the famous grottoes near the **Our Lady of Rosario** islet, or just to watch the old watermills turning creakily on the river banks.

In its glory days Silves was the home of some the greatest Arab poets. They recorded its ruin when the city fell to Portugal's King Sancho I in 1189: *"Silves, my Silves, once you were a paradise. But tyrants turned you into the blaze of hell. They were wrong not to fear God's punishment. But Allah leaves no deed unheeded,"* wrote Assilbia. His call may have been heard because in 1192 the Moors occupied Silves once more before it was finally re-conquered by the Portuguese.

Yemenite Arabs built the walled city, but the **castle** (on top of a Roman citadel, itself on top of neolithic foundations) and the defensive Albarra towers were heavily restored in the later Almohad period of the 12th and 13th centuries. The Moorish castle and Christian Sé (cathedral) dominate the city, the dark-red sandstone contrasting with the soft pinks and faded blues of the older surrounding houses. A sense of an-

cient history and poetry still permeates Silves and the castle—except in June when an international beer festival held within its walls considerably changes the atmosphere.

The Moorish cistern to the north surmounted by four seven-meter-high arches once supplied the city's water, and is architecturally similar to 13th century cisterns found in Palestine and in Cacares, Spain. These enormous systems, built both by Romans and Moors, were part of the advanced irrigation technology that transformed the Algarve into the garden of Portugal.

The Sé is originally of 13th-century Gothic, restored in the 14th century and almost destroyed by the earthquake of 1755. Its apse is decorated with square arches, pyramid-shaped battlements and fanciful gargoyles. The inner chapel of **João de Rego** dates from the 15th century. Various tombs here are said to be of crusaders who helped capture Silves from the Moors in 1244. One of the most interesting sights on leaving Silves on the road to São Bartolomeu de Messines is the Cross of Portugal, which is a 19 feet (six meter) crucifix thought to have been sculpted in the early 16th century. It pictures Christ nailed to the Cross on one side and His descent

The coast of Aljezur

from the Cross on the other.

Tourist delights: Once an important cork-curing center, today Silves depends more on tourism. In addition, barges on the Arade river bring citrus fruit, olive oil, almonds, figs and various grains. The town is known for its almond and fig sweets, as well as its cork and wrought-iron work.

South of Silves is **Lagoa**, where growers from around the area take their grapes to the central cooperative wine cellar. It's a great place to stop for a glass of wine after a cool walk through the town's parks. East of here is **Porches**, famous for its painted pottery, and to the south, through the almond groves, is **Cape Carvoeiro**, a craggy coastline of isolated beaches, like that of Algar Seco. Carvoeiro itself is a lively tourist spot.

Portimão lies west of Carvoeiro, and although its has no ancient monuments, it is a pleasant shopping town built right onto the ocean with a number of sidewalk cafes and a good fish market. Portimao is famous for its grilled sardines and pastry shops. Just outside the city is **Praia da Rocha**, a beach with amazing yellow-brown rock formations standing in the blue-green sea, its soft stone sculpted into freakish shapes by centuries of wind and water erosion.

Driving west you will come to **Lagos**, which some believe was founded by a Carthaginian chieftain, and later taken by the Romans in the 5th century B.C., when it was called "*Laccobriga*" or "fortified lake." The moors took it over in the 8th century and renamed it "*Zawaia*," or "lake." The city finally fell to the Portuguese during the reign of Afonso III.

In 1434 Gil Eanes left Lagos and became the first person to round Cape Bojador of northwest Africa, south of the Canary Islands—then the limit of the known world. Most of the city was rebuilt in the 18th century. Some evidence of the town's darker past still stands such as the columns and semicircular arches of Portugal's first slave market in the **Praça da Republica** (Portugal brought slaves in from Guinea and Senegal), or the modern **monument** by Portuguese artiest João Cutileiro making King Sebastião's departure to the disastrous battle of Alcacer-Quibir.

Take a walk through the city's winding streets and this will lead you to the **Church of Santo Antonio**, a sober-looking church on the outside. But, inside, however, is an extraordinary and beautiful example of gilded carving. The nave has an impressive painted wood barrel-vault with an 18th century shield in the middle, and Baroque

he athedral in ilves

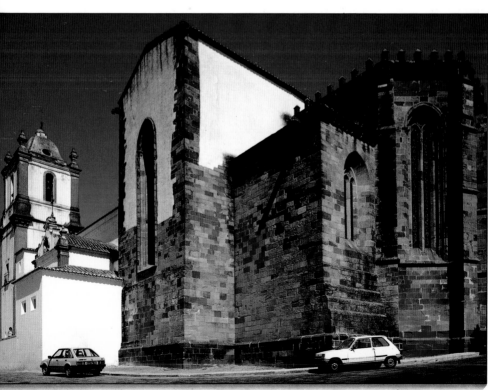

paintings on the side walls.

From Lagos you can walk along the shoreline's many beaches to Ponte **da Piedade**, which has a stunning view over the ocean. Try to hire a boat from local fishermen to explore the grottoes with their cathedral-like natural skylights.

The countryside changes drastically towards the west, particularly from **Salema** and **Figueira**, moving from coastal plateaus and tree-covered hills to a rockier and more undulating horizon. The trees, usually the hardier carob, fig and almond, get smaller and squatter, permanently bent from the unrelenting southwest wind.

The western Algarve is divided into two parts: the Atlantic coast and the Monchique mountains, known as the garden of the Algarve. In spring Monchique is covered in mimosa, narcissi, freesia, azeleas. Hundreds of wildflowers bloom in the deep green valleys between the **Foia** and **Picota** peaks. Foia is the highest point of the Algarve reaching 2,950 feet (900 meters) above sea level, but for the most breathtaking view go to Picota. Although its summit rises a more modest 2,500 feet (770 meters). The town of Monchique is rather disappointing if you merely drive through, but park the car and walk about the steep streets to get a better feel for the place.

The Monchique spas (*caldas*) are off to the right heading south, and are surrounded by chestnut, cork, pine, orange and eucalyptus trees. The spa has been in use since Roman times and the waters are believed to cure a number of ailments ranging from convulsions to rheumatism. There are eight springs, four of which are medicinal, that pour out an estimated 20 million liters (about four million gallons) of water a year.

The Algarve's dramatic coastline begins at **Odeceixe** and sweeps all the way down to Cape St. Vincent and Sagres, and is as yet unexploited. Odeceixe is a small Moorish-style village that reaches out to long sandy beaches and looming high cliffs. Further south is **Aljezur**, comfortably sprawled over the hills—and the last town to be taken from the Moors. Directly west are the **Monte Clerigos**, **Arrifana**, **Popa** and **Atalaia** beaches. At **Saiceira** there are large caverns and underground galleries to be explored, once the hide-out of pirates, now a refuge for many species of marine birds.

From Aljezur the road bumps down to the wild and windswept forked promontory of **Sagres** and **Cape St. Vincent**, the latter once believed to be a sacred meeting place

A house in Sagres

of the gods, as it stood teetering on the edge of the known world. Here, even on a calm day, waves crash against the dramatic cliffs with a violence that sends spray everywhere. In spring the smell of cistus fills the air, a bush with a perfumed oil on its leaves which the Egyptians had once used for embalming.

In Sagres, Henry the Navigator gathered the most renowned cartographers, astronomers and sailors of his day and founded the famous Navigation School in the 15th century. Although much of what stood then has been destroyed, a huge rose compass (*Rosa dos Ventos*) still lies on the stone floor of the fortress, stretching 130 feet (39 meters) in diameter. Today Sagres is a small fishing town that uses the **Baleeira Bay** as its fishing port. While here, make a point of seeing the **Torre of Aspa**, a natural rock formation that soars some 500 feet (150 meters) above sea level and is the area's highest point.

Sacred ravens: Sitting atop the impressive cliffs of Cape St. Vincent is a tall red lighthouse whose warning beams can reach ships as far as 50 miles (90 kilometers) away. Legend has it that in medieval times Christian followers of the martyr St. Vincent defied the Moors and buried his body somewhere on the cape, building a small shrine in his honor. Ten sacred ravens were said to have kept a permanent swooping vigil over the spot, and they can still be seen circling the skies today.

From here you can drive north to beaches with curious names like **Cor do Homem** (Color of the Man), **Barriga** (Belly), and **Cara da Teira** (Teira's Face). The area is wild—lynxes and birds of prey prowl here. Further north and inland is **Vila do Bispo**, an unspoiled town where rust-colored oxen still have the right-of-way, windmills are in use, and chattering women gather around the communal washing places to do the family's laundry.

Try to see **Castelejo**, a fabulous beach just north of here where the full force of the Atlantic crashes onto white-veined rocks. Back down again and going towards Lagos is **Salema**, a booming tourist town with a pre-13th century chapel of **Our Lady of Guadelupe**, believed to have been built by the Templars.

Perhaps the least traveled way to the Algarve is on the eastern edge of Portugal, on the road alongside the **Guadiana River** on the Spanish border which meanders through abandoned golden furze-covered hills dotted with corks, olive and fig trees.

The best part of traveling on this road is that it gives you a chance to branch off into as-yet-unspoiled Algarvian villages on either side of it. For example, just south of the Alentejo the road cuts off east to **Alcoutim**, one of the most serene and lovely towns on this side of the Algarve. Time seems to have stopped here. The only sounds are that of a donkey braying or a turkey gobbling. Sunning dogs in the only square in town have priority, so you'll have to park around them.

From the promenade built on the edge of the Guadiana River you can see the Spanish town of San Lucar de Guadiana settled in its nook of windmill-topped hills, reflected in the slow-moving water. The **village church**, also by the riverside, has interesting bas-relief carving on the baptismal font dating from the 16th century. Signs to the "castle" lead to an empty shell of walls—but the view from here is worth the short walk.

On down to the **Castro Marim** near the mouth of the Guadiana River, one of the oldest and historically most important areas of the Algarve. Once a major Phoenician settlement, it was also host to the Greeks and Carthaginians before the Moors and Romans invaded. Portugal's kings later used it as a natural point from which to fight the Moors to the east. The city was largely reconstructed after the 1755 earthquake, but the **castle** built by King Afonso III is still standing, overlooking the surrounding valley.

Surrounding the town is the **Castro Marim fen** or marsh, home of many migratory birds including storks and flamingoes, and hundreds of different species of plant life. Try the local *Servico de Parques e Reservas* for a guided tour and information. Next to the fen is the popular **São Bartolomeu** fair that sells local basketry and other handicrafts.

Further south, sitting right on the border with Spain is **Vila Real de Santo Antonio**, a city carefully laid out in geometric streets—the mark of the famous Marquês de Pombal who was responsible for redesigning old Lisbon. Pombal intended this town as an administrative, industrial and fishing model and he founded the Royal Fisheries Company here. But he lost favor with the court, and his plans never really took off until the Genoese arrived to take advantage of the fishing trade in the 1800s. However, constant fishing and modernization has depleted the supply of fish and today tourism is the main money-maker.

Left, a Tavira belltower. Right, Fortaleza in Sagres

Traveling west past the popular beach resort towns of **Monte Gordo, Praia Verde, Alagoas** and **Cacela** you will come to **Tavira,** known as the Venice of the Algarve. Tavira lies elegantly on both sides of the Sequa River, which becomes the Gilão as it slides under the seven-arched Roman-style bridge towards the sea. Mainly an estuary town, Tavira flourished in the 16th century because of its location. But trade rapidly dwindled as the fish disappeared, and this lovely town of narrow streets, palatial houses, miniature towers, domes, unusual four-sided roofs and minarets today stands strangely silent.

There are 15 churches and six monasteries in Tavira, of which the most interesting being **Senhora da Ajuda,** the **Igreja da Misericórdia** and the church of **Santa Maria** rebuilt on the site of the town's old mosque. (Guides are not always available, but detailed pamphlets of these monuments should be on hand either at the tourist center or town hall.)

From Tavira is a brief drive through **Fuzeta** to **Olhão,** a 17th century town built in the Moorish style, famous for its crowded indoor fish market. Get there early and be prepared to use your elbows to get to the slithery hills of fish which the women hawk at the top of their voices, poking them to prove their freshness. The best buys are gilt-head bream (*dourada*) bass (*robalo*) and sole (*linguado*). Nearby there is a fruit, vegetable and live fowl market.

With a basket full of fresh food, head back towards Tavira but veer off at the little fishing port of Fuzet. There, you can get a ferry to **Fuzeta Island** with its long strip of beach, and have a barbecue. Or alternatively, you can get a simple lunch from the only local *tasca.*

Fuzeta lies practically in the middle of the **Ria Formosa** a huge undeveloped wild life area that stretches some 30 miles (50 m) from Anciao in the west to Cancela in the east, hitting a width of some four miles (six km) around Faro.

This natural lagoon system, protected from the sea by a network of sand bars, is crucial, as it provides for 90 percent of Portugal's total harvest of clams and oysters. The Ria is also an important bird sanctuary, especially for waders like egrets, black-winged stilts, oyster catchers, and rare species like the purple gallinule. Tragically, the uncontrolled and heavy influx of people in this area and the absence of the necessary governmental infrastructures to deal with it today threaten the entire area.

church at Boliqueime

ÉVORA AND THE ALENTEJO

Alentejo, literally "beyond the Tejo" (the Tagus River), has a distinctive character and beauty unlike that of any other Portuguese province. Its vast plains, colored burnt ochre in summer, are freckled with cork oaks and olive trees which are the only shade for the small flocks of sheep and herds of black pigs.

Nicknamed "terra do pão" (land of bread) because of field upon field of wheat, oats and rice, the visitor will pass by acres of grapevines, tomatoes and other vegetable plantations.

The Alentejo is the largest and flattest of the Portuguese provinces; about the size of Belgium, it occupies one-third of Portugal's total land area. It stretches from the west coast eastward to the Spanish border and separates Ribatejo and Beira Beixa in the central regions from the Algarve in the south. The open countryside is punctuated by picturesque whitewashed towns and villages, many of which were built on the low hills which dot the horizon.

The Alentejo is rich in handicrafts. Rustic pottery with naive, colorful designs can be found everywhere. In addition, certain towns specialize in particular crafts or products: handstitched rugs from Arraiolos, loom-woven carpets from Reguengos; cheese from Serpa; tapestries from Portalegre; sugar plums from Elvas. All these can be purchased, of course, elsewhere in the Alentejo, or in Lisbon or Oporto, but for price, selection, freshness and adventure, isn't it more satisfying to go to the source?

By Portuguese standards, the roads which connect the towns are excellent. Most of the traffic is local and slow moving. You will need to equip yourself with a reliable road map—signposting is limited, and without a map you could drive miles before discovering you've taken a wrong turn.

The Portuguese in general are not renowned for their tidiness but the Alentejanos are the exception. The towns are litter free and there is always a *dona de casa* in view whitewashing her already pristine home. Cool and simple is the theme for the Alentejo architecture; low, single-story buildings are painted white to deflect the sun's glare, with a traditional blue skirting to reflect the sky. Large domed chimneys indicate chilly winters. This practical style is followed from the humblest cottage to the large hacienda-style homes of the wealthy

landowners; ornate and impressive architecture is reserved for cathedrals and churches.

Inland from the coastline, Alentejo temperature in the summer can reach inferno level: what little wind there is blows hot and dry from the continental land mass—no cooling sea breezes here. As you would expect from this dry, flat terrain, temperatures drop dramatically in winter, resulting in some bitter cold nights.

Geographically the province is split into two regions, Upper (*Alto*) and Lower (*Baixo*) Alentejo. Portalegre is the capital of the former and Beja of the latter. To the east are two low mountain ranges, the Serras of **São Mamede** and **Ossa**. Some of the towns in these ranges, particularly Marvão, have breathtaking, even precipitous settings. Portugal's third longest river, the Guadiana, flows through the province and in places provides a border between Portugal and Spain. This is by no means the only waterway. The region is crisscrossed by a network of small rivers and dams.

The Alentejo is steeped in history which goes back to the days of Roman colonization. Later, it was the seat of the great landed estates of the Portuguese nobility and home to former kings. Even as late as 1828 Évora—capital of the Alentejo—was considered the second major Portuguese city, an honor first bestowed on it by King João I (1385-1433).

Estremoz, whose ancient castle has been converted into a comfortable *pousada* (state-run hotel) was a nerve center to medieval Portugal. Vila Viçosa has a history which began in the Middle Ages and continued up to the early 20th century. It was the seat of the Dukes of Bragança, whose royal dynasty began in 1640 with the coronation of João IV and ended in 1910 with the fall of the monarchy.

Political change: Nowadays, modern Alentejo is a far cry from the days of aristocratic domination, although farming techniques of the smallholdings have changed little over the centuries. The greatest change is a political one: since the restoration of democracy in 1974 the Alentejo has been the heart of Portuguese communism.

Many of the great estates—so vast that they included villages, a school and even small hospitals—were taken over by the farmworkers during the Revolution. Some of the land-owning families were forcibly ejected, but the majority lived away from the farms for most of the year anyway, in other properties nearer Lisbon or Oporto. Unfortunately, lack of management skills has led many of the cooperative-run farms to near-bankruptcy, but others flourish. Government legislation is attempting to ensure that the former owners have their lands—or parts of them—reinstated and/or that they receive compensation for their losses. There is also a new land-owning generation that has a modern approach to agriculture and is skilled at effective farm management.

Farming, is the pulse of Alentejo, and the lives of its people revolve around the seasons. Aside from Évora the towns are small and the rest of the population is scattered in hamlets linked to farms. Secondary schools are restricted to the larger towns; in the more remote areas the general practice among young people is to leave school early to work in the fields.

Throughout the year, but particularly at harvest time, you will see the fieldworkers making their way to and from work on foot, by bicycle or crammed into open-topped trucks. Most rural *Alentejanos* adopt the traditional dress: black wide-brimmed hats for both men and women, black trousers, waistcoats, jackets and white collarless shirts for men, black shawls and thick black skirts for women under which are worn layers of petticoats. Neckerchiefs for extra

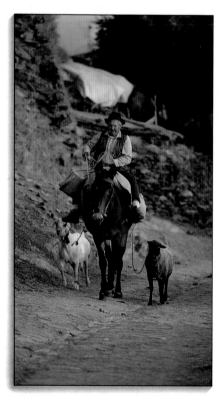

protection against sun and dust are loosely knotted around the men's necks, while women favor head-squares worn under their hats. The faces of the old *Alentejanos* are extraordinary—leathery skins baked a deep brown, furrowed like tree bark and colored like walnuts.

One of the traditional pastimes for the menfolk is a wild boar hunt. These animals are most populous near the Spanish border. It really is a case of out of the frying pan and into the fire for the poor creatures. They cross the border from Spain to flee the Spanish hunters, only to find themselves hunted here, although to a less extent. Hunting is especially popular in the open Alentejo terrain, and during the season (October-February), one will inevitably see men out with their shotguns, pouches and a gaggle of dogs.

Singing and dancing is popular across the length and breadth of Portugal, and the Alentejo does its share. Here, the folk songs are the domain of the men. The songs are slow, rather melancholic, but of a completely different style than the haunting *fado* heard elsewhere. A slow tempo is set by the stamping of the men's feet as they sing in chorus, swaying to the rhythm by the time they reach the end of the song. A performance is well worth listening to; ask at an Alentejo tourist office about where to hear one.

Évora is the largest and most important of all the Alentejo towns. It is a superb city, full of fascinating sights, all of which are in a good state of preservation. They are likely to remain so as the entire city has been proclaimed a historical monument by the international preservation organization World Patrimony, therefore qualifying for its financial aid.

It takes about two and a half hours to drive from Lisbon to Évora, and a tour could be comfortably managed as a day trip. But that would not leave time to see the lovely towns and villages along the way, nor those within striking distance of the city. To base yourself in Évora is easy; there are plenty of small guest houses and hotels.

To reach Évora leave Lisbon via the April 25th Bridge and head down towards the *autostrada* for Setúbal, and then turn eastwards on the N4 for Évora. You will not need a welcome billboard to tell you that you have just reached the Alentejo; suddenly the roads are wider and less potholed, and you will find yourself at the edge of the rolling plains. Look for the jumbles of twigs on top of the high walls and buildings— homes to the storks that flourish in the

Roadside attractions in Monsaraz

province. As you drive further inland you will also notice the waning breeze and the increase in temperature.

Pegóes is the first small Alentejo town on the route. It's a rather dry, dusty and deserted town nowadays, all of which you observe if you're delayed at the railway crossing there. It once must have been a thriving market town but it appears quite depressed today. A little further along the road is **Vendas Novas**. About the same size as Pegóes, it makes a great contrast. Shady, neat and with an air of affluence, it is not really worth a stop, but it is attractive to view from the car.

Montemor-o-Novo can be seen from quite a distant approach, its ruined medieval castle crowning its low *monte* (hill). The castle ramparts are thought to date back to Roman times. The town is divided into the upper old town and lower new town. As you might expect the old town is the one more interesting to stroll through. It was here that St. John of God (São João de Deus) was born in 1495. He was baptized in the ruined parish church, the only of part of which is still intact is the granite Manueline portal. In the square outside the church is a statue commemorating the saint, a Franciscan monk of great charity and humility. According to legend, he carried a beggar to the hospital one stormy night. Although they hardly boast the population to support them all, the town's religious significance has resulted in the building of five churches, three convents and two monasteries.

Évora: As you enter Évora on the main Lisbon road, there is a small tourist office just before the town's Roman walls. There is a larger tourist office in the center, but at this one you can pick up a street map with suggested walks marked to take in the most important sights. The best place to park is the center of the city at the **Praça do Giraldo**, a large square with arcades on two sides and a 16th-century **church** and fountain at the top end. From this central parking area you can explore the inner city with ease.

The history of Évora can be traced back to the earliest civilizations on the Iberian Peninsula. It derives its name from *Ebora Cerealis*, as it was called during the Luso-Celtic colonization. The Romans later fortified the city and renamed it *Liberalitas Julia*. It thrived under the Romans, who elevated it to the status of *municipium*, which gave it the right to mint its own currency. Its prosperity declined somewhat when it was conquered by the Visigoths, but rekindled under the long Moorish rule (early 8th century to 1165). Much of the architecture reflects the Moorish presence with arched, twisting alleyways, tiled patios and potted plants filling terraces.

Évora was liberated from the Moors by a Christian knight, Geraldo Sem-Pavor (Gerald the Fearless), in 1165. He did so in the name of King Afonso I, the first king of Portugal.

For the next 400 years Évora enjoyed great importance and wealth. It was the preferred residence of the kings of the Burgundy and Avis dynasties. During these centuries the courts attracted famed artists, dramatists, humanists and academics to Évora. Great churches, monasteries, houses and convents were built. The splendor culminated in 1559 when the last of the Avis kings, Henrique—who was also the Archbishop of Évora—founded a Jesuit university there. In 1580, following the annexation of Portugal by Spain, Évora's glory waned. The Castilians paid little attention to it, except as an agricultural and trading center. Even after Portuguese independence was restored in 1640, Évora did not regain its former brilliance.

The oldest sight in Évora is the so-called **Temple of Diana**, which dates back to the 2nd or 3rd century A.D. To reach it walk down Rua 5 de Outubro, off Praça do Giraldo. The temple is presumed to have been built as a place of imperial worship, dedicated, perhaps, to the goddess Diana. The Corinthian columns are granite, their bases and capitals hewn from local marble. The facade and mosaic floor have disappeared completely, but the six rear columns and those at either side are still intact. The temple was converted into a fortress during the Middle Ages and then used as a slaughterhouse until 1870. Although not an elegant role, this use saved the temple from being torn down; its brick walls helped preserve the columns as well. Until recently, you could actually wander among the columns, but sensibly the temple has been roped off to prevent further wear and tear.

There is a lovely viewpoint just across from the rear of the temple in the shady garden. From here you can look down over the lower town and across the plains: the tiny village of Évoramonte is just visible on the horizon to the northeast.

To the right of the temple is the **Monastery of Lóios** (also known as the church of John the Evangelist). The conventual buildings have been converted into an elegant *pousada* but the church is still a public one. Founded in 1485, its style is Romano-Gothic, although all but the doorway in the facade was remodeled after the earthquake in 1755. The nave has an ornate vaulted ceiling and walls lined with beautiful tiles depicting the life of St. Laurence Justinian, dated 1771 and signed by António de Oliveira Bernandes. Guided tours of the church, cloisters and chapterhouse can be taken.

Nearby the temple is **Cathedral** (*Sé*), dedicated to the Virgin Mary. An imposing, austere building, its granite facade was built in the 12th century, also in Romano-Gothic style. Its main portal is flanked by two grand conical towers. These towers are unusual in that they are asymmetric—the glittering blue tiled one is particularly lovely. Both were added in the 16th century.

Before going into the cathedral, take a close look at the main entrance. It is decorated with magnificent 14th-century sculptures of the apostles. The vast broken barrel vaulted ceiling inside is quite stunning; suspended from it are huge chandeliers, their supports appearing to be of interminable length. The cathedral has the most capacious interior in Portugal: its three naves stretch for 70 meters.

Once you've seen the cathedral, it really is worthwhile to pay the nominal sum to see its cloisters, choir stalls and Museum of Sacred Art lodged in the treasury. They are open at the usual visiting times (9 a.m. to midday and from 2 p.m. to 5 p.m., closed Mondays and public holidays).

A short climb up a staircase will take you to the **museum** which contains a beautiful collection of ecclesiastical gold, silver and bejewelled plate, ornaments, chalices and crosses. The Renaissance-style choir stalls, tucked high in the gallery, are fashioned with a delightful series of wooden carvings whose motifs are of both sacred and secular design. Particularly charming are those of day-to-day life: wine pressing, wheat threshing, singing and feasting. From the choir stalls you get a good birds-eye view of the cathedral.

The **cloisters** are 14th-century Gothic—large and imposing in their granite plainness, more awe-inspiring than encouraging of meditative contemplation. Next door to the cathedral is the **Regional Museum**, formerly the Bishop's Palace and now home to a fine collection of paintings, both Portuguese Primitives and Flemish. There is also interesting sculpture, furniture and decoration from local buildings.

14th-century Apostles greet visitors to Évora's Cathedral

More elegant and graceful cloisters are visible at the old **Jesuit University**. You have to follow a short road down to the east of the city to reach it. The marble of the broad **students' cloisters** seems to have aged not at all since the 16th century. The cloisters still maintain the peaceful atmosphere of the serious academic: it's the sort of place that makes you involuntarily drop your voice to a hushed whisper.

The classroom entrances at the far end of the cloister gallery are decorated with *azulejos* representing each of the subjects taught within. If you take a slow walk back up the hill and head for the church of St. Francis (São Francisco), you'll pass by another church—the **Misericórdia**, noted for its 18th-century tiled panels and Baroque relief work. Behind it stands the **Soure Mansion**, a 15th-century Manuline house formerly part of the Palace of Infante D. Luis.

As you walk, take notice of the houses. Nearly all have attractive, narrow, wrought-iron balconies at the base of tall rectangular windows. A rather odd tradition in Évora is that visiting dignitaries are welcomed by a vivid display of brightly colored bedspreads hung from these balconies. A forerunner to bunting, perhaps?

When you reach the Misericórdia Church, take a brief detour of the **Portas de Moura Square**. The gates there mark the fortified northern entrance to the city, the delimitation of construction and safety as it was in medieval times. This picturesque square is dominated by a Renaissance fountain, built in 1556.

Back on the road again, keep an eye out for the church of **Nossa Senhora da Graca** (Our Lady of Grace), just off the Rua Miguel Bombarda. Built in granite, it is a far cry from the austerity of the cathedral. A later church (16th century), its influence is strongly Italian Renaissance. Note the four huge figures supporting globes which represent the children of grace.

A mother's curse: The church of **São Francisco**—from the late 15th or early 16th century, has a remarkable chapel, the **Casa dos Ossos**. This bizarre and macabre room is entirely lined and decorated with bones of some 5,000 people. It was "created" in the 16th century by a Franciscan monk. At the entrance lies the inviting Latin inscription: *"We bones lie here waiting for yours."*

The skulls and bones have not merely been placed in a random fashion; a lot of creative thought has gone into their placement! Hung at the far end of the chapel are

One of the indignities of being a statue in Évora's public gardens

the corpses of a man and a small child. These centuries-old bodies are said to be the victims of a dying wife and mother's curse. Father and son were supposed to have made her life a misery—their ill treatment killed her. On her death bed she cursed them, swearing that their flesh would never fall from their bones. The corpses are far from fleshy, but there is plenty of leathery substance attached to their bones.

Braids of human hair dating to the last century are hung at the entrance of the chapel, *ex-votos* put there by young brides. The **chapterhouse** that links the chapel to the church is lined with *azulejos* depicting scenes from the Passion and contains an *altar dos promessas* (altar of promises) on which are laid wax effigies of parts of the body, particularly arms, legs, and feet. The ailing, or their friends and relatives, go to the altar and pray for a cure. If it comes, then an effigy of the cured part is placed in thanks on the altar.

Évora's **public gardens** near the church provide a very pleasant walk; if you're lucky you may catch the band playing on the park's old-fashioned wrought-iron bandstand. A delightful **palace** stands in the park, that of King Manuel (1495-1521). Luso-Moorish in style, it has typical paired windows in horseshoe arches. Exhibitions are held quite regularly in the long Ladies' Gallery.

During the last week of June, Évora is filled with visitors who come to enjoy the annual **Feira de São João**. This huge fair fills the grounds opposite the public gardens. If you don't mind the crowd then you'll enjoy what is offered: a local handicraft market, an agricultural hall, a display of local light industry, the general hodgepodge of open-air stalls selling everything, folk singing and dancing, and special restaurants serving typical cuisine.

If you're visiting Évora during the summer and want to cool off, go to one of the local swimming pools on the edge of town. Although well-patronized because they are inexpensive, they are spotlessly clean, with plenty of lawn on which to stretch out and dry. A cafe serves all kinds of snacks and drinks.

If you're not intent on going inside Évora's monuments, a night stroll displays its exterior architecture admirably. Nearly all the monuments are floodlit until midnight, and the winding narrow streets are very inviting on a balmy evening.

The Alentejo has a number of megalithic monuments scattered across its plains, and some of the most important are just outside Évora. The best preserved and most significant stone circle, or cromlech, on the Iberian Peninsula is seven miles (12 km) west of the city, close to the hill of Herdade dos Almendres. **Cromoleque de Almendres** has 95 standing stones.

Next to the Agricultural Department of the University of Évora in Valverde, which neighbors Évora, stands the largest dolmen on the peninsula. The **Zambujeiro Dolmen** stands some 17 feet (5 meters) high with a 10 feet (three meter) diameter and is dated about 3,000 B.C.

Estremoz is a lovely town steeped in a history which goes back to the Middle Ages. Although much smaller than Évora, it has its own fascinating monuments worth a few hours' visit.

The old part of this sleepy town, crowned by a castle now converted into a *pousada*, was founded by King Afonso III in 1258. The monument was a residence of King Dinis in the 1300s and it is with him that it is most often associated. His wife, the sainted Queen Isabel of Aragon is honored by a statue in the main square, and a **chapel** dedicated to her can be seen in one of the castle towers. To view this chapel ask either at the *pousada* or at the museum on the main square.

The Temple
of Diana, for
a time the
town slaugh-
terhouse

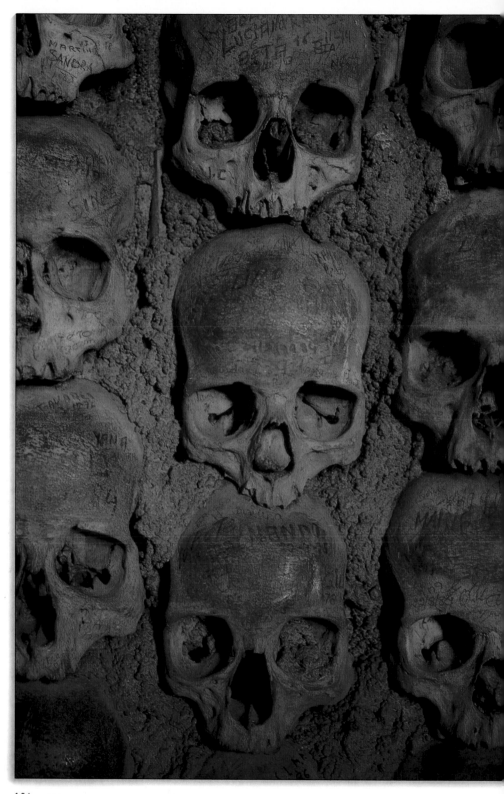

The chapel is at the top of a narrow staircase; small, and highly decorated, it is where she is said to have died. (Mind you, she is said to have died in the nearby **King's Audience Chamber** as well.) The chapel walls are adorned with 18th century *azulejos* and paintings depicting scenes from the Queen's life. The most famous incident, represented here, is the "miracle of the roses." Isabel was a very charitable woman, sometimes more so than her husband might have wished. Once when Isabel was distributing alms to the poor King Dinis came upon her. She hastily hid the coins in the folds of her skirts, but the king demanded to see what the gown held. When Isabel spread her skirt, the gold miraculously had turned to roses. Behind the altar is a tiny, plain room bearing a smaller altar on which the Estremoz faithful have placed their *ex votos*.

The most impressive part of the castle is the wonderful 13th-century **keep** which is entered via the *pousada*. To get to the top you need to be fairly fit—or make a slow and steady ascent. The second floor has an octagonal room with trefoil windows. From the top platform there is a breathtaking view. The red rooftops contrast beautifully with the whitewashed houses and the green plains beyond, much of which are planted with rows of olive trees.

Across the square from the *pousada* is the **Royal Palace of D. Dinis**. It must have been a beautiful palace, but all that remains standing after a gun-powder explosion in the palace arsenal in 1698 is the Gothic colonnade and star-vaulted chamber (D. Dinis' Audience Chamber). It is used nowadays for exhibitions by local artists. Having survived the narrow roads and hairpin bends on the drive up to the castle, the descent should seem easier. The upper town is connected to the lower town by 14th-century ramparts and fairly modern buildings: the wrought-iron balconies here are decorated with colored tiles.

Estremoz is famed for its pottery jugs and figurines, which can be bought throughout the town, but they are perhaps most attractively displayed at the Saturday markets **main square** of the lower town. If you're a lover of Portuguese wines then you're likely to be familiar with the name **Borba**, a co-operative wine company which produces a good red wine. The wines take their name from the ancient village of Borba, said to date back to the Gauls and Celts. There is not much to see there now except for a splendid fountain, **Fonte das Bicas**, built in 1781 from local white marble.

Just down the road from Borba is **Vila Viçosa**, the previously mentioned seat of the Dukes of Brangança. Vila Viçosa comes as quite a surprise after the Moorish-influenced towns perched on the top of hills. The town is cool and shady, its large main square (**Praça da República**) is filled with orange trees, and elsewhere there are lemon trees and lots of flowers. *Viçosa* means shade, and its elegant boulevards are a pleasure to walk through.

A lovely, if rather overgrown medieval **castle** overlooks the town square. It is very peaceful there, the only sound is the cooing of the white fan-tail doves which nest in the ramparts. The drawbridge is lowered across the moat (now dry), and the first floor has been converted into a modest archaeological **museum**.

Vila Viçosa is best known for the **Ducal Palace**, an enormous and elegant building which is open to the public for guided tours. Its furniture, painting and tapestries are very fine, and worth an hour or so. The palace also contains an excellent collection of 17th- to 19th-century coaches.

The palace overlooks a square in which stands a bronze statue of João IV, the first king of the Bragança dynasty. To the north of the square—on the Lisbon road—is a curious edifice, the **Knot Gate**, part of the

Left, the macabre Casa dos Ossos, embellished by Évora's deens. Right, the 16th-century Porta dos Nos at Vila Viçosa

16th-century town walls. It is so called after its design: the stone archway appears to be roped together.

Between Évora and Estremoz stands **Évoramonte**, a village at the foot of a recently renovated **castle**. It was in this village that the convention ending the civil war was signed on May 26, 1834. A plaque commemorating the event is placed over the house where the historic signing took place.

Évoramonte is a particularly high hill and the views from there are quite remarkable: well worth the detour and the clamber up to the top of the somewhat bland, if well-kempt castle. From there you can see for miles and miles.

Close to the Spanish border, about 30 miles (50 km) from Estremoz, is the strongly fortified town of **Elvas**. Founded by the Romans, it was long occupied by the Moors and finally liberated from them in 1230—nearly 100 years later than Lisbon.

The town was of great strategic importance during the wars of independence with Spain in the mid-17th century. The fortress of **Santa Luzia**, south of town, was built by a German, Count Lippe, for the purpose of repelling the Spanish. The older **castle**, above the town, was originally a Roman fortress, rebuilt by the Moors and enlarged in the 15th century.

If you walk around the ramparts you cannot fail to be impressed by the effective engineering which completely encircled the town. The town itself is particularly attractive, from the triangular "square" of Santa Clara, with its 16th-century marble pillory, to the main square, **Praça da República**, with its geometrically patterned mosaic paving.

Elvas has a nice *pousada* which used to have one of the most famous restaurants in the country. One of its specialties nowadays is a *Bacalhau Dourado*—slivers of salted cod fried with thinly-chipped potatoes, onions, olives and scrambled egg.

An interesting history surrounds the **Amoreira Aquaduct**, designed by a great 15th-century architect, Francisco de Arruda. It took nearly 200 years to complete, all five miles (7.5 km) and 843 arches of it. Its cost was borne by the people of Elvas under a special tax named the *Real de Agua*.

Handwoven rugs used to be manufactured throughout the Alentejo, but nowadays the small town of **Reguengos** is the only place where they are still made, in a factory that has been using the same looms for the past 150 years. Reguengos is another nucleus of megalithic stones and dolmens,

A sleepy afternoon in Vila Viçosa

156

found in several sites near the town.

Up the road from Reguengos is the delightful walled town of **Monsaraz**, so small it can easily be seen on foot—leave the car at the fortified gate. Its proximity to the Spanish border combined with its height made it of strategic importance. Once the threat from Spain had gone, however, Reguengos became gradually more influential. Monsaraz relaxed into a charming, peaceful village. Its main street, **Rua Direita,** is all 16th- and 17th-century architecture, yet, the town maintains a distinctly medieval feel.

The countryside surrounding the capital of the Upper Alentejo, **Portalegre**, is rather different from that in the lower lands. This area is in foothills of the Serra de São Mamede, and the cooler and slightly more humid climate makes it much greener.

Quite a large town by Alentejo standards, Portalegre is unusual in that it is not built on top of a hill. It is built on the site of an ancient ruined settlement called Ammaia. In the mid-13th century, King Afonso III instructed that a new city was to be built and called Portus Alacer: Portus for the customs gate which was to process Spanish trade and Alacer (which meant joy) because of its pleasing setting.

King Dinis ensured that the town was fortified in 1290 (although only a few of those ruins can be seen today) and João III gave it the status of city in 1550.

The lofty 16th-century interior of the **cathedral** (*Sé*) is late-Renaissance style. The side altars have fine wooden retables and 16th-and 17th-century paintings of Italian style. The sacristy contains lovely blue-and- white *azulejo* panels from the 18th century depicting the life of the Virgin Mary and the flight to Egypt. The cathedral's facade is 18th-century, dominated by marble columns, granite pilasters and wrought iron balconies.

Portalegre's affluence began in the 16th century, when its tapestries were in great demand. Continued prosperity followed in the next century with the establishment of silk mills. Don't miss the opportunity to see the tapestry workshops in the former Jesuit Monastery. The looms are still worked by hand, following modern as well as traditional designs.

Portalegre was home to one of Portugal's most famous poets: José Régio (1901 - 1969). His house has been opened as a museum. Of particular interest is his collection of regional folk and religious art.

Also of note is the 17th-century "Yellow

ilhouettes Monsaraz

Palace," formally called the **Palácio dos Albrancalhas**. The ornate ironwork is remarkable.

Marvão must be one of the most spectacular sights of the Alentejo. About 15 miles (25 km) north of Portalegre, it is a medieval fortified town perched on one of the São Mamede peaks. Its altitude (2,830 feet/862 meters) affords it an uninterrupted view across the Spanish frontier. The precipitous drop on one side made it inaccessible to invaders and an ideal defensive situation.

At this height the land is barren and craggy. The seemingly impenetrable **castle** was built in the 13th century from the local gray granite.

Clinging to the foot of the castle is the tiny village, a few twisting alleyways flanked by red-roofed whitewashed houses. Close by the church of **Espirito Santo**, on the street of the same name, is an austere Baroque granite **fountain**. On the same street is the sober-looking **Governor's House**: its only decoration is two magnificent 17th-century wrought-iron balconies.

On the road to Castelo de Vide are the ruins of the Roman settlement of **Medobriga**. Many artifacts have been found here, although most were removed to Lisbon. Completing the triangle of noteworthy upper Alentejo towns is **Castelo de Vide**, a delightful town built under the shade of an elongated medieval castle. The whole is situated on the summit of a foothill on the northern *serra*.

Castelo de Vide is a spa town. You can drink its curative waters from the plastic bottles in which it is sold in the supermarkets, or sip from one of the 300 fountains located in the town and environs. Perhaps its prettiest outlet is the quadrangled, covered fountain (**Fonte da Vila**) set in the small square below the Jewish Quarter. The Barque fountain has a pyramid roof supported by six marble columns. The central urn is carved with figures of boys and the water spills from four spouts.

Near Castelo de Vide you will find still more megalithic stones: these *Pedras Talhas* are everywhere, standing in fields, open scrubland or in local villages. The town itself was first a Roman settlement. Alongside it ran the major Roman road which traversed the Iberian Peninsula. The settlement was sacked by the Vandals at the beginning of the 4th century; occupied by the Moors during their domination of the southern part of the peninsula; and fortified by the Portuguese in 1180.

The rooftops of Marvão

As in nearly all fortified Alentejo towns, Castelo de Vide has two very distinct faces. The first is the older one, situated next to the castle. The most interesting and picturesque is the medieval **Jewish Quarter** (Judiaria). This host of back alleys, cobbled streets and whitewashed houses is splashed with green, as potted plants sprout their tendrils from every available niche, windowsill and step. Notice the doors: this section of Castelo de Vide has the most and best-preserved stone Gothic doorways in Portugal.

You don't see many young people here; the majority of the inhabitants appear to be old people who sit in the doorways of their homes calmly watching the world go by. Further down the hill is the newer part of town: essentially 17th- and 18th-century buildings with wider, less steep streets, more space, more order and more elegance. On the main square (**Praça D. Pedro V**) stands the grandiose 18th-century **parish church** and the old town hall (**Paços de Concelho**), remarkable for the huge 18th-century wrought-iron gate securing the main entrance.

Nisa is a small, rather spacious, town slightly north of Castelo de Vide. It has the mandatory medieval **castle**, walls and an unusual squat, round-towered **chapel**.

Homemade cheese is Nisa's speciality.

Some 15 miles (26 km) south of Nisa on the road to Estremoz is **Crato**, best known for the Brotherhood of Hospitaler—later known as the Knights of St. John—who were installed there. The main square is dominated by a splendid 15th-century stone veranda (**Varanda do Grão-Prior**), which is all that survives of the former priors' residence. Two royal marriages took place in this town. The first was that of Manuel I, who married Leonor of Spain in 1518 (his third marriage). The second was seven years later when King João III married Catarina of Spain.

Further south, in countryside filled with olive groves stands **Alter do Chão**, a medieval town interesting for its equine traditions. It is from here that the Alter Real horse takes its name. Based on Andalusian stock, the Alter stud was founded in the mid-1700s by the Bragança family. The horse thrived until the Napoleonic Wars when the best horses were stolen and the royal stables abolished.

Unspoiled beaches: An area of the Alentejo overlooked by most tourists is its coastline. If you like unspoiled cliffs and beaches, quiet roads and sleepy villages, then you'll love the area and hope that no one else discovers it. However, with the Algarve becoming more built up and crowded it probably is only a matter of time before the property developers creep up the coast. It borders on the open Atlantic and the ocean is therefore much rougher than on the south coast. But there are plenty of sheltered bays for swimming, although the water is chilly. And it's wonderful just to watch the waves crashing against the cliffs.

The Alentejo coast is not renowned for its nightlife. Bars, discos, and fancy restaurants simply do not exist; nor do large hotels, except at Vila Nova de Milfontes. There are campsites, however, and all the villages have at least one *pensão*. You'd better bring along your phrase book. Where tourists are rare, so are natives who speak English.

Access to the coast is easy; in fact, the coastal highway was the main north-south route until the faster inland road was built. Keep on the main Algarve road until you reach Grandola, then take the turn for the quaint town of **Santiago do Cacém**, which is crowned by a castle built long ago by the Knights Templar. From there it's just a short hop to the Alentejo's largest coastal town, **Sines**.

Sines is not what you'd call a beauty spot, but you may find it interesting as an exercise in misguided expansionist idealism. For centuries Sines was a pretty fishing village, known for being the birthplace of Vasco da Gama. The old part is still picturesque; but what surrounds it is horrible.

During the Caetano regime it was decided to build a massive oil refinery to process the oil from the hundreds of tankers which were expected to port there. They didn't. Sines was left with an ugly white elephant which dominates the town. It functions, as does a large power station on the northbound approach, but between them they produce pervasive smells of gas and chemicals and make the area look like some futuristic industrial forest.

To forget the ugliness of Sines, go and clear your lungs at the lovely village of **Porto Corvo**. The road which takes you there is tree-lined and virtually traffic-free. Several tracks lead from the main road down to shingly beaches. Porto Corvo is a tiny little village, with cobbled streets swept scrupulously clean. The main square, grandly named **Largo Marquês de Pombal**, is very small, bordered by homes and the tiny parish church. A few small trees and plentiful benches surround the square. Down by the sea you can find shops, cafes

Cork trees on the Alentejo plain

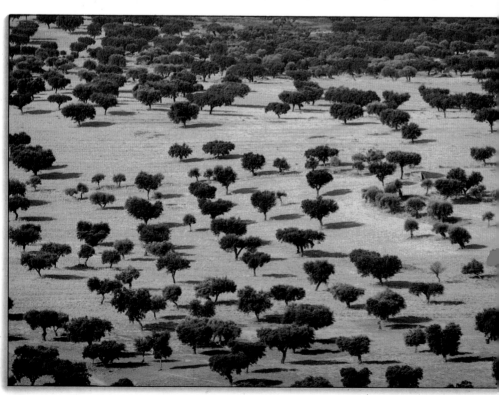

and a restaurant.

Just off the coast of Porto Corvo is the fortified **Ilha do Pessageiro** (Peach Tree Island), which in bygone days provided protection from raids by Dutch and Algerian pirates.

Some nine miles (15 km) down the road from Porto Corvo is the little village of Cercal, and here is the turn for **Vila Nova de Milfontes**, the busiest of the coast's resorts. If ever there was a perfect seaside town then Vila Nova de Milfontes is it. The only time it gets really busy is in high summer when many *Alentejanos* and *Lisboners* come for their annual holiday at the large campsite there.

Again, there is little nightlife but there are a few more seafood restaurants and a small beautifully kept hotel which overlooks the sea. This is converted from an ivy-clad fortress—drawbridge and all, its only drawback being that you have to pay a steep price for room and three full meals.

Vila Nova de Milfontes is set at the mouth of the Mira River, and this provides miles of golden beaches and calm sea. There is beach around the mouth which then opens out onto the Atlantic proper. Park out at the headland overlooking the ocean, and you can turn back to see the quaint town to your left, the winding river and the hills beyond—all very idyllic. If you are planning a day or two on this coast, then here is the place to stay as you can rent an apartment or stay at a guest house, the campsite, the castle/hotel, or a more modern, larger hotel complex just outside the town at Moinho Asneira.

Almograve and **Zambujeira** offer more stunning, deserted beaches and some fine clifftop viewpoints across the basalt cliffs to the sea. Between these two beaches is another one, **Cabo do Girão**. But it is naval property and access is prohibited.

If you have some extra time and feel like moving inland from here, in the lower Alentejo is the pretty village of **Odemira**, set on the banks of the Mira River for which it's named. It is a verdant town full of flowers and trees, so green that you are apt to forget that it is in the Alentejo. Water, water everywhere can also be found up at the nearby **Barragem de Santa Clara**, a huge dam which feeds the Mira as well as the local water supply. You might take some time and indulge in water sports here.

Ourique is a charming little agricultural town north of the dam. On its surrounding fields (**Campo do Ourique**) are grown fruit, olive and cork trees. These fields, however, have seen far more than just farm-

Left, refinery pipelines at Sines. Right, Gothic castle in Beja

ing. In the hamlet of **Atalaia**, archaeologists excavated an extraordinary Bronze Age burial mound, and it was on those fields, thousands of years later in 1139, that a significant battle was fought between the Portuguese and the Moors. Afonso Henriques had just been crowned the first King of Portugal. The victory on this battlefield strengthened his determination to rout the Moors from Portuguese soil, and gave a tremendous boost to his army's morale.

The capital of lower Alentejo, **Beja**, is possibly the hottest town (in air temperature terms) in Portugal during the height of summer. It takes about three hours by car from Lisbon and an hour or so from Évora. A town existed on the present-day site as early as 48 B.C. and when Julius Caesar made peace with the Lusitanians the settlement was named after this event, *Pax Julia*. During the 400-year Moorish occupation, the name was adulterated to Baju, then Baja, until it finally became known as Beja.

Beja is now a fairly prosperous town, its income derived from trade in olive oil and wheat. It has a large German Air Force base where fighter pilots are trained. Beja is not a beautiful town overall, but it does have some interesting sights. The 15th century Convent of Conception (**Convento da Conceição**) is a beautiful building and a fine example of the transition between Gothic and Manueline architecture. The Baroque chapel is lined with carved, gilded woodwork. The chapterhouse which leads to the cloisters is tiled with superb Hispanic-arabic *azulejos* dating back to the 1500s. Their quality is rivalled only by those in the Royal Palace at Sintra. The convent also houses the **regional museum**.

The small and modest **Santo Amaro** is the oldest church in Beja. It is thought to date back to the 7th century and is a rare example of Visigothic architecture. Beja's 13th-century castle still stands, and its castellated walls run around the town perimeter. At one corner is the tall keep which contains a **military museum**, and a narrow balcony on each side from which you can enjoy a remarkable view across the plains.

Driving in to **Serpa** is—as with so many small Alentejo towns—like driving into a time warp. The **castle** and fortified walls were built at the command of King Dinis. A difference here from other 13th-century walls is that these have an aqueduct built into them.

A well-preserved gate is the **Portas de Beja**, which, along with the rest of the walls, were almost sold by the town council in the latter half of the 19th century. Cooler heads prevailed and the walls were saved, though a great part of them had been destroyed in 1707 when the Duke of Ossuna and his army occupied the town during the War of the Spanish Succession.

There are several churches worth seeing, as well as the delightfully cool and elegant palace belonging to the Count of Ficalho. The **Paços dos Condes de Ficalho** was built in the 16th century. It has a majestic staircase and lovely tiles. The present Marquise, incidentally, is the granddaughter of Portugal's great 19th-century novelist Eça de Queiroz.

The **Guadiana** is a lovely river. It's the most peaceful of Portugal's three big rivers (the others being the Tagus and Douro), but an exception is at Pulo do Lobo near **Mértola**. This is a stretch of high and wild rapids, which can be reached by road and is worth a visit if you're in the area. Mértola, an ancient fortified town, is also worth a brief stop, set in the confluence between the Guadiana and the Oeiras Rivers. The **parish church** was originally a mosque. To see it ask at the house nearby. It is one of the few mosques in Portugal to have survived virtually intact.

The Alentejo's culinary specialities should not be missed. Try *sopa alentejana*—a filling soup of bread, lots of coriander (a herb used a great deal in Alentejo cooking), garlic and poached eggs; or *sopa da cação*, which is a rich fish soup. One of the classic meat dishes is *carne de porco à alentejana*—chunks of pork seasoned in wine, coriander and onions and served with clams. Two much heavier but delicious stewed dishes are *ensopada de cabrito*—kid boiled with potatoes and bread until the meat is just about falling off the bone, and *favada de caça*, a game stew of hare, rabbit, partridge or pigeon with broad beans. The best Alentejo cheese comes from Serpa. Made from sheep and goat milk it has a creamy texture and a strong, slightly piquant flavor. Évora has its own goat, cheese which is hard, salty and slightly acid. It is preserved in jars filled with olive oil.

Alentejo is a demarcated wine region. Its reds are full-bodied and mature well in the bottle. Most towns have their own cooperative winery from which you can buy stocks at rock-bottom prices. Most restaurants have a modestly priced cooperative house wine. To appreciate really good Alentejo wines, try the reds from the Reguengos cooperative or those from Quinta do Carmo in Estremoz (Borba region). White wines from the Vidigueira cooperative are far superior to any other Alentejo whites.

Capela de São Gens in Serpa

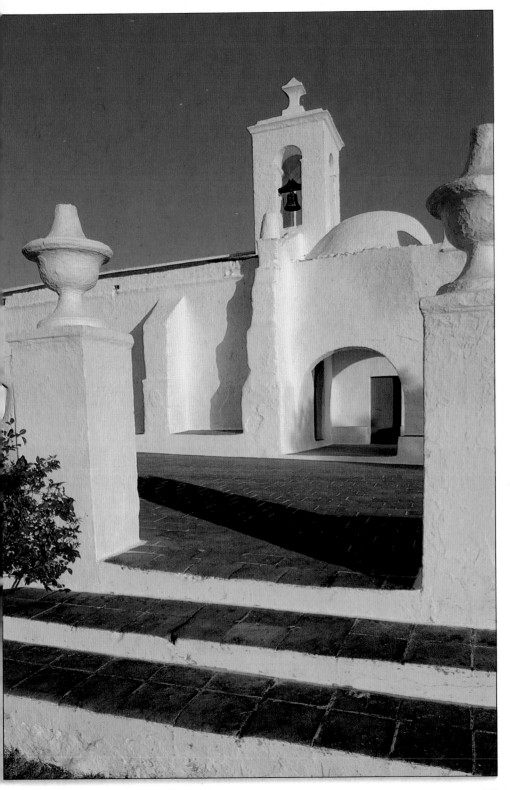

TREES OF THE ALENTEJO

The Portuguese are a people of the earth: they describe their country as garden sown on the edge of the sea; they weave their ancient legends around roses and almond blossoms; and a flower—the red carnation—is the symbol for the 1974 Revolution, which restored democracy. Many people still cherish the flowers, now pressed and dried.

But the land that the Portuguese have inherited does not make cultivation easy. Nowhere in the country is this more true than in the toilsome soil of the large, parched plains and craggy coastline of the Alentejo.

argue that the labor expended on raising sparse crops from barren soil could be turned to more productive account by using the land in a different way. The agronomists' answer to Portugal's farming problems is a return to the country's historic wealth—forests.

Centuries ago dense oak woods covered most of Portugal. They have largely disappeared. One third of the country, about 7.5 million acres, is now forested. Some experts believe the Portuguese economy would benefit greatly if the extension of forest was almost doubled so that trees covered 59 percent of the country. Massive

Alentejo balconies brim with hydrangeas and the white walls of houses are cloaked with purple bougainvillea in the late summer. But Portugal must work its land to produce useful crops, not decorative blossoms.

Almost a third of Portuguese workers are engaged in farming, three times the European average. But poor soil, a difficult climate and outmoded methods mean that most crops yield less than half the average per acre in Western and Eastern Europe. Struggling farmers have to cultivate every square inch of land to earn their livelihoods.

About half the surface of Portugal is devoted to farming. But experts estimate that because of the poor quality of the soil only half of that land is really suited to agriculture. Economic planners

planting projects are underway to achieve this aim, such as a plan funded by the World Bank to reforest a huge area of central Portugal north of the Tagus River. Similar plans will surely be instituted in the Alentejo before long.

Even now trees big business. The forestry industry employs some 100,000 workers in a sector that earns $1 billion a year in export revenue. Pine, said in Portugal to be of use to man from cradle to coffin, is used to produce timber for furniture and construction, as well as resin for pitch and turpentine. Pine accounts for about 40 percent of the country's wooded land. Driving through pine forests, you will see metal cups strapped below holes to collect sap. The openings are cut in the trunk with a special long-bladed axe. Each mature tree is tapped for resin once or twice in each of the last two years before it is felled and each tapping takes about a month, during which the resin is collected three times.

The main product of Portuguese forests is pulp used for manufacturing paper and cardboard. Pine has lost its place as the mainstay of the pulp, industry as demand grows for the short fiber pulp produced by the eucalyptus. The Australian eucalyptus, whose distinctive aroma fills the air, was introduced into Portugal in 1856. Today it accounts for 10 percent of all forested land. Eucalyptus oil also is used for various pharmaceutical products.

Pines and eucalyptus are found in many parts of Portugal, including, of course, the Alentejo. But other products are more specifically characteristic of this province. Perhaps most distinctive of all are sprawling cork-oak trees with their raw, stripped trunks spread over the grasslands in thousands.

More than half the cork in the world, from stoppers in bottles of the finest champagne to the linings of spacecraft, is supplied from these fields where pigs, turkeys and sheep amble between the trees, feeding on the acorns as the bark slowly matures to readiness over the decades.

Pulp manufacturers are lobbying to extend the cultivation of the eucalyptus, or gum tree. Their main concern is expediency, as the eucalyptus grows to maturity in 12 to 15 years, compared with 40 to 50 years for pine, and is hardy enough to grow on poor, sandy soil.

But some farmers oppose the spread of eucalyptus groves that they claim rapaciously draw up water needed for other crops if not managed correctly. The anti-eucalyptus lobby currently holds sway, with official planting programs for the tree amounting to about half those of pine.

Left, some of the groves that produce the piquant Portuguese olive oil. Above, the distinctively twisted and knotted cork trees

Cultivating cork is not a trade for the impatient. From the acorn, the spreading tree with its heavy, twisted branches grows for about 25 years before it is ready to yield its bark. The branches of shiny dark-green evergreen leaves with a grayish underside are carefully pruned to admit the sunlight and make the bark accessible to the cutters. What underbrush there is on the plains is periodically burned away.

At the height of summer, when the trunk has shrunk away from the gnarled, dull-gray outer skin, workmen skillfully begin the stripping. Using special axes ground to razor sharpness, they first make horizontal cuts around the circumference of the trunk and the lower branches. These are linked with vertical incisions and the roll of bark is stripped off, leaving the rich red, bare trunk beneath. Machines cannot replace the expertise of the strippers, who cut the bark with such skill that the tender trunk below is left undamaged.

The first stripping yields virgin cork that is used for specialized purposes such as life-jackets. Each tree gives between 60 and 100 pounds of cork at a cutting. It will be another nine years before a sufficiently thick layer of bark has grown back for another crop. A tree is usually stripped 12 to 15 times in a life of around 200 years. After sorting, the cork strips are piled high on trucks and transported to one of the 700 processing plants across the country. They are dried for up to a year to remove any viscous residue that might remain in the millions of minute, air-filled cells that make cork so light. An improperly dried cork could doom a vintage port! The strips are then

ever likely to replace bottle corks.

The Alentejo produces around 2,000 tons of cork a year but the tree, a *sobreiro* in Portuguese, also grows in the Algarve and parts of the Ribatejo. Portugal earns more than $200 million dollars a year in exports from this constantly expanding sector.

Older still than the cork oaks of the Alentejo are many of the olive trees found mainly in the Alentejo but also across all of southern and central Portugal and along the Douro Valley in the north. Experts believe some Portuguese olives are as old as the trees in the Garden of Gethsemane, shown by carbon-14 tests to date from the time of Christ. Whatever their age, the lovely groves of evergreen olives rising on gentle, grassy slopes with their gnarled trunks, tangled branches and dark-green silvery leaves are one of

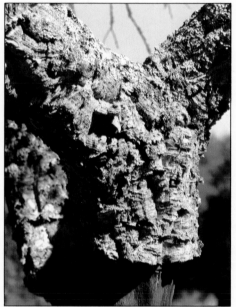

boiled in water for a day in huge copper vats to bond the cells and make the cork more flexible. The strips are smoothed out into flat sheets and dried again in the sun.

Cork is graded into almost 50 different categories that mark them for a huge variety of uses including heat insulation, floats, tiles, soundproofing, containers for radioactive materials, badminton shuttlecocks, table tennis bats and, of course, corks—or bottle stoppers as they are known in the cork trade. Workmen who manually punch out thousands of stoppers a day from strips of cork are now being replaced by machines. But mechanization cannot match their skills for crafting the perfect fits that are needed to cork fine wines and champagnes. Nor are artificial materials,which do not allow wine to breathe,

the strongest visual bonds between Portugal and its Mediterranean neighbors from Spain to the Middle East.

Olive oil, called "the thread of life," is as basic to Portuguese cooking as salt and pepper in other countries. The starting point of most dishes is a *refogado*, or base of chopped onions and garlic browned in olive oil. The oil is also poured onto boiled fish, potatoes and vegetables and into some soups. Much of the olive oil produced in Portugal, which has a slightly more tangy taste than in other countries, is used in the canning of sardines and tuna.

A great deal of labor goes into producing the oil. The tree, which reaches between 10 and 40 feet in height, does not bear fruit during its first 25 years of life, sometimes longer if frost affects its growth. The olives are picked in November, just before they ripen fully, between six and eight months after the tree flowers. Crops are erratic, varying from heavy one year to sparse the next. A white sheet, that was once made of linen but is more often of cotton or plastic today, is spread beneath the tree. The pickers shake the fruit onto the sheet with long poles, then climb into the tree to glean the rest. Today, some farmers use machines that grip the tree trunk in a large clamp and shake it mechanically.

Some olives are preserved in salt water and served as an appetizer or a garnish. Between 20 and 30 percent of the weight of the fresh fruit is oil. Traditionally, this was extracted by grinding the oil between two large stone wheels onto a granite slab. The pulp was then drained through a stack of rope baskets that are pressed so that the

oil most commonly used for cooking. Third pressings are usually refined for industrial uses. Complex methods of repressing and processing are used to produce other grades of oil.

Though the trees of the Alentejo are perhaps not as strikingly exotic as the lovely almond and carob of the Algarve to the south, the landscape is given its unmistakable texture by its own particular trees. The cork and olive lend character—scrappy, smallish, but indomitable—to the land. And there are other native beauties to be found. The *loquat*, another southern tree, is an evergreen of the rose family that originated in China and Japan. You can tell the tree by its stiff leaves and small, fragrant white flowers. The oval yellow, plum-like fruits grow between one and three inches long in large, loose clusters. Eaten raw, the juicy white flesh has a tart but pleasing taste.

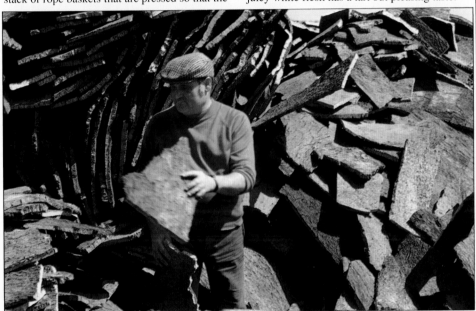

oil drips into metal containers of water beneath. The oil was poured off, leaving the impurities in the water. These traditional methods are still used on small farms in many parts of the country, but most farmers today sell their olive crops to cooperatives who use modern, mechanical presses to produce and refine industrial quantities of oil.

Lightweight, dark-green virgin oil of the highest quality is produced from the first pressing. The second pressing delivers a heavier oil, also of excellent quality, that is blended to make the olive

There are other crops, of course, although their roles are minor when compared to the great trees that do so much for the country as a whole. Only vineyards compare in importance nationally, and they are cultivated in every province, including a modest offering from the Alentejo. Vines take three years to bear grapes, and another three to produce mature fruit. Alentejo wines—Redondo, Borba, Beja and Vidigueira—are good. Dark fruity reds and pale, sharp whites, they are generally high in alcohol content. In the alluvial plains, as the Alentejo's rivers near the Atlantic, a fair crop of rice is produced.

Far left, the imposing and aromatic eucalyptus trees. Left, a half-naked cork trunk shorn of its valued bark. Above, Robinson's Cork Factory in Portalegre

The ubiquitous forests of carefully cultivated trees along with the irrepressible wildflowers combine to make the Alentejo a verdant, vibrant province.

COIMBRA

Perched on a hill overlooking the Mondego River, Coimbra is surrounded by breathtakingly beautiful countryside. The city itself is a mixture of ancient and new, rural and urban—a combination that is sometimes jarring but always interesting.

While there are few traces of the Roman occupation, vestiges of the Middle Ages still abound. Turning into some parts of old city is like stepping back in time.

The University is the most stalwart guardian of the past. Students clad in black capes, the traditional academic dress, resemble oversized bats as they flit around town. Note that the bottoms of the capes are slit: the number of slits depends on either academic or romantic prowess, depending on whose story you believe. These capes, by the way, have only recently come back into style, since for a time they were associated with Salazar's New State, and therefore not worn in the years after the Revolution.

In the spring of every year, the University celebrates the *Queima das Fitas*, the "burning of the ribbons," during which graduating students burn the ribbons that they have been wearing on their sleeves. The color of the ribbons depends on which department the students are in. The various celebrations last a week. The grand finale is a large, drunken parade of students that floats through the center of the city. It is the most elaborate academic festival in the country.

Another Coimbran tradition is *fado*. The music is the more serious and intellectual cousin of Lisbon *fado*. The somber tradition of Coimbra *fado*, in fact, requires one to clear one's throat in approval after a rendition, and not applaud. This type of *fado* has a slow, rhythmic beat and is performed only by men, usually graduates of the University.

Although the University has been and remains a great influence on Coimbra life, don't imagine that there's nothing else here. As the country's third-largest city, Coimbra has grown prosperous under the shadow of its ivory tower. It is the center of an agricultural region and has a large market. The students, by the way, are not the only ones in black: it is the traditional dress of many of the rural women who come in to town as well. Coimbra also has its share of manufacturing—fabrics, beer—and a lively handicrafts industry as well.

Roman roots: Coimbra traces its roots to the Roman municipality of *Aeminium*. The city gained in importance as the city of Conimbriga, a few miles south, proved vulnerable to invasion. Convulsions in the empire and various invasions brought an end to Roman rule in the city, and throughout Portugal. The Moors took over in 711, ushering in 300 years of Islamic rule, with a few interruptions. One such interruption occurred in 878 when Afonso III of Asturias and Léon captured the city. But Coimbra was not permanently taken by Christians until 1064.

Coimbra then became a base for the reconquest of other parts of Portugal from the Moors. It was about this time—the 11th century—that the city was originally walled. In the 12th and 13th centuries, Coimbra became the capital of Portugal.

The 12th century was an age of great progress for Coimbra, including plans for a bridge over the Mondego River, and construction of the city's most important monastery, Santa Cruz, which still stands. Both projects were started in 1131. The city was a lively commercial center and included both Jewish and Moorish quarters. Division was not only by religion, but by class as well. Nobles and clergy lived inside the walls; merchants and craft workers lived outside in what is today called the Baixa, the downtown area.

The University was founded in 1290—not in Coimbra, however, but in Lisbon. In 1308 the University moved to Coimbra, only to return to Lisbon in 1377. These shifts were the result of continual political conflict between the monarchy and the academic leaders. It was not until 1537 that the university settled permanently in Coimbra. A few years later, it moved to its present site at the top of the hill. Since then, the University and its students have been a continual influence on the character and growth of the city.

Most areas of touristic interest are easily reached on foot—that is, if you're willing to do some uphill walking. There is an extensive bus system, although the bus maps are difficult to read. It's probably more trouble than it's worth to have a car within the city, as streets become one-way at frustrating times, and parking is difficult. The old city and the University crown Coimbra's central hill. The Baixa, which is the main shopping district and also quite old, lies at the foot of the hill along the Mondego River. Santa Clara lies across the river.

Old city: Once located inside the city walls, the old city is a tangle of narrow streets and alleys, lined by ancient buildings and filled with squares and patios. If you can ignore the cars, you can look back in time as the historical vistas spread before you. Shortly after the University moved to Coimbra, King João III offered his royal residence to house it, and there, in the heart of the city, it has stayed. Buildings have, of course, been remodeled and added, but the University has preserved its dignified air.

The modern center of the university is the statue of Dom Dinis, founder of the University. Around it are the buildings that house the **Faculties**, as the schools are called, of **Science and Technology, Medicine and Letters,** and the **new library**.

Of more historical interest than these rather stolidly functional buildings is the **Patio das Escolas**, Patio of the Schools. To enter the patio, pass through the 17th-century **Porta Férrea**, a large portal decorated in the Mannerist style. This doorway leads to a large, rather dusty courtyard, which unfortunately now is used as a parking lot. Here are some of the oldest and stateliest buildings of the University.

The figure of João III, who installed the University in Coimbra, still reigns from the center of the patio. Behind him, there is a magnificent view of the river below.

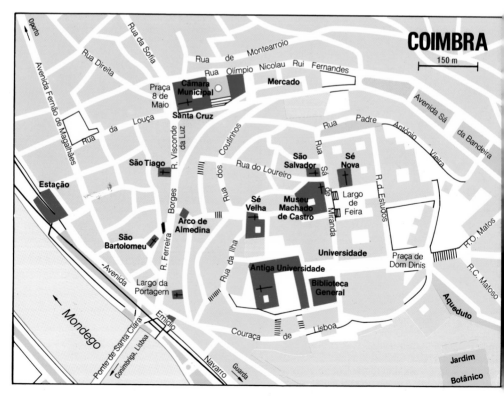

The building in the farthest corner from the Porta Férrea is the old **Library**, the most beautiful of all the university buildings. To enter, knock or ring and wait for the caretaker to open the door (closed for lunch, 12:00 p.m.-2:00 p.m.). The three 18th-century Baroque rooms were built during the reign of João V, whose portrait hangs at the far end. Bookcases, decorated in gilded wood and oriental motifs, reach gracefully to the second floor. Even the ladders are intricately decorated. Note the frescoes on the ceilings. The rare books that fill the cases make up a venerable and quite valuable collection that still is consulted by resident and visiting scholars.

Next door is **St. Michael's Chapel**, begun in 1517, and remodeled in both the 17th and 18th centuries. The chapel is notable for its "carpet" style tiles, the painted ceilings, the altar, and the Baroque organ. There is also a **museum of sacred art**.

The long terraced building to the right of the Porta Férrea houses several interesting rooms. The **Sala dos Capelos**, where many academic ceremonies take place, was probably a reception room in the royal residence. Portraits of the kings of Portugal hang from its walls. Other rooms into which the visitor should wander are the **Rectory** and the **Private Exam Room**.

To the left of the Porta Férrea is São Pedro College, a 16th-century building that has been remodeled several times.

Leaving the University grounds, one finds the nearby **Sé Nova** (new cathedral) whose sand-colored facade presides over an uninteresting square. Built for the Jesuits in 1554, it became a cathedral in 1772. Inside, the altar is of lavish gilded wood. Fourteen of the 16 paintings around the altar are copies of Italian masters.

The **Machado de Castro Museum**, open 10 a.m. to 12 p.m. and 2 pm. to 4:45 p.m., is housed in the old Episcopal Palace and the church of **São João de Almedina**, both 12th-century constructions. The former was the home of the city's early bishops. The museum is built over the ruins of a Roman crypt. It has an excellent collection, both extensive and varied. Unfortunately, much of it is unlabeled, which can be quite frustrating or quite liberating—every artifact can become a source of speculation. What labels there are, are all in Portuguese, and there is no complete catalog in either Portuguese or English. Still, the museum is certainly worth a visit for its collection of Roman artifacts, medieval Portuguese sculpture, a large collection of Portuguese painting from the 15th century onward, gold work, ceramics, tapestries, furniture, and even two coaches. There is also a great view of the Sé Velha (old cathedral) and the roofs of the old city from the courtyard.

The Sé Velha, renovated this century, was built between 1162 and 1184. It served as cathedral until 1772, when the episcopal see was moved to the Sé Nova. The fortress-like exterior is relieved by an arched door and an arched window directly above. The intricate Gothic altar within is of gilded wood, created by two Flemish masters in the 15th and 16th centuries. On the left side, a 16th-century door sports a beautiful sculptured medallion. The door, unfortunately, is in somewhat decrepit condition. There are several **tombs** in the church, including those of 13th-century Bishop Dom Egas Fafes (left of the altar) and Dona Vetaca, a Byzantine princess who lived in the Coimbran court in the 14th century. The **cloister** is early Gothic; construction began in 1218.

Construction on the **Colégio de São Agostinho**, on Rua Colégio Novo, began in 1593. The ecclesiastical scholars and monks who first occupied it would be shocked by the goings-on here today, for this pleasant building, lined with pretty *azulejos*, is now home to the University's Psychology Department.

Nearby, on Rua Sub-Ripas, the medieval **Torre** (Tower) **do Anto** was once part of the 12th-century walls of the city. Much later it was the home of poet António Nobre during his undergraduate days. Today it displays and sells traditional crafts from the Coimbra area, sponsored by the city council. The enthusiastic and knowledgeable manager will tell you all about the works in any one of seven languages, including English.

The **Casa de Sub-Ripas**, also on Rua Sub-Ripas, is an aristocratic mansion from the 16th century. Note the archetypal Manueline door and window, but don't bother knocking, it's still a private residence. Here, according to tradition, Maria Teles was murdered by her husband João, eldest son of the tragic Inês de Castro. João had been convinced by Queen Leonor Teles, who was jealous of Maria, that his wife—the queen's sister—was unfaithful.

The **Arco de Almedina**, an entrance to the old city just off of Rua Ferreira Borges (the main downtown street) was also part of the Coimbra walls.

The Baixa is the busy shopping district. **Rua Ferreira Borges**, with many fashionable shops, is the principal street. Other winding streets lead off toward the river. Although this district lay outside the walls

of the old city, it dates back to nearly the same time.

The **Santa Cruz Monastery**, in Praça 8 de Maio, off Rua Ferreira Borges, was founded in 1131 by Portugal's first king, Afonso Henriques. The facade and portal date from the 16th century, when the church was restored. Inside, although the church is small, it is light and spacious. Eighteenth-century *azulejos* adorn either wall: the right side depicts the life of Saint Augustine, the left scenes related to the Holy Cross. The prize piece of the church is the exquisite **pulpit** on the left wall, an intricately carved work by sculptor Nicolau Chanterene.

The sacristy is open from 9 a.m. to noon and from 2 p.m. to 5 p.m., and contains several paintings (the largest is the *Descent from the Cross*, by Andre Gonçalves), a silverwork collection, and some vestments. You can visit the **tombs** of the first two kings of Portugal, Afonso Henriques, and Sancho I, who are ensconced in truly regal monuments. You may also see the **Chapterhouse** and the lovely **Cloister of Silence**.

The Rua da Sofia, off Praça 8 de Maio, a 16th-century street, was extraordinarily wide for its time. It was the original home of several colleges of the University before they were moved to their present location on the hill.

Praça do Comércio, off Rua Ferreira Borges, is an oddly shaped square lined with 17th- and 18th-century buildings. At the north end stands the sturdy **Santiago Church**, dating from the end of the 12th century. The capitals are decorated with animal and bird motifs. At the south end is the church of **São Bartolomeu**, built in the 18th century.

The Santa Clara section of town lies across the river. **Santa Clara a Nova** (New Santa Clara) **Monastery** is worth a visit if only for the view of Coimbra from the praça in front of it. Inside, in a wildly Baroque setting, stands the **tomb of the Queen Saint Isabel**, the patron saint of Coimbra.

Closer to the river, too close for its own comfort in fact, is **Santa Clara a Velha**, the old Santa Clara Monastery, which is now partially submerged. This 12th-century edifice is simpler and lovelier than its replacement, for which it was abandoned in 1677.

Nearby, **Portugal dos Pequenitos** is an outdoor museum of small-scale reproductions of traditional Portuguese houses and famous monuments.

In other areas of the city, the **Celas Monastery** is notable for its cloister and the pretty church of **Santo António dos Olivais** was an old Franciscan convent.

There is a lot of sightseeing to do in Coimbra—perhaps too much; church after church becomes wearing. However, there are other ways to enjoy the city as well.

One is shopping in the Baixa. Shops range from the fashionable to the hole-in-the-wall, and it's always an adventure to let yourself get lost in the meandering and illogical streets of the shopping district. For those interested in traditional Coimbran ceramics and handicrafts, the city runs a showcase shop in the **Torre de Anto**, in the old city. For a different shopping experience, go to the **covered market** on Rua Olimpio Nicolau, not far from the Baixa, which is open every morning but best on Saturdays. The market vendors hawk fish, bread, fruit, vegetables, flowers, even live animals (chickens and rabbits). You'll get a real taste of Coimbra life.

Coimbra's many parks make delicious resting places. The **Botanical Garden**, on Alameda Dr. Julio Henriques, next to the aqueduct, is a lovely garden filled with a wide range of plant life. Unfortunately, not all the grounds are open to the public—but enough for a pleasant visit. Other nice parks are **Santa Cruz**, off the Praça da República, and **Choupal**, west of the city—a larger park good for walks and bike rides. The very small **Penedo da Saudade** has a nice view over the city.

Canoing in Coimbra: For those who want physical exercise, one option is to rent canoes from the municipal boat club near the **Santa Clara Bridge**, on the far side of the river. Another possibility is to walk on some of the smaller roads to or between the villages outside Coimbra—the countryside is beautiful and easily accessible.

Outlying districts accessible by bus or by car include **Penacova**, a village with a strikingly beautiful view—try lunch there at the Panorâmica Restaurant, which lives up to its name. The drive/bus ride there runs along the lovely Mondego River valley. There are windmills—somehow, always a surprising sight—on hilltops in the surrounding countryside. Or visit **Penela**, a village with a Moorish castle overlooking the area; or **Lousã**, a mountain town.

Coimbra is located 118 miles (188 km) north of Lisbon and 74 miles (118 km) south of Oporto on the Lisbon-Oporto highway and the Lisbon-Oporto train line. It takes an hour and 20 minutes to and from Oporto by fast train, and two hours 10 minutes from Lisbon. The tourist office is located in the center of town in **Largo de Portagem**. They will provide you with a good map of the city.

Alumni of the Medical School gather at the Old University

A WALKING TOUR OF CONIMBRIGA

The largest excavated Roman ruins in Portugal, complemented by one of the country's finest museums, lies not far from Coimbra, near the town of Condeixa. Conimbriga (pronounced with the stress on the second syllable: Co-NIM-briga) is a fascinating site that includes the remains of a Roman wall, several public buildings and private houses, and beautifully preserved mosaics which alone would be worth the visit.

Of an estimated 32-acre site, only a few hundred yards have been excavated. A glance out onto the hot, dusty field that is still off-limits to tourists reveals signs of further ruins, and, happily, the beginnings of more excavation. In fact, the site stretches much further than is obvious; archaeologists believe remains may be found as far away as the main highway and even under the homes of people in the nearby village of Condeixa-a-Velha.

Conimbriga probably was settled as early as the Iron Age (800-500 B.C.). The name Conimbriga itself suggests Celtic habitation, as *briga* is a Celtic suffix. The site was likely chosen for its natural defenses: it is protected on two sides by deep gorges.

It was not until the last part of the second century B.C. that Romans came to Conimbriga. Perhaps they first arrived as part of a campaign to subdue Lusitania, the Roman name for this part of the Iberian Peninsula. Two hundred years of conflict eventually ended, and the people of the area were gradually Romanized, their names Latinized and they adopted Roman gods. The local Romans, in kind, adopted some of the native deities and cults.

Prosperity accompanied peace. Conimbriga profited from its location along the Roman road between *Olisipo* (present-day Lisbon) and *Bracara Augusta* (now Braga). Some time around 70 A.D., the Roman Empire designated Conimbriga a *municipium* and bestowed the name of Flavia on it.

In the year 391, Christianity became the official religion of the Roman Empire. The earliest evidence of Christianity's spread to Conimbriga is a tombstone from 522.

Great Wall of Conimbriga: Conimbriga's prosperity was not to last. Crises in the Empire and Barbarian incursions into Iberia prompted the construction of the defensive wall still prominent today. The wall was built of bits and pieces of everything, including stone, remnants of old houses, and brick. To take advantage of the natural defensive position of the area, and to concentrate the area of defense, the inhabited area of Conimbriga was reduced and some parts of the

town were left outside the wall. Despite the new wall, in 464 Suevi successfully attacked the city; of this early raid we know that they captured the wife and children of the nobleman Cantaber, whose home, next to the wall, has been excavated. They returned four years later and overran the city, destroying much of the population.

Conimbriga continued to be inhabited, but it lost its status as an important center to its neighbor, the more easily defensible *Aeminium*. The population of Conimbriga decreased, and little or no new buildings were constructed. It is likely that the Episcopal see of the region was moved to

Aeminium during the 6th century. *Aeminium* even absconded with Conimbriga's name, which eventually was shortened to Coimbra.

As you enter the site, you are walking down the very road that gave Conimbriga its original importance—the highway between *Olisipo* and *Bracara Augusta*. In front of you is the enormous wall, built later, that cut off parts of the city.

Before the wall, and to your right, lie the ruins—still not entirely excavated—of a large house. The house was partially destroyed by the construction of the wall, which went right through the front of it. Indeed, pieces of this house were used to make the wall.

At the front of the house, the part closest to the wall, is the main entrance which leads into a small courtyard and atrium. Small service rooms lie on either side. Just beyond is the peristyle—a central courtyard with sculptured pool, which the Romans kept stocked with fish. Thick walls and central pools helped keep Roman houses cool even on the hottest of days—something you'll understand as you simmer among the ruins of Conimbriga in the middle of summer.

Several mosaics line the peristyle. Among them are a scene of Perseus and the sea monster; a man returning from the hunt with a rabbit; and a very small minotaur and a very large labyrinth. Mosaic scenes such as these served not only for decoration but also as a means of keeping mythical traditions alive among the part of the population that was illiterate.

The family's private quarters are on the side of the house closest to the road. There are bedrooms here, as well as a courtyard and an *impluvium* for catching rainwater. Here are other noteworthy mosaics, including one of stag-hunting and another of Silenus riding a donkey.

Opposite, on the north side of the house, is a lavatory. Overflow from the central pool may have been used for the flushing system. The rooms to this side served unknown purposes; there is another hunting mosaic in one of these. Finally, on the east side of the house, opposite the main entrance, is the main reception area and dining room.

Passing through the main entrance in the wall, and continuing along the path through to the right, you'll come to the arch of the aqueduct (rebuilt); parts of the aqueduct, and the remains of several buildings which might have been small shops.

Back to the main entrance, Cantaber's house stretches to the south (left, with your back to the entrance). The house is full of ornamental pools. The first is just beyond the entrance to the house; there are more flanking a reception room just further south. In the middle section of the house, up against the city wall, is a suite of rooms (which you can view by climbing a small staircase). These too have a pool; note the trident symbol of Neptune at the entrance to the suite.

Roman baths: Perhaps the most interesting part of the house is the baths, which lie at the extreme south end. They are easily recognizable by their hexagonal and round shapes, and by the heating system (of pipes) visible through the stone grid covering the floors. The *frigidarium* is the square room; this was the room for cold baths.

The *tepidarium* held warm water, and the *caldarium* hot. The Romans believed it was healthful to progress through all three temperatures during a bath. Beyond the house, on the south side of the ruins, are tombs and skeletons from a much later period.

Back around the other side of the wall, we can see more baths: the public ones, this time. The stacks of tiles piled on the ground indicate that these baths ran on a different, less expensive, system than the baths at Cantaber's home. While Cantaber's baths used a system of piped hot water, in the public baths the floor was raised off the ground by means of stacked tiles. A slave would stoke a furnace and pump bellows to push the hot air under the floor, which thus heated the room above.

The public baths were an important part of Roman life, and wealthy Roman men would spend hours daily bathing. It was both a health ritual and a place to discuss politics and other subjects. The Romans were particularly convinced of the salutary effects of bathing, and took great care in covering themselves with olive oil after a bath and then scraping their skins clean with a curved blade, to remove impurities.

Beyond the baths is an area of marvelously patterned mosaics. The colors were once much brighter than the pleasing pastels to which they have mellowed today. Note the delicate shading of the reds and yellows in some of the mosaics.

The museum is small but thoughtfully designed. A long case displays artifacts relating to ceramics, weaving, agriculture, lighting, writing, health and hygiene, jewelry, and other areas. There is also statuary and a very good model of the forum and temple, buildings that date from around 70 A.D. when Conimbriga became a *municipium*.

The room devoted to superstition and belief is especially interesting. A shelf of tombstones dominates the room; the inscriptions are translated to Portuguese, and include such dedications as "Aviro and Rufina dedicated this monument to their son Vegeto, dead at 18, hoping that the earth lie light upon him." A display case shows amulets that were used to ward off bad fortune and the disfavor of the gods. Another case is dedicated to the specific gods Conimbrigans worshipped. The final case illustrates the coming of Christianity to Conimbriga.

Conimbriga lies about 9 miles (15 km) south of Coimbra. The drive is easy; there is also a bus service. The site and museum are open 9 a.m. to 1 p.m. and 2 to 5 p.m. daily; the museum is closed on Mondays and holidays.

Left, a Roman mosaic from Conimbriga's House of the Fountains depicts Perseus holding out the head of Medusa to a sea serpent

SIDETRIPS FROM COIMBRA

Coimbra is the largest city in the province of Beira Litoral, which lies above the provinces of Estremadura and Ribatejo. All three are lush, green and laced with waterways. The Beira Litoral has a very ragged coastline, as the Atlantic constantly pushes in with greedy fingers, both at the Ria and south of it. Ricefields are planted in this low coastal area, which is sometimes known as "Costa da Prata," the Silver Coast. There are patches of pine trees that have been planted in some spots in an effort to stabilize the sand dunes. Inland, the ground begins to rise very gradually, and fruit trees and grain fields flourish.

Estremadura stretches below the coastal part of Beira Litoral like an arm reaching down to touch Lisbon and Setúbal. It was once the southern extremity of Portugal, a fact confirmed by its name, which means "farthest land on the Douro." It continues the beaches of the "Costa da Prata," and, indeed, the inland agriculture of its northern neighbor. Ribatejo, "bank of the Tejo (Tagus)," is a small strip to the east of Estremadura. It is an alluvial plain, again planted with grains. Wherever flooding allows, ricefields are sown. But most important are the large meadows on which graze the horses and bulls bred to participate in the grand sport of bullfighting. These beautiful animals are used all over Portugal, and the Festival of the Red Waistcoats, held each July in **Vila Franca de Xira**, is five days of bull running and celebration.

Fátima: There are many other colorful festivals in these provinces, but the most important celebration—indeed, one of the most populous Catholic events in the world, is the pilgrimage at **Fátima**. In 1917, three peasant girls here had a vision of the Virgin of the Rosary on May 13th. Thereafter, she appeared before the three children, and the townspeople that gathered with them on the 13th of every month until October, asking for peace in the world. The processions that now take place each year draw thousands from around the world. Two of the original girls died shortly after the miracle, but one, Lucia, is still alive, a nun in a convent near Coimbra. Today, the town has capitalized on its sacred history with ubiquitous merchandizing of religious souvenirs. Furthermore, unlike a few decades ago, when making the pilgramage was a genuine hardship

Batalha Monastery

because of scarce lodgings, today motels have proliferated.

Beira Litoral, Estremadura, and Ribatejo are pleasant for casual meandering, but they are full of historical points of interest as well—Batalha, Alcobaça and Tomar being the best known of these.

The largest town in these provinces, apart from Coimbra, is **Aveiro**. It is likely to be described as "the Venice of Portugal," a claim some of its inhabitants make. Don't be disappointed: Aveiro, although pleasant enough, is nothing like the Italian city.

The comparison with Venice stems from the canals that traverse the city and the boats that ply them. There is, in fact, only one main canal with two smaller canals along the edges of town; only a few boats harbor here. These canals lead to the real attraction of the area: the **Ria**, the lagoon that extends 29 miles (47 km) just inland of the coast.

As might be guessed, the Ria plays a large part in Aveiro's economy. The colorful boats with large, graceful prows, the *moliceiros*, are used to gather *moliço*, seaweed, for fertilizer. Next to the canals are large saltpans, another local industry. Other important industries are fishing, wood, cork, and ceramics from nearby Vista Alegre.

It is believed that Aveiro, then known by the Roman name Talabriga, once lay directly on the ocean. Later, a strip of sediment built up, creating the Ria and a perfect sheltered harbor.

Aveiro was a small settlement during the Middle Ages. In the 13th century it became a town, later encircled by fortified walls (1418) at the suggestion of Infante Prince Pedro (after whom the city park is named). Shortly after this, the king granted Aveiro the concession of a town fair, and the March Fair still goes on to this day. In 1472, the king's daughter, Joana, entered the convent of Jesus in Aveiro against her father's will. Today the convent is a museum, and the princess, Santa Joana Princesa, has several miracles attributed to her locally.

The 16th century was a time of growth and expansion for the town. With its easy access to the sea and the interior, Aveiro became a mercantile and trade center from which products of the entire Beira region were exported to the world.

The city makes an interesting study in geographic destiny. A fluke of nature cut short Aveiro's prosperity. In 1575 a violent storm shifted the sandbanks in the lagoon, blocking the canal to the sea. A dramatic decrease in population (to about one-third of the original number) accompanied the inevitable decline in Aveiro's importance

as a maritime center.

In 1808, another storm opened up the passage to the sea again, but it was not until the last half of the 19th century that Aveiro's fortunes picked up. A key figure in this economic redevelopment was José Estevão, whose statue stands in the **Praça da República.**

As well as serving as a base for a trip on the Ria, Aveiro itself holds some interest, and is worth a few hours' exploration. The city is divided into two parts by the principal canal. The southern part of the city is where the aristocracy once lived; the northern half is the old fishermen's section.

The southern half centers around the Praça da República. In the simple square, the nicest building is the solid and prim **town hall**, which stands directly opposite the tourist office. Its large clock tower presides over the statue of José Estevão in the middle of the square. On the east side of the square, the 16th- and 17th-century **Misericórdia** church boasts a lovely Renaissance portal and 19th-century tiles on its facade.

In a square further south the 17th-century **Carmelite Convent** housed the barefoot Carmelite order. Note the paintings on the ceiling which depict the life of Saint Teresa.

The devout sacrifice their knees at Fátima

Although the **museum** of Aveiro is not well-labeled, guides will take you through and answer questions. The museum is housed in the 15th-century **Convento de Jesús**. The **church** of the convent is a riot of gilded wood. Arching over the choir are lovely hand-painted ceilings, and off the choir is a chapel with beautiful tiles. Just outside the church is Santa Joana Princesa's **tomb**, done in intricately carved colored marble with statues supporting and crowning it. The tomb took 12 years to construct. The walls are also of marble.

The rest of the convent holds pieces of varying interest: many ornate altars, painted biblical scenes, a gruesome Christ covered in graphic sores. Perhaps the most interesting pieces are those that illuminate the life of the convent: the choir music stands, the Mother Superior's chair, the old convent pharmacy, where a bookcase holds containers for opium, belladonna, and cocaine extracts; drawers labeled for various herbs, scales to weigh the medicine, and books on pharmacology.

The **São Domingos Cathedral** is near the museum. Its Baroque facade has twisted columns and sculpted figures of Faith, Hope and Charity. Inside, an enormous skylight over the altar lends the church an airiness that many Baroque churches lack. The enormous blue altar rises strikingly in the all-white interior. The **tomb of Catarina de Atalíde** is here, a woman honored, under the name Natércia, by the poet Camões in his sonnets. The church was founded in 1423 and remodeled during the 16th and 17th centuries.

Several blocks away is the refreshing **Dom Infante Pedro Park**, on the grounds of the old **Franciscan Monastery**. Colorful flowers, lush trees, fountains, and a small lake where you can rent paddle boats make this a nice spot for a break.

North of the canal lies the fishermen's section, where narrow one- and two-story houses support facades that sometimes rise beyond roof levels. The arches and curves on the tops of these false fronts are reminiscent of the fishing boats themselves and their curved prows. The **fish market**, where the catch is sold each morning, is in this area. There is also the bright white, oddly shaped chapel of **São Goncalinho** and the church of **São Goncalo**. Inside this 17th- and 18th-century church gleam a gilt altar and newly placed tiles.

The beautiful Ria is the real reason for coming to Aveiro. You can tour its length by boat, car, or bus, although boat is by far the

One of the *moliceiros* of Aveiro

most rewarding. The Ria and its subsidiary canals extend as far south as Mira and as far north as Ovar. There are many camping areas around. You will see the traditional *moliceiros,* shorelines dotted with saltpans, forests and villages, glorious sea fowl plummeting into the water after fish, and the sandbar which protects the city's access to the sea.

There is regular bus and boat service along the Ria. The tourist office runs a boat tour to the area twice daily in summer. In addition, you may rent tour boats on an hourly basis from the tourist office; there are several itineraries from which to select.

Tomar, about 75 miles southeast of Aveiro and about 40 miles south of Coimbra, is a beautiful town that also happens to be the site of an important historical monument, the castle/church of the Knights Templar and the Order of Christ. The town population of about 15,000 is settled between the banks of the Rio Nabão and the woods which overlook the town from low hills. In the old part of Tomar, narrow stone-paved streets are lined with whitewashed buildings from which bloom exuberant flowers. Whether for its gentle ambience or for a chance to learn a little of Portugal's history, Tomar is worth exploring.

Tomar was the home of the Knights Templar in Portugal, an order which was formed in 1119, during the Crusades. The order spread quickly through Europe, gaining extraordinary wealth, including properties throughout the continent. They also made powerful enemies, and in the early 1300s, with accusations of heresy and foul practices, and finally the suppression of the order altogether, they took refuge at their property in Tomar. They re-emerged in 1320, though under royal, as opposed to independent or papal control, as the Order of Christ. They played an important role in the exploration of other continents later, in the age of Portuguese discoveries.

In Tomar they left behind the marvelous ruins of the old Templar castle and the still intact church and cloisters on the site. The **castle** is located on a hill above the city, and the 10-minute walk up commands a view of the roofs of the old town. The castle is set alongside a forest, and the grounds are extensive and tranquil.

The castle itself is a maze of staircases, passages, nooks and crannies. The seven cloisters (only four are open to the public) have been added at irregular angles, leaving eccentric spaces between. Even the main entrance is oddly tucked into a corner.

Another scene of Aveiro's canal

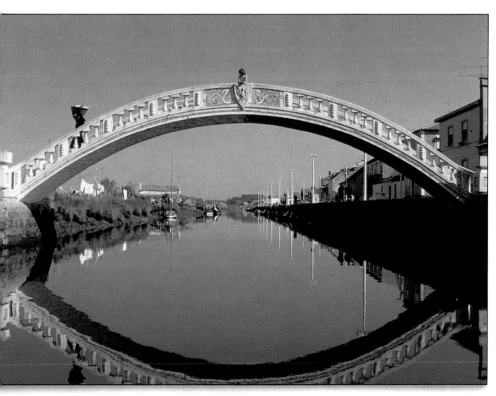

Inside the entrance, the original **Templar church** lies to the right. Begun in 1162, the octagonal temple was modeled on the Church of the Holy Sepulchre in Jerusalem. Here the knights would hear services while seated on their horses and pray for victory in battle. Despite its faded colors, the gilt painting on the walls still retains its majesty.

The **choir loft**, added much later, provides a sharp contrast to the original temple. Lighter, emptier and airier, this loft is an example of the Manueline style in full bloom.

Adjoining the original church is a 16th-century cloister with 17th-century tiles. Some of the tombs of the knights are found here. From here there is access to the upper level of the choir loft, then into the other cloisters. From the terrace of the small **Claustro de Santa Bárbara**, there is a view of the amazing, ornate, Manueline window structured around two deep relief carvings of ships' masts and decorated with knots, cork, coral, and seaweed. The whole is topped by a shield, crown and cross, symbol of the union of church and king.

From the opposite side of the building, there is a view of the surrounding forest and the castle yard where knights trained their horses and spent their free time. Also on this side lies an unfinished chapel, which was to be a copy of the entrance. Bad luck during construction led the superstitious knights to abandon it.

Tomar's **synagogue** is at Rua Joaquim Jacinto, 73. Although up to 70 percent of Portuguese have Jewish ancestry and Tomar was once the home of a thriving Jewish community, there are very few Jews left in Tomar or in Portugal. When in 1497 the Portuguese king married Isabella of Castile, part of the marriage contract was to expel the Jews from Portugal. Instead, Jews were allowed to remain if they converted, although practices were not closely monitored. Later, the Inquisition would brutally enforce these laws.

The synagogue/museum is simple and moving, decorated with gifts from all over the world. The director of the site will explain the synagogue's history and tell you about recent excavations and the ambitious plans for a bigger museum and library.

The church of **São João Baptista** has a dark wood ceiling and sombre atmosphere. There are 16th-century wood panel paintings on the walls depicting scenes including *The Last Supper* and *The Decapitation of John the Baptist*. On the left is a delicately carved pulpit.

Standing incongruously on an empty lot in the new part of town, **Santa Maria do Olival** is a lovely simple church dating from the 12th century. It was later remodeled.

The tourist office is located on Avenida Dr. Cándido Madureira, near the road to the castle.

The Martyred St. Irene: Santarém, the central town of Ribatejo, lies 30 miles down the Tagus River from Tomar. It was named for St. Irene, a young nun who was accused of being unchaste and so killed in 653 near Tomar. Her body, thrown into the river, washed ashore here, where apparitions attested to her innocence. The Romanesque-Gothic church of **São João de Alporão** contains a fine archaeological museum, as well as the beautifully carved tomb of Duarte, a son of Pedro I who died in the Battle of Alcacer-Quiber in 1458. It contains only one of Duarte's teeth, the sole relic retained by his wife.

Also in Santarém is the church of **Santa Clara**, originally part of a 13th-century convent. There are two tombs of Dona Leonor, the original and, below a lovely rose window, another from the 17th century. The church of **Nossa Senhora da Graça**, a bold Gothic structure with a beautiful nave, contains several tombs, among them that of Pedro Alvares Cabral, discoverer of Brazil.

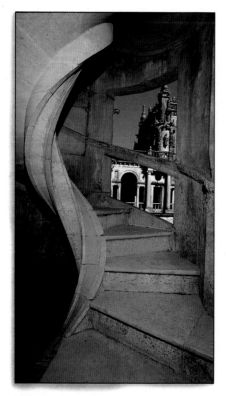

Detail of the Convent of Christ

Batalha's monastery perches like a wedding cake on one side of the Lisbon-Oporto highway. This incongruous sight rises suddenly around a bend in the road, and it's well worth getting off the highway to have a look. In fact, it's worth planning a special trip—by car or by bus—to one of Portugal's most beautiful monuments.

The **Santa Maria da Vitória Monastery** (the full name of Batalha's Abbey) traces its origins to Portugal's struggle to maintain its independence from Castile. One of the decisive battles for independence was fought at Aljubarrota, not far from Batalha. The Castilian king, Juan, based his claim to the Portuguese throne on his marriage to a Portuguese princess; he invaded Portugal to enforce the claim in 1385. The 20-year-old Dom João, Master of the order of Avis, illegitimate son of Pedro I, promised to raise a church to the Virgin Mary if the Portuguese won. With his young general, Nuño Álvares Pereira, João defeated Juan and became João I. Construction of the church began in 1388, and was completed—or, more accurately, was last worked on—in 1533.

The **front portal**, though large, is smaller than those of most Gothic churches. The arches sweep upward to a sculpture of figures representing the hierarchy in the heavenly court—as it was perceived in the Middle Ages. In the center is Christ surrounded by Matthew, Mark, Luke, and John.

Though the outside of the church is ornate, the interior is endowed with a simple Gothic elegance and dignity. The vaulted ceiling arches above a slender nave lighted by colorful stained glass. A feeling of light and spirit fill this room, intensified if you're fortunate enough to witness the organist playing.

The room to the right is the **Founder's Chapel** (Dom João's Pantheon), built around 1426 by João I. In the center are the tombs of João and his English queen, Philippa; the lovely carving on the top shows the pair holding hands. Other tombs, including that of Prince Henry the Navigator, are set into the walls under regal arches. The room is topped by a dome supported by star-shaped ribbing.

On the other side of the church you may enter **Dom João's Cloister**. Arches filled with Manueline ornamentation surround a pretty manicured courtyard. The arches are patterned with intricate, rope-like weavings decorated with vegetable motifs.

The **chapterhouse** is the first room off

the cloister. It has an unusual and beautiful ceiling with no support other than the walls. This seems to pull the whole room together to a central point. The impression is of precarious balance. The window is filled with a stained-glass scene of Christ on the Cross, remarkably rich in color. This room houses the tomb of two unknown soldiers, whose remains were returned to Portugal in 1921 from France and Mozambique. Above them, the sculpture of "Christ of the Trenches" was given by the French government in 1958. The lamp on the top burns Portuguese olive oil. The three armed soldiers guarding the tombs seem out of place in this otherwise peaceful setting.

Other rooms off the cloister house a **military museum** and temporary exhibits.

Another cloister abuts Dom João's: this is **Dom Afonso's**, a much simpler, austere construction with a lovely central garden. This cloister was built in the 15th century.

To reach Dom Duarte's Pantheon, or, as it is more commonly known, the **Unfinished Chapels**, it is necessary to exit the cloisters and walk along the outside of the monastery. This octagonal structure is attached to the outside wall of the church and, as it is abruptly roofless, it seems awkward. Ordered by Dom Duarte to house the tombs of himself and his family, the chapel was begun in the 1430s but never finished. No one is quite certain why, but it is likely that the building funds were redirected by the king to a project that interested him more.

The building contains simple chapels in each of seven walls. The chapel opposite the door holds the tomb of the king and Dona Leonor, his wife. The eighth wall is a massive door of limestone, with endless layers of beautifully detailed ornamentation carved in Manueline style.

There is little else to see in the village of Batalha. There is a shopping mall next to the monastery filled with tourist-oriented "handicraft" shops. The tourist office is located in the shopping mall.

About eight miles (12 km) south of Batalha lies the town of **Alcobaça**, named after two small rivers, the Alcoa and the Baça. At its center, and looking, oddly enough, right at home, is the huge, magnificent **Cistercian Abbey**. The first king of Portugal, Afonso Henriques, founded the monastery as thanks to St. Bernard for the capture of the town of Santarém from the Moors. Afonso laid the foundation stone himself, in 1148. There has been much alteration since, and now some sections are shut off for a variety of uses, including a home for the elderly.

The Unfinished Chapels of Batalha

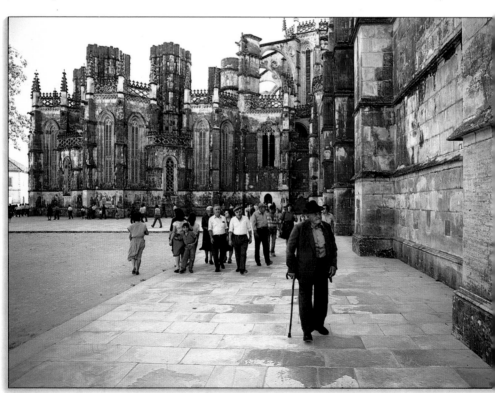

The Cistercian monks were a productive, vivacious bunch. Numbering, it is said 999 ("one less than a thousand"), they tilled the land around the abbey, making it to this day Portugal's greatest source of fruit. In 'Sebastião's reign, the exceedingly wealthy and powerful Alcobaça Abbey, or Santa Maria Abbey as it is also known, was declared by the Pope the seat of the entire Cistercian order. The monks were known for their lively spirits and lavish hospitality. They ran a school, perhaps the first public school in Portugal, at the abbey, and a sanctuary and hospice as well. In 1810, however, the abbey was sacked by French troops. In the Liberal Revolution of 1834, when all religious orders were expelled from Portugal, the abbey was again pillaged.

The long Baroque facade of the abbey, added in the 18th century, has twin towers in the center, below which are a Gothic doorway and rose window, the only part of the original facade left. Directly inside is the astonishingly serene and austere **church**. It is the largest church in Portugal, and the three equally tall aisles give a wonderful light to the clean lines. In the transepts are the justly famous, richly carved **tombs of Pedro I and Inês de Castro**, whose story is one of Portugal's most romantic (see page 17). Much of the damage to the carvings was caused by the French.

Off the south transept are several royal tombs, including those of Afonso II and Afonso III, and a sadly mutilated 17th-century terra-cotta of the Death of St. Bernard. To the east of the ambulatory, there are two fine Manuline doorways that were designed by João de Castilho.

An entrance in the north wall of the church leads to the **Cloister of Silence**. Several rooms branch off from the cloister, including the chapterhouse and, upstairs, a dormitory. There is a large but narrow **kitchen**, with an enormous center chimney and a remarkable basin—a rivulet runs through it which once provided the monks with not only water but a constant supply of fresh fish! Next door to the kitchen is the **refectory**, with steps built into one wall leading to a pulpit.

One other room of note is the **Sala dos Reis**, with statues, probably carved by monks, of many of the kings of Portugal. The panel in the same room, which tells the history of the abbey, is a rare example of a manuscript *azulejo* panel.

Also in Alcobaça is a ruined Moorish **castle**, which provides a fine view of the surrounding area.

Left, inside Batalha. Right, the beautiful lines of Alcobaça

FISHING COMMUNITIES

Women still gaze out over the sea along Portugal's Atlantic coast as they have since the rocky edge of western Europe was first settled by Phoenician sailors 3,000 years ago. Some wait anxiously for the fishing boats to return with their husbands, brothers, fathers and sons. Others, dressed in black, stare into waters that have claimed their menfolk for ever.

In a country whose character as well as its coastline has been shaped by crashing Atlantic breakers, fishing remains the trade most emblematic of the Portuguese soul. Skill in handling tides and winds, pioneering ship-building and navigational techniques, and the courage to explore the unknown took Portuguese navigators around the uncharted globe in the 15th and 16th centuries to discover new worlds.

Similar prowess and bravery—though toward humbler ends—is shown today by the hardy Portuguese fishermen who trawl for cod in the North Atlantic, harpoon whales off the Azores islands, or set sail in small boats into the treacherous Atlantic swell from the fishing communities that edge westernmost Europe.

A 90-minute journey northwest of Lisbon takes you to the port of **Peniche** and into the heart of the age-old Portuguese fishing industry. Like most of Portugal's coastal towns, Peniche has no natural harbor, only a bay sheltered by the rocky promontory of Cabo Carvoeiro, the second most westerly point in Europe. The town has built a seawall to protect the bay from the fury of Atlantic storms.

Peniche is an uncompromising town of some 15,000 people. Here, the waves beat against dramatic crags of black rock, and the spare white houses cling to the slopes for shelter from the sweeping northwesterly winds. Too stark and exposed for tourism to have taken hold, the town typifies life in Portuguese fishing communities, where the people labor to subsist from the sea in a daily struggle with the weather and the limitations of outdated equipment.

The **Fortaleza Prison** physically dominates the town. The veteran leader of Portugal's communist Party, Alvaro Cunhal, and others, who had been held there by the pre-1974 authoritarian regime, escaped in 1960. They climbed down the cliffs to a waiting boat that reportedly took them to a Soviet-bloc submarine. Later, Fortaleza served the nobler purpose of a refugee camp for

the *retournados*, who arrived after the colonies were declared independent. Today, the building serves as a museum, containing an interesting hodge-podge of local artifacts, crafts and natural history.

Most of the boats that work out of Peniche are small trawlers, or *traineiras*, about 80-feet (24-meters) long, powered by diesel engines with a cabin enclosing the wheel andequipped with a basic VHF radio of limited range. They are wooden-hulled with high, broad bows and, characteristic of all Portuguese fishing boats, painted in bright yellows, blues, reds and greens. These colors and designs, that lend such gaiety to fishing villages are not just an aesthetic whimsy. The unique creations, serve the eminently practical purpose of enabling skippers to recognize individual boats at a distance.

Traineiras, old and battered though many of them are, stand in the front rank of Portuguese fishing. Of the country's 11,000 working boats, only a small number are more than 40-feet (12-meters) long and two-thirds are powered by oar or sail. Most vessels are 20 years old or more, and little more than 100 are designed to fish in deep waters.

Peniche bustles with activity when the boats return, usually early in the morning, low in the water laden with their catch, the sea birds wheeling hungrily behind. The men hurl plastic crates packed with gleaming fish from the decks high up onto the quay where the women sort the catch before it is taken to the auction building, known as the *lota*, to be sold.

The catch varies, but the bulk of it is usually

Preceding page, Mira beach. Left, dawn at Nazaré. Above, mariner's workhorse at rest

sardines, the fish that accounts for more than a third of the 250,000 metric tons of fish harvested by Portugal each year. The other main catches are cod from Newfoundland and Greenland, accounting for about 10,000 metric tons, and some 8,000 metric tons of tuna from around the islands of Madeira and the Azores. Much of the sardine and tuna is canned for both export and domestic use, in factories such as the one in Peniche, using another of the country's main products, olive oil.

A good night's fishing could land a catch worth $5,000. The owner's share is usually a little more than half, out of which he has to meet high running and maintenance costs, particularly fuel. The remainder is divided between the crew of around 25 in decreasing sums depending on position. These would be high earnings in Portugal if they were consistent. But many nights at sea

force as you dip and rise across to the red granite outcroppings that loom 300 feet (90 meters) above the sea. The trip is nevertheless well worth taking. A 17th-century **fortress**, now converted to an inn, the **lighthouse** and a few fishermen's cottages are the only buildings. The entire island has been demarcated a national bird sanctuary, and seagulls and eider are everywhere. Officials patrol the make-shift paths to ensure that visitors don't wander into forbidden territory and distrub the birds. Rabbits and flowers abound, but the greatest excitement lies in taking a boat trip around the reefs, caves and smaller islands, past a breathtaking sea tunnel called the **Furado Grande**. The ferry runs from June to September; the trip takes one hour.

Sport fisherman often choose the Berlengas as a home base. It is a simple matter to catch more

yield catches of very little value or nothing at all; often the weather prevents boats leaving harbor for days on end.

Some 40,000 men are employed in the fishing industry, some spending long months in the freezing North Atlantic fishing for cod, others facing fire from Polisario guerrillas off North Africa and many plying Portugal's difficult coastal waters. Small open boats, age-old methods and obsolescent equipment put the mariner's safety constantly at risk.

A sense of the Atlantic swell that is the fisherman's constant companion and nemesis can be felt by taking the ferry from Peniche to the **Berlengas Islands**, seven miles (four km) off-shore. Once out of the shelter of the peninsula, the powerful current rocks the boat with unexpected

mackerel and sardines than you want, and with a little expertise and experience you can land a 100 lb. (45 kg) swordfish. Most off-shore fishing does not require a license. It is available all year (inland the season is limited to April through November). Complete fishing trips—including bait, tackle, and a professional craft—are available at Peniche, Ericeira and Nazaré.

The hazards faced by Portuguese fishermen are reflected in their strong Roman Catholic faith and the many religious festivals along the coast dedicated to blessing their vessels and praying for their safety. On the first Sunday in August, the people of Peniche hold a typical celebration in the festival of Our Lady of Safe Voyages (**A Nossa Senhora da Boa Viagem**).

The image of the Virgin, the fishermen's patroness, is carried by night from its shrine on the rocky cape to the harbor in a procession of boats gaily decorated with colored paper and lit by lanterns. Carrying candles, the townspeople gather on the quay beside the twinkling vessels as a priest, in a fishing boat moored alongside, blesses the small fleet.

For several days after this stirring convocation ceremony Peniche gives itself over to the *festa*. A fair fills the streets, brass bands play, fireworks burst over the harbor and the town dances into the early hours under the stars.

The daily labors of the Peniche fishermen and their seasonal celebrations are part of the general rhythm of life along the Portuguese coast. But every community has its unique character and traditions.

Thirty miles (48 km) north, the fishing port of

abound. But the life of the hardy fishermen goes on as it has for centuries, almost indifferent to the crowds of holiday-makers.

Because they had no natural harbor, the fishermen used to launch their boats from the beach. They managed this by pushing their craft down log rollers into the sea then clambering aboard and rowing furiously till they overrode the incoming breakers. When they arrived home again, the boats were winched ashore by oxen and later by tractors. The building of a modern anchorage at the south of the beach has relieved the fishermen of this arduous labor.

Similarly the traditional dress for which the Nazaré fisherfolk are famed—having become one of the most photographed populations in all of Portugal—is today seen more in souvenir shops than on the townspeople. But some women

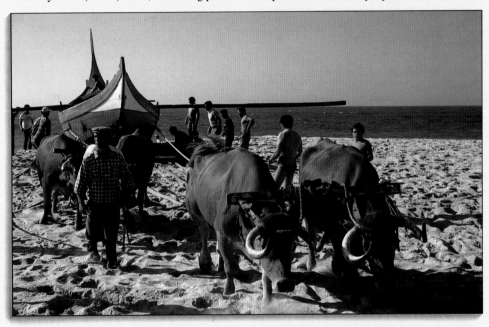

Nazaré nestles along a sweeping mile-long bay, a brightly-colored, gay and bustling town in striking contrast to the severity of Peniche. In summer, thousands of holiday-makers pack the beach in rows of peaked, striped canvas tents that create the rather romantic atmosphere of a Moorish battle camp.

The abundance of tourists vitiates some of Nazaré's charm, but it also assures that all the visitor's desires will be catered to. Pleasant seafood restaurants and small hotels line the sandy bay; esplanade cafes, bars and souvenir shops

Left, the "Good Voyage" promises many more. Above, winching the boats ashore at the end of a long day, the old-fashioned way

still wear the seven colored petticoats under a wide black skirt and cover their head with a black scarf or shawl; the men still favor woolen shirts in traditional plaids, but few wear the distinctive black stocking bonnets whose tops fall down to the shoulder.

The Nazaré fishing boat is traditionally about 18-feet (five-meters) long with a flat-bottomed hull and high bow rising in a spiked crescent. These boats with distinguishing eyes, stars and other symbols painted on the prow can still be seen at the south of the bay. But motorized *traineira* today account for the bulk of the fisher's catch. The yield is mainly sardines along with whiting, blue mackerel, sole and perch, and is sold at the *lota* or canned in a local factory.

Nazaré named from a statue of the Virgin that

a 4th-century monk brought to the town from Nazareth, lives literally on two levels. In the lower part of town, small, white-walled fishermen's cottages line the narrow alleyways. High above on the cliff that towers 360 feet (109 meters) above the old town is the quarter known as *Sítio*. Reached by a funicular that climbs the tallest cliffside in Portugal, Sítio is dominated by a large square and on its edge the tiny **chapel** built to commemorate a miracle in 1182 when Our Lady of Nazaré saved the local lord by stopping his horse from plunging off the cliff as he pursued a deer.

The 17th-century **Church of Our Lady of Nazaré** on the other side of the square is the focus for the annual religious festivities during the second week of September that include processions and bullfights in the Sítio ring. The steep,

narrow pathway and steps from the **lighthouse** west of the church affords stirring views of Atlantic breakers crashing against the rocks.

One of the most enjoyable aspects of becoming acquainted with Portugal's fishing communities is sampling the freshest of fish. Peniche and Nazaré are both ideal venues.

For excellent grilled fish, usually served with boiled potatoes, vegetables and a butter sauce, choose between *robalo* (bass), *cherne* (turbot), *salmonettes* (red mullet), *garoupa* (merou) and *peixe espada* (scabbard fish). *Espadarte* (sword fish), either grilled or smoked as an hors d'ouevre, is a delicacy worth paying a little extra for. Other delights probably less familiar to visitors include *tamboril* (monkfish) with a texture similar to shellfish, *lulas* (cuttlefish), *chocos*

(squid), *polvo* (octopus) and *safio* (conger eels).

Shellfish has grown expensive in Portugal as much of it is imported. But a visitor who can splash out a little on a local crayfish (*logosta*) or lobster (*lavagante*) is unlikely to regret it. An excellent setting is the picturesque fishing village of **Ericeira**, 30 miles (48 km) outside Lisbon and south of Peniche.

The village, which takes its name from the abundance of sea hedgehogs, or *ouriços,* found there, is on the clifftops looking down onto the rocky beaches. A winding path leads down to the tiny fishing beach protected by a jetty and concrete boulders piled into the sea to break the Atlantic current. From the wall high up above the small harbor, you can watch the fishermen unload their catch, mend their nets and repaint their boats.

The tiny chapel of **Santo António** above the harbor is the center of the summer festa. The chapel—and a replica of a fishing boat holding a statue of the Virgin—are filled with hundreds of candles lit by the townspeople as a prayer for the safety of the fishermen. The Virgin is carried at night in a procession down to the harbor where the priest blesses the brightly decorated boats.

A tiled plaque on the side of the chapel records the flight of King Manuel II and his family from the beach here in October, 1910, after the monarchy was overthrown and Portugal became a republic. The king sailed via Gibraltar to Britain where he lived the rest of his life in exile, devoting himself to amassing an important collection of early Portuguese books. Documents including British newspaper reports on the escape can be seen in Ericeira's small but interesting **municipal museum**. Ericeira becomes a bustling resort in the summer not least of all sought for its seafood, much of it raised in tanks on the rocky shore.

Ericeira, Nazaré and Peniche are similar in spirit to the many other fishing communities that have struggled for centuries to earn a living from the sea on the frontier where Europe meets the Atlantic. Each is unique; others that will reward a visit include **Sesimbra** nestled beneath the beautiful Arrábida Hills south of Lisbon; the beautiful bay of **São Martinho do Porto;** and **São Pedro de Moel** surrounded by Pine forest close to Nazaré.

In the north, **Vila do Conde** at the mouth of the Ave River is renowned for its lacemakers' procession in the third week of June, which winds across the candle-lit town to the beach. **Viana do Castelo** has prospered since the 16th century as the home of fishermen who brave the distant and icy Atlantic waters to fish for cod off Newfoundland.

Above, amateur fisherman still hoping to land dinner as the day nears its end. Right, a successful day's catch of sardines, destined for the *lota*

THE WINE DISTRICTS

Northern Portugal is wine country par excellence. Fine vineyards flourish throughout the land, but the best known wines, dating back to Roman times, come from the districts of Minho and Douro.

The two provinces make up an area shaped like a large L: From the Minho River on the northern border with Spain, south to the Douro, then along the river valley eastward to Spain again. Grapes are grown everywhere. They hang from trees, pergolas and porches, and climb along slopes and terraces. They grow in rocky, poor soil where little else flourishes.

There are still great old grape-growing estates but most grapes are produced on small farms and then sold either to cooperatives or to large companies. The *vindimia,* or grape harvest, is still done by hand and is a wonderful sight to behold. Harvesting occurs in September and October and lasts until early November. It is often a hazardous task, requiring towering 30-rung ladders to get at the elusive treetop grapes. In the hilly country, men still carry on their backs huge baskets of grapes weighing as much as 150 pounds (70 kilograms). On some back roads, squeaky oxcarts still transport the grapes to wine-presses. In these modern times, however, the fruit is generally transported in trucks.

While harvest is a festive occasion, it is no longer the unbridled merry-making of yore. In the old days, workers used to perform a kind of bacchanal dance, their arms linked and stamping on the grapes with their bare feet. It was said that this was the only way to crush the fruit without smashing the pips and spoiling the flavor of the wine. This was often accompanied by music and clapping, glasses of spirits and a good deal of sweat. Nowadays, mechanical presses are generally used to crush the grapes, although treading still takes place on some of the small farms. (For more information on Portugal's wines, see article "Moscatels, Ports and *Vinhos Verdes*" found on page 255)

The Douro: The name means "of gold" and the river, on certain glowing days, does resemble a twisting golden chain as it winds through the narrow valley between the steep hills and terraced vineyards. The countryside is exceptionally beautiful, particularly in spring and fall. To explore the Douro Valley, the point of departure is the city of

Oporto. The river wends its way for about 130 miles (210 km) in Portugal and then another 70 miles (110 km) along the border with Spain. One option is a bus tour to the port wine estates, offered by several travel agencies in Porto. The N108 road runs along the northern bank as far as Regua and the N222 follows the southern shores of the river, sometimes high above, sometimes along the water's edge. There is also a train that runs along the northern bank of the river, crossing at **Saõ João da Pesqueiro** and continuing along the southern bank until the Spanish border at **Barco d'Alva.** The ride takes about six hours.

The **Lower Douro** is technically *vinho verde* country although farther north, the Minho, is more closely associated with the "green" or young wines. The main town is **Penafiel**, between the Sousa and the Tâmega Rivers. There are some lovely old granite houses with gargoyles and wooden balconies and a 16th-century **parish church.**

A few miles to the northeast lies the charming town of **Amarante**, on the bank of the Rio Tâmega. The three-arched **bridge** was built in 1790. It leads to the convent of São Gonçalo, named after the local patron saint, protector of marriages. The festival held in the Saint's honor every June is a particularly raucous one—and distinctly phallic cakes are served during it.

The convent, however, is much more somber. It was begun in 1540 but not completed until 1620. Inside is the tomb of São Gonçalo, who died about 1260, and some lush gilded carved woodwork. There are two cloisters; above the rear one is the **Museu de Albano Sardoeira**, which includes some modern Portuguese painting— Sardoeira, was a cubist artist from Amarante.

Nearby is the **Quinta da Aveleda**, seat of one of Portugal's main wine empires and leading exporter of *vinho verde*. The Quinta is included on some wine-tasting tours. Individual visitors are welcome but advised to make prior arrangements at the company's office in Oporto. A tour of the 500 acre (200 hectares) Aveleda estate includes a visit to the **family chapel**, which was built in 1671. The luxuriant gardens contain a ruin from Prince Henry the Navigator's Palace in Oporto. One can also observe contemporary *vinho verde* production: miles upon miles of grapes; climbing poles, trellises and crosses; and mechanical crushers, modern concrete storage vats and mechanized bottling and labeling.

Preceding pages, the Rio Tâmega near Amarante; a round of cards in Gerês; a regional fair. Below, the Sandeman Port House

At the wine lodge visitors are invited to taste different types of *vinho verde*. Those who wish to purchase a bottle or a case may do so in the old distillery, now converted into a store.

Beyond, the road turns abruptly south, running parallel to the Douro. From **Mesão Frio**, on a steep hillside, there is a sweeping view of the Upper Douro twisting through the gorges and port wine country.

Portugal's authoritarian Marquês de Pombal staked out the Douro in 1756, making it the first officially designated wine-producing region in the world. Subsequent legislation designated the Upper Douro as the Port Wine Region. The area stretches along the Douro River Valley from **Barqueiros**, south of Mesão Frio, to **Barca d'Alva** on the Spanish border. It includes the valleys of tributaries.

The port wine vineyards grow on neatly terraced hillside farms along the Douro. Seignorial manors and whitewashed cottages perch among the vineyards and olive groves. The climate is cold, wet and foggy in winter. Summers are hot, and made hotter by the direct rays of the sun reflected on the schist, or crystalline rock.

Regua is a busy river port and headquarters of the Port Wine Institute, founded in 1932 to establish quality control. In the area lie some of the oldest British and Portuguese estates. Here the road crosses the Douro and runs along the southern bank, recrossing the river at **Pinhão**, another wine center.

Nearby lies the **Quinta Do Infantado**, an ancient wine estate that had once belonged to Prince Pedro. The Roseira family, which has owned the property since the turn of the century, recently began selling a drier "Estate Bottled" port directly, without going through the normal channels of shippers of Vila Nova Da Gaia. Other locally bottled wines, that have challenged the Gaia monopoly are Quinta Cotto and Roma Nera. A grape growers' association has since been established to stand up to the shippers.

At Pinhão, the traveler should make a side trip north to **Sabrosa,** the birthplace of Fernão de Magalhães, better known as Magellan, the man who led the first tour around the world in 1522—under the Spanish flag.

A couple of miles northwest is the village of **Mateus,** with its celebrated **palace** and **gardens.** It was built by Nicolau Nasoni in 1739-43 for António José Botelho Mourão. Today, an illustration of the palace graces the distinctive label of the less-than-distinctive rosé wine from this area. The handsome

Terraced vineyards and a port house on the Douro

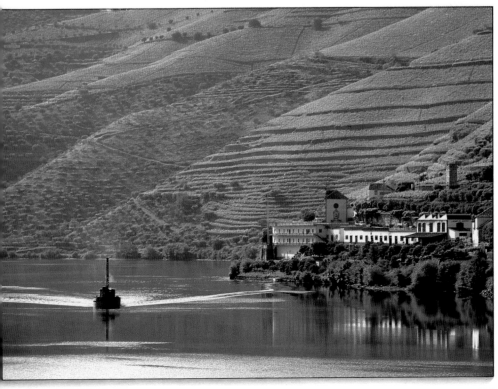

building with whitewashed facade, double stairway, and huge coat of arms has been restored and is open for visits.

To break the journey, a road leads southeast to the valley of the **Tua** with its orange groves, and crossing the Douro again, climbs along the terraced hills to São João da Pesqueira, on a plateau. Winding along the contours of the hills, past quaint churches and the ruins of a castle, one comes to **Vila Nova de Fozcôa** and the valley of the **Côa**. Then the road moves away from the Douro, heading either north or south. The railroad, however, continues along the Douro, with spectacular views of the steep vineyard. It ends in Barca d'Alva, at the Spanish border—which is also the end of port wine country.

The Minho: Nowadays the Minho is generally called Costa Verde, or the Green Coast, a reference to the vineyards and thick pine forests along the shore. It is beautiful countryside, with joyous fairs, festivals and pilgrimages. Foreigners do not often travel here. The Minhotos are naturally good-tempered and hard-working; they seem to enjoy life.

With Oporto as a starting point again, the best way to visit the Minho is to drive up the coast and return by an inland route. The Atlantic beaches are generally broad with fine sand, but the sea is cold and rough. A fishing town and resort, **Vila do Conde**, is the site of the vast **Convent of Santa Clara**, which was founded in 1318, the 16th-century parish church of **São João Baptista** and a lovely 17th-century **fortress**. Travelers are welcome to watch how fishing boats are made and visit the lace-making school. Nearby, **Póvoa de Varzim** is another popular fishing port-resort, with an 18th-century **fort** and a **parish church**. There's also a casino and a modern luxury hotel, the Vermar dom Pedro, with heated pools and tennis courts. Further north, **Ofir** is a delightful sea and pine forest resort. Just across the **Cávado** River is the town of **Esposende** with the remains of an 18th-century **fortress**. There are many new, often garishly-painted houses in towns and villages along the way; many of these have been built by remittances from Portuguese workers in France and Germany.

A lively fishing and ship-building port, **Viana do Castelo** was called *Diana* by the Romans. This was the center of Portugal's wine trade until the port declined in the 18th century and Oporto took preeminence. There is a good deal to see in Viana, starting with the 18th-century **Palace of Távoras**, **Play mariners**

now the main Tourist Office. On the central **Praça da República**, there's a beautiful 16th-century fountain and the remarkable **Misericórdia Hospital**, with its three-tiered facade supported by caryatids. Nearby stands the handsome 15th-century **parish church** with a Gothic portal and Romanesque towers. The town is dominated by **Monte Santa Luzia,** with a rather ungainly modern basilica. To the west, in a large field, the baroque **Nossa Senhora da Agonia** church is the site of a popular pilgrimage every August. Dancers, musicians, and other celebrants, wearing red- and-white traditional costumes, come from all over Minho to take part in the three-day festival.

Continuing north, the road leads to **Caminha**, an attractive town with echoes of its past as a busy trading port. The parish church, dating from the 15th century, has a beautiful carved-wood ceiling. There are a number of lovely 15th- and 16th-century buildings near the main square.

At the estuary of the **Minho River**, the road turns inland and follows the river, which forms the border with Spain. **Valença do Minho** is a bustling border town with shops and markets. Spaniards come here regularly to purchase items that include coffee, cigarettes and crystal chandeliers. The Portuguese, on the other hand, cross the border frequently to Tuy or Vigo to buy canned goods such as asparagus and artichokes, and ready-made clothing. The old town of Valença is still fairly intact with cobbled streets and stone houses with iron balconies. It is surrounded by 17th-century granite ramparts. The ancient **convent**, with a splendid view of the Minho River and Spain, that has been since converted into a *pousada*.

From **Monção**, a fortified town famous for its spring water as well as its wines, one takes the road south through the heart of the Minho province: lush green countryside, crisscrossed by rivers with medieval stone bridges; simple white churches with elaborate granite doorways and windows; and, of course, unending vineyards. Because of the high population density, the land has been divided and sub-divided for generations, so the average property is an acre or two. To get the most out of the land, the Minhotos train their vines to grow up, on trees, houses and hedges, leaving ground-space for cabbages, onions and potatoes. This free-wheeling system has made it difficult to modernize grape production, but in recent years, the larger farms have begun to use a system of crosses called *cruzetas*.

The road passes **Arcos de Valdevez**, a charming hillside town built on the two banks of the **Vez River**, with a magnificent view of the valley. Just a few miles south, **Ponte de Barca** on the left bank of the **Lima River**, has a lovely 15th-century **parish church** and an old **town square**, but the principal attraction is the fine stone **bridge** with arches, built in 1543 and restored on several occasions.

Here the traveler should turn westward, along the beautiful valley of the Lima River, which the Romans believed was the Lethe, the mythological river of oblivion. Situated here are great estates or *solares*, a tangible reminder of the glories of the old empire. Some are now guesthouses, and arrangements to visit these manors should be made beforehand in the Portuguese tourist office in Lisbon or Viana do Castelo.

Generally the owners or family members live in the *solares* and welcome visitors to share their way of life. This might mean hunting and fishing, taking part in the grape harvest, or simply holding long conversations by the fireplace. Each *solar* has its own history and charm. On the outskirts of **Ponte de Lima,** the original tower of the **Quinta de Sabadão** was built in the 16th century, and the house has been in the Abreu

Vila do Conde's aqueduct (1705-14) peers above the rooftops

Lima family since the beginning of the 17th century. The lady of the manor proudly shows visitors the family portraits, antiques and her great-grandfather's diary from the war against Napoleon.

Ponte de Lima is one of the loveliest towns in Portugal, mainly because of its location on the south bank of the Lima River. The town faces a magnificent long **Roman Bridge** with low arches. Remains from the old city wall still stand. A 15th-century **palace** with crenellated facade is now used as a hospital. Across the river, stand the 15th-century **São António convent** has beautiful woodwork, including two Baroque shrines.

Continuing towards Viana do Castelo, there are more *solares*, such as the **Casa de Cortegaça**, with its great stone tower dating back to the 15th century. This is a working manor, with wine cellars, flour mill and stable. Guests are welcome to take part in the farm life.

South of Viana, another inland road leads to the charming market town of **Barcelos**, on the northern bank of the **Cávado River**. Barcelos boasts 15th-century **fortifications**, a 13th-century **church** and a 16th-century **palace**, but more than that, it has one of the best handicraft fairs in the coun-

try. Every Thursday, merchants and artisans display their folk art and other wares at the fairgrounds in the center of town. It was here that the late Rosa Ramalho, Portugal's Grandma Moses, created her world of fanciful ceramic animals and people. These can be seen in the **Ceramic Art Museum**, which is connected to the parish church. Other popular items include copperware, hand-made rugs, wooden toys, bright cotton tableware, and of course the Barcelos cock, now the national emblem.

According to the medieval legend, a pilgrim from Galicia was suspected of committing murder and condemned to death. Protesting his innocence, the Galician pointed to a roast chicken on the magistrate's table, and declared, "As surely as I stand innocent, so will that cock crow when I am hanged." The cock obligingly crowed *before* the sentence was carried; the prisoner was set free and a monument built to mark the miracle.

Guimarães: A busy manufacturing town noted mainly for textiles, shoes and cutlery, Guimarães still possesses many reminders of its past glory as birthplace of the Portuguese nation.

In the year 1128, an 18-year-old boy named Afonso Henriques proclaimed inde-

The serenity and beauty of Ponte de Lima

206

pendence for the county of Portucale from the kingdom of León and Castille. It was in the field of **São Mamede**, near Guimarães, that the young Afonso Henriques defeated his mother's army, which was battling on behalf of Alfonso VII, king of León and Castile.

The city's Festival of Saint Walter, the *Festas Gualterianas*, dates from the middle of the 15th century. This three-day celebration, held on the first weekend in August, includes a torchlight procession, a fair with traditional dances and a medieval parade.

Guimarães has long been the center of the Portuguese linen industry. It still produces high quality, coarse linen from home-grown flax naturally bleached by the sun. The region is also known for its hand embroidery on linen. This, unfortunately, is gradually being replaced by machine.

A visit should begin at the 10th-century **castelo** on the northern side of town. It is believed that Afonso Henriques was born here in 1110, the son of Henri of Burgundy, count of Portucale, and his wife Teresa. The castle is a large mass of walls and towers on a rocky hill with magnificent view of the mountains. The dungeon and fortifications were restored many times. Early in the 19th century, the castle was used as a debtors' prison; it was restored again in 1940. At the entrance stands the small Romanesque chapel of **São Miguel do Castelo** with the original font where Afonso Henriques was baptized in 1111.

Heading into town, one passes the 15th-century Gothic **Palace of the Dukes of Bragança,** now occasionally used as an official residence by the President of the Republic. Otherwise, it is open to the public. This massive granite construction consists of four buildings around a cloister and has been completely restored. Outside is a fine statue of Afonso Henriques by Soares dos Reis. Visitors may also view the splendid wood ceiling of the Banquet Hall, the Persian carpets, French tapestries, ancient portraits and documents.

The **Rua de Santa Maria**, with its cobblestones and 14th- and 15th-century houses with wrought-iron balconies leads to the center of town. On the left lies the **Convento de Santa Clara**, built in the 17th century and now used as the Town Hall.

Nossa Senhora de Oliveira, originally of the 10th century, was rebuilt by Count Henri in the 12th century; it has since undergone several restorations. Still visible are the 16th-century watchtower and 14th-century western portal and window.

According to a 7th-century legend, an old Visigoth warrior named Wamba was tilling his field near Guimarães when a delegation came to tell him he had been elected king. He refused to take the office. Driving his staff into the ground, Wamba declared that not until it bore leaves would he become king. As these things happen, the staff turned into an olive tree. The church was named in honor of the miracle.

Adjacent to the church of Oliveira, the Romanesque cloisters have been converted into the **Museu de Alberto Sampaio**. This includes the church's rich **treasury** of 12th-century silver chalices and Gothic and Renaissance silver crucifixes as well as 15th- and 16th-century statues, paintings and ceramics.

The busiest square in Guimarães is the **Largo do Toural**. Just beyond, the church of **São Domingoes** was built in the 14th century and still has the original transept, rose window over the portal, and lovely Gothic cloister. The **Museu Martins Sarmento** is located in the cloister, built in 1271 and enlarged early in the 20th century. Here are artifacts and objects from Briteiros and other citânais—ancient Iberian fortified villages—of northern Portugal; statues, Roman votives, inscriptions, ceramics and coins.

Continuing along the broad garden called the **Almeda da Liberdade**, one reaches the church of **São Francisco**, founded in the 13th century. There is little left of the original Gothic structure. However, the sacristy is very fine with its 17th-century gilt woodwork and ceiling.

High on the outskirts of the city stands a most interesting building. **Santa Marinha da Costa** was founded as a monastery in the 12th century and rebuilt in the 18th century. The church functions regularly and may be visited. The cells of the monastery, which were badly damaged by fire in 1951, have recently been restored with great care and turned into a luxury *pousada*. Visible in the **cloisters** are a 10th-century Mozarab arch and vestiges of a 7th-century Visigoth structure. The veranda is decorated with magnificent 18th-century tile scenes and a fountain.

After seeing the Briteiros exhibit at the Martins Sarmento Museum, the traveler must visit the original site, only six miles north toward Braga. At first, the **Citânia de Briteiros** appears to be nothing more than piles of stones on a hillside, but is in fact one of Portugal's most important archaeological sites. Here are the remains of a prehistoric fortified village said to have been inhabited by Celts. It was discovered in 1874 by archaeologist Francisco Martins

Sarmento. At the summit, a small chapel and two round houses have been restored. Also visible are the remains of triple defensive walls, ancient flagstones and foundation walls of some 150 houses. Most houses were circular with stone benches running around the wall. A large rock in the center supported a pole that in turn held up a thatched roof. Several houses are larger, with two or more rectangular rooms. The town seems to have been well organized with a water system: spring water flowed from the top of the hill down gutters carved in the paving stones to a cistern and a public fountain.

Braga: Some people still refer to the Braga somewhat wistfully as "the Portuguese Rome." They point out that in Roman times, it was known as *Bracara Augusta* and was the center of communications in North Lusitania. In the 6th century, two synods were held here. Under Moorish occupation, Braga was sacked and the cathedral badly damaged. But in the 11th century, the city was largely restored to its former eminence by Bishop Dom Pedro and Archbishop São Geraldo. The Archbishop claimed authority over all the churches of the Iberian Peninsula, and his successors retained the title of Primate of the Spains for six centuries. Like a Renaissance prince, Archbishop Dom Diogo de Sousa in the 16th century encouraged the construction of the many handsome Italian-style churches, fountains and palaces. Zealous prelates restored many of these works in the 17th and 18th centuries, but often with unfortunate results.

Braga lost its title as ecclesiastical capital in 1716, when the Patriarchate was established in Lisbon. Even so, Braga is still an important religious center, the site of the most elaborate Holy Week procession in the country, with torches, floats, folk-dancing and fireworks.

Any visit to Braga begins at the **Sé**, built in the 11th century on the site of an earlier structure destroyed by the Moors. Of the original Romanesque building, there remains only the southern portal and the sculpted cornice of the transept. Although it has been greatly modified by various restorations, the cathedral is still an imposing edifice, with its great facade, twin towers, transept and dome. The interior contains a fine granite sculpture of the Virgin, an 18th-century choirloft and organ case and richly decorated chapels and cloister. The cathedral treasury is now a **Museum of Religious Art** with a fine collection of vestments

The gardens at Bom Jesús do Monte

going back to the 15th century, and silver chalices and crucifixes of the 10th and 12th centuries.

Nearby, in a garden with an 18th-century fountain, is the **Palace of the Archbishop,** built in the 14th century. It, too, has been reconstructed several times. The palace now houses the **Public Library**, with city archives dating to the 9th century, 300,000 volumes and 10,000 manuscripts.

On the other side of the **Agrolongo Square** stands one of the Rome-inspired churches, **Nossa Senhora do Pópulo**, built in the 17th century and remodeled at the end of the 18th century. It is decorated with tiles showing the life of St. Augustine.

The **Casa dos Biscainhos**, across the way, is a 17th-century mansion with lovely garden and fountains. Now a museum, the collection includes 18th-century tiles, ceramics, jewelry and furniture. Part of the museum has been set aside for artifacts from the recent excavations at **Colina de Maximinos**. Long known as the original site of *Bracara Augusta*, a protected zone finally was finally established in 1977—after some damage from modern construction. The university of Minho is directing the excavations, which have uncovered **Roman Baths**, a sanctuary called "**Fonte do Idilio**"

and the remains of a house called "**Domus de Santiago**." These may be visited.

On the northern side of the city, the church of **São João de Souto** was completely rebuilt in the late 18th century. But here is the superb **Chapel of Conceição,** built in 1525, with crenellated walls, lovely windows and splendid statues of St. Anthony and St. Paul.

There are many other churches and chapels of interest in the religious center, but the best known is **Bom Jesús**, on the wooded **Monte Espinho**, just outside the city. This popular pilgrimage center is remarkable, not so much for the building but for its grandiose stairway and the view from its terrace of the Cávado River valley and mountains in the distance. The double flight of stairs is flanked by chapels, fountains and terra-cotta figures at each level, representing the Stations of the Cross. If a visitor is not up to making the climb, there's a funicular and a winding road to the top. There, in a park of huge oak trees, eucalyptus, camelias and mimosa, stands the 15th-century church, rebuilt in the 18th century. In its **Chapel of Miracles**, there are many votives and pictures left by past pilgrims. Several hotels, souvenir shops and restaurants are also located near the sanctuary.

Thousands gather at the sanctuary of Bom Jesús do Monte each Pentacost

OPORTO

As its name implies, Oporto is the commercial center of northern Portugal and is the hub of the lucrative port wine trade. (The Potuguese spelling, by the way, is simply *Porto*.) Like Lisbon, Oporto is clustered on hills overlooking a river. But unlike the pastel walls and Mediterranean light of Lisbon. Oporto is a northern European city with granite church towers, stolid dark buildings, narrow streets and hidden Baroque treasures.

Posed majestically on the rocky cliffs overlooking the Douro River, Oporto is linked by three bridges to Vila Nova de Gaia, an industrial area where most of the wine lodges are located. Large ships often dock at the seaport of Leixões because of frequent silting of the Douro estuary; but coal barges, fishing trawlers and other small vessels still sail up the river.

The climate is temperate and the *Portuenses,* as the inhabitants are called, are traditionally industrious. The population of Greater Oporto is about one million.

In Roman times, the twin cities at the mouth of the Douro were known as Portus on the right bank and Cale on the left bank. During the Moorish occupation, the entire region between the Minho and Douro rivers was called Portucale. When Afonso Henriques founded the new kingdom in the 12th century, he took the name of his home province and called it Portucalia.

Closely linked to Portugal's golden epoch of the Discoveries, Oporto prospered from the seafaring exploits. Its shipyards produced the caravels that sailed around the world. Prince Henry, who founded the country's school of navigation, was born in Oporto. Also proudly numbered among the *Portueses* are the poet Almeida Garrett and novelist Julio Dinis.

The city's close English connections developed with the wine trade. According to some Portuguese accounts, it was actually the English who discovered port wine. They say that in 1678, two sons of a wealthy English merchant stayed for awhile in a monastery on the Upper Douro. They discovered that by adding a little brandy to the sweet wine of the Douro, it was sufficiently fortified to withstand temperature changes and long sea voyages. When the brothers returned to England, they reportedly took back large quantities of this fortified wine, which came to be known as port.

Pasquale Iocca, a wine authority with the Portuguese Trade Commission in New York, gives a different story. He notes that in the 17th and 18th centuries, the wines of the Upper Douro were robust table wines. Then in 1820, a "climatic accident" occurred, with very warm weather producing unusually sweet grapes and a wine appreciated by the British. In the following years, amid much controversy, the wine companies added *aguardente,* or brandy, to stop the fermentation and fix the sugar content. This was the beginning of the sweet fortified nectar as it is known today.

Whatever the history is, the Methuen Treaty of 1703 opened English markets to Portuguese wines, and the British shippers of Oporto became increasingly rich and powerful. In 1727 they established a Shippers Association, which regulated the trade and controlled prices paid to Portuguese growers. To combat the English monopoly, the dictator Pombal founded the Alto Douro Wine Company in 1757, which restored a measure of Portuguese control.

Rose Macaulay describes whimsically how British port wine shippers virtually "captured and occupied" Oporto in her delightful book, *They Went to Portugal.* She notes that the "Oporto families, some of

eft, plenty
f activity
long the
Douro in
porto.
ight,
onstruct-
ng port
arrels at
Vila Novo de
Gaia

them established in Oporto or Viana do Castelo since the 17th century, have the air of owning the city, so Britanically, so unconsciously arrogantly." The British presence still can be felt, although it is, most would agree, less overbearing.

Portugal's liberal revolution began in 1820 at Oporto. The severest fighting took place against absolutist King Miguel in 1832-3, leading to his exile and the restoration of liberalism.

In modern times, the city was the center of liberal opposition to Salazar's right-wing dictatorship. After the 1974 revolution, the city served as a bastion against the spread of Communism to the north.

Oporto today is a relatively prosperous commercial city, where people like to eat and drink well. Regional specialties include roast pork, fresh salmon, lamprey, trout and tripe.

Generally Oporto is a sober city. Apart from dining, there's not much nightlife. Visitors may hear *fado* at some restaurants such as Mal Cozinhado or Taverna de São Jorge. The Portuguese usually make a trip out of town for some entertainment. The younger set frequents discotheques at the suburb of **Foz do Douro,** while their elders prefer the nearby coastal resort of **Espinho** with its casino and night club.

The city's main festival is that of Saint John the Baptist on June 23 and 24. This coincides with the ancient celebration of the summer solstice, so the Christian feast is laced with pagan traditions. People take to the streets and slap one another teasingly with bundles of leeks, feathers and nowadays, plastic hammers. The most popular festivities occur at the **Alameda das Fontainhas,** a square overlooking the **Dom Luís I Bridge**, where people sing and dance around bonfires, drink *vinho verde* and feast on roast kid and grilled sardines.

The heart of the city is the **Praça da Liberdade,** with an equestrian statue of Pedro IV in the center. On the north side of the square is the broad **Avenida dos Aliados,** with bright flowerbeds and mosaic walks, leading uphill to the **Town Hall.** Here stands the modern stone statue of native son Almeida Garrett, liberal poet and novelist.

"From here, where it got its name, Old Portugal, the name will again rise up with distinction," Garrett wrote in 1819. "The brilliance, the honor, the healthy customs, pure love of native land, the sincere frankness, the noble independence of other epochs will resurge once more from here…"

To the southeast of Praça da Liberdade lies the **Praça de Almeida Garrett**, where the **São Bento Railroad Station** has a fine entrance hall, decorated with tiles showing historical scenes.

Heading south up the hill, one arrives at the **Sé**, or cathedral, with its square towers and small domes, dating back to the 12th century but greatly modified since. Here King João I wed the English Queen Philippa of Lancaster in 1387. The Gothic **cloister** is decorated with fine tiles. Nearby on **Pena Ventosa**, the site of an ancient citadel, stands the impressive 18th-century **Bishop's Palace**. Just beyond, the **House of Guerra Junqueiro**, a poet who died in 1923, is a museum with his memorabilia and furnishings.

Across the avenue stands the 15th-century church of **Santa Clara**, next to one of the best preserved parts of the old city wall. Santa Clara has been rebuilt several times but is noted for its splendid gilt-wood choirstalls and altars. Sacheverell Sitwell writes: "After it, every other building in Porto, even São Francisco, is drab and dull."

To the west, the church of São Lourenço better known as Grilos (for the crickets that lodge there), is one of the earliest examples of Portuguese Baroque, built in 1570.

At the end of Rua dos Ingleses stands the bastion of English life, the **Feitoria Inglesa** or the Factory House. Here the old British port wine shippers do their business, play billiards or cards, read English newspapers and enjoy English cuisine, as they have for the past 200 years. Outsiders must obtain special authorization from the British Port Wine Shippers Association to visit.

Around the corner, on Rua da Alfândega, stands the much restored **palace** where Prince Henry the Navigator was born in 1394. For a time it served as the customs house; it is now a museum.

Going by the **Praça do Infante Dom Henrique**, one reaches the **Church of São Francisco**, founded by King Sancho II in 1233 and rebuilt in the 14th century. The interior glitters in Baroque splendor with gilded columns, arches and statues. On the site of the convent, which burnt down in 1832, is the **Bolsa**, seat of the Commercial Association of Oporto and the stock exchange. It is noted for its opulent neo-Moorish reception hall.

Up the hill is the Port Wine Institute, a government agency established in 1932 to control the quality of port. Every year, the Institute establishes specific quotas for port production. About 40 percent of the

he Douro
makes
through
porto

region's grapes go into port; the rest are used for ordinary table wines.

Following the Rua Belmonte past lovely old homes with balconies and tiled walls, one arrives at the church of **São João Novo**, built in 1592. Across the way, stands the 18th-century **Palace of São João Novo,** a whitewash and granite building that houses the **Museum of Ethnography and History.** The collection includes archaeological finds going back to the Paleolithic Age, old wine presses and wine boats, fishing equipment, pharmacy, vases, ceramics, costumes, jewelry and folk art.

The road leads to the graceful **Torre dos Clerigos**, a six-story granite tower built in the 18th century as a landmark for ships coming up the Douro. It is worth climbing the 225 stairs for a spectacular view of the city.

Outside the city center, there are various sites that will interest visitors. To the east lies the busy square called **Praça da Batalha**, with a statue of Pedro V in the middle. On the square stands the imposing 18th-century church of **São Idlefonso** with a fine granite facade decorated with blue-and-white tiles.

The main shopping street is **Rua Santa Catarina**, where one may find good buys in a variety of local products from shoes and clothing to pottery. **Rua das Flores** has the best gold and silver shops.

Northwest of the center lies the main **university** building, a handsome granite structure built in 1807 as the Polytechnical Academy. Further north, stands the 12th-century **São Martinho de Cedofeita** church. "Cedofeita" means "done too soon;" the church was hastily built to honor the patron St. Martin of Tours.

On the western side of the city, in the old royal **Palácio dos Carrancas** where Wellington once slept, is a museum that should not be overlooked. The **Soares dos Reis Museu**, named after the important 19th-century sculptor, has a fine collection of archaeological articles, religious art, regional costumes, ceramics and contemporary paintings, as well as sculpture. A number of paintings by Grão Vasco are on display, among them *St. Catherine* and *St. Lucy.*

Past the modern **Sports Pavilion** is the **Solar do Vinho do Porto**, where one may test a wide variety of port wines.

Nearby lies the **Quinta da Macierinha**, where the former King Charles Albert died in 1849, after abdicating the throne of Sardinia. Called the **Romantic Museum**, this

Left, portrait of King Carlos, in the Stock Exchange. Right, the ebullient gilded woodwork at São Francisco

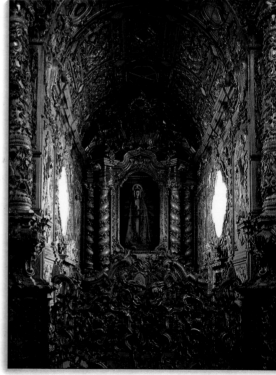

mansion is set in a rose garden and it contains most of its original furnishings and paintings.

Returning to the river, one should spend some time just strolling along the river bank, called **Cais da Ribeira**, the liveliest part of the city. Many small shops and restaurants are built right into what remains of the old city wall.

The splendid steel arch farther up river is a railroad bridge, **Ponte de Dona Maria Pia**, built in 1876 on a plan by the ubiquitous Alexandre Gustave Eiffel. On the Western side of the city, the modern concrete span called **Ponte da Arrábida**, is used mostly by the north-south travelers, wishing to avoid Oporto.

From the center of Oporto, travelers generally take the picturesque **Ponte de Dom Luís I**, built in 1886, which provides splendid views. This two-story iron bridge leads directly to **Vila Nova de Gaia**, an industrial zone that is rather black, with ceramic, glass, soap and other factories. But above all, Gaia is the real seat of the port wine industry, where most of the warehouses or lodges are found.

In springtime, the new wine is brought down from the Upper Douro by truck—less picturesque but considerably more practical

than by *barcos rabelos*, the flat-bottomed sailboats that used to sail the Douro. In the Gaia lodges, the wine is left to mature in 139-gallon (534-liter) oak casks called pipes. Here the blending takes place for most ports, with wines from different vineyards and years blended to produce the correct taste and color. Then the wine is bottled and again left to continue maturation until its time has come, depending on the type of wine.

Like museum pieces, a few *barcos rabelos* are kept docked at Gaia near the Dom Luís I bridge. Once a year, during the feast of São João on June 24, the boats participate in races on the Douro.

Visitors, however, may take a short launch cruise on the Douro, with fine views of Oporto and the three bridges. The excursion lasts 50 minutes and leaves hourly from a dock near the **Ferreira Lodge.**

There are about 60 port wine lodges located in Gaia. Many of them welcome visitors who wish to tour the installations and taste the wines. The **Sandeman**, **Ferreira** and **Ramos Pinto** companies have full-time guides for visitors. A French expert once calculated that a normal human being can only go through three such tasting visits in one day and remain lucid.

TRAS-OS-MONTES

The English translation of Trás-os-Montes sounds rather awkward—"Back of the Mountains," or "Behind the Mountains." But the meaning suits this remote northeast corner of Portugal. To most Portuguese the province of Trás-os-Montes could be on the other side of the moon. Most Lisboners are inclined to look at it with that distance—albeit with fierce affection as well. It is a province for the more adventurous traveler, for when journeying here, one occasionally has to do without modern comforts.

The word "trás"—"back" or "behind"—fits the region like a glove, for it is certainly "backward" in almost every aspect, cut off from the rest of the country by mountains, poor road and rail systems, and a grinding poverty which has driven the workforce of almost every village into migration to the larger urban areas, or emigration up into the more advanced economies of northern Europe, or overseas. It's quite possible that this ancient historic area is the single most "backward" pocket of civilized Europe—on par, perhaps, with the remoter areas and islands of Greece, and the hinterlands of Sardinia, Sicily or Yugoslavia.

The Portuguese, however, are proud of Trás-os-Montes. Those who come from there, or who go there to spend their holidays—or visit with relatives and childhood friends, unanimously praise the area. The place has its share of regional stories, anecdotes and ethnic jokes. But about the venerable if underdeveloped Trás-os-Montes there is a universal affection that comes across in every conversation one will have on the subject.

"You think we are poor?" queried a village priest from a tiny village in the Barroso district. He was seated on a stone slab inside the stone structure of the communal bake oven, the broiling sun outside the open doorway cooking the dust and dung that "paved" the village street. Against a far wall is an ox-cart with wooden wheels, a design used in the Middle Ages. A hand-held wooden plough, also designed for ox-power—a type used in pre-Roman times—leaned against the ox-cart, its metal digging tip freshly hammered into place by a local smith readying it for work the next day.

"Well, we are poor up here," he said with a broad smile, "but if you look around you—anywhere you go in Trás-os-Montes—you will not see people begging the way you see them in the streets of Lisbon or Oporto. We grow enough food up here to feed everybody. We eat well. Our wine is the best. Others should come and learn from our example..."

There is much higher emigration from the north of Portugal than from the South, and one of the principle reasons is due to the division of lands. The south is an area of *latifundios*—large landholdings, while the north has *minifundios*—small holdings. A farmer's land in the north is simply not sufficient to provide him and his family with a living. The northern people are conservative, and resist any form of cooperative farming venture such as those widely used in the southern province of Alentejo. Another reason for the *minifundios* is the terrain—high mountains and steep-sided valleys have made it difficult to organize farming on a large scale.

A more subtle factor affecting Portugal's conservative north is the Church. While all of Portugal might be viewed as Roman Catholic, the sheer remoteness of the northeast corner of the country has meant that national government has little impact, while native religion predominates. This has affected education, particularly; until recent years, often the only educated man in a village was the priest, whose wisdom and opinion would be sought on every matter ranging from the spirit to advice on crop harvesting.

One may enter the region, which is often overlapped with the Alta Douro, the upper valley of the Douro River, from a number of directions. Border crossings from Spain are at Vila Verde da Raia, on the road leading south to Chaves (this is a historical invasion route—employed by the armies of Napoleon in the early 1800s); at Portelo, in the Parque Natural de Montezinho; at Quintanilha, east of Bragança; and at Miranda do Douro and Bemposta, where the River Douro forms the frontier. From inside Portugal, the main routes into the region would be from Oporto via Vila Real; and from the south, from Lamego via Vila Real; or from Guarda via either Torre de Moncorvo or Freixo de Espada à Cinta. The region is split into two administrative districts, with capitals at Vila Real in the southwest and Bragança in the northeast.

Heading north, one is still in port wine country when one crosses the Douro from the direction of Lamego and enters Regua. There are two bridges crossing the river here—one a road bridge, the other a railway bridge that has never been used, but some 50 years ago was intended for a spur line con-

eceding
ages, con-
rsation in
arvicais;
ue love.
ft,
inning in
e Barroso
nshine

necting Regua with Lamego. Of greater curiosity is the tiny rail-link between Regua, Vila Real and Chaves, a south-north route built in 1890 which still uses original rolling stock—toy-sized carriages with wood-slat seats and a humorously primitive toilet system aboard. A conversation with Stationmaster Agostinho Bernardo dos Santos would be enlightening for any railroading buff. He has spent nearly 30 years as chief at Regua—and is particularly proud of the running record of the tiny Regua-Chaves line.

The original steam engine stands proudly displayed on a rusted old section of the narrow-gauge track behind the station—replaced by a specially-built diesel locomotive only five years ago. The train leaves, more or less on time, five times a day—and manages an average speed of 16 miles (27 km) an hour as it wends its way north. Some passengers, when in season, take along empty baskets on their journey; the blackberries one can pick off the bushes en route are delicious.

Driving north out of Regua, you can make a stop at Martha's port wine house in **S. João de Lobrigos**. Try a sweet port, at any time of the day. The trip to **Vila Real** gives one a first glimpse of the terraced vineyards of this province, where more than half of the working population is employed in agriculture.

Vila Real: An ancient settlement in the Terra de Panóais, Vila Real was founded and renamed by Dom Dinis, the sixth king of Portugal, in 1289. Its name literally means "royal town"—fittingly, as Vila Real boasts more noble families than any city other than the capital, and has ever since King Dinis first patronized it. Walking in the ancient streets, one will see many residences marked, often above the main entrance, with the original owners' coat of arms. Like as not, the same family is still living there. The famous 19th-century writer Camilo Castelo Branco lived in Vila Real, and wrote many of his most enduring works using the town as a backdrop.

"In what century are we on this mountain?" asks one of his characters.

"In what century?" comes the reply. "Why, it is the same 18th century here as it is in Lisbon."

"Oh!" says the first. "I thought time here had stopped in the 12th century."

Vila Real became a city proper only in 1925, but the importance of the region dates from 1768 when the vineyards were first developed commercially: The first of

The Corgo railway line which runs from Chaves to Régua

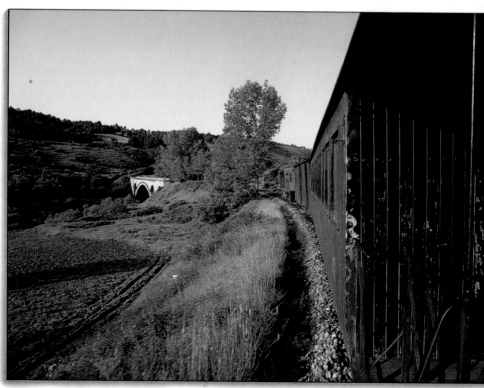

Portugal's port wines were blended here, and most of the region's red and white wines are labelled *reserva* to mark their excellence. The wines of Vila Real are exported to more than 150 countries.

Panóais, the original name given to the pre-King Dinis settlement, is also the name of a strange pagan sanctuary about three miles (six km) out of town in the **Vale de Nogueiras**, where a series of enormous carved stones rest, which are believed to have been used as altars of human sacrifice. Inscriptions in Latin invoke the ancient god Serapis, known to both Greek and Egyptian mythology. It is believed that an early Roman settlement existed here—dating to a time not very long after the birth of Christ, and possibly even earlier. It is known that Christianity had taken a firm foothold in this region by the second century A.D., and it is likely that the inscriptions predate the Christian era of the settlement.

The **Sé**, or cathedral, was originally the church of a Dominican convent. Although much of the present building dates from the 14th century, still remaining are Romanesque columns from and earlier structure.

Vila Real's oldest church is the ancient **Capela de São Nicolau** on a promontory of high land behind the municipal hall, over-

looking the valley of the **Rio Corgo**. Other churches of note are the baroque **São Pedro**, built in 1528, with a lovely coffered ceiling, and the Gothic cathedral of **São Domingos**.

There are also a number of fine houses dating from the 15th to the 18th centuries. An example is the **Casa de Diogo Cão**, an Italian Renaissance-style house that was, according to tradition, the birthplace of the navigator who discovered the mouth of the Congo River.

In the area of handicrafts, the Vila Real region is particularly noted for the black pottery of Bisalhães, and the woolen goods of d'Agarez, Caldas do Alvão and Marão.

Addressing modern interests, Vila Real has become known as the motorcycling capital of the country, with a circuit that runs within the city's limits. International motorcycle meets and races are held in June and July.

Serra de Alvão: Two scenic routes lead north out of this capital city, one on each side of the high Serra da Padrela—to Chaves in the north, and Bragança in the northeast. But the adventurous traveler may strike northwest into the rugged Serra de Alvão, and be treated to one of the most lavish mountain vistas the country has to offer. The road leads through a small natural park and across the **Rio Olo** to **Mondim de Basto** on the banks of the **Rio Tâmega**. There it forms the border between Trás-os-Montes and Minho.

Granite gives way to slate—many of the houses are roofed by it—and in the high passes, one can hear the rushing of mountain waters, the tinkle of goat bells, or the calling of a herder to his dogs. In the winter there is snow here, but at other times of the year one is likely to encounter a profusion of wild flowers—whole mountainsides of purples or yellows—and everywhere the smell of pine forest. Pine resin, used in making paints and turpentine, is a major product of this area.

A side trip of some eight miles (12 kilometers) from Mondim de Basto will take one to **Atei**, a delightful little village containing numerous archaeological remnants of Roman occupation. From here a curious subterranean road of either Roman or Arab construction leads down to Furaco on the banks of the Tâmega.

Leaving Mondim de Basto, the road winds northwards to **Cabeceiras de Basto**, which is actually in the Minho province, at the head of a small "peninsula" that juts up into Trás-os-Montes. Stop at the imposing baroque **Refojos Monastery** before heading into the high Serra de Cabeceira and back into Trás-os-Montes at **Póvoa**.

Barroso District: One soon joins the main Braga-Chaves road that runs beside **Barragem do Rabagão**, a gigantic expanse of lake formed behind a dam, but here again another side trip is called for—to Mont'alegre, the towering Serra do Larouco, and the primitive villages of the Barroso district.

In truth, one could spend weeks or more in this area; anthropologists and sociologists have spent lifetimes studying this extraordinary corner of Portugal, for the region lends some understanding to life in medieval Europe.

As the largest town in the area, **Mont'alegre** might be considered the "capital" of Barroso. Given a charter in 1273 by King Afonso III, and restored and expanded in turn by King Dinis and King Manuel I, Mont'alegre (*monte* meaning hill, *alegre* meaning happy or cheerful) is thought to have possibly enjoyed its villa status from a much earlier time, for the pillory in the center of town carries the coat-of-arms of King Sancho I, who was on the throne of Portugal from 1185 until 1211.

The hill on which the town stands commands a view over a wide area, so it is hardly surprising that it has been a military center for some dozens of centuries. Mont'alegre is rich in archaeological finds. It was a center for the ancient Lusitanians, the Romans, Suevi and Visigoths. There have been no finds of Moorish occupation, although they did play an important role in the history of nearby Chaves. At **Outeiro Lesenho**, near Mont'alegre, in the 18th century were found two gigantic granite statues of warriors. They are thought to be from the Iron Age, and have been attributed to Celtic influence. Both are to be found today in the Ethnology Museum of Belém in Lisbon.

A magnificent four-towered **castle** stands at Mont'alegre and was in constant use during the many wars that Portugal fought against Spain. North of the region rises the mass of the **Serra do Larouco**, second highest range of mountains in the country (after the Serra da Estrêla), with a number of passes leading into Spanish Galicia.

The district of Barroso stretches from the foothills of the Serra do Larouco to some nine or 12 miles (15 or 20 km) northwest of the city of Chaves. There is no absolute boundary, but it would include such villages as Meixide, Padornelos and Tourem Pitões, to name a few. If one can shut out the "emigrant architecture" that blights the vil-

Archaic building methods survived until recently in Barroso

lages in northern Portugal—uncontrolled modern housing that is built with money saved by the Portuguese who work abroad—one will find in these settlements vestiges of a bygone era, a sense of history utterly remote in time.

The ancient houses are built of enormous granite or slate blocks. Doors, windows, balconies are of weathered antique wood. Until recently, many houses were thatched, although tiled roofs are now more the rule. Streets are dirt, or simple bare rock. In many villages, electricity was installed only within the past decade. Almost every church is in Romanesque style—early Middle Ages—with the typical facade rising to a twin-columned peak to house the church bell. Ox-carts are still standard transport between the villages and the surrounding arable fields. It is rare to see a tractor; most ploughs are hand-held, wooden-stocked and pulled by oxen.

For centuries the people of Barroso lived out their lives cut off from the outside world. They developed their own customs, songs, festivals and habits. In many corners of the world under similar circumstances, local people may treat outsiders with suspicion or alarm. This is certainly not the case in Barroso. It is hard to imagine a more warm-hearted, hospitable people, eager to share the peculiarities of their daily lives with others who come to visit them. By tradition, the bread oven, which is fired up once a week, is both meeting place for each village, and local hostel for travelers seeking shelter for a night or two. Winter or summer, the bread ovens are never cold—but they are housing at its most primitive—residents must supply their own sleeping bags!

Local cultural groups keep alive the ancient customs and folklore. Along with the recognized need to modernize there is, happily, a proud awareness of the area's link with the past.

One of the region's most colorful festivals is the annual *Chega dos Toiros*, an intervillage competition which means "The Arrival of the Bulls." Each village takes enormous pride in its bull, a communal animal bred especially for the purpose of covering the various cows owned by the individual farmers. This bull, by both tradition and breeding, is the biggest and most ferocious animal imaginable—one feels that his breeding is as much to gain the honors at the annual competition as it is for stock purposes.

Held in June, July and August, the *Chega* is essentially a bullfight, where the bull of

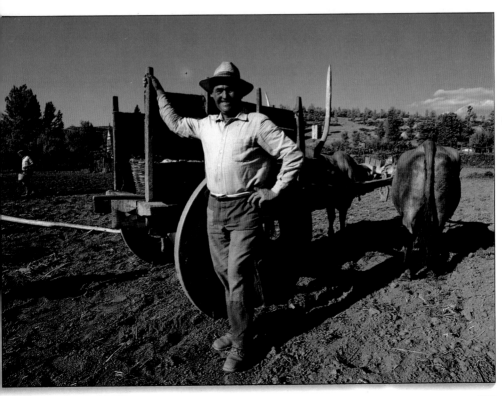

one village is pitted against another in a duel. Each animal is decorated and feted by his villagers, and paraded with bands and crowds with much color and hoopla.

The fight itself is deadly earnest, with the champions of each bull shouting and goading their animal into battle. The fight continues until one animal is killed, or turns and runs away. The victor is lead away by his villagers with much celebration to be prepared for the next fight.

At the end of the season there will be a regional champion—and this is the lucky animal who'll be put out to pasture with the region's cows. He is a source of great pride to the residents of the village from which he comes.

Chaves: Chaves, just a few kilometers down the road from Barroso, seems a world away. Itself an ancient city (the fortified Lusitanian village of the present site was captured by the Romans in the year 78 A.D.—the Emperor Flavius founded the city of *Aqua Flaviae* there, inaugurating the still popular hot springs and baths), Chaves is a bustling center with a population of about 15,000. It is an agricultural and textile center, famous for its ham, and boasts the largest *taverna* or *tasca* in Portugal.

Situated on the Rio Tâmega, Chaves commands a strategic position in a wide valley that extends from the Spanish frontier into the heart of Trás-os-Montes. Just about every invader who set his heart on Portugal, or chunks of it, routed his armies through this channel. Thus, at one time or another, Chaves has hosted Celts, Lusitanians, Romans, Vandals, Suevi, Moors, Spanish and French.

In addition to fortifications and the baths, the Romans built here the largest of their bridges ever to be built in the Iberian Peninsula. Completed in 104 A.D., it has 20 arches, is 150 yards (140 meters) in length—and is still very much in daily use. In the middle of the bridge are two inscribed Roman milestones.

Chaves means "keys" in Portuguese, but actually this is not the derivation of the name of the city. The ancient *Aqua Flaviae* was much later shortened to *Flavias*, and local mispronunciation eventually produced the current name.

Sights include the **parish church**, originally rebuilt in the 16th century; and the Baroque **São João de Deus**, a church near the bridge.

Prior to the formation of Portugal, the fortified city was made a part of the original County of Portucale. Various of Portugal's

Scythe-seeing near Aldeia Santo Andre in Barroso

early kings added significantly to its **castle**, one of the most important in the land. A second castle, in its day also an integral part of the defenses of this strategic valley, still stands at **Monforte de Rio Livre**, about eight miles (12 kilometers) east of Chaves.

Heading eastwards towards Bragança one will pass the old town of **Vinhais** high in the **Serra de Montesinho**, on the south flank of the natural park of the same name. There was a castle long since destroyed at Vinhais, and it is known that there was a significant population here long before the formation of Portugal as a country. For lovers of nature, the high parkland is well worth a visit of at least several days. And, like Barroso farther to the west, the villages of this region are steeped in ancient history, the customs and culture of centuries past.

The area is famous for its agriculture, particularly vines. Fine woodwork, weaving and basket-making are traditional handicrafts throughout Montesinho.

A mountain, **Ciradela**, rises behind Vinhais. Over it passed the Roman road that led from Braga to Astorga; today this ancient route is rich in archaeological discoveries.

In the 11th and 12th centuries there was a general movement of the population of this area towards the more fertile farm lands

of the south. To prevent this, various monasteries were founded and encouraged by the early rulers of the region to develop their own agriculture and cottage industries. One of the most important of these monasteries was the magnificent **Mosteiro de Castro de Avelãs**, a few miles west of Bragança. Parts of the church of the Benedictine abbey have been incorporated into the present-day parish church.

A visitor to the region is well advised to stop at the tourist office in Bragança and ask specifically for the book available on the Parque Natural de Montesinho. In it one will find a detailed map of the park area—and it would be of value to spend a few minutes studying it before heading out on the intricate road system through the park. Many of the roads are paved—but many are not. Whichever direction one takes, one is guaranteed a journey through spectacular countryside. But be sure your car is up to it, and that you carry plenty of fuel. There are no gas stations.

Bragança: Bragança is, at least to many travelers, the most fascinating spot in all of the province. With a current population of some 30,000, it is the administrative capital of the province. A university town, it is also an agricultural trade center (livestock, vine-

A "novelty store" in Chaves

yards, olive oil, grains), a thriving textile industry, and has been famous for its ceramics since prehistoric times (in a nearby cave at **Dine**, archaeologists have found bits and pieces of pottery dating well into the Paleolithic Period).

Known as *Brigantia* to the Celts and *Juliobriga* to the Romans, Bragança received its first *foral* (royal franchise) from King Sancho I in 1187—the same year that the family of the Dukes of Bragança started building their feudal castle there.

The Braganças—still pretenders to the throne of Portugal—provided the land's kings and queens consistently from 1640 until the formation of the republic in 1910, and the emperors of Brazil from 1822 to 1889. The title of Duke of Bragança was traditionally held by the heir to the throne. In 1661, Catherine of Bragança became Queen Consort to Charles II of England, thus renewing the age-old friendship between the two nations.

Traditionally, the possessions of the Bragança family support the *Fundação da Casa de Bragança*, a foundation of the Portuguese state. Its headquarters, a library, a museum and a lecture center, are all based at the family's 16th-century residence in Vila Viçosa, in the Alentejo province.

Bragança's ancient **castle** still stands,—with a **Princess's Tower** full of tragic ghosts. The keep of the castle houses a very fine **military museum**. Nearby, still within the castle walls, one will find the 12th-century five-sided **Domus Municipalis**, the oldest municipal hall in the land. The town walls with their 18 watch towers are still largely intact, and the city boasts a particularly fine Renaissance **cathedral**.

Basing oneself in this historic city, it is relatively easy to make short day trips out into the surrounding region—north into the Montesinho, or south into the center of the district where there are a number of villages that have been specially built, it would seem, to boggle the mind of the latter-day Childe Harold.

Firstly, to the north, in the farthest corner of Portugal, there is **Rio de Onor**, a tiny village that actually straddles the border.

"Bragança has forgotten us up here," complains one of the locals, in reference to the nonexistent bus service. "As for Lisbon—well, the president made a big show of coming up here once, but he didn't arrive by public transport!"

Cut off from civilization for so many centuries, the people of Rio de Onor have actually developed their own dialect. In **Bragança's medieval mien**

228

their music and folk dances a common instrument is the *gaiteiro*—a bagpipe, which although more commonly associated with Scotland, Ireland and parts of northern England, is more accurately associated with the Celts.

A good time to visit many of the villages that reach in an arc from Vinhais, across Bragança, and down as far as Miranda do Douro and Freixo de Espada-a-Cinta, would be between Christmas Day and Epiphany (January 6th), when the local population celebrate a number of feasts connected with the Christian calendar. The "Christian" element is really a modern addition to celebrations, complete with ferocious masks and unearthly costumes, which date back to the dawn of time when the simple agrarian people of these pastoral regions practiced fertility rites and paid more than passing attentions to strange magical forces that emanated from the bowels of the earth.

Carnival, of course, is another good time to visit. Forty days before Easter the masks come out again, and one cannot be sure if it is the Christian spirit or the bogeyman that dominates the season.

South of Bragança one may head towards the Spanish frontier at **Miranda do Douro**

where the Douro River has cut a deep gorge into the rock. This charming village is the site of a former **cathedral**, a 16th-century granite building with a series of gilded wood altarpieces.

The river flows southwesterly towards **Freixo de Espada-a-Cinta** in the bottom corner of the province. There are five dams built along the Douro here, jointly operated by Spain and Portugal. This route will lead one through the area inhabited by the Mirandês—a word that denotes both the people living in the villages of this zone and the language they speak. In fact, this language, close to Vulgar Latin, is considered such a valued relic of Portugal's cultural past that it is currently being revived and taught as a subject in the region's schools.

Freixo, as it was first known, is one of the oldest towns in the province, and had initially been fortified by Lusitanians, then Romans, Visigoths and Moors—though nothing now remains of their works. However, an important **castle** was built there when Dom Afonso Henriques first granted the town its charter. The castle's beautiful seven-sided tower, known as the **Cock's Tower**, and remnants of its walls remain.

To promote settlement in a town lying so near—only two and a half miles (four kilometers)—to Spain, Freixo was granted the status of sanctuary for fugitives. Here selected condemned people might receive their freedom once again, although certainly none who had committed treason.

Freixo's Manueline **parish church** was built over a very long period and concluded only in the 17th century. It has a fine Gothic doorway, and, inside, a notable carved chancel.

Taking a more interior route south from Bragança, one may visit such beautiful villages as **Chacim**, in the **Serra de Bornes**, or **Vila Flor**, a little farther south.

Lovers of castles will want to see the impressive ruins at **Algoso**, south of Vimioso. Since the 12th century, this fortress has guarded the area surrounding its lofty perch—a hill called **Cabeço da Penenciada**—while 1,650 feet (500 meters) below, the **Rio Angueira** flows westward until it joins the **Rio Maçãs**.

And in the south center of the province, the castle of **Ansiães**, lonely atop its craggy peak, deserves special mention. As a fortification, the castle and its village grew in importance during the reign of Dom João I. In the 18th century most of the families living there drifted away; now this imposing fortress guards only a sleepy little village—and a realm of silence.

BEIRA ALTA AND BEIRA BAIXA

The provinces of Beira Alta and Beira Baixa, the Upper and Lower Beiras, constitute a large rural section of eastern Portugal—reputedly the poorest geographical region in a country already considered the "poor boy" of western Europe. But it is a richly historical area, because it was for centuries riddled with invasion routes for both the Spanish and Moors: the many castles and remnants of fortresses in these provinces clearly illustrate that. The area has its natural attractions as well: whether the dramatic mountains of the Alta or the stark plains and plateaus of the Baixa here are some of the most beautiful natural landmarks in Portugal.

The region is bounded by the Spanish frontier in the east, the Douro River in the north, and the Tagus River in the south. The western boundary is a ragged line that starts at the Rio Douro some 38 miles (60 km) east of Oporto.

Guarda is the principal city and administrative capital of the Beira Alta's eastern district. The charter of Guarda was granted by Sancho I, Portugal's second king, in 1199. It was already established by 80 B.C., though, when it had a role in the attempted secession from Rome.

Roman gates: There are still traces of Roman occupation. Ruins of the period can be found just outside of town, near the Romanesque chapel of **Póvoa de Mileu**, notable itself for a small rose window and nicely carved capitals. Three town gates, the **Torre de Ferreiros** (Blacksmith's Tower), the **Porta da Estrêla** (Star Gate), and the **Porta do Rei** (King's Gate), still stand from the 12th- and 13th- century castle and town walls, along with the castle **keep**. From the top there is a magnificent view of the mountains, and the broad plains to the north.

The **Sé** (cathedral) was built of granite cut from the surrounding area. An earlier cathedral, close to the city's original walls, was destroyed before this one was begun; it was believed to be in an unsafe position. Work on this "new" edifice started in 1390 and was not completed until 1540, so that there were many Renaissance and Baroque elements added to the original Gothic architecture. The renowned builder Boytac worked on the cathedral, which bears some resemblance to Batalha. The exterior boasts flying buttresses and fanciful gargoyles. Inside, the 16th-century stone **retable**, later

highlighted with gilt, represents scenes in the lives of the Virgin and Christ. A beautiful Renaissance doorway, off the north aisle, leads to the **Capela dos Pinas**, which contains a late Gothic bishop's tomb.

Local people from Guarda call it "the city of four F's—*feia, forte, farta e fria*," which means roughly, "ugly, strong, plentiful and cold." Ugly would be a matter of taste: perhaps the predominance of heavy gray granite makes it look dull, but the old parts of the city are charming. Strong alludes to Guarda's history as a defense point against the Moors and Castile. Plentiful refers, no doubt, to the rich land surrounding the town, noted particularly for its wine and sheep farming. Cold it certainly is, in winter. Situated some 3,500 feet above sea level, Guarda in Portugal's highest city—high enough to ensure abundant snowfall during winter months, a rarity in this southern country.

South of Guarda is a ring of majestic Crags of such disturbing shapes that the town in its midst, entered through massive Gothic gates, is called **Sortelha**, "magic ring." This area has long been the legendary home of witches and werewolves. Ancient civilizations may have shaped some of the rocks, and they certainly mined in the area—there are entrances that have been closed for countless centuries.

Stretching southwest of here is the **Serra da Estrêla**, the highest mountain range in Portugal and the source of Portugal's most delicious cheese. Its tallest peak, the Torre or **Malhão da Estrêla**, is 1,993 meters (6,537 feet). Near the Torre is a pilgrimage site, a huge statue of the Virgin carved into the rock, to which the faithful journey on the second Sunday of August. Dramatic crags and ravines make this area a stunningly beautiful drive or hike.

Covilhã, an ancient Roman town on the eastern side of the range, is Portugal's only winter resort. This picturesque town also have several churches of interest, including the 15th-century **Santa Maria** fronted with *azulejos*, and the 16th-century **Chapel of Santa Cruz**.

Covilhã is low enough that it seldom receives snow itself, but it is the principle gateway to the high *serra*, and from there it is a short drive to the ski area at **Penhas da Saúde**. The skiing, mind you, is not to be compared with Kitzbühel, but skiing there is, with a lodge, school facilities and equipment to be rented. The season runs from January through May—although the snow in May may be disappointing.

Edging the Serra on its western side, actually in the Beira Litoral province, is the beautiful **Buçac Forest**. For many centuries this area has been protected, and the 400 native and 300 exotic species of trees have flourished. Various springs and flower-lined walks make the forest a joy to visit.

Benedictine monks established a *hermitage* here in the 6th century, and later Augustine canons took over and guarded the area vigorously. Beginning in 1622 women were forbidden by Pope Gregory to enter. The Carmelites, who built a monastery in 1628, began thorough-going cultivation, planting species brought back from the Portuguese discovery voyages. Species include Himalayan pines, monkey-puzzles, Japanese camphor trees, huge Lebanese cedars, and ginkgoes. In 1643 the pope promised excommunication to anyone harming the trees of Buçaco.

In September 1810, Wellington routed Napoleon's army here, as the French attempted for the third time to conquer Portugal. There is a military museum devoted primarily to the battle.

A **royal palace** was built in Neo-Manueline style at the end of the 19th century next to what remained of the convent. It became a spectacular hotel in 1907, when

The exotic Buçaco Forest

the monarchy was abolished. The hotel is well worth a visit, preferably a stay if possible. There is a small **church**, the **cloister**, and several **monks' cells** remaining from the monastery. In one of these small cells, Wellington spent the night before the Battle of Buçaco.

Near Buçaco is the village of **Luso**, famed for its water which flows freely here from fountains and is available bottled throughout Portugal.

The eastern district of Beira Alta is governed by the city of **Viseu**, which, at a population of 20,000, is a third again larger than Guarda. In the 2nd century B.C., the Romans built a fortified settlement here—some of their road system can still be seen, along with a number of Latin-inscribed stones and signs from the same period.

A thorn in the side of the Romans was a rebel Lusitanian chieftain named Viriathus, who harassed local Roman legions until he was finally betrayed and killed. A monument to this hero has been erected in a park here—the **Cava de Viriato**. It is on the site of a Lusitanian and Roman military encampment. Here one can still see the old earthworks used by the Romans after the campaign of Brutus Calaicus in 138 B.C.

Viseu was made a bishopric during the time of the Suevian-Visigothic kingdom, and a record still exists in the form of a signature of th Bishop of Viseu, dating from 569 A.D.

The city suffered alternating invasions of Moors and Christians from the 8th until the 11th centuries. Fernando the Great of Castile and León captured it for good, and for the Christians, in 1057. Teresa, mother of the first king of Portugal, granted the city its first charter in 1123.

From the 14th to the 16th centuries, building in Viseu seems to have been concentrated in the upper part of town. About this time also an active Jewish colony evolved here. In 1411 the Infante Dom Henrique (Prince Henry the Navigator) became Duke of Viseu, and toward the end of that century the town walls were completed. But the area was becoming a center for the vigorous agricultural activity in the surrounding area, and by the 16th century, much of the town was outside the walls, and there were empty spaces inside.

Perhaps this was fortunate, because over the next two centuries, many of these spaces were filled with a lavish assortment of barque churches, chapels, mansions and fountains. Today the architectural richness lends a dignified air to the enclosed city.

The pure Baroque facade of the Church of the Misericórdia

Pure Baroque: Of the specific sights, the 13th-century cathedral would be one stop worth making. The ribbed vaulting overhead is beautifully carved to look like knotted cables, and the ceiling of the **sacristy** is extravagantly filled with numerous carvings of lively satyrs, animals and plants. The twin-towered **Misericórdia church** is up the hill from the cathedral. This whitewashed building is pure Baroque. The hill it crowns may have once been a Celtiberian settlement.

One should also take in the **Grão Vasco Museum**, many of the works being representative of the fine school of Portuguese Primitive painting that flourished here in the 16th century. The museum's name comes from the nickname of the school's most famous member, Vasco Fernandes. There are also modern Portuguese works and other attractions.

The São Mateus Fair, held annually in August and September, is a major event; the Festival of St. John the Baptist is another, held each June 24th. A Tuesday market is held throughout the year, with plenty of fresh produce, bolts of cloth, pots and pans, and handicrafts. Viseu is well known for its lace, carpets, and black pottery.

Some 25 miles (30 km) west of Viseu, on the main road toward Aveiro on the coast, one enters the valley of the Vouga River, a beautiful river which divides the mountain ranges of the **Serra de Arada** and the **Serra do Caramulo**. The town of **Caramulo**, a spa, has a notable **museum**, with medieval decorative arts, and impressive collection of 19th- and 20th- century European paintings. There is also an exhibit of more than 50 antique cars and motorcycles, including an 1898 Peugeot and a 1902 Darracq.

Nearby is the small town of **São Pedro do Sul** and, a few kilometers farther on, the **Termas de São Pedro do Sul**—possibly the best known and most frequented hot springs in the country. Sinus, rheumatism, hangover or foul temper, the springs are said to cure them all and more.

To the south is the **Barragem de Aquieira**, a gorgeous lake—especially considering it is man-made. Its shores provide popular retreats for campers and boat enthusiasts. A few kilometers away is the charming village of **Mortagua**.

A short hop will land one in the town of **Santa Comba Dão**, which, though a very pleasant spot, is known principally for being the birthplace of Portugal's notorious former dictator, António de Oliveira Salazar. His humble home, now abandoned, belies

Azulejos panels brighten Viseu's streets

the station he ultimately achieved in life. Political divisions within the old town are marked. Following the Revolution of 1974, zealots in opposition to the dictator's legacy decapitated a bronze statue of Salazar outside the local courthouse. Angry and outraged Salazarists immediately ordered a new head founded. But the opposition had the final say. Within days, a bomb exploded at the foot of the offending statue; it and the courthouse windows were blown to smithereens. To date the little town is still without a statue of its most famous son.

There are several other delightful little villages to visit in this region. Just south of São Pedro do Sul is Vouzela, in the valley of the Vouga River, with a lovely 13th-century **parish church**. Vouzela also has the Rococo **São Gil** chapel. Not far from here is the village of **Cambra**, clustered around the remnants of its **castle**. Just to the south is another Celtiberian site, **Cova de Lobishomem** (Werewolf's Cave). And near Caramulo is the pretty village of **Tondela**. South of Viseu, on the way to Nelas is the village of **Santar**, a gem of a place once known as the "court of the Beiras." On the western side of the Serra is the town of **Oliveira do Hospital**. It once belonged to the Hospitalers. Tombs of the Ferreiros, in

the **parish church**, are crowned on the wall above by a carving of an equestrian knight. There is also a beautiful 14th-century **altarpiece** showing the Virgin Mary with St. Joachim and St. Anne. In the village of **Lourosa** is an extremely old **church**. In 911, Ordoño II ordered the Mozárab building begun. In the shape of a basilica, it uses Roman columns and has elegant, typically Visigothic windows.

Returning to the Vouga River and journeying northeasternly from São Pedro do Sul, the traveller will find a particularly lovely stretch of road that runs between the **Serra de Montemuro** and the **Serra De Leomil** toward Lamego, and passes through the high town of **Castro Daire**. The Romans used this site as a garrison and built an important bridge here, the **Ponte Pedrinha**, over the **Paiva River**. A recently discovered stone says the bridge was built during the governorship of Caius Julius Caesar.

Lamego itself is a city of considerable historical importance. Although the Lusitanians had finally been subjugated by the Romans (after nearly two centuries of fighting), the tribes people of this area arose in revolt, refusing to pay the heavy taxation. In retaliation, the Romans—never much for diplomacy—burned the town to the ground.

The daily news in Viseu

But it was an important defensive location, so Emperor Trajan ordered it rebuilt.

By the 4th century A.D., the town had turned to Christianity, and was granted the status *civitas*, the Roman equivalent of city franchise. Then came the invasions of the Suevi and Visigoths—and then the Moors. For years Christians and Moslems fought over Lamego. One side would pull down the walls, then the other. Finally, in the same sweep that won him Viseu, Fernando of Léon and Castile took the city, aided, in fact, by the legendary mercenary El Cid. Fernando allowed the Moslem *wali* to continue to govern Lamego—as long as he converted, and paid tribute to the king.

Perhaps the city's most significant role in Portugal's history was as the site where, in 1143, the *cortes* met for the very first time. At this meeting, the nobles declared Afonso Henriques to be Afonso I, first king of Portugal.

Lamego's 12th-century **castle**, on one of the city's two hills, preserves a fine 13th-century **keep**, with windows that were added later, and an unusual vaulted **cistern**, very old, possibly Moorish, with monograms of master masons.

Atop Lamego's other hill is perhaps its most important building, the pilgrimage church of **Nossa Senhora dos Remédios**. The first chapel of this sanctuary was founded by Durando, Bishop of Lamego, in 1361, and dedicated to Saint Stephen. In 1564, it was pulled down, and a new one built. From that time, there has been a steady steam of the faithful seeking cures. The present sanctuary was started in 1750, and was consecrated 11 years later—but the magnificent Baroque-style **staircase** leading up to it, started in the 19th century, was not completed until the 1960s. Fountains, statues and pavilions marking the 14 Stations of the Cross dot the 600 steps.

The **Cathedral**, a Gothic structure, was built by Afonso Henriques in 1129. Only the Romanesque **tower** is left from the original building. The city **museum**, housed in the 18th-century Bishop's palace, has a fairly good collection, which includes 16th-century Flemish tapestries and works by Grão Vasco. Also to be seen in Lamego are several 17th- and 18th- century **mansions**.

Near Lamego, the village of **Tarouca** has a former monastery, the first Cistercian one to be built in Portugal. It contains lovely **Choir stalls** and the impressive **tomb** of Conde Pedro de Barcelos, illegitimate son of King Dinis, who assemble *Livro das Linhagens*, an early register of the country's nobility.

North of Lamego, in the valley of the **Balsemão River**, stands **São Pedro de Balsemão**, a Visigothic church that is believed to be the oldest in Portugal.

There is a fine **castle** at **Penedono**, a particularly graceful structure with two lovely detailed towers and a well-designed arch between them. The castle, which is known to have existed before 960, is thought to be the birthplace of Alvaro Gonçalves Coutinho, known as *O Magrico* (The Paladin). He was immortalized for his bravery and gallantry by Portugal's national poet-hero, Luis Vaz de Camões, in Canto VI of *The Lusiads*.

Miracle legend: Traveling in the Viseu district, one should also keep an eye open for **Sernancelhe**, a little south of Fonte Arcada. There is a miracle legend associated with the sanctuary here, that the Virgin Mary appeared before a mute shepherd girl and gave her the power of speech.

Other villages of special interest—there are many—might be **Ermida do Paiva**, where there is a 12th-century **church** built by the Augustinians, and **Carvalhal**, where there are **thermal springs**. Both of these villages are close to the town of Castro Daire. **Vila Nova de Paiva** and villages near it have been dubbed the **Terras do Demo**,

Strange denizens of the pilgramage church of Nossa Senhora dos Remédios

Lands of the Devil, made famous by a number of Portuguese literary figures—notably Aquilino Ribeiro in his 19th-century romance *Malhadinhas*.

Aguiar da Beira lies very near Vila Nova de Paiva. An exquisitely preserved example of a medieval town, the largely granite site includes a **town square** with an ancient **keep** and an unusual **council chamber**, atop a squat structure and open to the sky. Also here is a small **castle**, built entirely without mortar, and believed, therefore, to possibly date from the Iron Age.

Traveling south toward the Beira Baixa, one encounters the **Zêzere River**, which forms the northwest border of the province. In recent years, this river has become a favorite for canoeists looking for a little rough and tumble. The river flows most swiftly from early April through June. There are other water sports to be had in the **Barragem de Castelo do Bode**, a long, many-armed lake that runs south into the province of Ribatejo. Both the river and the lake have rather fine fishing.

Another dam, on the **Tagus River** at **Fretel**, marks the southern limit of Beira Baixa. Upstream the Tagus reaches and crosses into Spain. Here, on both the Portuguese and Spanish sides, is desolate scrub country. The gorge formed by the river is steep-sided and virtually inaccessible to vehicles other than four-wheel-drive jeeps. It is, nonetheless, an extraordinary part of the Rio Tejo. On the Portuguese side along much of the river here runs an **ancient road** built by the Romans. Originally it was the route from **Vila Velha de Rodão** to the Spanish town of Alcántara. Water now conceals large chunks of the work, but where the road rises above the surface, one can see a formidable engineering structure: instead of building the road with flat stones, the entire way is paved with local slate stood on edge, its upper surface rutted by centuries of cart traffic. Twisting in and out of all the gullies and indentures along the river bank, it is an impressive sight.

Both Beira Alta and Beira Baixa have a notable number of castles, not surprising when one considers the geographic development of Portugal's tumultuous history. There are dozens of stories associated with every castle, but a fitting choice to discuss would be that of the village of **Monsanto** in Beira Baixa, once declared "the most typical Portuguese village."

Built around and atop a steep rocky mass in the center of a broad valley some 30 miles (50 km) northeast of the city of Castelo Branco, Monsanto is located bang in the middle of what was major invasion route of the country. The Castle commands a superlative view in every direction and, being close to the Spanish frontier, it has been the scene of many a battle.

It is thought that this *monte* has been fortified since Neolithic times, and in fact the castle is so well-integrated into the natural rock that it looks like it simply grew here.

Rice-filled calf: Some say it was during the Roman invasion in the 2nd century B.C., others claim it was some 1,400 years later during a Moorish invasion, that the people of Monsanto, under a long siege and nearly out of food, showed their spirit to their attackers by killing a calf, filling its belly with rice, and hurling it off the ramparts to the soldiers below. The attackers were so impressed, the story goes, that they packed up and left. Today one of the biggest feast days is May 3, when young villagers, singing and celebrating, tramp up to the battlements and toss down pitchers filled with flowers.

Much of the castle was destroyed at the beginning of the 19th century. One Christmas Eve, there was a tremendous thunderstorm, and a bolt of lightning hit the castle's gunpowder magazine. Divine retribution, the people of the village believed, for that

Working in the vineyards near the village of Parapito, near Lamego

year the unpopular governor had forbidden the traditional burning of a cork oak tree trunk in front of the parish church. Instead, he had ordered the ceremonial log to be carried into his own home, and set alight in his hearth. At that point, however, the gunpowder exploded, and the and irons flew from the hearth and struck the governor dead.

The ruins of the Romanesque **chapel of Sao Miguel**, outside Monsanto's walls, lie in the midst of the original village. Nearby are several **tombs**. There is another ruined **chapel** inside the castle.

The folk music of Monsanto is charming if strange. Half chanted, half sung, there is nothing quite like it in the country. Its rhythm (one cannot really call it a melody) is beaten out with the assistance of a square tambourin-like instrument known as an *adufe*.

The great **Idanha Plain** stretches all the way south to Castelo Branco and beyond— a vast area of cattle-raising country, bitterly cold in winter, scorching in the summer. Near Castelo Branco, there are large areas of pine and a eucalyptus trees.

Castelo Branco, with 25,000 inhabitants, is an ancient city the origins of which, like so many communities in Portugal, are lost in time. It dates its "modern" history back to 1182 when it and the surrounding area—then called Vila Franca de Cardosa—were given as a gift to the Knights Templar by Dom Fernmão Sanches. It received a charter in 1213, and became a city in 1771, in the reign of José I.

The battlements of the old Templar **castle**—the "white castle" of the city's name, provides a fine view, though the castle itself is not noteworthy. The old town is delightful, with narrow winding streets. Points of interest include two churches, **Santa Maria do Castelo** and **Misericórdia Velha**, the latter a 16th-century structure with a particularly nice doorway; and the **Praça Velha**, also known as the Praça de Camões—a fine medieval square off which one can find the ancient **municipal library**.

Certainly the most important thing to see in Castelo Branco is the splendid **Episcopal Palace**, built on the order of Dom Nuno de Norunha, Bishop of Guarda, in 1596. It served as the winter residence of the bishops of the diocese. It now houses the **Museu de Francisco Tavares Proenca Júnior**, with prehistoric pieces from the area and Portuguese art.

In 1725 Bishop João de Mendonca commissioned the building of a garden at

The ruined fortifications at Monsanto

the side of the palace—the **Bishop's Garden**, today considered to be one of Portugal's most treasured national monuments. It is not a particularly large garden; one can walk around it in a matter of minutes. But certainly it is an extraordinary sight, if only for the multitude of statues erected along the course of every pathway and at every corner.

These statues are all named, and have been placed in homage to just about everybody and everything the bishops thought important: the kings of Portugal, of course (it is amusing to note that the two hated Spanish rulers of Portugal, Felipe I and II, are represented here, but by smaller figures); the saints, apostles and evangelists, along with the virtues of the religious; but also the seasons of the year, the signs of the zodiac, and the elements of the firmament. It is hard to believe that there once were even m*ore* statues, but apparently the invading French armies of 1807 carted off the best of the works—some in bronze, some in granite—as spoils of the war. The plinths of the stolen statues have been left standing in their places, in many cases with the name of the missing item clearly engraved. Frenchmen are thus encouraged to look on with shame. Their invasion of Portugal is not remembered too kindly.

If you are looking for your own spoils to cart off, you might consider a bedspread made in Castelo Branco. Since the 17th century it has been the custom for brides-to-be to painstakingly had-embroider their wedding bedspreads. From this tradition and skill a cottage industry was born. Traditionally the spreads are white, but in recent years, they have become available in interwoven colors. Earlier patterns were extremely geometric, echoing Persian carpets, but other decorative themes have since become popular as well.

Northeast of the city, **Idanha-a-Velha** was an episcopal see until 1199, when it was moved to Guarda. There remains here a strange, ancient **basilica** with dozens of Roman inscriptions inside. It is said that Wamba, the legendary king of the Goths, was born here. There is a Roman **bridge** in the village, still in use, and various coins, pottery and bones have been found.

Other charming villages in the Beira Baixa include **Proenca-a-Velha, São Miguel d'Acha, Bemposta, São Vincente da Beira, Castelo Novo**, and **Alpedrinha**. There is a tourist office in the center of Castelo Branco, and it is worthwhile calling in to obtain literature about the district.

The garden of the Episcopal Palace, Castelo Branco

THE LUSTY FOOD OF PORTUGAL

To dine in Portugal is to taste the presence of other countries, other cuisines. It is to conjure up images of empire. Brazil, Angola, Mozambique, Goa—these and others all belonged to Portugal once; in a manner of speaking, each helped to stir the pot.

The period of Portuguese Empire, when this nation smaller than the state of Alabama reached out across the terrifying "Green Sea of Gloom," as the Atlantic was called, has long passed. Yet Portugal, left with only Macão, the Azores, and Madeira, has preserved the flavors of other cultures in its cooking.

Prince Henry the Navigator, less than 30 years old when he started his School of Navigation, was a true scientist in an age of superstition. He ordered his 15th-century explorers to bring back from new lands not just riches and wild tales, but fruits, nuts and plants as well. In 1420, Prince Henry sent settlers to colonize the newly discovered island of Madeira. With them went plants he believed would thrive in Madeira's volcanic soil and subtropical climate—including grapevines from Crete and sugar cane from Sicily, both are indispensable today. Even more significant for Portuguese cooking, was Vasco da Gama's discovery of the water route to the East in 1497-98, five years after Columbus's aborted attempt and accidental discovery of the West Indies.

Black pepper was what Vasco da Gama sought, but cinnamon, which he also found in Calicut, would soon become equally precious to Portuguese cooks. Indeed, one boatload of cinnamon sticks, history tells us, fetched enough money to pay for an entire expedition to India. Cinnamon is perhaps the most beloved spice in Portugal today, certainly for the famous egg sweets (doces de ovos), which may not only contain the heady brown powder but also be decorated with it. Spaniards, on the other hand, prefer vanilla for their puddings and flans. There's good reason for this. It was the Spaniards who found Montezuma sipping vanilla-spiked hot chocolate in Mexico and learned the trick of curing vanilla beans, the seed pods of a wild orchid. Perhaps this is why chocolate, too, is more popular in Spain than in Portugal.

More surprising than the Portuguese appetite for cinnamon, however, is their fondness for curry powder (another bonus of Vasco da Gama's voyages). In the beginning, only the rich and the royal could afford the precious yellow stuff, which pepped up the blandest dish—and also retarded spoilage.

Today, packets of curry powder can be found in supermercados everywhere. Its function,

rather than to set food afire, is to mellow and marry the other ingredients, and add a mysterious muskiness to a large repertoire of soups and stews. The spiciest Portuguese dishes, incidentally, are not found on the mainland but in the Azores and Madeira. These islands were ports-of-call for the navigators, who would barter with the natives—offering spices in exchange for fresh fruits, vegetables and meats (and no doubt the local brew, too).

New Food for the Old: During Portugal's lavish Age of Empire, Portuguese navigators became couriers, bringing New World foods to the Old and vice-versa. Mediterranean sugar cane, for example, was cultivated in Brazil. Brazilian pineapples were introduced to the Azores, a colony established under Prince Henry. They still flourish there in hot houses, ripening under waftings of woodsmoke. Azorean pineapples, chunky, honey-sweet and tender to the core, are teamed today with rosettes of Portugal's mahogany-hued, air-cured presunto (prosciutto-like ham) and served as an elegant appetizer in fashionable Lisbon restaurants.

Tiny, incendiary Brazilian chili pepper took root in Angola early on, another important Portuguese colony, and became so essential to cooks there that today they're known by their African name, piri-piri . Since the collapse of Angola as a Portuguese colony in the mid-1970s and the subsequent influx to Lisbon of thousands of Angolan refugees, piri-piri sauce (an oil and vinegar mixture strewn with minced chilies) is as popular a table condiment in mainland Portugal as salt and pepper. Other exchanges thanks to the Portuguese: African coffee was transplanted in Brazil, which today produces about half of the world's supply; Brazilian cashews landed in both Africa and India; and Oriental tea plants arrived in the Azores (interestingly enough, the Portuguese word for tea—chá—is almost identical to the Cantonese one—ch'a).

All of this fetching and toting of seeds, leaves, barks, roots, stems, stalks and cuttings by Portuguese explorers across oceans and continents dramatically affected Portuguese cooking.

New World tomatoes and potatoes came to Portugal about as early as they did to Spain—in the 16th century. But Portuguese cooks, unlike the Spanish, might drop a few garlic cloves into the soup or stew along with the tomatoes and potatoes, or tuck in a stick of cinnamon.

It's unlikely that anyone grows nuttier, earthier potatoes today than the Portuguese. Indeed, along the New England coast in the U.S., where so many Portuguese families have settled, there's an old saying: "*If you want your potatoes to grow, you must speak to them in Portuguese*."

Tomatos respond to the Portuguese touch, too, and those harvested in the vast Alentejo province, east of Lisbon, are as juicy, red and deeply flavorful as any on earth. Not for nothing does that French menu phrase, "*á la Portugaise*," mean richly sauced with tomatoes.

Onions and garlic, indispensable to any respectable Portuguese cook, were probably introduced by the Romans, who established colonies in Portugal. The Romans are believed to have brought wheat to Portugal, too. They aimed to

and the Moors is found. It is seen in the snow-white cubistic villages that spill down red sandstone cliffs to embrace beaches, in the filigreed chimney pots (the Algarve status symbol), even in the paintbox-bright fishing boats of Albufeira, Lagos and Portimão, whose turned-up prows and lateen rigs clearly smack of the Arab dhow.

It was the Arabs who set up the water wheel in Portugal, who dug irrigation ditches there, who first planted rice (it now grows up and down the west coast), and who covered the Algarve slopes with almond trees. The Algarve's almonds were ground into paste, sweetened, and shaped into

make Iberia the granary of Rome. They also probably introduced olives (a major source of income today), and grapes as well. From shards found in the Alentejo, it's known that the Romans were making wine there as early as the 2nd century A. D.

The Moors, who occupied a large chunk of Portugal from the early 8th to the mid-13th centuries, enriched the pot even more than the Romans. The southern provinces were the Moorish stronghold—the Algarve and Alentejo, in particular—it is here that the look of North Africa

Preceding pages, snacking at Cascais; more elegant dining in Pousada ds Almeida Nossa Senhora da Oliveira in Guimarães. Above, *carne de porco á alentejana*

miniature fruits, birds and flowers of intricate detail. To this day the sculpting and painting of marzipan is an art that requires years to perfect.

The Moors also introduced figs and apricots to the Algarve together with the tricks of drying them under the relentless sun. They planted groves of lemons and oranges and, as it was their custom, they combined fish with fruits and fruits with meats.

Innovative Cooks: Finally, it was the Arabs who invented the *cataplana*, a hinged metal pan, a sort of primitive pressure cooker shaped like an oversize clam shell that can be clamped shut and set on a quick fire. The food inside—fish, shellfish, chicken, vegetables or a medley of them all—steam to supreme succulence. What goes into a *cataplana* depends upon the whims of the cook (and on what's available), but the most famous cataplana recipe is *amêijoas na cataplana* , clams tossed with rounds of sausage and cubes of ham in an intensely garlicky tomato sauce.

It's been said that this unlikely pork and shellfish combination was created at the time of the Inquisition to test one's Christian zeal. Pork and shellfish, of course, were forbidden to Jews and Moslems alike. What the *cataplana* does prove is the Portuguese cook's uncanny gift for combining unlikely ingredients.

There is no shortage of examples that attest to this culinary ingenuity. No one but a thrifty Portuguese cook with an eye on her *escudos* would have made bread a main course by layering yeast dough into a pan with snippets of chicken and sausage and two kinds of ham (this classic from the remote northern Trás-os-Montes is *folar*).

The cod-fishing continues today, with the men putting to sea in spring and not returning until fall. Sometimes, of course, the men do not return and to see their widows dressed in black, some of them barely 20 years old, is to understand why so many of Portugal's poems, stories, folk sayings, even *fado* songs focus upon the nation's proud but bittersweet seafaring tradition:

"O Waves from the salty sea,
From whence comes your salt?
From the tears shed on the
Beaches of Portugal."

It was as early as the 16th century, that Portuguese fishermen learned to salt cod at sea to last the long voyage home, to sun-dry it into board-stiff slabs that could be kept for months, later to be soaked in cool water before cooking.

Cod is still sun-dried on racks the old way on

Or who would have thought to crumble yesterday's bread into shrimp cooking water and come up with another favorite, this is an Estremadura classic known as *açorda de mariscos* . Or to braise duck with bacon and rice as it's done in the Serra da Estrêla, or to smother red mullet the Setúbal way with tiny tart oranges, or to scramble flakes of salt cod with eggs and shoestring potatoes as it's done all over the country?

Cod Country: Dried salt cod, or *bacalhau* (pronounced bockle-YOW), is a purely Portuguese invention. António M. Bello, first president of Portugal's gastronomic society, wrote in his *Culinária Portuguesa* published in Lisbon in 1936, that the Portuguese were fishing Newfoundland's Grand Banks for cod within just a few years of Columbus's discovery of America.

the beach at Nazaré, although much less of it now than in past decades. The Grand Banks have become so overfished that the Portuguese have taken to importing *bacalhau* from Norway just to be able to meet their annual demands. This, puts the price of salt cod beyond the reach of the very people it sustained for centuries—the poor.

Someone once said that the Portuguese lived on dreams and subsist on salt cod. Not quite, although they do claim to know 365 ways to prepare it, one for each day of the year. The best and most famous bacalhau dishes are *bacalhau á gomes de sá* (cooked in a casserole with thinly sliced potatoes and onions, then garnished with hard-boiled eggs and black olives), *bacalhau à brás* and *bacalhau dourado* (two quite similar recipes composed of scrambled eggs, onions and shoe-string potatoes), *bacalhau á conde de guarda* (salt cod creamed with mashed potatoes) and *bolinhos de bacalhau* (cod fish balls, a particularly popular *hors d'oeuvre*). All of these once-humble recipes are served with pride today in the most expensive restaurants of Lisbon.

Very nearly as popular as salt cod are the sardines netted off the Portuguese coast. These are what the tartan-clad fishermen of Nazaré go out for day after day in their gaily colored boats decorated with mermaids, stars and "eyes of God." Portuguese sardines are considered the sweetest and fattest in the world and Portuguese women grill them right on the streets in every town and village, using little terra cotta braziers. But only in spring, summer and early fall—the unofficial "sardine season." As every Portuguese knows, sardines are too bony to eat between November and April.

If salt cod and sardines share top billing as the favorite fish in Portugal, pork reigns supreme as the king of *carne* (meat). With good reason—Portuguese pork is incomparably sweet and tender because of its life of leisure and diet of acorns, truffles and chestnuts.

In the northerly Trás-os-Montes province, they say if you want good pork in the autumn you must feed your hogs twice a day in August. Some farm women even go as far as to cook potatoes for their hogs. Small wonder the hams (*presunto*) and sausages (*salsicha*) are so highly prized here. (the best of all are said to come from Chaves). Small wonder, too, that *charcuterie* figures so prominently in the lusty regional soups and stews. Cooks here even wrap freshly caught brook trout in slices of presunto, then bounce them in and out of a skillet so hot the ham is transformed to a crisp, deeply smoky sort of "pastry."

But Portugal's most famous pork dish comes from the Alentejo in the nation's midriff where hogs are no less pampered. It's *porco à alentejana* for which cubes of pork are marinated in a paste of sweet red peppers and garlic, browned in the very fruity local olive oil, then covered and braised with baby clams, still in the shell. The clams open slowly under the gentle heat, spilling their briny juices into the ambrosial red muddle. What accounts for the distinctive nut-like flavor of Alentejo pork is that the hogs are turned loose each autumn to forage in the cork orchards. Here they nibble upon acorns, wild herbs, and yes, the occasional truffle, too.

Sausage-making is as great a culinary art in the Alentejo as it is in the Trás-os-Montes, and this region's garlicky *chouriços, linguiças, farinheiras* (porridgey sausages plumped up with cereal) and chunky, smoky *paios* are without peer. As

Bacalhau a gomes de sa, one of the 365 receipes that keep Portuguese eating salted cod all year round

Portugal's food authority, Maria de Lourdes Modesto, writes in her masterwork, *Cozinha Tradicional Portuguesa*, "The grand destiny of the pig in the Alentejo is to become sausage."

Here, every part of the pig is used—ears, snouts, tails, feet, even it would seem, the squeal. At Carnival time, for example, the centerpiece of each Feast Day (*Mardi Gras*) banquet is *pezinhos de porco de coentrada*, dainty pig's feet braised with onions, garlic and gobs of fresh coriander.

Another province famous for its pork is the seaside Beira Litoral, particularly the little town of Mealhada, nothing more, really, than a wide place in the road about 12 miles (20 km) north of Coimbra. Here both sides of the highway are lined with restaurants that make suckling pig (*leitão assado*) specialty. The piglets are rubbed with secret their blends of oil and herbs, skewered from head to tail, then spit-roasted over white-hot hardwood coals until their skin is as crisply brittle as an onion's and their milk-white flesh so meltingly tender it falls from the bones at the touch of a fork.

Cabbage Patch: The Portuguese national dish, ironically, is built neither upon salt cod nor pork. It's key ingredient is cabbage, specifically a richly emerald, non-heading, tender-leafed variety (*couve gallego*) much like the collards of the American South. The dish, itself, is *caldo verde* , a bracing, jade-green soup brimming with potatoes, onion, garlic and filament-thin shreds of green cabbage. Sometimes it's fortified with slices of *chouriço* or *linguiça* although in the humblest Minho versions (it's here that the recipe originated), it often contains nothing more than water, potatoes, onion, garlic, cabbage and perhaps a tablespoon or two of robust olive oil.

To some people, "robust" may seem a kind euphemism. Portuguese olive oil, *azeite*, is richly aromatics—to critics, "*rank*." The distinctive flavor comes from harvesting methods. The festive December olive harvest is a casual event. The olives, beaten down from their branches, are left to age on the ground, only gathered after a week or so. That in addition to the hot-water pressing methods, accounts for their intense flavor.

Every Portuguese province now calls *caldo verde* its own, and it's not unusual to find kettles of it steaming on the backs of stoves. Indeed, *caldo verde* is such a staple in the Portuguese diet that plastic bags of minutely shredded *couve gallego*, ready to drop into the pots of potato broth bubbling back home, can be bought at Lisbon's rollicking **Mercado da Ribeira** (city market)—the ultimate in convenience food.

Country women, whether they grow their own cabbage or buy it at the local market, must cope with the whole head. A purely Portuguese sight is a small, ramrod-straight woman balancing cabbages on her head, sometimes six or eight of them at a time, as she goes about her shopping or chats with friends, completely oblivious to the burden she carries. Anyone who drives the back roads of Portugal will be awed by the inventory of items that Portuguese women balance atop their heads: crates of squawking chickens, wicker baskets of laundry, terra cotta water jugs, tables, chairs, even, incredible as it seems, sewing machines!

As for the preparation of *couve gallego* , every country girl learns, by the time she's head-high to the kitchen table, to shred it with the speed of light. It is not difficult once this technique is mastered. The leaves are stacked, perhaps five or six deep, rolled into a fat cigar, then literally shaved as a razor-sharp knife is whisked back and forth across the end of the cabbage roll so fast the movements are scarcely visible. The fineness of the cut is what makes a bowl of *caldo verde* resemble molten jade, also the cabbage is tossed

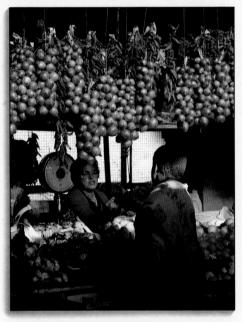

into the pot just minutes before serving so that its color intensifies but does not "turn."

The food of Portugal has often been refered to as the food of farmers and fishermen. And nowhere is this more evident than in the making of soups and stews. Fishermen brew giant drums of *caldeirada* (literally, "kettle of fish") on the beaches at Sesimbra, Nazaré, Albufeira and Sagres, beginning with water (sometimes sea water), adding tomatos, onions and garlic, then lean and oily fish in roughly equal proportion, and if their catch has been especially good, squid and/or octopus, too.

No two *caldeiradas* are ever alike, indeed they vary from day to day depending upon whatever the fishermen's nets have fetched up. One of the pleasures of visiting a deserted *praia* (beach) in

Portugal is the chance of running into a group of fishermen boiling up their latest catch. They're always willing to share.

Farmer's soups and stews are ever-changing, too, as country women constantly improvise with odds and ends—a bit of chicken from the Sunday dinner, a few *favas* (beans) left over from lunch, a handful of carrots, a dab of rice, some crumbles of yesterday's bread, and maybe some freshly minced mint or coriander. This is the way many of Portugal's great classic recipes were created.

Next to *caldo verde*, Portugal's most famous soup is probably *açorda á alentejana* , a coriander-strewn, bread-thickened, egg-drop soup seasoned, as someone once quipped, "with enough garlic to blow a safe." The soups and stews of Portugal—whether they're made of chick peas and spinach (another Alentejo classic), of tomatoes and eggs (a Madeira specialty), of pumpkins and onions (a Trás-os-Montes staple), or of dried white beans and sausages (the universally beloved *feijoadas*)—are frugal and filling, nourishing and soul-satisfying. All they need for accompaniment are a glass of wine, a chunk of cheese and a crust of bread.

Does any country bake better bread than the Portuguese? Not likely. The simple country breads usually contain only four ingredients— flour milled from hard wheat, water, yeast and salt—but they're kneaded until their dough fairly springs to life. And because they're baked in wood-stoked brick or stone ovens, they have a faintly smoky flavor. There are fancier breads, to be sure, notably the sweet festival breads (*pão doce* of Easter and fruit-studded *bolo rei* of Christmas). There are huskier breads, too, the rough round barley breads and most famous of all, the *broas*—yeast-raised corn-breads of the Minho that are sold by the truckload at the merry market in the river town of Barcelos.

This country market is Portugal's biggest and best. Held every Thursday in a vast tree-shaded square, it's divided into quadrants: one for breads, cakes and other baked goods; one for fresh produce (everything from potatoes to poultry); one for farm and wine-making equipment, and the fourth for the lace tablecloths, fancifully painted brown pottery and exuberantly decorated ceramic roosters of the region (these have become a national symbol).

Cheeses can also be bought here, too, as they can at country markets everywhere. The queen of them all is the ivory-hued *queijo da serra*, a cheese so strictly demarcated it can be made only from the milk of sheep grazing on the wild mountain herbs of the Serra da Estrêla. At the peak of its season—winter—a properly ripened "*serra* " is as biting, buttery and runny as the finest Brie.

Portugal also produces a number of other cheeses that are a match for the world's best: the nutty, semi-dry *serpa* from the Alentejo town of the same name, which connoisseurs rank as the nation's second best (it's cured in caves and brushed regularly with paprika-laced olive oil); *beja*, a buttery semi-hard cheese from Beja, near Serpa; *azeitão*, lovely little rounds of gold, tangy and creamy, that come from the village of Azeitão on the Arrábida Peninsula just across the Tagus River from Lisbon. Finally, there are the *queijos frescos*, snowy, uncured cheese much like cottage cheese, which calorie-conscious Portuguese sprinkle with cinnamon and eat in place of the country's devastating egg sweets.

The Moors are thought to have introduced egg sweets to Portugal during their 500-year occupation. It may be so. What is known, however, is that the 17th- and 18th-century nuns of Portugal glorified them—one reason, no doubt, why so many egg sweets bear such amusing names as "bacon

every Portuguese restaurant, no matter how simple or sophisticated the presentation, is at the pastry cart, a glittering double-decker trolley laden with *doces de ovos* (egg sweets) brought round at the meal's end.

Usually there are five or six choices—sunny little hillocks bathed in clear sugar syrup, flans decorated with siftings of cinnamon, individual goblets of rice pudding (*arroz doce*) as radiant as molten gold, flat yellow sponge cakes twirled up around orange or lemon custard fillings, tiny translucent tarts (*queijadas*) reminiscent of the American South's chess pies, and snowy poached meringue ring known as *pudim molotov* (one of the few egg sweets made out of the whites).

The egg sweets of Portugal look irresistible, even to the most resolute dieter. And they should be tried. But most of them, alas, are excruciat-

from heaven" (*toucinho do céu*), "nun's tummies" (*barriga-de-freira*) and "angel's cheeks" (*papos de anjo*).

Regardless of their names, what the dozens of different egg sweets share in common is a prodigious use of egg yolks and sugar. Many are flavored with cinnamon, others with lemon or orange or almonds. Each, moreover, is shaped in its own traditional way—like little bundles of straw, for example, or miniature haystacks, even like lamprey eel. The Portuguese so love this ugly river fish they make golden egg effigies of it for festive occasions. A ritual practiced at nearly

Portuguese cooks demand fresh food, which keeps the markets hopping. Left, Ribeira Market in Lisbon, and above, the fish market in Setúbal

ingly sweet and too rich for non-Portuguese palates. The Portuguese, on the other hand, whose sweet tooth is legendary, find that nothing complements—or follows—an egg sweet like a silky, syrupy wine. A vintage port, or a madeira.

When you do choose a *doce* from the cart, you can at least be assured of good cup of coffee to cut the sweetness. Coffee houses are a national institution, a gathering place morning, noon and night. It's actually not surprising for a country whose former colonies—Brazil, Angola, Timor—produce some of the world's finest coffee. The native choice is usually a*bica*, a powerful espresso-like brew. *Café* is closer to American standards, but if you really miss your morning coffee, order *carioca*: half-café, half-hot water; it will still be plenty strong and, very good.

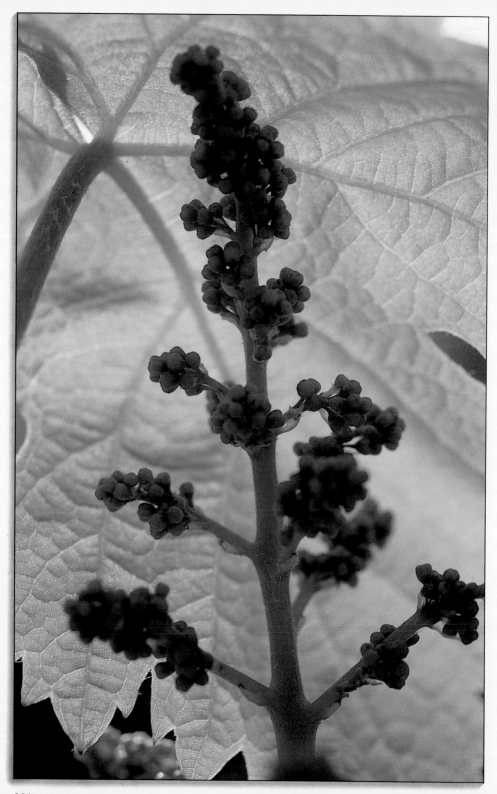

The wines of Portugal have only begun to gain popularity in the United States. Except for port, the famous fortified wine of the Upper Douro Valley, fine Portuguese wines are mostly unknown. Two immensely popular and inexpensive rosé wines, Mateus and Lancers, come from Portugal, but they give no hint of the diverse, unique, world-class wines that flow from this ruggedly handsome country.

Grape vines are cultivated in Portugal as far south as the Algarve. Eight of the best and most distinctive areas, all with long histories of winemaking, are given attention in this article. Starting from the north, they are: the Minho, the Upper Douro, the Dão Bairrada, and the environs of Lisbon—Carcavelos, Bucelas, Colares and Setúbal. Through their wine, each region offers the receptive traveler the unabashed flavor of their countryside—sometimes eccentric, sometimes sublime, yet always with the gregarious pride that typifies this inviting corner of the continent.

Portuguese wines may be divided into two basic categories: *vinho verde* and *vinho maduro*. The wine lists of Portugal's restaurants often show them this way. *Vinhos maduros* translates as "mature wines," wine that is made for aging and maturing in the bottle. *Vinhos verdes*, or "green wines," which demand less patience, are unique to Portugal.

The Minho: From the northwest corner of Portugal, in a province called the Minho, come these most distinctive wines. They can be either red or white; they are "green" only in figurative sense. Their youthful, stimulating acidity and charged effervescence take credit for the title.

Along with the four Lisbon regions and the Dão area, the Minho wine region was officially demarcated by the government in the early 1900s. The decree defined not only the boundaries of region, but also the characteristics of *vinho verde*, the types of grapes to be used and the viticultural techniques for making it.

The Minho encompasses an area of over two million acres of which some three percent are planted in vines. Within the Minho, six official subzones have been created: Amarante, Braga, Basto, Lima, Monção and Penafiel. They acknowledge the difference of each area's climate, which makes the wines distinctive.

The terrain of the Minho is green, lushly forested with oaks, pines and chestnuts. The *vinho verde* vines are allowed to grow practically everywhere, climbing around trees and trained up high to create oases of shade. The look of the land is one of verdure and fecundity. The height above the ground at which these vines grow serves to produce grapes that are lower in natural sugar and higher in malic acid—characteristics of unripe grapes. In the fall, they are harvested by ladder-toting pickers, who bring the relatively immature grapes to the *quintas* (estates) for vinification. First, they are fermented to convert their natural sugars into alcohol. Then a secondary fermentation, called the malolactic, takes place, induced by naturally occurring bacteria. As you might guess from its name, this process converts malic acid to lactic; a harsher, more unpleasant acid into a milder, more palatable one. While this secondary fermentation is common to wines made in many countries, the *vinhos verdes* are distinguished by their retention of the fermentation's by-product: carbon dioxide. Hence, a sparkle or light fizz in the wine, which can vary—depending upon age, technique and storage—from a light tingle on the tongue to a spritely carbonation. This is the hallmark of *vinhos verdes*.

The *vinhos verdes* comprise almost a quarter of the production of wines in Portugal. There are some 80,000 growers of grapes in the Minho region, most quite small operations. Over half of them produce no more than two pipes (about 110 cases) each of wine. This is a clear indication of the endless varieties of the wine. Moreover, there are many grape types allowed in the region. Amongst the whites are the Azal Branco, Dourado, Trajadura, Avalrinho, and Loureiro; the red varietals include the Azal, Padeiro, Borracal and Vinhão. The attributes of a typical white *vinho verde* will be low alcohol (8-11 percent) a straw yellow color, and a bright and fragrant bouquet. To taste, it will display alacritous zest and crisp finish. In the warm local weather, they can be marvelously thirst-quenching.

It is curious that the white *vinhos verdes* that are acknowledged as being the best depart from the features with which the wine is so identified. These are the wines from Monção, where the rare Avalrinho grape is grown. Paradoxically, it most resembles a *vinho maduro*, in that its carbonation is far more subtle, its alcohol content slightly higher, and its capacity to improve with age a proven fact. To acquaint yourself with the wines of Monção, try the "Cepa Velha," produced by Vinhos de Monção Lta. It has won many awards in international competitions and is definitely worth seeking out.

Left, a vintage in the making? Young grapes ripening on the vines of the Estremadura province

In white wine, an effervescence is not entirely unexpected. Many young white wines, upon their uncorking, will temporarily exhibit a light "spritz," or tingle. Unlike that of champagne, this feature "blows off" or vanishes after several minutes of exposure to air. In red wine, however, the presence of this verve can be disconcerting.

For the uninitiated, the first taste of red *vinho verde* may produce contorted facial expressions as one struggles to gain some gustatory equilibrium. Lightly fruity, effervescent, firmly tannic, the melange of sensations are like no other. Appropriately, Portuguese cuisine provides some compelling partners for this wine. Grilled sardines, for example, with their dense oily flesh, help the wine reveal its logic. My own memories of this lunch in the fishing village of Nazaré always recall the flavors of that uniquely sensible wine with the charred, delectable fish.

Red *vinho verde* makes up almost 70 percent of the entire Minho production. It is an important wine locally, but has made few inroads on international markets. The whites, however, have begun to appear in the United States. Two factors have contributed to this. First, improved shipping conditions preserve the wine's charm and freshness. Secondly, and rather ironically, the marvelous petillance, or sparkle, for which the U.S. government levies a stiff protective tariff has been stifled in the wines for export—to make the proposition economically feasible. Which is why they must be tasted here!

Port: The wines of Portugal are best known around the world by their eminent ambassador, port. With a long and fascinating history, port has earned its place beside the other great dessert wines: Sauternes, Tokai and Madeira. It is a fortified wine, the grapes for which are grown in the rugged, mountainous terrain of the Upper Douro River. The wine can be red or white, though it is from the red that port has gained its fame. To be fortified means that the natural conversion of grape sugars into alcohol has been arrested at a calculated time by the addition of Portuguese grape brandy. This bolstering brings the wine's alcoholic content up between 15-24 percent by volume, and makes for a medium sweet, hearty product.

Port as we know it today, has been made since the 1830s. It developed by dint of the historic commercial alliances between the British and Portuguese. The British invested considerably in both the research and development of port, thus controlling the industry. Needless to say, the British populace acquired a healthy thirst for these wines and for hundreds of years were the primary bottlers and consumers of the product. Today, among the port lodges of Vila Nova de Gaia, the blending and storing place for these wines, one still finds a high percentage of British names representing Portugal's finest wine.

Port wine begins its life in a region called the Upper Douro, an officially demarcated region whose boundaries cling to the banks of the Douro and its tributaries. A number of approved grape types grow here. The reds include Tinta Roriz, Tinta Francesa (a descendant of the French Pinot Noir), Touriga Nacional and Bastardo; among the whites, Malvasia, Esgana Cão and Rabigato.

The earth of the Upper Douro is the slate and granite "soil" of the river's banks, a craggy terrain that often approaches a slope of 60 degrees. Into this unabiding territory countless hours of manual labor have been spent to create the terraced grounds in which the vine can prosper. The slate and granite had to first be broken up. Support walls were then built with the shattered stone to harbor the vine from erosion. Driving along the river, one sees thousands of these walls, many of

them nearly 300 years old. A haunting sense of timelessness pervades the area. Day-to-day maintenance of vineyards in such an area is onerous. One must climb from terrace to terrace. At harvest time, the work becomes ever more arduous: the harvested grapes are carried up and down the steep paths in baskets on the backs of men and women. This is how it has been for hundreds of years. At harvest time, the Upper Douro breathes of cultural richness. Ancient songs, the primitive music of pipe and drum, the night-long treading of the grapes with the feet (still done to a considerable degree here), all contribute to a sense of strange, romantic ritual.

As new vineyards are planted, modern techniques—bulldozing and dynamiting—have made expansion economically feasible. In turn, the port wine area has grown tremendously since its inception, increasing to almost 20 times its original size. Virtually all of the new area has been forged upriver, in the valleys of the Douro and its tributaries: the Pinhão, Tua, Torto and Távora Areas which comprised the region through the 18th and 19th centuries, around the town of Régua and the Rio Corgo, are now thought of as lesser wines. The regions producing the finest ports presently center around Pinhão, some 14 miles east of Régua, and extend to the Spanish border.

The famous shipping houses have their *quintas* in the hills of the Douro. These are spacious white houses, often clad in vines, that offer sanctuary from the heat and glare of the region. They can generally be visited if arrangements are made in advance. It is here in autumn that the fermentation process takes place. It is of course interrupted by the addition of grape brandy, creating the raw, fortified wine. Young port then spends the winter at the *quinta*. In springtime, it is transported to the port lodges in Vila Nova de Gaia, by train or truck, where it is blended and matured into a variety of styles. In times past, the port was shipped to the lodges by boat, in the lovely "Barcos Rabelos," narrow ships with large, square riggings. A retired "Barcos" can still be seen moored at the docks in Vila Nova de Gaia.

Vila Nova de Gaia is the town at the mouth of the Douro, on its south bank, facing Oporto. It has more than 80 port lodges, most of which have regular visiting hours—many with English-speaking guides. It is here that one can be instructed in the basic differences of port styles, aided, delightfully, by sampling the product itself. What follows are brief descriptions of the varied styles of port that one may encounter.

Vintage Port: The most famous and most expensive of the ports is vintage port. Representing only two percent of the entire annual port production, it is the crown jewel of Portuguese wines. It is produced from a single harvest's grapes and is "declared" only in years when the quality is deemed extraordinary. This decision—to declare a vintage—comes only after much testing, sampling and deliberation. With minor exceptions, one finds that the shippers declare vintages as a group, the regions' climate affecting the grapes more or less uniformly. Vintage port is bottled after two or three years in wood. For example, the great 1963 vintage must, by law, have been bottled between July 1, 1965, and June 30, 1966. This is what distinguishes vintage from all other ports: the majority of its aging takes place in glass, not wood. From a legal standpoint, vintage

port must identify itself as such, stating the name of its maker, the year of the vintage and carrying the governmental seal of approval, the "selo di origim."

As bottle aging progresses, vintage port "throws" a heavy sediment, the simple phenomenon of heavier particles in the wine succumbing to gravity. In appreciation of this, it is important that the wine be stored correctly: horizontally, yet at a slight incline, wine in contact with the cork. This measure will permit the bulk of the sediment to settle into the punt, or base, of the bottle. When vintage port—or any aging red wine, for that matter—is then opened, its contents will be disposed to decanting. Decanting is a simple procedure whereby the clear wine is poured away from the accumulated dregs. A properly stored bottle will facilitate this procedure.

Vintage port can be drunk as soon as 10 years after its vintage date, but most would agree that the wines hit their stride after 15 to 20 years. Vintage ports which I have enjoyed over the years have come from Taylor-Fladgate, Graham and Croft for the English houses, Fonseca and Quinta do Noval for the Portuguese.

Crusted Port: Crusted port differs from vintage port in that it needn't be from a single year, or vintage. It is mostly created from two or three different harvests. Crusted port spends extra time in wood, accelerating the wine's maturation. This extended aging makes for a lighter-bodied wine. Like vintage port, however, crusted port throws a sediment and needs to be decanted.

Late Bottled Vintage: Late bottled vintage (LBV) sees even more time in wood—from four to six years—than the aforementioned wines. As its name implies, the wine comes from a single year's harvest, but is much lighter in color than vintage port and need not be decanted. To comply with the law, both the date of the vintage and the date of bottling must appear on the label. Those who are exploring the world of port should be advised that ordering a glass of "vintage" port does not always yield true vintage port; late bottled vintage is sometimes served in its place. As an aid, it is thus worth remembering that the shipper's generally do not offer late bottled vintage in the same years as real vintage port. Knowing the more recent vintage declarations can help to avoid any misunderstandings. With minor exceptions, most of the port houses declared vintage wine in: 1985 (declaration made in early 1987), 1983, 1982, 1980, 1977, 1975, 1970, 1966, 1963 and 1960. Thus one tends to see late bottled vintage dates of 1981, 1978 and 1974.

Port with a Date of Vintage: A confounding offshoot of the vintage-dated wines is "Port of the Vintage" or "Port with Date of Vintage." Not to be confused with late bottled vintage, port with a date of vintage will come from a single year, but will have been aged in wood for no less than seven

Left, tawny port, so called because of its relatively light coloration, a result of being kept in the cask for seven years or longer

years. The bottle will often say *Colheitas* (which means "vintage")19xx, will have the date of bottling and some indication that the wine has been aged in wood. Port with a date of vintage can be found dating back to the early 1900s. The house of Nierport has a wonderful stock of these *Colheitas* wines. For all intents and purposes, these wines are the first step into tawny ports; that they are from a single vintage, however, prevents them from legally being so titled.

Wood Ports: Wood ports are the bread and butter of port trade. They are blended wines—from several harvests—that are matured in cask until they are ready for drinking. Because they are blended, it is the goal of the shipper to define his style through this wine so that year after year the customer can expect a consistent product. Three main types are: ruby, white and tawny.

Normally, white ports are sweet and served after the meal, but they are no competition for the reds. In response, winemakers have sought to popularize them by fermenting out the sugar, then adding brandy, and marketing them as dry, aperitif wines. These, however, are no competition for a good Fine Sherry. So they have yet to find their market. My first taste of the white port in the lodge of Villa Nova de Gaia was shortly accompanied by the hurling of the balance of my glass over my shoulder onto the sawdusted floors of the caves! Yet where there is wine there is hope: white port has became a viable accessory in the cuisine of today's chefs. More than once have I tasted dishes whose subtleties were enhanced by the addition of white port.

Last, but by no means least, there is tawny port, a special blend of port wine from different vin-

Ruby is young and hearty, not complex and not expensive. To a port drinker, it is the staple wine, attractive for its full, overt flavor. It is aged for two or three years in cask before bottling. One offshoot of ruby port is called "Vintage Character" port. This wine will have the same general features of ruby, but will be of a higher quality, usually older, and certainly more expensive. Unfortunately, such an appellation can only help to blur the distinctions between the several ports which appropriate the word "vintage." Vintage Character, however, will show no date.

White ports are also matured in wood. They can come from either red or white grapes. A white or clear color can be gotten from red grapes by separating the juice from the skins during fermentation before the color has been extracted.

tages which sees many years in cask. Through the more rapid oxidization process within a barrel, this wine matures rather quickly, evolving its tawny color and fabulously scented bouquet. Tawny port is thus more mellow in style than the "vintage-dated" ports, but it is refined, pensive and self-esteeming. True, old tawnies are rather expensive, priced in correlation to the long years the wine has spent aging in barrel. They should not be confused with the cheap tawny port so readily available in the United States. Cheap tawny port owes its existence to the strong world demand for a less concentrated, eminently drinkable port wine. The port shippers have handled this demand by concocting inexpensive tawny port, a blend of ruby and white port. The product is a simple wine of pinkish hue, in contrast to the fading russet of a true tawny. It will have none of the complexity that real tawny port gains through long aging. Since the name "tawny" can apply to either wine, the consumer must rely on color and price to distinguish between the two. Real tawny is not cheap; cheap tawny should never be expensive! True tawny port is a wonderful wine. I have always found the Taylor 10, 20 and 30-year-olds to be fine examples of tawny port. Only the "real thing" will reveal why this is the wine which many port houses most prize.

Dão Wines: The Dão region is the primary producer of Portugal's *vinhos maduros*, or aged wines. It is a mid-altitude area in central Portugal, delineated by no fewer than six mountain ranges. It is shaped and irrigated by a number of rivers including the Rio Dão, from which the area takes its name. This network of rivers, along which

grape quality. While there is little geological differentiation within the area—the soil consists primarily of granite—informed opinion will have it that the wine made between the rivers Mondego and Dão, around the towns of Nelas and Mangualde, are the best products.

In the past, the wines of the Dão were made by many small winemakers, who didn't trouble to make the fine distinction between the grapes that fared best in the environment and lesser varietals. To some extent this is still true today, despite the diligent prodding of the area's wine administration, the Federacão dos Vinicultores do Dão. The goal is to convince farmers of the relative superiority of certain varietals and encourage the eradication of the inferior species. Needless to say, change in the old country takes time.

The primary approved varieties producing the

much of the best planting is done, runs in a general southwest direction, and has by the time it reaches Coimbra converged with the Mondego, the region's main river.

The Dão covers approximately 1,000 square miles, only five percent of which are under vines. Driving through the territory, one is struck by its minimal composition: green geometries of vine, tortuous bands of pine forest, stark expanses of raw granite. It is divided into three main subregions, based upon the general consensus on

Left, the older the better: vintage 1863 botles of Ferreira Port Wine. Right, the barrels of port await their judgment

best Dão reds are the Tourigo, Tinta Pinheira, Tinta Carvalha, and the Avarelhão. More successful white varieties include the Dona Branca, Arinto and Barcelo. Reds are traditionally fermented in large granite tanks, then transferred to wood barrels where a slower fermentation continues under cooler conditions. This retarding and extending of the fermentation process graces the Dão reds with the trait for which they are most appreciated: a glyceral, velvetly feel on the palate. The reds then spend three years aging in wood; the *reservas* even longer. The whites must age in cask for at least 10 months before bottling. They comprise a very small percentage of total production, some three percent. White Dãos mature in a relatively short time—two to three years— and when good have a clean, rather nutty bouquet, and a dry, medium-bodied weight in the mouth.

As Portugal has modernized, the wine industry, which accounts for some 20 percent of its export revenues, has benefited from government incentives. In the Dão region, tremendous cooperatives, like the one located at Mangualde, have been built in the past 20 years. The local landholding growers have accepted the facilities and increasingly bring their grapes there to be processed into wine. After fermentation in the fall, their wine generally remains at the cooperative no later than summer, at which time it is brought to the *adega* (cellar) of the purchaser to age.

The larger growers, whose wine is rarely sold in its entirety, use an unusual interim storage facility: the concrete balloon. This bizarre construction is made by inflating an enormous rubber

Standard Dão reds see about three years of wood aging. This is where the wine evolves, appropriating the attributes of the barrel, slowly oxidizing through the wood's porousness and developing complexity during this introspective stage. The *Reservas* spend even more time in wood and the *Garafeiras*—loosely, "private cellar selection"—are often kept in wood for as long as seven years.

The acceptance and use of the new facilities have unquestionably taken Dão wines to a higher level of quality from the wines of years past. They give the consumer the sought-after balance of price and quality. Concurrently, however, one is obliged to acknowledge a certain homogeneity, that slights the Dão wines of their charismatic individuality.

While French and Italian wines are recogniz-

balloon and enclosing it with a dense grid of curving steel rods. Cement is then sprayed over the monstrosity. When the insides are sealed with a suitable resin, these huge white balls become halfway houses for wines in transit. They have capacities up to 96,000 gallons and can be seen all over Portugal. In the Dão they serve a function beyond mere storage. Each balloon frequently stores a different kind of wine: some will have been made with extended skin contact and thus be colorful and quite tannic; another may contain soft, fruity, free-run wine.

To the winemaker, each offers its own virtues to blending, so that an established flavor and house "signature" can be designed and maintained. When the "assemblage" is complete, the wine is channelled into wooden barrels to age.

able by any of a number of factors—estate, grape type, producer, etc.—many Dão wines lack the cult of personality that would encourage a worldwide popularity. On the other hand, Dão wines have one compelling advantage over their Continental counterparts. They can be enjoyed at the peak of their development at prices that would make any traveler relax. While it would be irresponsible to give any hard and fast data regarding the vintages of Dão wines (so hard to do anywhere, really) the 1954, 1957, 1964, 1970, 1973 and 1978 years are fairly safe bets.

As the producers go, the cooperative facilities have narrowed the gaps in quality between most producers. The following are wines I have regularly found rather pleasing: "Conde de Santar" from Carvalho, Ribeira & Ferreira. "Grão Vasco" from the Vinicola do Vale do Dão, "Terras Altas" from Jose Maria da Fonseca, "Dalva" from the Caves da Silva, "Porto dos Cavaleiros" from the Caves São João.

Don't let this list deter you from sampling the other Dão wines. Do remember that the notations *Reservas* and the *Garrafeiras* usually mean far better wine at a mildly higher price.

Bairrada: To the west of the Dão, stretching southward from Oporto to the university town of Coimbra, is the recently designated wine region called Bairrada. An area which has produced wine as long as any other in Portugal, Bairrada was nonetheless overlooked during the demarcation of 1906. Finally, as a result of concerted pressure from the local lobby, this legitimately estimable area was formally sanctioned in 1979. It is not an area frequently visited by tourists, but it does offer the renowned Buçaco Forest.

Both red and white wines are made here, the bulk of the white being used to make rather good sparkling wine by the "méthode champenoise." It is the red wine, though, that deserves attention. Made from the Baga grape, which dominates the region's acreage, the Bairrada reds require years of aging to reach their peak.

While somewhat tannic in its youth, the Baga repays patience with the elegance of its maturity. Deep, brilliant ruby in color, with the fine, cedary fragrances of an old Bordeaux from the St. Julien area, Baga wines unfurl layers of fruit and flavor on the palate. Its tannins, so prevalent in the wine's youth, faithfully endure, but adapt and give balance and structure in the wine's maturity. Such are my memories of a 1958 Buçaco that confirmed my beliefs in the fine wines of Portugal. But you will not find these wines in many city shops. Why not venture up into the "Green Cathedral," as Buçaco is known?

With a lunch in Sintra, an afternoon coffee in Coimbra among the students at the university, Buçaco and its Palace Hotel can be leisurely reached from Lisbon before nightfall. As you drive, the ground becomes higher, the vegetation greener, darker and taller. The dense, fairytale forest, thickened with exotic species, is broken by lonely, winding footpaths. Up you go, until you arrive at an absolutely eccentric palace. Begun as a monastery in the early 14th century; built into a Neo-Manueline palace in the 16th century; converted to a royal hunting lodge in the 18th century; "The Palace Hotel" is a quixotic amalgam, with remarkable first-class quarters. The rooms are ornate and furnished with antiques.

Dining proves to be an exercise in old-world leisure and elegance. Five to six-course meals are the norm, served by attentive, accommodating waiters. Yet the biggest thrill comes as you open the wine list and discover the treasured cellars of Buçaco.

Available only through the properties of Mr. Alexandre d'Almeida (at the Metropole in Lisbon; Das Thermas in Curia; the Astoria in Coimbra and the Praia-Mar in Carcavelos), the wines of Buçaco are not available for export. These wines are made on the premises at Buçaco in the old method of foot-stomping fermentation. The cellars, which contain over 200,000 bottles, are readily displayed to anyone interested. Both a red and a white are produced and selections can be made from vintages dating back into the 1920s. Invariably, a wine-lover's vacation slows down here. One can luxuriate for days in this wine list, sampling 30-year-old whites and 40-year-old reds! Reasons to visit this unusual palace are numerous—the forests are enchanting—but none better than to taste the finest red table wines this country has to offer.

Lisbon: In the environs of Lisbon, there are four officially demarcated wine regions, two on the verge of extinction and two eking out a living despite the onslaught on modernity. While none of the four are of great commercial importance, they are each quite distinct, with long traditions of wine-making.

To the west of Lisbon, just north of Estoril, lies the vanishing area of Carcavelos. Swinging northwest onto the actual shores of the Atlantic is the remarkable, yet endangered region known as Colares. Almost due north of Lisbon, the Bucelas zone maintains most of its original shape, producing some of the country's best whites. And to the south, one can explore the vineyards of the famous sweet Muscat wine: the Moscatel de Setúbal.

Carcavelos, like many Portuguese wines, gained a reputation through the Anglo-Portuguese economic alliances of earlier centuries. Its proximity to Lisbon—about 15 miles (25 km)—was once a boon to its popularity. Today, however, real estate developments in the resort towns of Estoril and Cascais, have reduced production of this wine to a mere trickle. When you can find it (your best chance of doing so is in the better Lisbon restaurants) Carcavelos is a nutty-flavored, fortified wine. On the sugar scale, it will vary from moderately dry to medium-sweet. For those eager to seek out this endangered species, the best lead that can be offered is the name Quinta do Barão, the sole remaining property, owned by Raul Ferreira & Sons Ltd.

Colares makes some of the most unusual red wine in the world. The town itself sits between the hills of Sintra to the east and the beaches of the Atlantic Ocean to its west. The best Colares vines are planted in the sand of the Atlantic shoreline through exceedingly labor-intensive methods.

Left, they grow in every single province of Portugal. Here, vineyards in the Ribatejo

The varietal used in winemaking is called the Ramisco, a small, dark blue grape.

Planting the vine in sand is no mean feat. A trench must first be dug down to the layer of Mesozoic clay below. Into the clay the roots of the plant are laid. During this work, the laborers often place baskets atop their head to ensure a channel of oxygen if and when the walls of sand cave in. The work is so physically difficult that rather than plant individual vines, the vine is cropped in such a way as to have one "mother" plant course through the ground. The final visual effect is of many seemingly individual plants sprouting upward; thus a row of vines is created.

The single most fascinating fact of the Colares vines is that their original root stocks have survived intact. Those who know their viticultural history will recall that Europe was plagued in the 1870s by the invasion of a parasite named the phylloxera aphid. The louse had arrived from the United States during viticultural exchanges with the Continent. It ravaged the vineyards of Europe by burrowing into the soil and chewing the roots of the vine for sustenance. In several years, virtually all of the vine-growing areas of the continent had been attacked. Many inventive cures were tried, yet nothing seemed to help. Eventually, the crisis was remedied, in an ironic manner. Root stocks from grape vines of the United States, huskier and largely immune to the phylloxera, were shipped to Europe, where the European vines were grafted onto its new root host with a kind of jigsaw fitting. This surgery was successful and today even the great classified growths of Bordeaux—no doubt to the chagrin of the French—have American rootstocks.

Not so with Colares. What saved their roots was the extremely dense soil—packed sand—into which the phylloxera could not burrow. So the plants and thus their wines remain much as they were over a hundred years ago. The red, which are the wines of note, are rather astringent in their youth, with firmly entrenched tannis. They become approachable after six or seven years, as the wine improves distinctly with age. When the wine is at its best, Colares tannins have relinquished their hold on the wine: the bouquet is fully fruited and bright. In flavor, Colares is medium-bodied, somewhat briary, with a concentrated, impressive finish. When dining, take the advice that I did: order, if possible, the "Colares Chita," produced by Antonio Bernadino Paolo Da Silva. In this case, the older, the better.

Some 15 miles (25 km) northwest of Lisbon lies the tiny wine-making region of Bucelas. Encompassing a mere 450 acres, production of Bucelas rarely exceeds 75,000 cases. The vines are grown both on the gentle slopes and the valley floor of the Trançao River, in soil that is predominantly clay. There are only two grapes—both white—grown in the region, the Arinto and the Esgana Cão. Like other wine regions surrounding Lisbon, wine-making in Bucelas—or Bucellas, as one sometimes sees on wine labels—has declined to practically one main producer: Camillio Alves, which bottles its wine under the label Caves Velhas.

In its youth, Bucelas wine is pale greenish-yellow. The bouquet is fine and fragrant, the taste, clean and dry, with a light but marked acidity. The young Bucelas spends very little time developing in wood. Despite the miniscule production, these young wines are geared for export and can be found in several of the EEC nations. The traveler's mission then becomes to locate an older Bucelas, or a "garrafeira." Mature Bucelas, which can spend years in Brazilian oak before bottling, will show far more exotic fruit flavors, and a dry, nutty finish. The older ones are some of Portugal's best white wines.

Setúbal: Moscatel de Setúbal is a fabulous dessert wine whose description has coaxed poetry out of all but the most perfunctory of oenophiles. Moscatel de Setúbal is sweet, perfumed, ethereal. Grown in an area south of Lisbon, across the bridge on the Arrábida Peninsula, the wine takes its name from the nearby port of Setúbal. Moscatel de Setúbal earned its "selo de origem," or governmental sanction, back in 1907. The area is presently being rezoned so that a distinct region for the local red wine will be recognized. Moscatel de Setúbal may be red or white, the majority being white. The small amount of red Moscatel, made with the Moscatel Roxo and rarely seen outside of Portugal, is worth the search if one is adventurously inclined.

Moscatel de Setúbal is fortified wine whose grapes grow rather wildly around the villages of Palmela and Azeitão. The grape "must"—crushed grapes—is vinified in cement vats and the fermentation is arrested by the addition of grape brandy at a specific sugar level. The vinified wine is then transferred to large cement containers, where lightly crushed grapes and skins are added to the must. The added contents are allowed to steep in the original concoction and their marvelous effect is to impart the signature aroma of the Moscatel grape at its freshest. After a single pressing, the wine is held, spending some time in cask, until ready for bottling and sale.

The two white wines commercially available are the six-year-old and the 25-year-old Moscatel de Setúbal. Both are intensely sweet and quite alluring as a finale to a summer's meal. The younger wine exhibits the intense varietal beauty of the grape; the fully mature 25-year-old does the same, with the added complexity and smoothness of age, as well as a dark, cosmetic brilliance.

Right, wine casks must be tended with great care; blends are added at specific times over the years

POUSADAS AND MANOR HOUSES

If waking up in a bed that once belonged to a Portuguese queen, or staying in an opulent remodeled convent, or even eating homemade bread and cheese in a shepherd's cottage sounds like an exciting change of pace from standard hotels, try the government-run *pousadas* (inns) or the privately-owned *turismo de habitacão* (tourist lodging) networks. The *pousadas*, now numbering more than 30, have justly earned a good reputation for comfort, luxury and service, and are easily located by abundant road signs. The quality of the tourist lodging varies widely, as these are private homes now open to the public.

If you happen to be traveling in the lush green and thick-forested northwestern corner of Portugal, you will come to the town of **Valença do Minho** and the **Pousada de São Teotonio**. This elegant *pousada* sits on a high point inside the ancient walled city and has a spectacular view of the Minho river across to Spain and the Galician mountains. It is also perfectly located for walks around the medieval town of tiny winding streets and stone houses.

The **Pousada D. Diniz**, named after the 14th-century Portuguese king, is in **Vila Nova da Cerveira**, just west of Valença, and also overlooks the Minho river. The inn is actually built into the town's ancient castle and has a small 18th-century chapel around the corner. The rooms, housed in several separate buildings, are large and feature lovely carved beds.

To the east is the **Pousada de São Bento**, a comfortable ivy-covered stone building on a hill inside the **Peneda-Gerês National Park**, a beautiful dense forest veined with cool streams. Its floor-to-ceiling windows overlook the Caniçada Dam and the surrounding countryside. This inn has a swimming pool and tennis court.

The **Pousada de Santa Marinha da Costa** is further south, in **Guimarães**, the town known as the "cradle of Portugal"—the first king of the country was born here. Do not confuse this *pousada* (some three miles outside of town) with the more modest but charming **Santa Maria** in Guimarães proper. The Santa Marinha is a beautiful converted 12th-century monastery, luxurious with all its original stone walls and windows—including the large center hall where the last owner is rumored to have exercised his horses! Some of the small rooms here used to be monks' cells but don't think you will feel incarcerated; many have balconies with a view of a charming courtyard that saves them from feeling cramped.

The north of Portugal is the birthplace of the tourist lodging plan, which was created as a means of conserving some of the country's most beautiful private manor homes and palaces. The owners of these magnificent homes can no longer afford the expensive maintenance and have opened them up to tourists. One of the most pleasant aspects of these lodgings is that visitors are usually treated as guests of the family and are expected to respond as graciously.

One of the most impressive examples of tourist lodging in the northwestern tip of the country is **Paço de Calheiros**, a three-century-old manor house and chapel. The house has been the home of the Count of Calheiros since 1336, and the

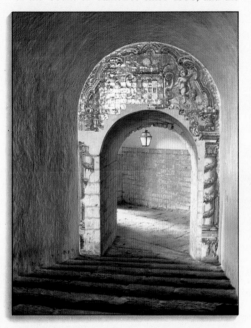

present count now lives here with his mother and family.

There are 10 rooms here, all restored with antiques and, where possible, with original materials, and all done in impeccable taste. Be sure to sample the homemade jams as you dine using the family's heirloom silverware.

The bedrooms are all wonderful, but perhaps the most romantic experience is to sleep on Portugal's Queen Carlotta Joaquina's original bed, a precious antique decorated with wood carved legs in the shape of dolphins crowned with flowers.

Another breathtaking home in the north is **Paço da Gloria** in **Arcos de Valdevez**, just northeast of Calheiros. This 17th-century stone palace, which once belonged to the Count of

Santa Eulalia, is now owned by an Englishman, Colin Clark. The house, with its large book-end towers, sits on a hill surrounded by vineyards and a garden. The interior has been decorated with a hospitable international sophistication—note the highly-polished entry-hall floor of black basalt and orange brick relecting the busts on their pedestals.

The bedrooms here have spacious bathrooms. One of the loveliest features of the house is its arched veranda. Have a seat and gaze out at the ice-blue pool and the tailored green lawns.

Further south, the **Viana do Castelo** and **Ponte de Lima** areas offer a wide range of lodging homes. North to Meadela on the road to Ponte de Lima stop at **Casa do Ameal**, a gracious shell-shaped building with a flower-framed pool. The house has three double rooms, four apartments,

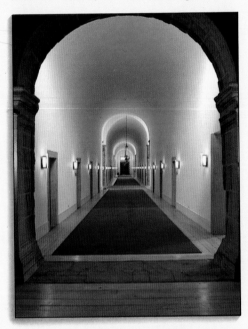

sitting rooms and an attractive garden.

In Ponte de Lima itself, try **Casa do Outeiro**, a large, comfortable 18th-century house framed by large shade trees and well-kept grounds. It is fitted with all the modern conveniences, yet has lost none of its original charm. Not far away is **Casa do Antepaço**, tucked away in a lovely *quinta*, or estate. This house has been carefully restored, and guests can stay in the one private apartment or in one of the four double rooms

Preceding page, the Pousada da Santa Marinha in Guimarães. Left, an outside stairway at Pousada de São Filipe in Setúbal. Above, the hall down which the former owner ran horses at Pousada da Santa Marinha

available, and enjoy the comfortable living room complete with fireplace, the library, or the terrace which overlooks the garden and Lima River.

In the same area, near Facha, rising suddenly out of a curve in the road, is **Casa das Torres**, a magnificent example of King João V (1706-1750) architecture, with stone-framed windows, thick white-washed stone walls and gracefully tiled tower roof-tops. There is one double room in the main house and a separate annex apartment. Visitors are welcome to make full use of the swimming pool and gardens.

For those who prefer a more rural setting and more privacy, **Quinta da Aldeia** in Crasto-Ribeira is a lovely if small *quinta* with an ivy-covered entrance. It offers an entire apartment complete with kitchen, bathroom and living room, all furnished with rustic wood furniture.

Your own watermill: Minho de Estoroes, also near Ponte de Lima, is a delightful small, old stone watermill sitting on the banks of the Esteroes brook that has been carefully refurbished to fit one family. Don't be surprised if you share the brook with a group of local women who kneel at the rocks to wash their family's clothing.

These are just a few of the 50 or so different houses dotted around this area, known as the *Costa Verde* or "Green Coast." Every house is very different, and every owner will receive you in his or her own personal way.

In the Douro Valley there are a few Tourist Lodging houses, two of the most interesting being the **Villa Hostilina** in Lamego and **Casa dos Varais** in Cambres. The villa overlooks the old city of Lamego and has been totally refurbished to include a gym, sauna, massage room, tennis courts and a swimming pool. In the Casa dos Varais you can enjoy the full beauty of the Douro, for its large stone house, terraces and gardens overlook the river and nearby hillsides. This house has only two double rooms and a separate sitting room for guests.

Deep in the heart of the **Serra da Estrêla** is the town of Manteigas and the **Pousada São Lourenço**, a modest building of stone with a red-tiled roof. The rooms are plain but comfortable with wooden four-poster twin beds. Rooms on the second floor have little verandas with dramatic views of the mountains and the town below. The inn has a lounge and snug television room, and a fireplace warms up the dining room. Regional specialities, such as the famous Serra da Estrêla sheeps' milk cheese, is served here. You should also try the local *gerupiga* wine, usually served in unmarked bottles.

One of the best spots in the Serra is **Sabugueiro**, a tiny mountain village of narrow cobblestone and mud streets and granite houses. Any villager can show you the way to the **Casa do Sabugueiro** run by Dona Teresa da Graça Trinidade, who also happens to run the local tavern, selling shot-glasses of red wine to tired shepherds wearing brown felt hats and overcoats. Staying here gives you a real taste of rural Portugal (although with considerably more comfort than in the houses around you). Expect to wake up to the tinkle of sheeps' bells and the low calls of the shepherds before sunrise.

Dona Teresa has remodeled the inside of two granite houses into charming white-walled bedrooms, neat bathrooms and sitting rooms with small corner fireplaces. She has also set up a small dining room where she serves homemade rye bread, cheese and heaping platefuls of the meal of the day. One of her nieces makes cheese by hand over a wood fire, as well as fresh cottage cheese. This is a dying art, so ask if you can watch the process—but be prepared to wake up at 5:30 a.m. to do so.

vent of Christ, and a little way out of town, in Castelo do Bode, is a *pousada* perched above a large blue-water dam on the Zêzere River. This inn is surrounded by olive and pine trees. The bedrooms are smallish but very comfortable with plain wood furniture and floral print curtains. The breakfast room is full of sunlight in the morning and looks out over the dam.

Just south of Batalha is Porto de Mós, with its massive castle. The rambling Quinta do Rio Alcaide, recently remodeled, is set in the side of the mountains, with columned terraces and red-tiled roofs overlooking the wide gardens. The quinta has four sections: the main house, the "middle" house, the old "bread-oven" house, which has been transformed into a self-contained apartment, as has the "windmill" house that sits on a hill overlooking the *quinta*.

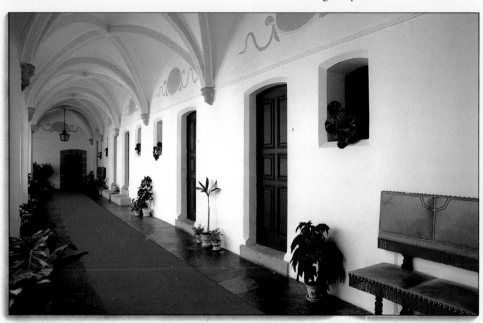

At the foot of the Serra is Alpedrinha, a small town huddled under the mountainside. Turn right off the main street and you will come to a 19th-century-style house called Casa do Barreiro. Here you will be ushered through several rooms full of overstuffed chairs, pianos, thick carpets, and numerous knick-knacks and antiques. The walls of the houses are decorated with antique fans, tapestries and tiny crowded vitrines. If you come in winter be prepared for the cold. A glimpse underneath those floor-length tablecloths reveal small pans filled with coal—heating the old-fashioned way. The bedroom has a 19th-century-style canopy bed, chaise lounge and small eating table, for breakfast served in your room in the morning.

The town of Tomar boasts the intriguing Con-

Southwest of here and just north of Lisbon is the graceful walled town of Óbidos. The Pousada do Castelo, which is built into a section of the old castle, is very small and popular, and therefore difficult to reserve. If you miss out on a room, it's still more than worthwhile to stop in and have a drink.

Closer to Lisbon is Torres Vedras and Quinta do Hespanhol, a 16th-century manor which still has much of its original Manueline detail. The house, has four double rooms and various sitting rooms, is bordered by large shady trees and has a lovely columned veranda on the top floor. Some three miles (five km) outside of Torres Vedras, in S. Mamede de Mertola, is the Moinho do Loural, an old windmill converted to a tiny two-bedroom apartment, complete with kitchen, bathroom and sitting room with fireplace.

Following the Tagus River north, the traveler comes to **Santarém** where two families have opened up their homes to guests. **Casal da Torre** is the more modest of the two, a small house on the edge of a cobblestone street with flowering bushes covering its front and plants sprouting from its roof. The house has three bedrooms, sitting rooms, and a small garden where you can share an open-air barbecue.

Quinta da Sobreira is larger and more elegant, with an arched entranceway and tower on one side. This early-19th-century home has a swimming pool and riding facilities, Santarém being famous for its horses. There are only three bedrooms here, each with a private bathroom.

A view to Spain: If you head east from here, you will arrive at the border town of **Marvão**, a 14th-

hostess will provide large logs in winter) in the open sitting room, a cozy loft bedroom with white-on-white bedspreads and a lovely arched window seat and kitchenette. There are two more bedrooms downstairs, so the house is big enough for three couples or a family.

A few of the houses in the greater Lisbon area live up to the beauty and grace of the houses in the north of the country. One example of this is the **Quinta da Capela** in Sintra, an exquisite place that fits in perfectly with the Byronesque setting of the Sintra hills. The palace belongs to the Marchioness de Cadaval and is arranged in perfect taste with fresh orchids on the windowsills; the dining room in soft shell-pink tones; and the extensive gardens carefully tended. The *quinta* has one suite, with four double rooms in the main house. Two apartments large enough for four

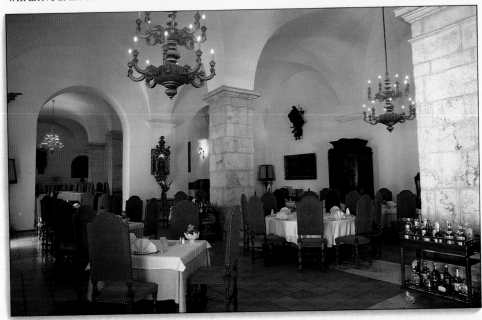

century whitewashed walled town perched like an eagle's nest at the top of the mountain. Inside the medieval walls is the **Pousada Santa Maria**, simply decorated with red tile floors, wood-beamed ceilings and fireplaces, and a glassed-in terrace with a panoramic view into neighboring Spain. The bedrooms are comfortable but small, and the restaurant's menu includes local game.

If you prefer to have a house of your own here, for a few days or a few weeks, try **Travessa do Terreirinho**, owned by Margarida Leite Rio. The house is typical, with a huge fireplace (the

Left, the vaulted ceilings of Pousada dos Lóios in Évora. Above, the dining room of Pousada da Rainha Santa Isabel in Estremoz

people each have been set up on the grounds.

Also in Sintra is **Quinta de São Thiago**, close to the **Seteais Palace**. The seven double rooms here are all luxuriously fitted, as are the various lounges, the bar and the sitting room. The *quinta* also has a large garden with magnificent shade trees that surround the modern swimming pool and tennis court.

Directly south of Lisbon is **Palmela** and the impressive **Pousada Castelo de Palmela**. This *pousada* is part of a 15th-century monastery built in the reign of King João I and faces the Palmela Castle. All the large airy bedrooms have sweeping views over the countryside, and there is also a gorgeous sun-filled cloister in the center, protected by a series of stone arches.

Not far away is Setúbal, whose **Pousada de**

São Filipe is actually inside the walls of the São Filipe Castle. Most of the high-ceilinged rooms have a view of the bay, as does the restaurant, which specializes in regional dishes. There is a pleasant outdoor lounge on the old stone terrace for a drink before dinner.

Traveling toward Spain you will come to **Elvas** and **Estremoz**. The **Pousada de Santa Luzia** in Elvas is best known for its cuisine and lavish servings of food. Many people just stop in for lunch. The rooms, however, are perfectly adequate.

You should make a point of staying in the fantastic **Pousada Rainha Santa Isabel** in Estremoz, which sits elegantly above the small town. This inn has been brilliantly restored with 17th- and 18th-century antiques. A majestic marble staircase leads to the bedrooms upstairs, all ro-

tions of the ancient castle. Today completely refurbished, it is a fabulous inn with high ceilings and granite and marble arches. A carved marble staircase leads upstairs to the bedrooms. The sitting room here is all hand-painted and decorated with antiques, and the dining room has been set around the glassed-in interior garden and fountain.

The tourist lodging in Évora is also exceptional. The towers that formed the original gates to the city dating from Moorish times now form one of the walls of the **Casa do Conde da Serra**, owned by Sra. Sousa Cabral. The house came into the hands of the first Count da Serra da Tourega in the mid-1600s, and his coat of arms is still displayed on the front of the house.

Inside, the house is filled with precious furniture and artful decor. An impressive 17th-century

mantically furnished in deep rich colors, and all with good views. The dining room is made up of a series of low arches and huge stone pillars which are softly lit in the evening, and the menu branches out from local specialities to include Steak Diane and Crepes Suzette, cooked at your table.

In between Estremoz and Elvas, slightly past Borba, is **Vila Viçosa** and the elegant **Casa dos Arcos**, named after the slender arches that embellish its entrance. The grandest features of this 16th-century home are the original frescoes that cover the walls of the sitting room. The rooms are not as inspiring, but they are pleasant, airy and private.

In Évora, the **Pousada dos Loios** was originally a 15th-century mansion built on the founda-

oil painting depicting Christ's cruxifiction on four arched wooden panels adorns a huge stairway. Some of the bedrooms have their own gracefully tiled fireplaces and Arraiolos rugs on the floor. Breakfast is served in the main dining room, which is furnished with 18th-century commodes, a vitrine of *lignum vitae* dating from the reign of King João V, and a Dutch cupboard that dates from 1625.

Not far from Évora and just a few kilometers from the village of Redondo is the magnificent **Convento da Serra D'Ossa** which has been in the family of Sr. Henrique Leotte for over 150 years. Originally built by monks of the Order of Saint Paul around 1070, other sections were added in the 14th and 18th centuries. The surrounding countryside is covered in olive, pine and eucalyptus trees. The rooms are converted monks' cells which branch off a main corridor, itself a work of art, with panels of blue- and -white tiles dating from the 18th century.

A wonderful outdoor patio, also decorated in original tiles, faces a Florentine fountain with archways overhead. The original chapel, which is open to guests, displays frescoes dating from the 17th and 18th centuries and tiles depicting biblical scenes, which have the rare feature of being signed.

On the west side of the Alentejo, not far from the Roman ruins of Mirobriga, is **Santiago do Cacém** and the **Pousada de São Tiago**, a small ivy-covered building with a garden full of flowers and a swimming pool. There are four bedrooms in the original part of the inn, all with a pleasant rustic flavor, with wood floors and whitewashed

absolutely perfect for hours of star-gazing.

And finally to the Algarve, Portugal's southernmost province. The **Pousada São Brás** is a peaceful whitewashed inn located some two miles (three kilometers) above the town of **São Brás de Alportel**. The rooms are plain, but have a view over the valley below and beyond to the coast. The glassed-in semicircular dining room also has a panoramic view, and the lounge is comfortably decorated with leather furniture and throw rugs on the floor.

Pousada do Infante, named after Prince Henry the Navigator, is on the Atlantic edge of the Algarve in Sagres. It is a sprawling modern building with pleasant, airy rooms that overlook the coast. With the dining room fireplace, thoughtfully selected art and amenities, and the carefully tended, lush green lawn that reaches out to the

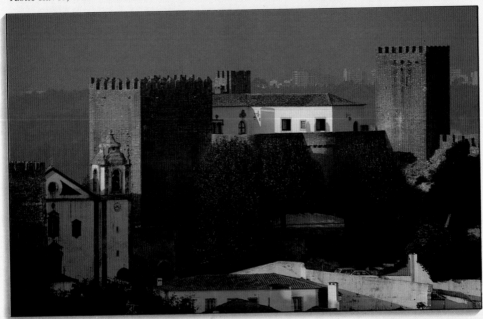

walls, and there are additional bedrooms in the annex. This *pousada* has a calm and welcoming feeling about it.

Seeing stars: Heading south, almost on the border with the Algarve, is **Pousada Santa Clara** overlooking the vast blue waters of the **Santa Clara Dam**. This *pousada* is a little hard to get to, as it is off the main road, but it is worth the extra drive. The dining room looks out onto a stone terrace and a sloping garden planted with orange trees. During the day you can go for long walks around the lake, and the darkness at night is

Left, exterior of Pousada de Santa Marinha da Costa outside Guimarães. Above, Pousada do Castelo in the walled town of Obidos

cliff's edge, these comfortable lodgings are reminiscent of an American country club.

Tourist lodging is not as developed here as it is in the north, but there is one place worth staying, the **Quinta do Caraçol** just at the entrance of **Tavira** on the east side of the Algarve. The owner recently converted the quinta and did a lovely job, picking up on the Tunisian blues and soft yellows traditional for this region. The house is sparkling white and low, covered in occasional splashes of purple bougainvillea, reflected in the crisp blue water of the mini-pool tucked into the back of the house. There is also a tennis court and small bar open to guests, who are made to feel comfortable in this gem of a home. (For information about reservations, see "Where To Stay" in the Travel Tips section)

ART AND ARCHITECTURE

Portugal's unique geographical position, cut off from Europe by Spain on one border, facing out toward the New World on the other, is reflected in its art and architecture. In order to counter the natural tendency toward isolation, Portuguese artists and architects have for centuries looked outside for influence and affirmation. Even today, a kind of magical aura surrounds cultural events that occur *lá fora*—literally "out there," meaning abroad, overseas. Simultaneously, because it serves as a bridge, Portugal has attracted numerous foreign artists, as will be seen below. Thus, a kind of filtering process has occurred, where local traditions have blended with imported ideas. At its best, Portuguese art has forged out of foreign influences powerful and original stylistic languages.

Romanesque

In Europe, the reiteration of Christianity in the face of encroaching Moslem faith was represented not only by the Crusades, but also by the reforms introduced by the new religious orders, especially those of Cluny and Cister, whose influence spread far and wide.

In Portuguese art, a discussion of the Romanesque period, the period that began with the 12th century is essentially a discussion of religious architecture. Other than a few illustrated manuscripts, very little except architecture has survived from that time. The predominance of religious architecture is hardly incidental: the founding of the kingdom corresponds to the reconquest of Portugal from the Moors; and hence, to a period in which Christianity was strongly felt. The construction of cathedrals during this period followed the path of reconquest from Braga to Oporto, southwards to Coimbra, Lamego (reconstructed in the 18th century), Lisbon and Évora.

The man who, enlisting the aid of the Crusaders, led this sweep of Portugal and became its first king was Afonso Henriques. His father, Henri, had arrived from Burgundy in the late 11th century. These Burgundian roots of the kingdom were instrumental in the development of Portuguese Romanesque architecture. The close relations of the duchy of Burgundy with the Order of Cluny meant that this order became especially influential—numerous monks from Cluny and Moissac became bishops of Oporto and Braga. Portuguese Romanesque cathedrals, especially those in the west of the country along the route to the pilgrimage church of Santiago de Compostela (in what today is Spanish Galicia), have an affinity with the Clunian churches of Auvergne and Languedoc.

The building of Romanesque churches in Portugal continued into the 14th century in the north, at which time the Gothic style was already spreading throughout the rest of the country. Portuguese Romanesque is an architecture of simple, often dramatically stark forms, whose sturdiness is frequently explained by the need for fortification against the continued threat of Moorish or Castilian invasion. This fortified appearance is enhanced in the cathedrals of Lisbon and Coimbra by the crenellated facade towers which seem to balk against intrusion.

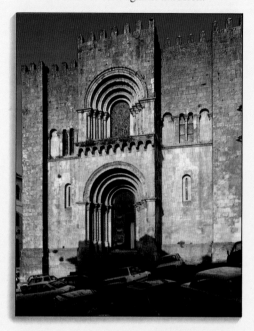

Portuguese Romanesque is largely an architecture of granite. This stone abounds in the northern regions, where numerous monasteries were built—of which usually nothing more than the churches have survived. The hardness of granite renders detailed carving impossible, thus favoring a simplicity of form. Absent, therefore, are the ornately carved tympana of French and Spanish Romanesque churches. In areas where the softer limestone abounds, such as the central belt of the country (including Coimbra, Tomar and Lisbon), carved decorations are more common.

Although there are regional variations, these Romanesque churches share a certain robustness; a method of construction based on semi-circular arches and barrel vaults; a cruciform plan; and a solid, almost sculptural sense of form in the interior which allows for a play of light and shade. All these features serve to enhance a sense of mystery, indeed of Divine Mystery. This sobriety is accentuated by the paucity of decoration, which is frequently reduced to the capitals of columns and the archivolts surrounding the portals. When the tympana are not bare, the simplified carvings are usually stylized depictions of Christ in Majesty, or the *Agnus Dei* (Lamb of God) or simply of a cross. In some cases, animals and serpents climb up the granite columns, as in the *Sé Velha* (Old Cathedral) of Coimbra or in the unusually richly decorated principal portal of the early 13th-century Church of São Salvador in Bravães in Minho.

Gothic

In France, new methods of construction involving pointed arches and ribbed vaults allowed for lighter, taller architectural forms. As the main weight of the building was now borne outside at fixed points by flying buttresses, the walls could be pierced at frequent intervals. The light filtering into these Gothic interiors became a metaphor for Divine Light, replacing the Romanesque emphasis on Mystery.

The first building in Portugal to use these new construction methods was the majestic church at the Abbey of Alcobaça, commissioned by Afonso Henriques. With its great height and elegant, unadorned white interior bathed in a milky light, Alcobaça is one of the most serene and beautiful churches in Portugal. Begun in 1178 and consecrated in 1222, it is almost purely French in inspiration: its plan echoes that of Clairvaux, the seat of the Cistercian Order in Burgundy—a nave and two side aisles of almost the same height, a two-aisled transept, and an apse whose ambulatory fans out into various chapels. Other Portuguese churches at this time did not employ this Cistercian plan and usually followed the scheme of a nave and two side aisles, a salient well-lit transept, and an apse consisting of three or five chapels, without ambulatory.

The true affirmation of the national Gothic style came after the Portuguese armies defeated the invading Castilians at the Battle of Aljubarrota. In fulfillment of a religious vow made prior to the battle, King João I commissioned the construction of a magnificent monastery. In 1388 work began on the now famous Dominican Monastery of *Santa Maria da Vitória* (St. Mary of the Victory), better known as Batalha, which means "battle."

The stylistic heterogeneity of Batalha is due to the many years it took to build. Its construction can be divided into three stages. The first, lasting until 1438, was initially supervised by architect Afonso Domingues, who died in 1402, and then by a figure known as Huguet, whose nationality is unknown. Domingues' plan was entirely Portuguese in inspiration, following the general scheme of the churches of the Mendicant Orders (Franciscans and Dominicans), which were now gaining ascendance. The central nave is illuminated by clerestory windows; simple ribbing supports the vault; and the chancel gives on to two pairs of chapels, without ambulatory.

Offset by Domingues' scheme, Huguet's contributions, which include the Founder's Chapel and the famous chapterhouse vault, have a greater refinement and elegance, influenced by English Gothic architecture. Indeed, similarities have been noted between Batalha and the Cathedrals of York and Canterbury. Contact with England was close at this time as João I's wife, Philippa of Lancaster, was the daughter of John of Gaunt. But these and other foreign influences were subject to modifications, especially in the relatively low proportions of the nave, in a certain oriental flavor in the Founder's Chapel, and in the large, airy cloister characteristic of Portuguese Gothic churches. With Huguet's sudden death in 1438, the chapels of the octagonal pantheon remained incomplete.

The second stage, under Martim Vasques and Fernão de Évora, lasted until 1481, during which time a second cloister was built. The third stage was supervised by Mateus Fernandes and Diogo Boytac, and corresponded to the Manueline (see below) phase of the building, culminating in the arcade of the incomplete chapels and the Royal Cloister.

The stylistic influence of Batalha is felt in various churches throughout the country, examples being the Cathedral at Guarda and the ruined Church of Carmo in Lisbon, which were both begun at the end of the 14th century. The state of ruin in which the latter stands today is a poetic if somber commemoration of the Lisbon Earthquake of 1755.

In general, the austerity imposed by the Mendicant Orders meant that the national Gothic style leaned toward temperance rather than flamboyance. Soaring pinnacles and the dissolution of form into light did not suit either the religious orders or the national temperament.

If Portuguese Gothic architecture retains something of Romanesque sobriety, this is not the case with its Gothic sculpture. In addition to the decoration of capitals and columns, three-dimensional sculpture became increasingly common. In free-standing pieces in both wood and stone, the image of the Virgin presides. Emphasis is given to those aspects of her relationship with her Son that are most human and tender—from pregnancy in the *Senhora do O* (such as the beautiful example by the renowned Master Pero, now at the Machado de Castro Museum in Coimbra, to suckling (sometimes while caressing the Child's foot), or carrying the Infant on her raised hip, as at the cathedrals of Braga and Évora. The hieratic sternness of Romanesque carvings is replaced by the humanization of Christ and his Mother. The handling of the drapes also becomes less stylized: now ample, they follow the curves of the body they clothe.

By far the most important category of sculpture in the 14th and 15th centuries was that of tombs, often carved with representations of their inhabitants. Previously, burial within the church walls was not practiced, and exterior tombs were seldom extensively carved. It was only well into the 13th century that sculpted sarcophagi began to

proliferate. Coimbra was the most important focus for this tradition, as a result of the abundance of soft limestone there. While the sarcophagi of Lisbon and Évora are generally archaizing, the tomb (1330) at the Church of Santa Clara-a-Nova in Coimbra of the *Rainha Santa* (Holy Queen) lying serenely, clothed in the Franciscan habit of the Order of St. Clare, is a moving example of early Gothic naturalism. The sculpture has no Portuguese precedents. It is thought that it was inspired by the School of Aragon, which was then the most important center for sculpture in the Iberian Peninsula.

The two tombs that together emerge as the crowning glory of Portuguese 14th-century funerary sculpture are those of King Pedro and his lover Inês de Castro in Alcobaça. The illicit,

passionate love affair, the brutal murder of Inês, Pedro's unmitigated sorrow and horrible revenge—this sad and beautiful story has been sung by the nation's greatest writers and poets. (see page 26) The sarcophagi do justice to the dramatic tale. Of unknown authorship and hybrid influence, they outshine all preceding funerary sculpture in their monumentality, plasticity, refinement of naturalistic detail, and richness of symbolism. With the tombs facing each other in opposite transepts, come the Day of Judgment, the lovers, as Pedro planned, will rise gazing into each other's eyes.

Inês lies calmly, surrounded by angels and crowned at last, in earth as never in life, as Pedro's queen. The sides of her tomb are carved with scenes from the life of Christ and the Virgin, while the head and foot depict scenes of Calvary and the Last Judgment respectively. The latter, a favored theme of European portal sculpture, is especially interesting for being the only one of its kind in Portugal.

The sides of Pedro's sarcophagus display incidents from the life of St. Bartholemew. Carved on the head of this tomb is a magnificent rosette—two concentric circles, the themes of which have been controversial. Some scholars see in them the narration of the story of Pedro's love for Inês; more frequently, the rosette is considered to be a wheel of fortune, representing life's vicissitudes. The masterful grace in the carving of these twin tombs brilliantly executes both symbolic and narrative detail.

Of a later date (ca. 1433) is the double tomb in the Founder's Chapel at Batalha of King João I and Philippa of Lancaster. The tomb itself is unadorned but for a Gothic inscription. The King clasps the sword of Aljubarrota, and his armor bears the crest of the House of Avis, the dynasty he founded. The crowned couple lie open-eyed and hand in hand. Although common in England, this type of double tomb was rare in the Peninsula; it seems possible that it was made by English sculptors who came to work at Batalha at the request of the queen.

The 15th century was the first great age of Portuguese painting. Almost no paintings of the 12th through 14th centuries have survived, although frescos were certainly painted in churches. One fragment of an early 15th-century fresco is an interesting, rare example of secular painting—the allegory of justice entitled *O Bom e o Mau Juiz* (The Good and the Bad Judge) in a Gothic house that was probably a court of law, in the town of Monsaraz. The most notable surviving religious fresco of the same period is the *Senhora da Rosa* in the sumptuous Church of São Francisco in Porto. It has been attributed to an Italian painter, António Florentino, who, it is thought, may also have painted the portrait of João I now at the Museu Nacional de Arte Antiga in Lisbon.

By far the most brilliant contribution to painting during this period was the introduction of *retábulos*—painted panels, or altarpieces. The importance of Flemish art to this development has often been noted and is undeniable. In 1428, the celebrated Flemish master Jan Van Eyck was invited to the court of João I to paint the portrait of the Infanta D. Isabel, future wife of Philip the Good (1396-1467), Duke of Burgundy. The Netherlands were, at the time, under the control of the dukes of Burgundy who were renowned for their excellent taste in art. When the Flemish artists turned from illumination to the painting of altarpieces, they added to their own love of realistic detail the Burgundian passion for gemlike decoration. To aid them in these pursuits, they developed and perfected the heretofore little-used medium of oil painting.

The most outstanding 15th-century Portuguese *retábulo* is the polyptych of St. Vincent attributed to Nuno Gonçalves, in Lisbon's Museu Nacional de Arte Antiga. The mystery that enshrouds this work has increased its aura. The panels were "lost" for some centuries, and there are various conflicting accounts of their reappearance at the end of the 19th century. No sooner were they cleaned and hung publicly than an angry polemic arose as to the identity of their author as well as of the figures therein depicted. Scholarly arguments have raged ever since. A touch of drama was added when one eminent scholar committed suicide after a dispute concerning two documents which radically altered the direction of the research. The documents were later proved false by a commission of inquiry.

The eminent Portuguese art historian José de Figueiredo, who was responsible for hanging the polyptych at the Lisbon Museum in 1910, was also primarily responsible for its attribution to Gonçalves. He based his argument on the 16th-century *Treatise on Ancient Art* by Francisco de Holanda, which mentioned that a great Portuguese artist had painted the altar at the Church of St. Vincent, then the patriarchal see in Lisbon. Holanda later praises one Nuno Gonçalves, royal painter at the court of Afonso V, for his panels depicting St. Vincent. Figueiredo was convinced that the polyptych he installed in the Lisbon Museum and the St. Vincent altarpiece mentioned by Holanda were one and the same. Later research supported these findings through detailed comparisons of the dates of known events in the life of Gonçalves, with the dating of styles in dress and arms. The panels thus could not date before 1467, and were probably painted around

1467-70. The work includes a portrait of King Afonso V, and it is known that in 1471 Gonçalves was still a favorite royal painter. In light of these clues, Nuno Gonçalves is generally regarded as the author of these famous panels.

The theme of the polyptych has also given rise to dispute. Some see in it the veneration of the *Infante Santo*—D. Fernando, uncle of Afonso V, who died at the hands of the Moors. But nowadays, it is generally thought to represent the adoration of St. Vincent, patron saint of the kingdom and of the city of Lisbon. While many of the figures have still to be identified, the important point of departure was the identification of the Infante D. Henrique (Prince Henry the Navigator) to the left of the saint in the third panel from the left. This identification was based upon the similarity of this depiction with a portrait of the

Prince in an illuminated chronicle. A snag: Henrique had died in 1461. The dating of the work, however, is still plausible, as the prince's haircut and Burgundian hat were somewhat out-of-date for 1467-70. His portrait in the polyptych is thus assumed to be posthumous, although possibly based on an earlier one by the same painter.

The panels, from left to right, are known as the Panel of the Monks (the white-robed monks of the Cistercian Order), the Fishermen, the Infante, the Archbishop, the Cavalry and finally, the Relic Panel. Among the characters identified are the king himself in profile beneath the Infante D. Henrique in the Infante Panel; his brother D. Fernando along with the Archbishop in the Archbishop Panel; the Archbishop (D. Jorge da Costa), the chronicler Gomes Eanes de Azurara

Left, detail from the great polyptych showing Prince Henry the Navigator and the future João II. Above, detail from the sepulchre of Inês de Castro

278

holding an open book in the Relic Panel; and the second Duke of Bragança and his children in the Cavalry Panel. The panels are thought to have originally flanked a central votive sculpture.

The polyptych uses neither the linear perspective of the Italians nor the aerial perspective of the Flemish, who often included landscapes in their altarpieces. Instead, the composition of figures filling up the format echoes tapestry design. While the chromatic richness and exquisiteness of handling seem of Flemish influence, the drawing of the heads and the almost sculptural drapes is Italianate—broader and more synthetic than that of the northern masters.

While arguments may continue about influence, the work's real genius and originality lie in the fineness of the portraiture—its masterful attention to realistic detail as well as its psychological dimension. The work is monumental, heroic. Without actually portraying any historic events, it reads like an epic poem of King Afonso's dreams of conquest and of the magical world of the Infante D. Henrique's navigations—blessed, as it were, by the patron saint of the kingdom.

Manueline

In the 15th and 16th centuries, the Portuguese rulers were forerunners in supporting the navigation of the Atlantic. The exhilaration resulting from their discoveries had a marked effect on art, architecture and literature. The term "Manueline" was first used in the 19th century to refer to the reign of Manuel I (1495-1521) during which Vasco da Gama reached the coast of India (1498), Afonso de Albuquerque conquered the Indian city of Goa (1510), and the art of the Discoveries reached its zenith. The term is now used more broadly to refer to certain stylistic features predominant during the Avis dynasty (1383-1580), especially in architecture.

Manueline architecture does not have major innovative structural features—the twisted columns, such as those at the Church of Jesus in Setúbal, perform the same function as do plain ones. Rather, Manueline can be seen as a heterogenous late Gothic, its real innovation lying in its stone decoration, the exuberance of which reflects the optimism and wealth of the period. Inspired by the voyages to the New World, it is ornate and imposing, uniting naturalistic maritime themes with Moorish elements and heraldic motifs: during the reign of Manuel I, the king's own emblems are usually included—his military sphere or coat of arms, or the cross of the Order of Christ. These emblems were also used in the

churches built in the newly "discovered" overseas territories.

The Monastery of Santa Maria de Belém in Lisbon, better known as Jerónimos, is one of the great *hallenkirchen* of the period—that is, a church whose aisles are as high as its nave. The construction was at first supervised by Diogo Boytac who, as mentioned was also responsible for the Royal Cloister at Batalha, as well as for the Church of Jesus at Setúbal. The apse of Jerónimos was rebuilt along more classical lines after an earthquake destroyed the original one in 1571, and the happy marriage of Manueline and Renaissance features account for the extraordinary interior space of this church.

Perhaps the most notable feature of Manueline architecture is the copious carving surrounding portals and windows. These are often contained

in semi-circular arches rather than the pointed Gothic ones. The imposing southern portal of Jerónimos and the window of the chapterhouse at the Convent of Christ in Tomar well deserve the acclaim they receive. Construction on the latter began in the 12th century with the famous Templar *Charola*—a chapel with the circular floor plan. When the Order of the Templars was dissolved in 1314, the convent became the seat of the Order of Christ. During the 16th century, the conventual buildings, including four cloisters, were added. The lavish Manueline decoration of the church culminates in the famous window, which is designed with two great ship's masts on either side, covered with carvings, topped, like the southern portal at Jerónimos, by the cross of the Order of Christ.

Left, *Calvario* by Gregório Lopes, from the School of the Master of Tomar. Above, the fantastically ornate Manuline window at the Convent of Christ at Tomar

Cloisters were now also richly ornamented, and there are many fine examples: Batalha's Royal Cloister, the Cloister of Silence at the Santa Cruz Monastery in Coimbra, and the cloisters of Jerónimos, as well as those of the churches of Jesus at Setúbal and Lóios at Évora.

Manueline architecture also adopted and modified certain Moorish features, known as *morisco*. At the Palácio Nacional at Sintra, for instance, restored during Manuel's reign, *morisco* features include the use of tiles, merlons, and windows divided into two lights by columns reaching the parapet. Another *morisco* feature is the horseshoe arch, as in the chapterhouse at the Convent of Lóios in Évora. In the Alentejo province, especially around Évora and Beja, numerous palaces are strongly *morisco* in their decoration, which includes flat lattice-worked ceilings.

During the reign of João II (1481-1495), when the navigations occupied the energies of the nation, there was a lull in painting activity. However, with the discovery of the sea-route to India and the consequent prosperity, painted *retábulos* again became a dominant form of expression. At the end of the 15th century, Portugal was one of the largest importers of Flemish paintings. Many of the altarpieces in Portuguese churches were Flemish, and some can still be seen today, such as the *Fons Vitae* at the Misericórida Church in Oporto, and the magnificent altarpiece originally at the Cathedral of Évora (now in the Évora Museum). Furthermore, like Afonso V before him, Manuel I invited Flemish masters to come and work in Portugal. Some—including Francisco Henriques and Frei Carlos—then settled there.

The visiting Flemish artists attracted local disciples and had a marked influence on national painting. Nevertheless, Portuguese painting maintained local features, giving rise to the "Luso-Flemish" style. Manueline painting has thus been characterized by the following features: monumentality, a fine sense of portraiture, brilliant gem-like colors, a growing interest in the naturalistic depiction of architectural and landscape backgrounds and an increasing preoccupation with expressive detail.

It is essential to remember that at this time, painting was not the expression of an individual sensibility, but more often the collaborative effort of a master and his assistants. Attribution, then, is extremely difficult, and often paintings are known as the products of particular workshops rather than individual artists. The two principal Portuguese workshops were that of Vasco Fernandes in Viseu and that of Jorge Afonso in Lisbon.

Vasco Fernandes, better known as Grão Vasco, is doubtless the most celebrated regional Manueline painter. For many years, the myth of "Grão Vasco" obscured his real work in a plethora of attributions—Gothic and Renaissance paintings alike were thought to be of his authorship, although a single lifetime would not have sufficed for so large an output. Since the 19th century, a clearer and more historical image of Vasco Fernandes has emerged. It has now been established that he was responsible for the altarpiece originally at the Lamego Cathedral (now in the Lamego Museum), dating 1506-1511, as well as the one for the Viseu Cathedral (Grão Vasco Museum, Viseu) of a slightly earlier date. The stylistic differences between the two works befuddled scholars for some time, but it is now assumed that Flemish assistants at Lamego account for the differences. The panels for the chapels of the Viseu Cathedral (also in the Grão Vasco Museum), of which those of the *Calvary* and *St. Peter* are the most renowned, are also attributed to him, although dating to his mature phase (1530-1542).

Noteworthy for their emotional strength and drama, these works are also characterized by a denser application of paint than that of the Flemish masters. Furthermore, the faces of the Portuguese works tend to be less stylized, more expressive, and, it would seem, often drawn from specific local models, just as the landscape backgrounds are drawn from the Beja region rather than being imaginary or purely symbolic.

The Lisbon workshop was under the aegis of Jorge Afonso, royal painter from 1508. Many artists are known to have worked there, including Grão Vasco himself, Francisco Henriques, Cristovão de Figueiredo, and Gregório Lopes, whose works can be seen in churches and museums in various parts of the country. As for Jorge Afonso himself, documents from the reign of Manuel I show that he was involved in various royal projects, but none has helped to identify which works were actually by him. It is possible that he painted the "anonymous" panels at the Tomar *Charola*.

Two of the most important artists to emerge from Jorge Afonso's workshop were his son-in-law Gregório Lopes, royal painter to Manuel I and João III, and Cristovão de Figueiredo. Of all the works attributed to the former, the one that is in the best state of repair is the *Martyrdom of St. Sebastian* (Museu Nacional de Arte Antiga) painted for the Tomar *Charola*. As for the latter, little is known about his life except that between 1515 and 1540 he was extremely prolific and exercised great influence on Portuguese painting. One of his most impressive works is the *Deposition* (also in the Museu Nacional. de Arte Antiga in Lisbon). This work is remarkable for its emotional power and its portraiture, especially that of the two donor figures on the right.

The discussion of Manueline painting would not be complete without mention of the *Santa Auta* altarpiece, whose panels now hang separately in the Museu de Arte Antiga. This work was commissioned by Queen Leonor; a case has been made for the authorship of Cristovão de Figueiredo, who is known to have been a favorite painter of the queen's, but this is not certain. The central panel represents the martyrdom of eleven thousand virgins pierced by the arrows of the Huns, and includes a shrimpnet, which was Leonor's emblem. One of the side panels depicts the arrival at church of the saint's body and includes what is assumed to be a portrait of the queen. The Manueline portal with Leonor's coat of arms and the Della Robbia medallion identify this as the Church of Madre de Deus in Lisbon, which indeed is where the work originally hung.

Renaissance and Mannerism

The Renaissance has been described as a narrow bridge crossed the moment it was reached; this was certainly the case in Portugal. In their art and architecture, the Portuguese shied away from the Renaissance rationalism, instead inclining toward naturalism or toward the drama of the Romanesque—and later the Baroque. The Renaissance in Portugal, then, was best represented by foreign artists. Foreign sculptors were frequently invited to decorate the portals and facades of Manueline buildings, introducing elements of Renaissance harmony and order within the general flamboyance of the Manueline decorative

Above, a 16th-century portrait of the reckless and ill-fated King Sebastião by Cristavão de Morais

scheme. The temporal coincidence of Manueline and Renaissance and later of Renaissance and Mannerist forms explains the hybrid style prevalent during this period.

Mannerism uses elements of Renaissance classicism but the sense of an ordered, harmonious whole—intrinsic to the Renaissance style—gives way to an exaggeration of these elements. Applied to painting, this often means a certain elongation, which is considered the most characteristic feature of Mannerism. It can also mean unexpected highlighting of a seemingly incidental section of the work, rather than the typically Renaissance orientation towards a central incident. In architecture, Mannerism is characterized by a stress on detail, a shift away from the basic classical proportions and Greco-Roman vocabulary.

To the drama of the art of the Discoveries, the French sculptors Nicolas de Chanteréne and João de Ruão added a touch of Mediterranean rationalism and sobriety. The heraldic motifs and abundant foliage of the former were transformed into the plaques, medallions, and symmetrical foliate arabesques typical of the latter. Chanteréne's work includes the portal sculptures of Manuel I and his second wife, Queen Maria, on the western portal of Jerónimos. The pulpit at the Church of Santa Cruz in Coimbra has been variously attributed to both Chanteréne and João de Ruão. The latter was most prolific and introduced classicizing elements to Portuguese carving, especially in the region around Coimbra, in works such as the altarpiece at Varziela.

Architects, too, immersed themselves in an Italianate vocabulary. The Spaniard Diogo de Torralva is thought to have designed one of the finest examples of Renaissance construction in the Peninsula—the Chapel of *Nossa Senhora da Conceicão* (Our Lady of the Conception) in Tomar (ca.1530-40), with its simple exterior and diffusely lit, barrel-vaulted interior. Also in Tomar, Torralva's Great Cloister at the Convent of Christ evokes the balance and harmony of Palladian classicism. After Torralva's death in 1566, this majestic cloister was completed by the prestigious Italian architect Filipo Terzi.

Terzi, a specialist in military architecture, had been invited to Portugal by Philip II of Spain, who ascended the Portuguese throne in 1580 after the tragic battle of Alcacer-Quiber, which lost Portugal its king—the young Sebastião—and its independence. Terzi also designed some of the most imposing works of the period, such as the Castle of St. Philip in Setúbal and the fortress in Viana do Castelo.

The imposing Church of St. Vincent in Lisbon, previously attributed to Terzi, is now thought to be by Herrera, architect of the Escorial. The plan is in the shape of a Latin cross, with intercommunicating chapels. The huge central nave is spanned by a barrel vault. The exterior, dominated by two towers and three equally sized portals, is divided into two stories, the bottom with Doric arcades the top with Ionic, in the manner of an Italian *loggia*. This facade became a prototype for many Portuguese churches, especially of the Benedictine and Carmelite Orders, which, however, were frequently more ornate, thus being considered Mannerist rather than typically Renaissance.

From the late 16th through the 17th centuries, the spirit of the Counter-Reformation was pervasive, and another type of church became predominant. The Jesuit Order of St. Ignatius Loyola insisted that the interiors of its churches should be ample, and that the pulpit should be clearly visible from all parts of the church. This, in effect, meant a broadening of the central nave, disposing of the side aisles and giving rise to a centralized plan with ambulant chapels. The first church to be built along these lines in Portugal was that of *Espírito Santo* (Holy Ghost) in Évora, whose construction began in 1567, one year before that of the Church of Gésu in Rome, long thought to be the first of its type.

The magnificent Jesuit Church of São Roque in Lisbon, which unfortunately suffered much damage during the 1755 earthquake, was begun in the late 16th century, following a plan by Terzi. Simple and austere on the exterior, the interior is richly decorated with tiles and gilded woodwork. It is, nevertheless, extremely spacious and sober, in keeping with the Jesuit tradition.

With the death of Gregório Lopes (ca.1550), the great age of the Manueline *retábulo* had come to an end. During the reign of João III, many artists went to Rome, and Italian influence replaced that of Flanders. Altarpieces, for instance that at the Cathedral of Portalegre, became overtly Italianate, with their emphasis on modeling and *chiaroscuro*. This was also the period in which portrait painting came into its own. The fine, aristocratically elongated portrait of King Sebastião (Museu de Arte Antiga), attributed to Cristovão de Morais, is but one example.

Baroque and Rococo

The Baroque is considered to be that stylistic range which, although it uses a basic classical vocabulary, strives for dissolution of form rather than definition. Emphasis is given to motion, to the state of becoming rather than being. This obliteration of clear contours—whether by brushstrokes or as an optical illusion in sculpture and architecture—is further enhanced by a preference for depth over plane. These features all stress the grand, the dynamic and the dramatic.

The first truly Baroque Portuguese church is Santa Engrácia in Lisbon with its dome and undulating interior walls. This building was not actually completed until 1966. The octagonal plan, like the oval used in Italy, dispenses with axiality: instead of being oriented in one direction, one is engulfed by a more fluid space. The richness of the colored marble lining the walls and floor, the dynamic interior space, and the general sumptuousness of the edifice are typical of construction during the reign of João V (1706-1750).

The wealth from Brazil and the munificence of João V rendered the early 18th century a period of great opulence. It was this king who commissioned the Chapel of St. John the Baptist at the Church of São Roque in Lisbon. The entire chapel was built in Rome, blessed by the Pope, shipped to Lisbon in three ships and reassembled in the church, where it shines with bronzes, mosaics, rare marble and precious stones.

The most extravagant project that was launched by João V was the construction of the huge complex of church, palace, and convent at Mafra, near Sintra. The king commissioned the German silversmith-turned-architect, Johann Friedrich Ludwig, frequently known by the Latinized name Ludovice, and construction began in 1717. The plan of the complex is a huge square; the church is at the center of the principal facade, flanked by wings belonging to the palace, with a monumental turret abutting at each end. Hybrid influences are evident in the imposing Italianate facade and the Germanic bulbous domes; local features are, on the whole, absent.

While the construction of Mafra dominated the south, in the north the major centers for the development of the Baroque were Oporto and

Braga. Here, the influence of the Tuscan architect-decorator Nicolau Nasoni, who reached Portugal in 1725, predominated. He introduced a greater buoyancy and elegance, and rich contrasts of light and shade. Unlike Ludwig, he incorporated local characteristics as well. His elliptical-naved Church of Clérigos in Oporto was without successor. But his secular buildings, such as the Freixo Palace in the same city, with their interplay of whitewash and granite, established a large following.

The Chapel of Santa Madalena in Falperra and the Casa do Mexicano in Braga, although following Nasoni, are already Rococo—drama is replaced by fantasy and a love of flourish and ornament. In the former, the portal is bordered by exuberant granite volutes playing against the white wall; this sense of contrast is less effective in the latter, whose facade is dressed in tiles. In addition to the love of fanciful, sensuous ornament, the Rococo was also marked by a growing interest in landscaping. The type of church represented by Bom Jesus in Braga became popular: surrounded by gardens, it sits atop a hill, and is reached by a sweeping succession of stairways which at a distance seem to cascade downward from the twin-towered facade.

In Lisbon the Rococo was more sober than in the north. The architect Carlos Mardel designed many of the city's public fountains, including those of Rua do Século and Largo da Esperança. he was also responsible for a section of the Aguas Livres Aqueduct, which was commissioned by João V and has been for over two centuries a handsome and familiar part of the Lisbon cityscape. Mardel was one of the architects involved in the Pombaline reconstruction of downtown Libson after the 1755 earthquake. Much of what characterizes the Lisbon of today dates to this period. The masterpiece of the reconstruction of the city was Praça do Comércio, the majestically proportioned, arcaded square giving onto the mouth of the Tagus River. As the point of contact between the city—indeed the Portuguese kingdom itself—and the ocean much traversed by Portuguese navigators, the square is a kind of symbol of the nation itself. From its center, mounted on his horse, King José, immortalized in bronze, casts his eye towards the horizon. The square is more commonly known as Terreiro do Paço—the Palace Square—for the royal palace was here, on the square's prototype, until destroyed by that fateful earthquake.

One of the truly singular features of this period was the use of azulejos—ceramic tiles. Any visitor to Portugal cannot fail to be amazed at their abundance and variety. They were first used in

the mid-15th century, gained importance in the mid-16th century, and by the 17th century they were nearly indispensable. Impressive examples are in the Church of Marvila at Santarém or that of São Lourenço in Almansil in the Algarve. At the end of the 17th century, the improved economic conditions allowed for much restoration and reconstruction of older buildings, and many azulejo panels date from this period. Both Oriental and Dutch porcelain, in blue- and- white, temporarily substituted the local polychrome tradition. While vast decorative schemes of azulejo panels filled churches and palaces alike—a notable instance of the latter is the Palace of the Marquês de Fronteira in Lisbon—the tile also enjoyed humbler use in settings such as kitchens and stairways. In addition to the murals, the use of small floral panels, or single tiles, in the Dutch manner, adorned with motifs such as flowers, birds or human figures were also popular. In the 18th century, decorative azulejo panels sumptuously adorned gardens such as those of the Palace of Queluz or of the Quinta dos Azulejos at the Lumíar Palace in Lisbon.

In religious architecture, exteriors continued to be quite austere until relatively late. Interiors, however, became increasingly ornate: the use of azulejos was often accompanied by that of carved and gilded woodwork known as talha dourada. Used first mainly on altars, this carving soon came to invade the entire interior space. This was particularly, although not uniquely, the case in the north. The Convent of Tibães near Braga, for example, and the smaller Church of São Francisco in Oporto, have walls encrusted with an overwhelming confection of gilded putti and floral arabesques.

The reign of João V saw another influx of foreign artists. The first of these was the French sculptor Claudio Laprade. His tomb of Bishop D. Manuel de Moura at the Chapel of Nossa Senhora da Penha (Our Lady of the Cliff) in Vista Alegre, with its angels securing a billowing drape, is the most Baroque of Portuguese funerary monuments. The bishop, founder of the Chapel, is depicted not serene in death but propped up on his elbow, gazing upwards.

Laprade spent his last years at Mafra, where João V had also commissioned numerous works from Italian sculptors, all in the tradition of Bernini—swirling drapes and suspended motion were the order of the day. Alessandro Giusti, who came to Lisbon from Rome in 1747 in order to reassemble the St. John the Baptist Chapel at São Roque, was commissioned to carve a marble altarpiece at Mafra; there he formed a school which attracted a large following. Undoubtedly the most gifted Portuguese sculptor to emerge from Giusti's school was Joaquim Machado de Castro who was the author of the first Portuguese equestrian statue, which we have already en-

Left, the pilgramage church of Nossa Senhora dos Remédios in Lamego (1750-1760) is a fine example of Baroque architecture

countered—King José at the Praça do Comércio. He also made polychrome clay figures—a national popular tradition which flourished in the 17th and 18th centuries—such as those at the Regional Museum of Aveiro, where the arabesques formed by the drapes, their intricate gilded patterns, the rosy luster of lip and cheek, were already typically Rococo.

While the 17th and 18th centuries were particularly rich with regard to architecture, carving, and the *azulejo*, painting receded in importance. Nevertheless, this period saw the flourishing of portrait painting, in Portugal as indeed elsewhere in Europe. Perhaps the most celebrated 17th-century portraitist was Domingos Vieira (1600-1678), known as "the Dark" to distinguish him from his contemporary Domingos Vieira Serrão. His nickname stemmed from his predilection, in works such as the Portrait of D. Isabel de Moura (in Museu de Arte Antiga in Lisbon), which dramatically contrast the deep, velvety backgrounds and the rich, creamy whites of ruffs and headgear.

Neoclassicism and Romanticism

The Pombaline style of the reconstruction of Lisbon is closer in many ways to classical models than to the contemporaneous Rococo constructions in the north of Portugal. The Neoclassical style proper, with its interest in Greco-Roman colonnades, entablatures and porticoes, was introduced in Lisbon in the last decade of the 18th century. It was given court approval when used for the Royal Palace of Ajuda which was begun in 1802 (and never actually completed) after a fire destroyed the wooden building that had been the residence of the royal family since the 1755 earthquake.

The Basilica of Estrêla in Lisbon (1789) was the last church to be built in the Baroque Grand Style. With the dissolution of the monastic orders in 1834, religious architecture lost its privileged position in Portugal. This had a negative effect on the development of large-scale public architecture. In Lisbon, after the Palace of Ajuda, perhaps the only noteworthy public building to be built in the first half of the 19th century was the Theatre of D. Maria II (1843), with its white Greco-Roman facade.

In the north, the middle-class ambience of Oporto proved fertile ground for conservative Neoclassicism to take root. The large English community connected to the port-wine industry favored this style, perhaps because of its affinities to the architecture of Richard Adam. It was the British Consul John Whitehead who commissioned not only the *Feitoria Inglesa* (literally English Trading Depot, actually more of a club) in Oporto, but also the Hospital of Santo António—perhaps the finest Neoclassical building in the entire country.

The return to the Greco-Roman aesthetic principles of Neoclassicism is also evident in such works as João José de Aguiar's statue of Queen Maria I, flanked by allegorical figures representing the four known continents, now presiding over the driveway at the Palace of Queluz, itself an example of Neoclassical architecture.

At this time, two painters emerged as especially outstanding: Francisco Vieira, known as Vieira Portuense (1765-1805), and Domingos António Sequeira (1768-1837). The two met in Rome, which was the essential venue for any serious artist. Vieira Portuense also spent some time in London, where the classicizing Roman influence was tempered by that of Sir Joshua Reynolds, as is evident in the elegant *Portrait of an Unknown*..., which is in the Museu Nacional de Arte Antiga in Lisbon.

The work of Sequeira offers an ideal study in the transition from Neoclassicism to Romanticism, a rare example when a single life can encapsulate two eras. He was nominated court painter in 1802 by João VI, and was thus charged with executing paintings for the rebuilt Palace of Ajuda. Political turbulence forced Sequeira to emigrate to France and then Italy, where he died. Thus, his work can be divided into three stages: the first, largely academic and Neoclassical in inspiration, corresponds to his first sojourn in Rome and to his work as a court painter; the second stage (1807-1823) which includes the *Alegoria de Junot* (Soares dos Reis Museum, Oporto), is stylistically freer and more individualistically inspired, with Goyaesque contrasts of dark and light, rapid brushstrokes and sudden bursts of luminous white; the last phase corresponds to his visits to Paris, where he won a gold medal at the Salon for his *Death of Camões*, since lost, and Rome. The late works show great painterliness and luminosity. The four cartoons for paintings in the Palmela collections, again in the Museu Nacional de Arte Antiga in Lisbon, are some of his most inspired, mystical works.

If Neoclassical art and architecture represented an escape from the turmoils of the present into a restrained, harmonious classical ideal, another form of escapism became an important ingredient in Romanticism. The flight into the past (medievalism) or into other cultures (orientalism), or into other states—the dream, madness, trance—are all forms of escape. The most extraordinary architectural manifestation of this was the Pena Palace in Sintra, commissioned by the Prince Fernando of Saxe-Coburg-Gotha (consort of Maria II). The building is a strange agglomeration of medieval and orientalizing forms, includ-

Right, the work of Domingos António Sequeira offers an ideal study in the transition from Neoclassicism to Romanticism

ing Manueline, Moorish, Renaissance, Baroque, and incorporating parts of the site's original structure, a 16th-century monastery. The whole is a rather overwhelming pastiche of English Neo-Gothic revivalism.

While the importance of sculpture receded yet again in this confused period of ideological tumult, painting styles echoed the architecture. Alongside the slackening of religious interests came the dissolution of the "Grand Style." Heroic, religious and ceremonial works gave way to more intimate and personal pieces. This also corresponded, in Portugal as elsewhere in Europe, to the rise of the middle-class. Courtly art had breathed its last. The liberal revolutions questioned the long upheld notion of history as the unfolding of a predetermined order, in favor of a relativism which heralded our modern times.

also gave increasing emphasis to the sitter's inner life. In Miguel Lupi's *Sousa Martins' Mother*, in Lisbon's Museu Nacional de Arte Contemporanea, the illuminated areas correspond to the face and hands—the most expressive parts of the body—and convey a sense of dignified pensiveness tinged with a certain restrained melancholy.

The foundation of the Artistic Center in Oporto (1879) and of the Lion Group in Lisbon (1880) were of seminal importance, especially as contact was established between them and the artistic milieu in Paris. Individuals, as well as these groups, admired the "City of Lights." Whether settling in as members of the vivacious emigré culture, or simply sampling the new ideas bursting everywhere in the newly recrowned capital of artistic innovation, the Portuguese joined the rest of the world in turning toward France. Paris was

Similarly, the idea that art expresses timelessly valid principles gradually gave way to the subjectivist and individualist notions which continue to hold sway in art today.

Sequeira represented the mystical, religious side of early Romanticism. With his death, Romanticism took a turn: nature became the new religion. The humbling of man before the larger, inscrutable forces of nature was a contemporaneous theme of English Romanticism, in both painting and literature. In Portugal, Tomás da Anunciação became the foremost romantic landscapist of this generation, along with Cristino da Silva.

Not surprisingly, the portrait, too, continued to enjoy popularity. Portraiture not only became the art form of the bourgeoisie par excellence, but

to remain the focus for the next generations of Portuguese artists. The individualism which colored the late 19th century makes any stylistic generalization difficult; this is true again in the 20th century. As in France, in landscapes and portraits, romanticism gave way to naturalism: the difference between them is often merely one of emphasis. While the former stresses the perceiving subject through whose eyes the landscape or sitter is seen, the latter stresses the objects of the artist's perception.

At the end of the 19th century, Silva Porto, José Malhoa, and Henrique Posão were the foremost naturalists. As opposed to their loose, painterly, luminous outdoor scenes, Columbano Bordalo Pinheiro (1857-1929) continued in the tradition of studio painting. Columbano, as he is known, is considered the Grand Master of Portuguese 19th-century art. He studied under Miguel Lupi at the Academy of Fine Arts (founded in 1836) and then spent three years in Paris. There, in 1882, he painted the renowned *Concert of Amateurs* (in Lisbon's Museu Nacional de Arte Contemporanea) where the dramatic illumination in no way conflicts with the naturalistic observation. On his return to Portugal, he joined the Lion Group, and painted a group portrait of its members in 1885, also in the Museu Nacional de Arte Contemporanea. His later portraits especially reveal him as a colorist; they are lighter, airier, with a masterly quick touch.

Columbano's brother, Rafael Bordalo Pinheiro, was perhaps a figure of even greater popularity in his day. A celebrated ceramicist working within popular caricatural traditions, he founded a porcelain factory in 1884 which became a veritable school for ceramicists. He was also a sketch artist known for his biting political caricatures.

Modernism

The first few decades of the 20th century saw an unprecedented ferment of artistic activity and invention, first in Europe and then in America. In Portugal, the political turmoil that resulted in the end of the monarchy (1910) did not provide a propitious context for this artistic revolution. Not long thereafter, the absolutist regime, which governed the country from 1926 to 1974, closed the doors to external cultural influence. For these reasons, many of the modern movements arrived late or in diluted form to Portugal. Indeed in architecture, the most interesting works were those which reappraised local traditions such as the Pombaline style. Expectably, this was a period not only of reappraisal of what constitutes "Portugueseness" but also of urban expansion and extensive renovation to public buildings.

For painters, 1911 was a turning point, for it saw the founding of the Museu Nacional de Arte Contemporanea in Lisbon, the transformation of the Academies into Schools of Fine Arts, and the establishment of the first Salon of Humorists in Lisbon—a turning away from conventional salon painting. Paris remained an important venue for forward-looking artists, and the point of contact with the Modernist avant-garde. Many painters of the first generation of Portuguese Modernists were, however, forced to leave Paris at the outbreak of World War I. Of this generation, the most daring and interesting were Santa-Rita and Amadeo Souza-Cardoso. The premature deaths of both these artists within six months of each

other in 1918 signalled the end of that generation. Santa-Rita was an eccentric personality who brought Futurism, with its talk of speed and dynamism and progress, to Portugal. Almost none of his work survives, as it was destroyed by his family, according to his wishes, after his death. Amadeo, many of whose works are in the collection of the Center for Modern Art at the Calouste Gulbenkian Foundation in Lisbon, was deeply influenced by Cubism, and by Robert and Sonia Delaunay, whom he met in Paris. In his works of 1913-14 this is particularly clear, as the figures delineated are merely a pretext for interplay of the brightly colored arcs.

One of the brightest lights of the 1911 exhibition of Humorists was José Almada Negreiros (1893-1970), who was to become one of the most fascinating, charismatic and energetic cultural figures in Portugal in the 20th century. Painter, draftsman, poet, and playwright, he also flirted with choreography and dance. He was a polemicist and theoretician of some import, and wrote, among other texts, an explication of the 15th-century Polyptych of St. Vincent, with which he was obsessed. His early caricatures drew the attention of the poet Fernando Pessoa, who became a friend and whose celebrated posthumous portrait he painted in 1954 (in Lisbon's City Musuem) and again in replica in 1964 (now in the Calouste Gulbenkian Foundation). One of his most important commissions was that for the frescoes for the port of Lisbon in 1943-48. He also designed stained-glass windows, ceramic tiles and tapestry cartoons. His last major project was the mural for the lobby of the Calouste Gulbenkian Foundation in Lisbon. While for most of his life Almada painted the world he saw about him, he turned in his later years to abstraction based on complex geometrical and metaphysical precepts. The title of this last work—*Comecar* (Beginning)—indicates a sense of spiritual rebirth at the end of his life.

Although all the major modern movements found expression in Portugal, Salazar's regime closed the doors to outside stimulus and meant effectively that forward-thinking, confrontational intellectual and artistic exchange was either clandestine or short-circuited. The military coup which initiated Portugal's democracy in April 1974 breathed new life into the arts, which had become invested with a great exploratory energy. The fervent activity bespoke the sense of exhilaration after years of repression and censorship. With access to external artistic events, Portuguese artists have been able to enter the contemporary artistic discourse, often modestly, sometimes boldly. The conflict between the relative value of imported and indigenous ideas—the conflict between "in here" and "out there" is now, as it has been for centuries, one of the central concerns of Portuguese art. This tension is perhaps also its most interesting feature.

Left, portrait of the poet Fernando Pessoa, painted by Almada Negreiros, originally commissioned for the Cafe Irmãos Unidos

TRAVEL TIPS

DESTINATION PORTUGAL

Air: Portugal's national airline, TAP Air Portugal, has daily flights in summer between the United States (New York or Boston) and Portugal. There are less frequent flights in winter. All flights land at Lisbon's Portela Airport, where you can make connections to other parts of the country.

TWA also flies daily in summer and less often in winter, with all flights flying to and from New York's Kennedy Airport.

TAP, British Airways, and DANAIR fly the Portugal-London route. There are direct flights to and from Lisbon, Oporto, and Faro. Also available are frequent charter and package deals that can be surprisingly inexpensive. Between the three regular airlines and charter companies, there are quite a few weekly flights.

Rail: A daily train makes the Paris-Lisbon run; another runs from Paris to Oporto. (Actually it's the same route from Paris to the French-Spanish border). The Lisbon branch passes through Coimbra as well. This grueling 24-hour trip is made on the well-worn Sud Express, and should be avoided if possible. Most connections for parts of Europe outside Iberia are made from Paris—even southern destinations, as it's usually faster to head north, then south again. If you hire a *couchette*, you can make the journey directly; otherwise, you must change at the French-Spanish border.

Two daily trains make the 10-hour Madrid-Lisbon and Lisbon-Madrid journey. There are other connections from northern Spain—Galicia to Oporto—and from southern Spain—Seville to Ayamonte to the Algarve. The latter is extremely time-consuming, involving three poorly coordinated trains and a boat.

INSIDE PORTUGAL

Passport and Visa: All non-European Community visitors must show a valid passport to enter Portugal. On arrival, your passport will be stamped with a 60-day tourist visa. To obtain an extension, contact the *Serviço de Extrangeiros* (Foreigner's Service). In Lisbon this is located at Rua Consilheiro José Silvestre, 1º; tel: 714-1027. No one with a tourist visa is permitted to work in Portugal.

European Community citizens may enter Portugal with a national identity card. Citizens of Great Britain, which issues no national card, must use a passport.

Currency: There is neither a minimum nor a maximum for buying Portuguese currency. While you may want to buy a small amount of *escudos* before you leave home, you'll get a much better exchange rate if you wait until you're in Portugal. Once you have bought *escudos*, however, it may be difficult to re-exchange them for foreign currency. The best policy is not to change large amount and risk having lots of money left over, but to change money as you need it.

Money is best exchanged at banks (rather than hotels or travel agencies); outside of banking hours, there are currency exchanges at Santa Apolónia train station and the airport.

Travelers checks are accepted in all banks; it is best not to spend them in stores, where, if they are accepted at all, you can be certain that they're being changed at a rate disadvantageous to you. Major credit cards can be used in the more expensive hotels, restaurants, and shops.

The *escudo*, which is divided into 100 *centavos*, is the basic unit of currency. The coin with the smallest denomination is the 50-*centavo* piece; the largest is the new 50-*escudo* coin. 1,000 *escudos* is usually called a *conto*. Don't accept any 20 *escudo* notes, or any of the older 1,000 *escudo* notes (they are larger, more colorful and don't have a picture of Dom Pedro V); these recently were removed from circulation.

The symbol for the *escudo* is the same as for the dollar sign, but it is written after the number of *escudos* (and before the number of *centavos*). Thus, 75$00 is 75 *escudos*; 75$50 is 75 *escudos* and 50 *centavos*. In numerals, a period is used instead of a comma (and vice-versa). For example, 1.000 means one thousand; 1,000 means one.

Geography

Portugal is roughly the shape of a rectangle, bordered on the east and north by Spain and the west and south by the Atlantic Ocean. It is about 360 miles (560 km) north-south and 130 miles (220 km) east-west—approximately the size of the state of Indiana. A 500-mile (830 km) coastline borders the country.

The mountainous northern half of the country is more populated. The intense greens of the northern valleys, the winding riverbeds, and the mountain peaks (the highest of which is the Serra da Estrêla, at 6,500 feet (2,000 meters), make central and northern Portugal extraordinarily beautiful.

Northern Portugal can be divided into several regions; the Douro Valley, the rich wine country of the northern coast; Tras-os-Montes, literally "Behind the Mountains" in the northeast corner; and the Beira Alta and Beira Baixa, in the north central Portugal.

The southern half of Portugal contrasts strongly with the north, and has an unusual beauty of its own. Dry, flat, and less populous than the north, the southern plains (the Alentejo) are sprinkled with bright villages surrounded by fields of wheat. The far south—the Algarve—is mountainous, and boasts long stretches of beautiful beaches, nearly all of which has been discovered by vacationers.

Climate

Spring and summer are definitely the best times of year to visit Portugal. Especially in the north and central regions, including Lisbon, winters are rainy, and while not frigid, are surprisingly chilly. Furthermore, few homes, restaurants, and inexpensive hotels are heated or insulated, so to keep warm you must have an adequate supply of sweaters. In the mountains it's even colder, and quite a lot of snow falls on the Serra da Estrêla between November and February. (There is enough, for ski enthusiasts, although conditions are far from ideal.) Winters are short, beginning in November or December and ending in February or March. The weather starts getting warm in May and June and usually stays so through September. The weather is changeable and difficult to predict from year to year; winters can be considerably shorter or longer; the rainy season heavy or light.

Nights can be cool even in summer, especially along the coast of north Lisbon. Along the western coast, the Atlantic tends to be cool until July. It warms up earlier along the southern coast. Summers in the Alentejo are extremely hot. The Algarve is moderate year-round, with a generous share of sun even in winter. It is far from hot, however, between November and April.

Supplies

Bring enough prescription medication to last through your stay, if only to avoid confusion with brand names and/or language. Toiletries and personal effects are all available locally, and are often much cheaper than in other countries. The exception is newer or less common articles, such as contact lens solution, which are more expensive. Common methods of contraception are available with the exception of contraceptive cream specifically for use with diaphragms.

Bring batteries with you: they'll be of better quality and longer lasting. Film and photographic equipment are cheaper outside the country.

Tipping

A tip of 10 percent is sufficient in restaurants and for taxi drivers. Barbers and hairdressers receive the same or a little less. Theater ushers get a tip of five or 10 *escudos*.

Business and Banking Hours: Most stores open for business Monday through Friday 9 a.m. to around 1 p.m., and from about 3 p.m. until 7 p.m. Stores are open on Saturdays from 9 a.m.-1 p.m., and are closed Sundays and holidays. Banking hours are Monday through Friday 8:30 a.m.-11:45 a.m. and 1 p.m.-2:45p.m., closed Saturday, Sunday, and holidays.

Etiquette: The Portuguese are extremely polite. A few minutes to learn the basics, and liberal use of these thereafter, will serve you well. "*Obrigado*" (if you're a man) or "*obrigada*" (if you're a woman) is thank you. Please is "*por favor*." To get someone's attention when you want service, say "*faz favor*" (pronounced "fash fuhVOOR"). Greet people with "*bon dia*" in the morning, "*boa tarde*" in the afternoon, and "*boa noite*" at night. Take leave in the same way.

Other hints: If you are invited to someone's house, it is polite to bring flowers for the hostess or a small toy if there are young children. Don't bring wine.

There are always orderly lines at bus stops. Be certain to respect them.

For some reason, stretching in public—on the street or at the table—is considered rude. Otherwise, use common sense and a smile.

Electricity: The electrical current in Portugal is 220 volts AC, with a Continental (round-prong) plug. If you plan to bring electrical appliances on you trip, bring a voltage converter as well.

Weights and Measures: Portugal uses the metric system of weights and measures. While conversions are given below, here are a few tips:

—100 grams of cheese or cold cuts is more than enough for a sandwich.

—Shellfish in restaurants is usually sold by the gram. About 300 grams is sufficient for one person.

—To convert Celsius temperatures to Farenheit (roughly), multiply the Celsius temperature by two and add 32. Thus, 20°C x 2 + 32 = 72°F.

Conversion chart

1 meter = 1.09 yards
1 yard = 0.92 meters
1 km = about 5/8 miles
1 mile = 1.6 km
1 kilo = 2.2 pounds
1 pound = about 0.46 kilo
1 liter = 1.76 pints
1 pint = about 0.57 liter
1 cm = about 0.3 inch
1 inch = 2.56 cm

Postal Services: Post offices open Mondays through Fridays 9 a.m. to 6 p.m.; smaller branches close for lunch from 12:30 p.m. to 2:30 p.m. In larger cities the main branch may be open on weekends. Mail is delivered Monday through Friday; in the central business districts in the larger cities, it is delivered twice a day.

To buy stamps, stand in any line marked *selos*. To mail or receive packages, go to the line marked *encomendas*. Postage rates are as follows.

—letters and postcards inside Portugal cost 25$00 for the first 20 grams, and usually take one to two days to arrive.

—letters to Europe cost 57$00 for the first 20 grams; postcards cost 51$00. These can take anywhere from two days to two weeks, depending on destination.

—letters to North America cost 74$50 for 20 grams; postcards cost 68$50. Letters take a week or so to the East Coast of the US and two to three days more to other parts of the country.

Be certian to write *Via Aerea* on all airmail items. To send large packages home, consider less expensive sea mail, which takes two to six months to cross the Atlantic.

The post office also provides services such as express mail (*expreso*), postal money orders (*vales*), general delivery (*posta restante*), registered mail (*registos*), insurance on packages (*seguro*), and telegraph and telephone services (see below).

Telegrams: You may place telegrams by phone (tel.10) or from the post office. The following are telegram rates.

—To the US: 1045$00 plus 68$00 per word.

—To Europe: 1045$00 plus 43$00 per word.

—In Portugal: 82$50 plus 3$00 per word.

The cheapest way to send a quick message outside of Portugal is to use the Telecopy service available only in the Praça dos Restauradores post office in Lisbon. For a little over 1,000 *es-*

cudos, you can write (or even draw) as much as you want within a given space. The copy reaches its destination within a few hours.

Telephones: There are plenty of pay phones in most cities; the problem is finding newer phones, which are easiest to use. Newer phones equipped for international calls are located in city centers. Instructions are written in English. The older phones are close to incomprehensible no matter what language you speak. They cannot be used for international calls; even for local calls, you'll need patience and good luck, as well as a large supply of small coins.

If you lack the proper change, you can make calls—both international and local—from the post offices. Go to the window for a cabin assignment and pay when the call is finished. In Lisbon there is also a phone office in the Rossio, open everyday from 9 a.m.-11 p.m.; in Oporto, there is one in Praça da Liberdade (same hours).

Most bars have telephones. Phone first, pay later, but be prepared to pay more than double the rate for pay phone or post office calls. This also applies to calls made from hotels.

To reach an English-speaking international operator, dial 098 (intercontinental service) or 099 (European service). To dial direct to the US or Canada, dial 097-1, plus the area code and phone number. For the UK, dial 00-44 plus the full phone number. Dial slowly.

Embassies

Lisbon

Australia
Avenida da Liberdade, 244
(tel. 523-350)

Canada
Rua Rosa Araujo, 2
(tel. 563-821)

Great Britain
Rua São Domingos, 37
(tel. 661-191)

Ireland
Rua da Imprensa, 1
(tel. 661-569)

United States
Avenida Forças Armadas
(tel. 726-6600)

Porto

Great Britain
Avenida Boavista
3072, 4100 Porto
(tel. 02 684-789)

United States
Rua Júlio Dinis
826-3º 4000 Porto
(tel. 02 630-94)

Tourism Information

Tourist Offices

Lisbon
Praça dos Restauradores
(tel. 01 363-314)

Cascais
Arcada do Parque
(tel. 01 268-0113)
Faro
Rua Ataide de Oliveira, 100
(tel. 089 240-67)

Lagos
Praça Marquês de Pombal

(tel. 082 630-31)

Évora
Praça de Geraldo
(tel. 066 226-71)

Elvas
Praça da Republica
(tel. 068 622-36)

Beja
Rua Capitão João Francisco Sousa, 25
(tel. 084 236-93)

Oporto
Praça Dom João, 25
(tel. 02 258-05)

Guimarães
Al. Resistência Fascismo, 83
(tel. 053 412-450)

Braga
Casa dos Crivos, Rua São Marcos
(tel. 053 769-24)

Viana do Castelo
Avenida Candido dos Reis
(tel. 058 226-20)

Coimbra
Largo da Portagem
(tel. 039 237-99)

Aveiro
Praça da Rebublica
(tel. 034 236-80)

Tomar
Avenida Dr. Candido Madureira
(tel. 049 330-95)

Viseu
Avenida Gulbenkian
(tel. 032 222-94)

Bragança
Avenida 25 de Abril
(tel. 073 222-72)

HOLIDAYS

The following is a list of public holidays in Portugal. All banks and most stores are closed on these days.

New Year's Day
January 1

Anniversary of the Revolution
April 25

Portugal and Camões Day
June 10

Saint Anthony's Day
(Lisbon only)
June 13

Saint John's Day
(especially in Oporto)
June 24

Day of the Assumption
August 15

Republic Day
October 5

All Saints' Day
November 1

Independence Day
December 1

Day of the Immaculate Conception
December 8

Christmas Day
December 25

Other holidays are Mardi Gras (February or March), Good Friday (in April), and Corpus Christi (in June).

ON THE MOVE

INTERCITY TRANSPORT

Buses: Rodoviária Nacional (RN) is the national bus company. RN runs direct and regional service between most cities and towns. Outside the routes between major cities, the bus is often faster than the train, and the bus system is certainly more extensive. This is particularly true in the north and between the smaller towns in the Algarve and Alentejo.

RN is not your only choice; there are dozens of private bus lines which tend to specialize in particular routes or areas of the country. Often, they have more direct routes to smaller towns. Many travel agencies can book tickets on a private line, or may even run their own.

Trains: Trains in Portugal range from the comfortable and speedy *rápidos* to the painfully slow *regionais*. Generally the most efficient routes are the Lisbon-Coimbra-Porto and the Lisbon-Algarve lines.

Rápidos, which run only on the two routes mentioned above, are quick and punctual and cost more to ride. Some *rápidos* have first-class carriages only; others have a very comfortable second-class as well. Next in line are the *directos*, which make more stops and travel more slowly. These have both first and second-class compartments; second-class here is likely to be less comfortable than in the *rápidos*. Finally, the *semi-directos* and especially the *regionais* seem to stop every few feet and take longer than one could have believed possible. On *directos*, *semi-directos*, and *regionais*, sec-

ond-class seats are not assigned, and CP (Caminhos de Ferro Portugueses, the train company) has no qualms about issuing more tickets than seats, if the need arises. If you want to be certain of a seat, board early.

On rural routes, trains are almost always regional. Furthermore, to reach more remote—or even not-so-remote—destinations, it may be necessary to change trains, and schedules are seldom coordinated. Except for the *rápidos*, which are punctual, leave yourself plenty of time between transfers, as trains are regularly late.

There are four train stations in Lisbon. Cais do Sodré and Rossio are commuter stations. International and long distance trains with northern and eastern destinations leave from Santa Apolónia Station, about a mile and a half to the east of Praça do Comércio. For trains to the Alentejo and the Algarve, catch a boat at the Terreiro do Paco station (across from the Praça do Comércio). The price of the boat is included in the train ticket, which you can buy at the boat station. Just be certain to buy the right one; there are two boat stations next to each other. For the train link-up, use the eastern station, i.e., the one to the left as you face the river.

Oporto and Coimbra each have two train stations. Porto's São Bento and Coimbra A are located in the respective town centers. Most long-distance trains, however, arrive and leave from Oporto's Campanhã station and Coimbra B station, outside the cities. There is frequent shuttle service between São Bento and Campanhã and between Coimbra A and B.

Car Rentals: Portugal is a trying place for drivers. In the cities, traffic is heavy, road construction hinders movement, parking is close to impossible, and cars and pedestrians regularly ignore both the rules of the road and plain common sense.

Outside cities, conditions are not much better. Highways are all too often in poor condition. Many are very narrow, making it difficult to pass slow-moving rural trucks and tractors. On winding mountain roads, driving takes great skill and concentration. Portuguese drivers are medium macho: relatively safe, but occasionally frightening when they pass at the last minute on the ubiquitous two-lane high-

ways. And wherever you are, gasoline is expensive.

If you're still determined to drive, there are Yellow Pages full of car rental firms. The big two—Hertz and Avis—are there, along with many other smaller and lesser-known (and often cheaper) companies. With Hertz and Avis, you can rent before leaving home, and this, inexplicably, is often less expensive.

A typical price in 1987 for the smallest available car was 4.200$00 per day plus 1.100$00 daily for insurance, plus tax; alternatively, 14.000$00 per week plus 22$00 per km (plus insurance and tax). Deposits can be quite substantial.

It's advisable to shop around, as costs vary and many agencies offer special packages from time to time. There are various options to choose from, including having a driver or not. The type of car you can hire ranges from the tiny Mini to much larger machines. To get more information and to compare prices, look up car rentals in the local Yellow Pages under *Automóveis— Aluger com e sem Condutor*. Most companies employ staff that speak English.

To rent a car in Portugal, most agencies require you to be at least 21 years old and to have had a valid driver's license for at least a year. An international license is not necessary.

Air: TAP Air Portugal is the national airline. There is daily service between Lisbon and Oporto, Faro, and Covilhã. Flights run several

times weekly between Lisbon and Bragança and Lisbon and Portimão. As of 1987, there are no service to Coimbra, although there is an airport some distance from the city.

CITY TRANSPORT

Lisbon

CARRIS, the city bus company, maintains an extensive system of buses, trams (*eléctricos*) and funiculars. Bus stops are clearly marked by signposts or shelters. All stops display a diagrammatical map of the bus route; many have a map of the entire city system.

The orange and white CARRIS information kiosks scattered throughout the city provide information about buses and trams and sell tickets and passes. If you're lucky, they may even have city bus maps in stock. Two of the most convenient kiosks are located in Praça da Figueira, near the Rossio, and near Eduardo VII park (the Marquês de Pombal statue).

An alternative for tourists is to buy a three-day or seven-day tourist pass, which gives unlimited access during the period of validity. If you have no pass, you may pay a flat rate when you board. Less expensive are the pre-paid *modules* that you can buy in packs of 20 from the kiosks (405$00). It is unwise to board the bus without paying, ticket inspectors appear from time to time, and the fine is steep.

The pre-World War I trams often ply the smaller,

steeper streets where buses are unable to navigate the narrow passages. Some of them are quite beautiful, inside and out; they are slower and cheaper than the buses and are a good way to see the city.

CARRIS also runs two funiculars and an elevator. The Santa Justa elevator located near the Rossio, leads to the Bairro Alto. One funicular climbs and descends the steep Calçada da Gloria, from Praça dos Restauradores, and another funiculer is in São Bento. Pay the driver only after boarding the funicular.

Metro: The Metro, with 20 stops, is quite limited, and principally useful for travel in the central zone of the city. The line is V-shaped, with the point of the "V" in the Rossio, and the two arms stretching up Avenida da Liberdade and Avenida Almirante Reis. The system is limited, and easy to use.

A tourist pass is valid on the Metro. You can also buy books of 10 tickets or single tickets. You must validate your ticket at the machines next to the ticket booths. As with buses, it is inadvisable to try to ride for free.

Trains: There are four train stations in Lisbon. Commuter trains to Cascais (stopping in Oeiras, Carcavelos, Estoril, and other towns along the western coast) depart from Cais do Sodré, located along the riverfront. Depending on the day of the week and the time of day, trains depart every 15 to 20 minutes; they arrive in Cascais (the end of the line) between 33-40 minutes later (again depending on the time of day).

Trains to the northwestern suburbs, including Sintra, leave from the Rossio station at 15-minute intervals. The trip to Sintra takes about 45 minutes. This station houses an information center which can inform you about trains all over the country.

For more information about long distance trains, see section on Intercity Transport.

Oporto and Coimbra

Oporto's public transportation is limited to buses and trams, and Coimbra's to electric buses. Both these systems run on the same principal as Lisbon's system: You may either pay the driver a flat fee, or buy prepaid modules and validate the number required by the length of the journey. You may buy modules and get information from bus company kiosks in both Oporto and Coimbra.

Taxis: In all of Portugal's cities, taxis are plentiful and cheap. The great majority of them are black with green roofs. In the city, they charge a standard meter fare, with no additions for extra passengers. (They carry as many as four people.) Outside city limits, the driver may run on the meter or charge a flat rate, and he or she is entitled to charge for the return fare (even if you don't take it). Tip taxi drivers about 10 percent.

FOOD DIGEST

WHERE TO EAT

Portuguese food is simple and fresh, abundant and filling. There is not an overwhelming variety in a country that can afford to import little. Portuguese rely on hearty basics; no complicated sauces, but broad flavors and lots of garlic, olive oil, and salt. Canned and frozen foods are almost unknown, or if known, scorned. Portions are more than filling, and you'll have to work hard to clean your plate in most establishments.

Soup is made especially well in Portugal. Perhaps the best—certainly the most famous—is the traditional *caldo verde*, a kale and potato puree with a piece of *chouriço* (sausage) in every bowl (some claim that the *chouriço* is required by law). For garlic lovers, there's *açorda á alentejana*, a bread-thickened garlic broth with egg. *Canja* is chicken soup; *sopa de mariscos* is seafood chowder; both are mouth-watering.

Fish, of course, is abundant. *Bacalhau* (codfish) is a national obsession. There are, supposedly, 365 ways to prepare it, and almost every restaurant features at least one of the ways. Shellfish ranges from the miniature clam-like *conquilhas*, to lobster, and everything in between including snails, squid, and octopus.

Carne de porco à alentejana (clams and pork with coriander) is a favorite meat dish. So is *cozida à portuguesa*, a stew. Other popular meats are goat, rabbit, suckling pig and chicken.

The Portuguese make wonderful regional cheese. Try *queijo da serra*, from the Serra da Estrêla, in northern Portugal. While the real stuff is difficult to get in Lisbon, There is no shortage of *queijo tipo serra*, its imitation.

Other deserts are sweet. They include *arroz doce* (rice pudding), flan (custard), mousse (at its best, homemade and thicker than the French variety), and a wide selection of pastries and cakes.

Portuguese wine is delicious. There are three basic types: red, white, and green, the last being young and slightly sparkling, and not green in color. Port, for after dinner, comes in both red and white. Most wines are inexpensive, and a low price does not indicate low quality. It's generally safe to stick with the house brand. Wine is drunk at both lunch and dinner.

Beer (*cerveja*) is ordered by the bottle (*garrafa*), the mug (*caneca*) or the glass (*imperial* or *fino*).

A small, strong cup of coffee is *bica*; this same portion in a large glass filled with milk is a *galão*. If you want less milk and more coffee, order a *meio de leite* (may-oh duh late).

Portuguese meal times are slightly later than what the Americans are accustomed to. Lunch is anywhere between 1 p.m. and 3 p.m.; dinner can start anywhere between 8 p.m. and 9:30 p.m. The following is a list of regional specialties.

In the North

The Douro and the Minho
Port and green wines (including red "green" wine); *caldo verde*; *Tripas a moda do porta* (tripe with butter beans)

Tras-os-Montes
Alheiras (flour sausage); *chouriços de sangue* (blood sausage); *feijoada* (bean stew); veal; goat; rabbit; trout; lamprey.

Serra da Estrêla
Queijo da serra (serra cheese); Dão wines; roasted kid; varieties of sausage.

Coimbra and Aveiro
Chanfana (kid stew); *leitão* (roast suckling pig); *pasteis de Tentugal* and *pasteis de Santa Clara* (pastries).

In the South

Alentejo
Açorda de alhos or de coentros (a bread stuffing heavily spiced with garlic and/or coriander); *carne de porco à alentejana* (clams and pork with coriander); lamb dishes.

Algarve
Ameijoas na cataplana (clams with ham and sausage, spiced with parsley and pepper); fried sardines; snails; seafood in general.

Restaurants

Restaurants are rated on a scale of one to four, depending on expense, decor, and service. The quality of food does not necessarily relate to the rating; there are plenty of great one and two-star neighborhood places. The list has a few recommended restaurants in several cities. There are, of course, many more. Throughout the country, the *pousada* dining rooms are of consistently high quality (and are usually expensive).

Northern Portugal

Braga

A Narcisa
Largo do Monte de Arcos (tel. 229-48)
A very charming moderately priced restaurant.

Retiro do Cacador
Nogueira
(tel. 265-50)
Serves good inexpensive Portuguese and regional cuisine.

Bragança

Hotel Bragança
(tel. 225-79)
A high-class restaurant.

Arca de Noe
Avenida do Savor
(tel. 227-59).
For less expensive fare.

Chaves

O Arado
Rua Ribeira Pinheiro
(tel. 219-96)
A noteworthy restaurant
with a panoramic view.

Oporto
You'll find a number of
homey restaurants in the
Ribeira area:

Casa Filha da Mae Preta
Cais da Ribeira, 40
(tel. 315-515)
A local favorite for traditional entree; inexpensive.
Nearby is the slightly more
expensive **Bebobos**, also
very good.

Mal Cozinhado
Rua Outeirinho
(tel. 381-319)
A somewhat expensive *fado*
house.

Mamuda
Rua do Campinho, 30
(tel. 233-51)
A very good restaurant officially known as "Montene-
gro." Expensive.

Portucale
Rua da Alegria, 598
(tel. 570-717)
A high-class restaurant with
a panoramic view.

Viana do Castelo

Os 3 Potes
Rua Beco dos Fornos, 9
(tel. 234-32)
Offers regional dishes in a
traditional atmosphere;

moderately priced. The restaurant at the **Hotel Santa
Luzzia**, on the top of the hill
overlooking the city, is more
expensive and very good.

Viseu

O Cortiço
Rua Augusto Hilario, 47
(tel. 238-53)
An excellent restaurant spe-
cializing in regional dishes.
Moderate to expensive.

Aveiro

A Cozinha do Rei
Rua Dr. Manuel das Neves
65 in the Hotel Afonso V
Portuguese and international
food. Expensive.

Avenida
Avenida Dr. Lourenco
Peixinho Moderate.

Centenário
Praça do Mercado
Regional specialties.
Moderate.

Galo d'Ouro
Travessa do Mercado, 2
Moderately priced Portu-
guese specialties.

Imperial
Rua Dr. Nascimento Leitao
in the Hotel of the same
name.
A first-class restaurant.
Expensive.

Sheik
Largo da Praça do Peixe,3
Near the fish market. Large
portions at small prices.

Coimbra

Adega Paço de Conde
Rua Adelino Veiga, off the

Praça do Comércio in the
Baixa.
Nice atmosphere; grill spe-
cialties. Inexpensive.

Big Ben
Avenida Emídio Navarro,
opposite park. Expensive.

O Alfredo
Avenida João das Regras, on
the far side of the bridge.
Seafood. Moderate.

O Patio
Patio da Inquisicão, near
Praça 8 de Maio.
Good food; modest and in-
expensive.

Piscinas
Over the municipal swim-
ming pool on Rua General
Humberto Delgado.
Expensive.

Praça Velha
Praça do Comércio.
Good food outdoors.
Moderate.

Real das Canas
Antiga Estrada de Lisboa
(on the old road to Lisbon).
Excellent view. Moderate.

Sereia
Rua Dr. Henriques Seco,
near Santa Cruz Park.
Counter service downstairs,
restaurant upstairs. Friendly
service. Inexpensive.

O Ticino
Rua Bernardo Albuquerque,
in Olivais section of town.
Swiss-Italian specialties.
Moderate.

Outside Coimbra

Conde de Marialva
In Cantonhede, about 21 km

northwest of Coimbra. Expensive.

O Escondidinho
In Figueira da Foz.
Goanese cooking.
Moderate.

O Verde Moinho
Casal do Lobo, near Vale das Canas, 5-6km (3-4 miles) outside of Coimbra.
Unusual specialties in an atmospheric setting.
Moderate.

Panorâmica
Penacova, about 23km (14 miles) northeast of Coimbra.
Beautiful view of the Mondego valley. The drive there is also scenic. Moderate.

In and around the Serra da Estrêla

Seia

O Camelo
On the main street. A large restaurant with pleasant atmosphere, good service, and good food. Moderate.

Oliveira do Hospital

A Onda
Small, friendly and bright.
Limited menu but the food is good. Inexpensive.

Lisbon

It is wise to make reservations at the more expensive restaurants, especially on weekends.

Expensive

Avis
Rua Serpa Pinto, 12-B
(tel. 328-391)

Chic atmosphere, international menu.

Bachus
Largo da Trinidade, 9
(tel. 322-828)
Sophisticated atmosphere.

Casa da Comida
Travessa das Amoreinas, 1
(tel. 685-376)

Casa do Leão
In St. George's Castle
(tel. 875-962)
Elegant decor, and the best view in town.
Open daily for lunch only.

Escorial
Rua das Portas de Santo Antão, 47, near Restauradores Square
(tel. 363-758)
Shellfish specialties.

Gambrinus
Rua das Portas de Santo Antão, 25, near Restauradores Square
(tel. 321-466)
A popular splurge for Lisboners. Noted for its fish and seafood.

Pabe
Rua Duque de Palmela 27-A, near Marquês de Pombal Square
(tel. 535-675)
Portuguese and international dishes.

Tavares Rico
Rua da Misericórdia, 37
(tel. 321-112)
Best-known luxury restaurant in town. Beautiful gilt and mirrored dining room.

Moderate

Adega da Tia Matilde

Rua de Benificencia, 77
(tel. 772-172)
Regional Portuguese dishes.

Casa Transmontana
Calçada do Duque, 39
(tel. 320-300)
Portuguese specialties.

Mercado de Santa Clara
Campo de Santa Clara, where the Feira da Ladra flea market takes place.
(tel. 873-986)

Michel
Largo de Santa Cruz do Castelo, 5, just outside São Jorge's castle.
(tel. 864-338)

Pap' Acorda
Rua da Atalaia, 57, in the Bairro Alto
(tel. 364-811)
In a remodeled bakery. Extremely popular; difficult to get a table on a Friday or Saturday night.

Porto de Abrigo
Rua dos Remolares, 18
(tel. 360-873)
An excellent seafood restaurant near the waterfront. Try the *pera doce* (sweet pear) for dessert.

Xele Bananas
Praça das Flores, 29
(tel. 670-515)
Popular with the Portuguese.

Inexpensive

Antigua Casa Faz Frio
Rua Dom Pedro V, 96
(tel. 361-860)
Excellent *paelha* (rice with seafood).

Bomjardin
Travessa de Santo Antão, 11

near Restauradores Square (tel. 324-389) Three annexes on the same street. The best roast chicken in town.

Bota Alta
Travessa da Queimada, 35 (tel. 327-959)
A nice, popular restaurant in the Bairro Alto.

Casa do Alentejo
Rua das Portas de Santo Antão, 58
(tel. 328-011)
Alentejano specialties in a lavishly tiled interior with several dining rooms.

Cervejaria da Trindade
Rua Nova da Trindade, 20-C (tel. 323-506)
A beautiful converted convent with lovely tiles and a garden. Although it's large, it fills up on Friday and Saturday nights. Get there early.

O Bichano
Rua Atalaia, 78

(tel. 372-546)
A tiny place in the Bairro Alto with good food.

Os Anarquistas
Largo da Trindade, 14 (tel. 323-510)
Another Bairro Alto favorite.

Portugalia
Rua Almirante Reis, 117 (tel. 520-002)
Well-known for its steak sauce. A large, spacious interior.

Évora

Two excellent and very elegant places to eat are **A Cozinha de Santo Humberto**, Rua da Moeda, 39 (tel. 242-51); and **Fialho**, Travessa das Mascarenhas, 14 (tel. 230-79). Other good, but more moderate choices are **Lagoa**, Rua Cándido dos Reis, 19 (tel. 268-82) and **O Taco**, Largo Luis de Camões, 19 (tel. 233-01).

For very good food at very reasonable prices, the best deal in town is O Sobreiro, Rua do Torres, 8.

The Algarve

Faro offer lots of good splurges, but perhaps the best is **Cidade Velha**, Largo da Sé (tel. 227-45); very expensive. The **Hotel de Faro** has a larger restaurant (tel. 220-76); very expensive. The **Clube Naval**, (tel. 234-34) next to the dock, serves less expensive seafood dishes.

Nearby Olhão has several good and inexpensive places, including **O Escondidinho**, Rua Leonardo (tel. 726-74).

In Lagos, try **Marafado**, on the highway to Lisbon (tel. 638-39), with a panoramic view; moderate. Sagres offers several seafood restaurants. The **Mar A Vista** is moderately priced and has a lovely view.

IN TRANSIT

WHERE TO STAY

The Portuguese tourist office divides accommodations into several categories: hotels, residentials, and pensions are the most popular. Hotels are usually bigger than other types of accommodation, and offer amenities such as restaurants and room service. All rooms have bathrooms. Hotels are rated from one to five stars:

five stars denote a luxury hotel; four stars, while not luxury, is pretty close; three-star hotels are typically clean but slightly run-down; one- and two-star hotels are sometimes depressing.

Residentials offer fewer amenities than hotels, and are rated from one to four stars. Pensions, usually smaller than residentials, are also rated from one to four stars. Despite being less expensive and "lower" on

the scale than hotels, many residentials and pensions are lovely and clean and offer a more personal atmosphere than the larger hotels.

Prices for luxury hotels range from 10.000$00 to 25.000$00 a night for a double. Four-star hotels are in the 8-12.000$00 range. Three-star hotels run 6-8.000$00. The highest-priced residentials can go to 10.000$00 but this is unusual. A top residential is more likely to be in the 4-6.000$00 range for two, and lower-rated residentials as well as pensions cost 2-4.000$00.

As an alternative to the above, the Portuguese tourist office maintains a list of private houses converted for guest use. Most of these are old, renovated mansions; some are owner-occupied, some not. For more information, visit the local tourist office, or contact the Direção-Geral do Turismo, Turismo de Habitação, Rua Alexandre Herculano 51-3º, Direito, 1200 Lisboa (tel. 681-713).

Finally, an expensive but worthwhile option is the government-run network of *pousadas*, first-class accommodation in historic castles, palaces, and monasteries, or in specially built sites. *Pousadas* are divided into three categories. Category "B" *pousadas* range 5-7.500$00, depending on the time of year; Category "C" *pousadas* run 6.400-9.750$00; category "CH" cost 9.500-13.100$00. (Prices quoted valid in 1987.) For a complete list of *pousadas*, see the end of this section. For reservations, contact a travel agent or: Empresa Nacional de Turismo, Central de Reservas, Avenida Santa Joana Princesa, 10.1700 Lisboa (tel. 881-221).

The list below includes a small sample of places to stay in Portugal. You'll find many others by walking down any street: most towns in Portugal are crowded with them. Remember, however, that you'll have difficulty finding a decent room in July

and August if you haven't made a reservation. The following are listed by area, beginning from the north and moving south.

Guimarães

Estalagem São Pedro
Riba de Ave
(tel. 053 931-338)
Four stars.

Hotel Fundador Dom Pedro
Avenida Dom Afonso Henriques, 274
(tel. 053 931-338)
Four stars.

Bragança

Albergaria Santa Isabel
Rua Alexandre Herculano, 67
(tel. 073 224-27)
Four stars.

Hotel Bragança
Avenida Arantes Oliveira
(tel. 073 222-42)
Three stars.

Oporto

Five-Star Hotels

Hotel Infante de Sagres
Praça Filipa Lencastre, 62
4000 Porto
(tel. 02 281-01)
Near the central square.

Hotel Meridien
Avenida da Boavista, 1466
4100 Porto
(tel. 02 668-863)
A little bit farther out than the above.

Hotel Porto Atlantico
Rua Afonso Lopes Viera, 66
4100 Porto

(tel. 02 694-941)

Hotel Porto Sheraton
Avenida da Boavista, 1269
4100 Porto
(tel. 02 668-822)

Four-Star Hotels

Grande Hotel da Batalha
Praça da Batalha, 116
4000 Porto
(tel. 02 205-71)
Near the center.

Hotel Castor
Rua Doze Casas, 17
4000 Porto
(tel. 02 384-151)

Hotel Dom Henrique
Rua Guedes Azevedo, 179
4000 Porto
(tel. 02 257-55)

Hotel Inca
Praça Coronel Pacheco, 50
4000 Porto
(tel. 02 384-151)

Hotel Ipanema
Rua do Campo Alegre, 156/174
4100 Porto
(tel. 668-061)

Hotel Porto Boega
Rua do Amial, 607
4200 Porto
(tel. 02 825-270)

Three-Star Hotels

Grande Hotel do Porto
Rua Santa Catarina, 197
4000 Porto
(tel. 02 281-76)
A few blocks east of the central square.

Hotel Corcel
Rua de Camões, 135
4000 Porto

(tel. 02 380-268)
Just north of the town center.

Hotel do Império
Praça da Batalha, 127
4000 Porto
(tel. 02 268-61)
In the center of town.

Hotel Tuela
Arq. Marques da Silva, 200
4100 Porto
(tel. 02 667-161)

Others

Pensaõ-Residencial Pão de Açúcar
Rua do Almada, 262
4000 Porto
(tel. 02 224-25)
Three stars. A large, clean, standard place right in the middle of town.

Residencial Castelo Santa Catarina
Rua Santa Catarina, 1347
4000 Porto
(tel. 02 495-599)
Four stars.

Residencial Rex
Praça da Republica, 117
4000 Porto
(tel. 02 245-48)
Four stars. In the center of town.

Aveiro

Hotel Afonso V
Rua Dr. Manuel das Neves, 65
3800 Aveiro
(tel. 034 251-91)
Three stars. A few blocks from the center.

Hotel Arcada
Rua Viana do Castelo, 4
3800 Aveiro
(tel. 034 230-01)

Two stars. A bit drab, but very centrally located along the canal.

Hotel Imperial
Rua Dr. Nascimento Leitão
3800 Aveiro
(tel. 034 221-41)
Three stars. Very modern and central, but on an uninteresting street.

Pensão Residencial Estrêla
Rua José Estevão, 4
3800 Aveiro
Three stars. Across from the Arcada Hotel.

Residencial Paloma Blanca
Rua Luis Gomes de Carvalho
Four stars. A sweet place with a lovely courtyard/garden. Near the train station, a few blocks from the center.

Coimbra

The four best hotels in Coimbra all have three-star ratings.

Hotel Astoria
Avenida Emídio Navarro, 21
3000 Coimbra
(tel. 039 220-55)
Across from tourist office.

Hotel Bragança
Largo das Ameias, 10
3000 Coimbra
(tel. 039 221-71)
Near Coimbra A Train Station.

Hotel Oslo
Avenida Fernão de Magalhães, 23
3000 Coimbra
(tel. 039 290-71)
Behind the Bragança.

Pensão Rivoli
Praça do Comércio, 27
3000 Coimbra
(tel. 039 255-50)
Centrally located. A beautiful courtyard, friendly management; slightly run-down.

Lisbon

Five-Star Hotels

Most hotels are located in the newer part of town.

Hotel Alfa Lisboa
Avenida Columbano Bordalo Pinheiro
1200 Lisboa
(tel. 726-2728)
A bit out of the way.

Hotel Altis
Rua Castilho, 149
1200 Lisboa
(tel. 522-496)

Hotel Avenida Palace
Rua Primeiro de Dezembro, 123
1200 Lisboa
(tel. 360-151)
Smack in the old center of town, between the Rossio and Praça dos Restauradores. The most centrally located of the luxury hotels.

Hotel Lisboa Sheraton
Rua Latino Coelho, 1
1000 Lisboa
(tel. 563-911)
Good for short stays and business trips. Otherwise, there are better hotels for the price.

Hotel Meridien
Rua Castilho, 149
1200 Lisboa
(tel. 690-900)
Elegant. Overlooking the park.

Hotel Ritz
Rua Rodrigo Fonseca, 88
1000 Lisboa
(tel. 657-523)
High-quality rooms and service. Overlooking Eduardo VII Park. The top of the luxury hotels.

Hotel Tivoli
Avenida da Liberdade, 185
1200 Lisboa
(tel. 530-181)
Big and beautiful, between the old and new parts of town. Friendly service.

Four-Star Hotels

Hotel Diplomatico
Rua Castilho, 74
1200 Lisboa
(tel. 562-041)

Hotel Florida
Avenida Duque de Palmela, 32
1200 Lisboa
(tel. 576-145)
Near the Marquês de Pombal Square. Standard, clean rooms.

Hotel Lisboa Plaza
Traversa do Salitre, 7
1200 Lisboa
(tel. 370-331)
Just off Avenida da Liberdade.

Hotel Principe Real
Rua da Alegria, 53
1200 Lisboa
(tel. 360-116)
Beautiful, small, and quiet, a few blocks from Avenida da Liberdade in an interesting residential area near the Bairro Alto.

Hotel Tivoli Garden
Rua Julio C. Machado, 7
1200 Lisboa

(tel. 539-971)
Run by the same people in charge of the five-star Tivoli, right next door.

Three-Star Hotels

Hotel Britania
Rua Rodrigues Sampaio, 17
1100 Lisboa
(tel. 575-016)
Clean, if slightly shabby, and on a nice street near Avenida da Liberdade but far from the noise.

Hotel Dom Carlos
Avenida Duque de Loulé, 121
1000 Lisboa
(tel. 539-769)
On an unattractive but centrally-located street.

Hotel Eduardo VII
Avenida Fontes
Pereira de Melo, 5-C
1000 Lisboa
(tel. 530-141)
Right next to the park of the same name. A beautiful view from the restaurant and the front rooms. Slightly dark, but clean.

Hotel Flamingo
Rua Castilho, 41
1200 Lisboa
(tel. 532-191)
Near the Marquês de Pombal, but on a quieter street.

Hotel Miraparque
Avenida Sidónio Pais, 12
1000 Lisboa
(tel. 575-070)
Decent rooms; poor service; a good location on a quiet street overlooking the park.

Hotel Rex
Rua Castilho, 169
1000 Lisboa

(tel. 682-161)
For those who can't afford the Ritz or the Meridian, the Rex is a nice place next door.

RESIDENTIALS AND PENSIONS

York House—Residencia Inglesa
Rua Janelas Verdes, 32
1200 Lisboa
(tel. 6624-35)
Four stars. In a class by itself: comfort and charm combined. This place draws raves. In an old and interesting neighborhood, about 15 minutes by bus from the Rossio. Reserve well in advance. The annex is down the street at number 47 (tel. 668-143).

Albergaria Senhora do Monte
Calçada do Monte, 39
1100 Lisboa
(tel. 862-846)
Four stars. Beautiful views overlooking Lisbon, not far from the Alfama.

Residencia Roma
Travessa da Gloria, 22-A
1200 Lisboa
(tel. 360-557)
Four stars. The size and amenities of a hotel: private baths and TVs in every room. Don't let the shabby outside phase you; the inside is well kept and very clean.

Residencia Dom João
Rua José Estevão, 43
1100 Lisboa
(tel. 543-064)
Three stars. In quiet, residential neighborhood, a bit off the beaten track, but only a 15-minute walk to the Marquês de Pombal Square.

Pensão Ninho das Aguias
Costa do Castelo, 74
1100 Lisboa
(tel. 860-391)
Three stars. One of the few pensions in the Alfama. Come for the charm, if not the comfort. Some rooms have great views; others none at all. Some people love it; others don't.

Residencia Florescente
Rua das Portas
de Santo Antão, 99
1100 Lisboa
(tel. 326-609)
Two stars. Simple, lovely, and inexpensive. Tiled hallways and bright, clean rooms, some with full baths. Very centrally located, near Restauradores Square.

Évora

Évora is small enough so that nothing is more than a few blocks from the center. The *pousada* (see following list) has the best location, right between the Cathedral and the Temple of Diana.

Albergaria Vitória
Rua Diana de Liz
7000 Évora
(tel. 066 271-74)
Four stars.

Estalagem Monte das Flores
Monte das Flores
7000 Évora
(tel. 066 125-018)
Four stars.

Hotel Planicie
Largo de Àlvaro
Velho, 40
7000 Évora
(tel. 066 240-26)
Three stars.

Residencia Diana
Rua Diogo Cão, 2
7000 Évora
(tel. 066 220-08)
Three stars. A nice little place near the Cathedral.

Residencia O Eborense
Largo da Misericórdia, 1
7000 Évora
(tel. 066 220-31)
Three stars. In a converted mansion.

Residencia Riviera
Rua 5 de Outubro
7000 Évora
(tel. 066 233-04)
Four stars.

The Algarve

Faro and Surrounding Areas

Hotel Atlantis Vilamoura
Vilamoura, Quarteira
8100 Loulé
(tel. 089 347-01)
Five stars.

Hotel Dom Pedro Vilamoura
Vilamoura, Quarteira,
8100 Loulé
(tel. 089 347-01)
Four stars.

Hotel Dona Filipa
Vale do Lobo
Almansil
(tel. 089 568-48)
Five stars.

Hotel Eva Dom Pedro
Avenida da República
7000 Faro
(tel. 089 240-54)
Four stars. Highest class hotel in the city.

Hotel Faro
Praça Dom Francisco
Gomes,
8000 Faro
(tel. 089 220-76)
Three stars.

Estalagem Aeromar
Praia de Faro
8000 Faro
(tel. 089 235-42)
Four stars. On the beach.

Pensão O Farão
4 Largo da Madalena
8000 Faro
Three stars.

Residencial Samé
Rua do Bocage, 66
8000 Faro
Three stars. In the center of town.

Lagos and Surrounding Area

Albergaria Casa Sao Gonçalo
Rua Cándido dos Reis
8600 Lagos
(tel. 082 621-71)
Four stars.

Albergaria Cidade Velha
Rua Dr. Joaquin Telo, 7
8600 Lagos
(tel. 082 620-41)
Four stars.

Hotel Golfinho
Praia Dona Ana
8600 Lagos
(tel. 082 620-81)
Four stars. On the beach.

Hotel de Lagos
Rua Nova da Aldeia, 83
8600 Lagos
(tel. 082 620-11)
Four stars.

Hotel Meia Praia
Meia Praia
8600 Lagos

(tel. 082 620-01)
Three stars. On the beach.

Hotel Riomar
Rua Cándido dos Reis
8600 Lagos
(tel. 082 630-91)
Three stars.

Sagres
There are many private rooms to let in Sagres—just look for the signs in the windows. Aside from these and the *pousada*, there's the three-star **Hotel da Baleeira**, Baleeira, 8650 Sagres, Vila do Bispo (tel. 082 642-12).

POUSADAS

For reservations and information on the Tourist Lodging (except for the Costa Verde region) in manor houses and other private homes, contact: Direccao-Geral de Turismo, Turismo de Habitacao, Rua Alexandre Herculano 51-3.o dto., 1200 Lisboa, Portugal. Tel: (1) 681713. For reservations in the Costa Verde, contact: Delegacao de Turismo de Ponte de Lima, 4990 Ponte de Lima, Portugal. tel: (58) 942335, telex: 32618. Either office will supply you with a complete list of the houses available. Some information is also available in major tourist offices. The following is a complete list of *pousadas* and manor houses by area.

Northern Portugal

The Douro, the Minho, and Tras-os-Montes

Pousada São Teotónio

Valença do Minho
(tel. 051 222-42)
Category C. North of Viana do Castelo, on the border with Galicia.

Pousada Dom Dinis
Vila Nova da Cerveira
(tel. 051 956-01)
Category CH. North of Viana do Castelo. Inside the walls of the village's old castle.

Pousada São Bento
Canicada
(tel. 053 571-90)
Category C.

Pousada Santa Maria Oliveira
Guimarães
(tel. 053 412-157)
Category C.

Pousada Santa Marinha
Guimarães
(tel. 053 418-453)
Category CH. Area showcase *pousada*, in an exquisitely renovated monastery.

Pousada São Gonçalo
Amarante
(tel. 055 461-113)
Category B. East of Oporto.

Pousada Barão Forrester
Alijó
(tel. 059 954-67)
Category B. Near Vila Real.

Pousada São Bartolomeu
Bragança
(tel. 073 224-93)
Category B.

Pousada Santa Catarina
Miranda do Douro
(tel. 073 422-55)
Category B.

North-Central Portugal

Pousada Ria
Murtosa
(tel. 034 483-32)
Category B. Near Aveiro, right on the lagoon.

Pousada Santo António
Serem
(tel. 034 521-1230)
Category B. Near Aveiro.

Pousada São Jeronimo
Caramulo
(tel. 032 862-91)
Category B. Between Viseu and Aveiro.

Pousada Santa Barbara
Oliveira do Hospital
(tel. 038 522-52)
Category C. Between Coimbra and the Serra da Estrêla.

Pousada São Lourenço
Manteigas
(tel. 075 471-50)
Category B. In the Serra da Estrêla.

Pousada Senhora das Neves
Almeida
(tel. 071 542-83)
Category C. East of the Serra da Estrêla.

Pousada São Pedro
Castelo do Bode
(tel. 049 381-75)
Category B. Near Tomar.

Pousada Castelo
Obidos
(tel. 062 951-05)
Category CH. Tiny but lovely, part of the original castle.

Pousada Mestre Afonso Domingues
Batalha
(tel. 044 962-60)
Category C. Right next to the

famous abbey.

Pousada Santa Maria
Marvão
(tel. 045 932-01)
Category C. Near Portalegre.

Southern Portugal

Pousada de Palmela
Palmela
(tel. 065 235-0410)
Category CH. Near Setúbal. Very well designed, inside castle walls.

Pousada São Felipe
Setubal
(tel. 065 238-44)
Category CH. Located again in an old fortress, overlooking the harbor.

Pousada Santa Luzia
Elvas
(tel. 068 621-94)
Category B.

Pousada Santa Isabel
Estremoz
(tel. 068 226-18)
Category CH.

Pousada dos Loios
Évora
(tel. 066 240-51)
Category CH.

Pousada Vale do Gaio
Alcacer do Sal
(tel. 065 661-00)
Category B. Southeast of Setúbal.

Pousada São Tiago
Santiago do Cacem
(tel. 069 224-59)

Category B. Just east of Sines.

Pousada São Gens
Serpa
(tel. 084 903-27)
Category B. East of Beja.

Pousada Santa Clara
Santa Clara-a-Velha
(tel. 083 982-50)
Category B. Between Sines and Portimão.

Pousada São Bras
São Bras de Alportel
(tel. 089 423-05)
Category B. North of Faro.

Pousada Infante
Sagres
(tel. 082 642-22)
Category CH. Each room has a small balcony overlooking the ocean.

ACTIVITIES

THINGS TO DO

NIGHTLIFE

Nightlife in Portugal is different things to different people. For some, it's a jug of wine and a night of *fado*. For others, it's a flashy disco, or a night at the neighborhood cafe.

Much of Portugal's nightlife takes place in Lisbon, and much of Lisbon's nightlife—from *fado* to disco—takes place in the Bairro Alto, an odd mix of the historical and the trendy. Towns and smaller cities—anything smaller than Oporto, tend to get very sleepy at about 10 p.m. or 11 p.m., and you'll find very little to do besides going to an odd disco or two. There are two exceptions: the tourist centers in the Algarve, where summer visitors like to stay up late; and any town, village, or city on the night of a festival.

For a list of just about everything going on and everywhere it's happening, consult the weekly newspaper *Sete*, which comes out on Wednesday. Even if you can't read Portuguese, the listings are comprehensible.

Movies in Portugal are subtitled, not dubbed, so they're accessible to non-Portuguese speakers. Seats are assigned, and the usher should be tipped five or 10 *escudos*.

Music—in *fado* houses, concert halls, and nightclubs alike—tends to start fairly late, perhaps around 10 p.m. Bars with live music—and often dancing—are called "boites" or "dancings." Discos occasionally have live music as well.

MUSIC AND DANCING

Lisbon

In or near the Bairro Alto,

Rato, and São Bento three areas located just west and up the hill from Avenida da Liberdade.

A Lontra
Rua São Bento, 157
(tel. 661-083)
A bar with small dance floor; people usually end up dancing all over the place, anyway. Live African music.

Clave di Nos
Rua do Norte, 100
(tel. 368-420)
Live music.

Copo do Tres
Rua Marcos Portugal, 1, in Praça das Flores
(tel. 670-230)
Live music ranging from string quartets to jazz to Brazilian bands.

Fragil
Rua da Atalaia, 128
(tel. 369-528)
The trendiest disco in town. Good music.

Gafiera
Calçada de Tijolo, in the Bairro Alto
(tel. 325-953)
A lively Brazilian bar; exotic drinks, Brazilian bands, lots of sambaing, and lots of fun.

'India a Noite É Uma Crianca
Praça das Flores, 8
(tel. 663-545)
Portuguese, Brazilian, and Latin American folk music, live. Nice and cozy, but it gets crowded.

Longas Noites
Largo do Conde Baráo, 50 (in Casa Pia Athletic Club)
Open on Fridays, just about all night. The name means "long nights," and if you've made it to this place, you've probably had one—it's the place to be at about 4 a.m., after everything else has closed. Unpretentious; lots of room, lots of people.

Elsewhere in Lisbon

Hot Clube de Portugal
Praça de Alegria, 39
(tel. 367-369)
The place for jazz.

Jamaica
Rua Nova do Carvalho, 6 near Cais do Sodré train station
(tel. 321-859)
DJ'd American music and dancing. In the city's red-light district.

Primorosa de Alvalade
Avenida dos Estados Unidos da America, 128-D
(tel. 771-913)
Disco.

Rock RendezVous
Rua Beneficencia 175
(tel. 774-402)
Live rock music in a nice setting.

Fado Houses: *Fado* is a nostalgic—though not necessarily unhappy—music, a popular art which goes back several hundred years. Long associated with traditional, working-class neighborhoods, it is now more of a province for tourists. The *fadista*, a powerfully-voiced singer, is usually backed by *guitarras*—the twelve-stringed Portuguese version—and *violas*—what we would call a guitar. The Portuguese say it takes more than a good voice to become a *fadista*—it takes a lot of soul as well.

Many *fado* houses are located in the Bairro Alto. There are others in the older neighborhoods—the Alfama, Alcântara, and Lapa. The houses usually serve dinner (optional) and often charge a fairly steep entrance or minimum consumption charge. Singing starts around 9:30 p.m. or 10 p.m. It's best to reserve in advance.

A Cesária
Rua Gilberto Rola, 20
(tel. 665-745)

Adega Machado
Rua do Norte, 91
(tel. 360-095)

A Sévera
Rua das Gáveas, 5
(tel. 364-006)

Lisboa À Noite
Rua das Gáveas, 69
(tel. 368-557)

Mascote de Atalaia
Rua da Atalaia.
Traditional *fado*, for the neighborhood, not the tourists. The local *fadistas* come to sing the night away in a small tavern. No food, no fancy decor—only wine and *fado*.

Oporto

D. Uracca
Rua Padre Luis Cabral 1090 in Foz Velha
"Medieval" decoration and modern music.

Flying Dutchman
Centro Comercial Dallas

Avenida da Boavista, 1588. Attracts a more sedate crowd. The organist plays old favorites.

Griffon's
Rua Julio Dinis
Centro Comercial Brasília.
Downstairs, a disco; upstairs, relative peace and quiet, and tables for resting.

Luis Armastrondo
Rua dos Mercadores 132, in the Ribeira.
Live music, some of it jazz.

Postigo do Carvão
Rua Fonte Taurina, 26/34, in the Ribeira.
A bar with a piano if you feel like playing.

Splash
Centro Comercial Dallas
Avenida da Boavista, 1588.
Live music.

Coimbra

There are two interesting places to be on a Friday or Saturday night in Coimbra. In the **Diligência**, off Rua da Sofia, there's usually a group who pick up the restaurant's guitars and sing *fado* and folk songs. It you're lucky, the music will be good. If not, just enjoy the *sangria*. Music starts around 10 p.m.; the Diligência closes at midnight. The other place to be is the **Agora**, which starts and ends much later than the Diligência. The Agora has a variety of live music, much of it a simple setting. Check also the **Gil Vicente Theater**, which usually has a weekly program of concerts, dance groups, or movies. Keep an

eye out for posters of other events—there is usually a concert or two. The tourist office also keeps a list of events.

MUSEUMS

Lisbon overflows with museums, Oporto has several, and any self-respecting town in Portugal has at least one. You won't be overwhelmed by the size of any museum in Portugal; they are all small enough to be manageable. Some of the most interesting are the local handicrafts museums, which are not museums in the purest sense, but rather showcases where works on display are sold. Most museums are open from 10a.m.-noon. and 2p.m.-5p.m., and closed Mondays. There is generally a small admission fee is charge.

The following is a list of museums in several cities and regions in Portugal.

The Algarve

Faro

Infante Dom Henrique Archaeological Museum, in the Convento de Nossa Senhora da Assunção. Roman and Arabic artifacts; tiles and ceramics.

Regional Ethnographic Museum, Praça da Liberdade, 2. Models of Algarvian life; handicrafts; photography.

Lagos

Regional Museum of Lagos, in the annex of Santo

António Church. Archaeology, religious art, and handicrafts.

The Alentejo

Beja

Queen Leonor Museum, in the Convento da Conceição. Archaeology, ceramics, and religious art.

Évora

Museum of Évora, between the Cathedral and the Temple of Diana. Archaeology, Roman sculpture, good Portuguese Primitives.

Sacred Art Museum, in the Cathedral. Old costumes, intricate embroidery, silver pieces, sculpture.

Handicrafts Museum, Rua da Republica, across from São Francisco Church. Display and sale of local crafts.

Coimbra and Surrounding Areas

Aveiro

Museum of Aveiro, Convento de Jesus, Rua Santa Joana Princesa.

Coimbra

Machado de Castro National Museum, Largo de Dr. José Rodrigues. Important collection of sculpture; Roman galleries.

Museum of Conimbriga Archaeological Site. Pieces from and explanation of the Roman ruins.

Tomar

Abraham Zacuto Luso-Hebraic Museum, in the old synagogue.

The Mountains and Tras-os-Montes

Guarda

Regional Museum, in the old Paço Episcopal. Archaeology, painting, sculpture.

Viseu

Grão-Vasco Museum, next to the Cathedral. A collection of 16th-century paintings.

Bragança

Regional Museum, Rua Abílio Beca.

The Minho and The Douro

Braga

Sacred Art Museum, in the Cathedral. Beautiful tiles, sculpture, religious costume, jewelry, and other objects in rather musty rooms.

Dom Diogo de Sousa Museum, Roman Archaeology.

Museum of Regional Art and History, Palácio dos Biscainhos.

Guimarães

Alberto Sampaio Museum, in the annex to the Church of Nossa Senhora da Oliveira. 14th- to 19th-century art.

Martins Sarmento Museum, in the Convento de São Somingos. Archaeology; modern and contemporary art.

Sacred Art Museum, in the old Convento das Dominicas.

Oporto

Guerra-Junqueira Museum, Rua D. Hugo, 32. Collection of art objects and furniture from the 16th-19th century.

Museum of Archaeology and Prehistory, Praça Parador Leitão.

Museum of History and Ethnography, Largo São João Novo, 11.

Sacred Art and Archaeology Museum, in the old College of São Lorenzo.

Soares dos Reis Museum, in the Palácio das Carrancas, Rua D. Manuel II. Art from prehistory to the 19th century, including the sculptures of Soares dos Reis.

Viana do Castelo

Municipal Museum, in the old Solar dos Macieis. Pottery, furniture, archaeology, anthropology.

Lisbon

Calouste Gulbenkian Museum, Avenida de Berna, 45 (tel. 735-131). The city's largest museum houses a permanent collection of Egyptian, Oriental, Greek/Roman and European art. The museum's Modern Art Center is next door, on Rua Nicolau Bettencourt. Usually one or two excellent special exhibitions in addition to the regular collection. Open Tues., Thurs., Fri. and Sun. 10 a.m.-5 p.m. (both museums). The Gulbenkian opens Wed. and Sat. 2 p.m.-8 p.m. The Modern Art Center 10 a.m.-7 p.m.

National Tile Museum, in the Convento de Madre de Deus, Rua Madre de Deus, 4 (tel. 824-132). Lovely museum of antique and modern tiles. Open 10 a.m.-12:30 p.m. and 2 p.m.-5 p.m.

National Art Gallery (Museum Nacional de Arte Antigua), Rua das Janelas Verdes, 95 (tel. 676-001). The most important national collection of European painting; worth a visit. Cafeteria and garden on the premises. Open 10 a.m.-1 p.m. and 2:30 p.m.-5 p.m.

National Coach Museum, Praça Afonso de Albequerque, in Belém (tel. 638-022). A collection of antique carriages, one of the most complete of its kind. The oldest is from 1619. Open 10 a.m.-5 p.m.

Popular Art Museum, Avenida de Brasilia on the docks in Belém (tel. 611-282). Folk and popular art: filigree, porcelain, embroidery. Open 10 a.m.-12:30 p.m. and 2 p.m.-5 p.m.

Maritime Museum, Praça do Império, Belém, next to Jerónimos Monastery (tel. 612-541). Maps, instruments, and detailed models of ships. Open 10 a.m.-5 p.m.

Calouste Gulbenkian Planetarium, Praça do Império, Belém, next to Jerónimos Monastery (tel. 610-192). Open Wednesdays, Saturdays, and Sundays with sessions at 3:30 p.m. and 4:45 p.m.

Vasco da Gama Aquarium, Dáfundo, near Algés, on the Cascais train line (tel. 419-6337). Open every day 10 a.m.-5:30 p.m.

Decorative Art Museum, Largo das Portas do Sol, in the Alfama (tel. 862-183). In an 18th century palace. Furniture, tapestries, and an interesting mix of other articles. Open Mondays through Saturdays between 10 a.m.-1 p.m. and 2 p.m.-5 p.m.; Opening hours on Sundays are 1 p.m.-5 p.m. Workshops on decorative arts open Wednesdays.

Costume Museum, Estrada do Lumiar, 2 (tel. 759-0318). A lovely museum of antique dress and toys. A section detailing spinning and weaving processes. A good restaurant on the grounds. Open 10 a.m.-1 p.m. and 2:30 p.m.-5 p.m.

Rafael Bordalo Pinheiro Museum, Campo Grande 382 (tel. 759-0816). Pottery and drawings by the 19th-century artist. Open 11 a.m.-5:30 p.m.

City Museum, Campo Grande 245, in Pimenta Palace (tel. 759-1617). Traces Lisbon's past and present. Open 10 a.m.-1 p.m. and 2 p.m.-6 p.m.

Ethnological Museum, Avenida Ilha da Madeira. Artifacts from all over the world, principally from former Portuguese colonies in Africa. Open 10 a.m.-12:30 p.m. and 2 p.m.-5 p.m.

Archaeological Museum, Largo do Carmo, at the top of the Santa Justa Elevator. In the ruins of the old Carmo Convent. Roman and medieval artifacts. Open 11 a.m.-6 p.m.

Museum of Sacred Art, Largo da Trindade, in the Bairro Alto (tel. 360-361). A small museum in São Roque church. Open 10 a.m.-5 p.m.

National Museum of Contemporary Art, Rua Serpa Pinto, 6 (tel. 368-028). Open 10 a.m.-12:30 p.m. and 2 p.m.-5 p.m.

Military Museum, Largo do Museu de Artilharia, near Santa Apolónia station (tel. 867-135). Weapons and armor from the 15th century to the present. Open 11 a.m.-5 p.m.

Parks and Natural Areas

Peneda-Gerês National Park

Portugal's only official national park is Peneda-Gerês, which extends over some 50,000 acres (20,000 hectares) and is located in the far north of the country. The park is bordered by Spain, and encompasses parts of the Peneda and Gerês mountain ranges, the Lima River, a branch of the Cavado river, and countless streams and dams. The highest peak on the Peneda-Gerês measures 5,095 feet (1,544 meters) with a view of the Minho, Tras-os-Montes, and across the border into Galicia.

The lush plant life is fed by heavy rainfall. The park is the home of 17 species of plants to be found nowhere else, as well as extensive forests of oak and pine. Wild ponies, deer, wolf, golden eagles, wild boars and badgers, as well as many other animals, live within the boundaries.

You may fish, ride horseback, hike and mountain climb amid the breathtaking scenery in the park. You can also visit picturesque villages including Castro Laboreiro and Cidadelhe, probably of prehistoric origin; Soajo, probably Roman, and Lindoso, medieval. There are also dolmens perhaps 5,000 years old, and milestones that once marked the old Roman road to Braga.

Entrance to the Peneda half of the park—the northern section—is from Melgaço, just at the Galician border. To Gerês, there are entrances from Ponte da Barca and from the Braga-Chaves road (follow the turn off to Caniçada). There is a *pousada* at the edge of the park, in Caniçada.

Tourist offices in the Minho, especially Braga, can provide information about the park.

Montesinho Park

Resting in the far northeastern corner of Portugal, Montesinho lies between Bragança, Vinhais, and the Spanish border. Like Peneda-Gerês, varieties of flora and fauna abound; there is not only breathtaking scenery but also ancient villages. These villages preserve age-old customs, and a few even speak their own dialect. Entrance is from Bragança or Vinhais.

Serra da Estréla

Granite peaks, glacial valleys, and streams and lakes are all part of the Serra da Estréla. The highest peaks in Portugal are also among the most beautiful, winter or summer; They are quite accessible by car, as well (though in wintertime roads may be blocked). In winter, this is the place for the little that Portugal has to offer in the way of winter sports. Visitors ski here, despite poor facilities, but mostly they scu. (Scu is a combination of the words ski and *cu*, which means rear end in Portuguese. To scu, grab a plastic bag, sit on it, and slide downhill.)

There are places to stay in the larger towns in or near the Serra, which include Gouveia, Seia, Covilhã, and Guarda. There is a *pousada* in Manteigas. The Serra is about two hours by car from Coimbra.

Serra da Arrábida

Just south of Lisbon, the Serra da Arrábida's natural beauty is accessible to anyone with a car. The peaks are modest, but beautiful nonetheless, as are the preglacial forests and the beaches. The Serra da Arrábida lies along Highway 379-1, which runs west from Setúbal.

SHOPPING

Portuguese handicrafts range from hand-carved toothpicks to wicker furniture to blankets and rugs. The most famous Portuguese handicrafts include ceramic tiles (*azulejos*) and pottery, Arraiolos rugs, and embroidery and lace work. Different varieties of ceramic work are produced all over the country; in the Alentejo, for example, you'll find examples of barro pottery, a simple brown clay, sometimes decorated, sometimes glazed. Decorations on ceramics tend to be paintings of fruit or flowers, or sometimes scenes of rural life. Fine pottery from around Coimbra often carries animal motifs, and looks quite intricate in comparison with the simple Alentejano decorations. Farther north, blue-and-white glazed pottery appears.

Arraiolos rugs, by contrast, come from only one place: Arraiolos, in the Alentejo. (They are, however, sold in other parts of the country, especially Lisbon.) The art of designing and stitching these rugs probably goes back to the Middle Ages.

While many regional crafts are sold in Lisbon, there is usually a wider and more authentic selection in the provinces. The following is a list of traditional crafts by area.

Alentejo

Cane and wicker work, cork products (baskets, coasters, sculpture), wool blankets, Arraiolos rugs, ceramics (barro), traditional hand-painted furniture, copper goods and lace.

Algarve

Palm and wicker work, copper and brass articles, candles.

Coimbra and the Beiras (including Aveiro)

Ceramics (colorful animal motifs from near Coimbra; elegant Vista Alegre ceramics from the Aveiro region; black clay pottery from the Viseu region); woven rag quilts (from the Serra da Estréla); lace and embroidery.

Douro and Minho

Ceramics, wickerwork, straw baskets and hats; embroidery, crochet, and regional costumes (especially from the Viana do Castelo area), religious art (from Braga). The Thursday market in Barcelos, north of Oporto, has lots of handicrafts for sale.

Tras-os-Montes

Blankets; weaving and tapestries; black pottery from Bisalhões (near Vila Real).

SPORTS

Football: Football (what Americans call soccer) dominates Portuguese sports life. From the 10-year-olds playing in the street to the hundreds of professional, semi-pro, and amateur teams, to the massive coverage the sport is given on TV and in the papers, football in Portugal is inescapable. The three most important teams in the country are F.C. Porto, from Porto (the 1987 European champions), and Benfica, and Sporting, both from Lisbon. Every Portuguese, no matter where he's from, is a loyal fan of one of the three.

The football season stretches from September or October to July. Tickets for the big three are difficult to get, as there are many season-ticket holders. In Lisbon, try the ABEP ticket kiosk located in Restauradores Square; elsewhere, try the stadiums themselves. Games are usually held on Sunday afternoons.

Bullfighting: Portuguese bullfighting is different from the Spanish . It is considered less violent because the bull is not killed inside the ring (but later outside). Nonetheless, it is not for those with weak stomachs, as the bull is poked and prodded and stabbed until it is quite bloody. Unlike Spanish bullfighters, the Portuguese are on horseback; the horses are beautifully bedecked and highly trained.

Bullfighting is popular primarily in the Ribatejo (just outside Lisbon) and in Lisbon itself. The season begins in the spring and ends in the fall. In Lisbon, fights are held in the Campo Pequeno bullring. There is also a ring in Cascais. The most famous bullfights, however, are held in Vila Franca da Xira, a Ribatejana suburb of Lisbon. (Take the train from Santa Apolónia.)

Ribatejana festivals, which are frequent during the summer, almost always feature bullfighting and the freeing of bulls in the streets.

Participant Sports

Golf

Lisbon

All golf facilities are located outside the city proper.

Estoril Golf Club
Avenida da República
Estoril
(tel. 268-0176)

Estoril-Sol Golf Club
Estrada da Lagoa Azul, 3
Linho, near Sintra
(tel. 923-2461)

Marinha Golf Club
Quinta da Marinha,
near Cascais
(tel. 226-3244)

Lisboa Country Club
Quinta da Aroeira
Monte de Caparica
(tel. 226-3244)

Lisbon Sports Club
Casal da Carregueira
Belas, near Queluz
(tel. 431-0077)

Setúbal

Troia Golf Club
Torralta, Troia
(tel. 065 441-51 or 442-36)

Costa de Prata

Vimeiro Golf Club
Praia do Porto Novo
Vimeiro, about 65km north of Lisbon
(tel. 061 981-57).

Northern Portugal

Miramar Golf Club
Praia de Miramar
Avenida Sacudura Cabral
Valadares, near Porto
(tel. 02 762-2067).

Oporto Golf Club
Pedreira, Silvada, near Espinho
(tel. 02 720-008)

Vidago Golf Club
Vidago, about two hours from Porto
(tel. 076 971-06)

Algarve

Palmares Golf Club
Meia Praia, near Lagos
(tel. 082 629-53 or 629-61)

Penina Golf Club
Penina, near Portimao
(tel. 082 220-51 or 220-58).

Quinta do Lago Golf Club
Almancil, near Loulé and Faro
(tel. 089 945-29)

Vale do Lobo Golf Club
Vale de Lobo, near Loulé
(tel. 089 941-45)

Vilamoura-1 and Vilamoura-2 Golf Clubs
Vilamoura, near Loulé
(tel. 089 336-52 and 336-53).

Tennis: In Lisbon, the **Marinha Golf Club**, **Lisboa Country Club**, and **Lisbon Sports Club**, listed above, have tennis courts. Try also the **Clube Ténis Estoril**, in Estoril, near the Casino (tel. 268-1675). There are two municipal courts in the city—one in **Monsanto Park**, the other in **Campo Grande** (tel. 638-073 or 648-741).

In Oporto, the **Miramar Golf Club** has facilities. There are also municipal courts at the **Clube de Tenis do Porto**, Rua Damala Góis (tel. 488-506).

In the Algarve, there are courts at the **Penina**, **Quinta do Lago**, **Vale do Lobo**, and **Vilamoura-1** Golf Clubs.

Watersports: There are very few rental facilities outside of the Algarve. In the Lisbon are, try **John David Snack Bar**, on the beach in Cascais, near the Palm Beach Disco. They rent waterskis, windsurf boards, and paddleboats. In Porto, the **Oporto Golf Club** (see above) has skindiving facilities. Try the **Leca de Palmeira Beach** (to the north) for sailing.

In the Algarve, most of the larger tourist beaches and towns have some facilities. Near Lagos, there are windsurfing and waterskiing facilities at **Luz, São Roque** (Meia Praia) and **Alvor** beaches; the latter two also have sailing facilities. **Praia da Rocha** has sailing, windsurfing and waterskiing facilities; sailing and windsurfing are practiced at **Armacão de Pera**, near Albufeira. **Vilamoura** has extensive watersports facilities, as does **Vale de Lobo**.

LITERATURE

FURTHER READING

Although the Portuguese have a long and rich literary tradition, few books have been translated into English; fewer are still in print. The following is a partial list of works available in English.

Luis de Camões, *The Lusiads*. An epic poem, written in 1572, celebrating the Portuguese Era of Discoveries. Written by Portugal's premier poet and national hero.

Almeida Garrett, *Brother Luis de Sousa*. Almeida Garrett was an important 19th-century poet and playwright.

Eça de Queiroz, *The Maias*, *The Illustrious House of Ramires*, *The Mandarin and Other Stories*, *The Relic*, and *The Sin of Father Amaro*. One of Portugal's best-known and most enjoyable authors. Eça wrote in the latter half of the 19th century.

Fernando Pessoa, this early 20th-century poet is second only to Camões in the long list of illustrious Portuguese writers. Many of his poems have been translated into English; others were originally written in English. Pessoa wrote under the names of Alberto Caeiro, Ricardo Reis and Alvaro de Campos; not simply changing from pseudonym to pseudonym, but transforming his style with each persona as well.

Fernando Namora, *Mountain Doctor*. One of the Portuguese "neo-realists" who tried to capture the ordinary texture of life. Another good neo-realist is Mario Braga, who wrote short stories.

Ferreira de Castro, *The Emigrants* and *The Mission*. Another modern Portuguese author of interest.

Antonio Lobo Antunes, *South of Nowhere (Os Cus de Judas)*. Lobo Antunes writes psychological novels of great intensity.

Books About Portugal

Again, the selection in English is not wide, and sometimes hard to find. The following is a short compilation of historical, anthropological, and sociological books about Portugal, listed in rough chronological order according to the time periods they cover.

Marques, A.H. de Oliveira, *History of Portu-*

gal, Vol. I, From Lusitania to Empire, and *Vol. II, From Empire to Corporate State.* Columbia University Press, 1972. The best general history of Portugal.

Nowell, Charles E., *Portugal*. Prentice-Hall, 1973. Also, *A History of Portugal*, Van Nostrand Co., 1952.

Livermore, H.V., *Portugal, A Short History*, Edinburgh University Press, 1973. Also, *A New History of Portugal*, Cambridge University Press, 1976.

Boxer, C.R. *The Portuguese Seaborne Empire 1415-1825* Harmondsworth, 1973. Figueiredo, Antonio de, *Portugal: 50 Years Of Dictatorship.* Harmondsworth, 1975. A general survey by a former political exile. Also, *Portugal and Its Empire: The Truth.* Gollancz, 1961.

Gallop, Rodney, *Portugal, A Book of Folkways.* Cambridge University Press, 1936. A fascinating collection of Portuguese folklore.

Cutileiro, José, *A Portuguese Rural Society.* Clarendon Press, 1971. A study of Portuguese village life.

Sunday Times, *Insight on Portugal: The Year of the Captains.* Andre Deutsch, 1975. A journalistic survey of the events of the Revolution.

Mailer, Phil, *Portugal: The Impossible Revolution?* London, 1977.

Graham, Lawrence S. and

Makler, Harry M., eds., *Contemporary Portugal, The Revolution and Its Antecedents.* University of Texas Press, 1979.

Harvey, Robert. *Portugal: Birth of a Democracy.* Macmillan, 1978.

Soares, Mario, *Portugal's Struggle for Liberty.* Allen and Unwin, Ltd., 1975. By Portugal's current president, one of the key figures in the Revolution.

Graham, Lawrence S., and Wheeler, Douglas L., eds., *In Search of Modern Portugal, the Revolution and Its Consequences.* University of Wisconsin Press, 1983.

Robinson, Richard Alan Hodgson, *Contemporary Portugal.* Allen and Unwin, 1979.

Buneau, Thomas C., *Politics and Nationhood: Post Revolutionary Portugal.* Eastbourne Praeger, 1984.

Music

The Portuguese musical tradition is much broader than simply *fado*. Folk music, very different from *fado*, is a surprisingly vibrant current. Portuguese rock music, born after the Revolution, ranges from the mediocre to the superb. Below are some of the better musicians that play in Lisbon or that have albums available.

Fado

Amália Rodrigues, of course. Her two-volume *Greatest Hits* was released in 1986, and covers a wide range of her work. Other well-known *fadistas* include Carlos do Carmo, João Braga, and Manuel de Almeida.

Folk/Popular

Vitorino. Folksy, traditional ballads, many from the Alentejo.

Janita Salome. Vitorino's brother sings folk music with an Arabic influence. Brigada Vitor Jara. This Açorian group collects folk songs from all over Portugal.

Carlos Paredes. Traditional Portuguese guitar. Beautiful instrumentals.

Julio Pereira. Portugal's best *cavaquinho* player; the *cavaquinho* looks like a baby guitar and is the ancestor of the ukelele.

Popular baladeers include Fausto and Paulo de Carvalho.

Rock

Rui Veloso. The "father" of Portuguese rock music, influenced by soul and blues. His first album, from 1980, is *Ar de Rock* and his most recent is *Rui Veloso*. Both are excellent.

GNR. An energetic band whose latest album is *Psicopatria*.

Other bands include: Radio Macau, Trouvante, and Xutos and Pontapes.

ART/PHOTO CREDITS

All photographs are by Tony Arruza except for those listed below:

12	Museu do Azulejo, Lisbon	35	Museu Militar, Lisbon	53	Notícias e Capital Empresa Pública dos Jornais
14-5	Museu Militar, Lisbon	36	Biblioteca Nacional , Lisbon	272-273	Notícias e Capital Museu Nacional de Arte Antiga, Lisbon
20R	Museu Militar, Lisbon	37	Biblioteca Nacional , Lisbon	276	Museu Nacional de Arte Antiga, Lisbon
21	Museu da Cidade, Lisbon	38	Museu Militar, Lisbon		
22	Museu Nacional de Arte Antiga, Lisbon	39	Museu da Cidade, Lisbon	278	Museu de Évora, Évora
28	Museu Nacional de Arte Antiga, Lisbon	40	Museu da Cidade, Lisbon	281	Museu Nacional de Arte Antiga, Lisbon
30	Museu da Marinha, Belém	41	Museu Militar, Lisbon	284	Museu Nacional de Arte Antiga, Lisbon
31	Museu da Marinha, Belém	43	Biblioteca Nacional , Lisbon	286	Museu da Cidade, Lisbon
33	Museu Nacional de Arte Antiga, Lisbon	46	Empresa Pública dos Jornais Notícias e Capital		
		48	Empresa Pública dos Jornais		

Endpaper: Museu Militar, Lisbon

INDEX